One Shaker Life

One Shaker Life

Isaac Newton Youngs, 1793–1865

GLENDYNE R. WERGLAND

UNIVERSITY OF MASSACHUSETTS PRESS
Amherst and Boston

LC 2005019235
ISBN 1-55849-523-1 (library cloth ed.); 522-3 (paper)

Designed by Dennis Anderson
Set in Sabon by dix! Digital Prepress, Inc.
Printed and bound by The Maple-Vail Book Manufacturing Group

Library of Congress Cataloging-in-Publication Data
Wergland, Glendyne R.
One Shaker life : Isaac Newton Youngs, 1793–1865 / Glendyne R. Wergland.
    p.   cm.
Includes bibliographical references and index.
ISBN 1-55849-523-1 (library cloth : alk. paper) —
ISBN 1-55849-522-3 (pbk. : alk. paper)
1. Youngs, Isaac N. (Isaac Newton)
2. Shakers—New York—New Lebanon—Biography.
3. New Lebanon (N.Y.)—Church history.
I. Title.
BX9793.Y68W47 2006
289'.8'092—dc22
[B]

                              2005019235

British Library Cataloguing in Publication data are available.

FRONTISPIECE: Interior of the New Lebanon Shaker meetinghouse
in 1856, with balding brother in foreground. Drawing by Benson J. Lossing.
Harper's New Monthly Magazine, July 1857.

Contents

Illustrations follow page 94.

Acknowledgments

I OWE A DEBT of thanks to the people who piqued my interest in Isaac Newton Youngs and supported me with encouragement, help, and advice as I worked through his life story. After June Sprigg introduced me to Isaac, the Frances Perkins program at Mount Holyoke College offered me wonderful opportunities to round out my undergraduate education. Lynda Morgan taught me that history can be interesting. Jane Crosthwaite encouraged me in Shaker scholarship, directed me to graduate school, and continued to offer useful advice. Ken Hafertepe started me working through my ideas on the Youngs family clockmakers. Daniel Czitrom helped me understand what I needed to tell about Brother Isaac's background. And Christopher Pyle provided a once-in-a-lifetime academic opportunity for total immersion in living history.

My graduate work in nineteenth-century history at University of Massachusetts Amherst provided a foundation for my understanding of Shaker life. I especially appreciated Bruce Laurie's ideas on artisanry and apprenticeship. My studies with Kathy Peiss and Joyce Berkman also led me to think about workers in new ways. *One Shaker Life* grew, however, from my honors thesis at Mount Holyoke, not from my doctoral dissertation.

Many Shaker scholars were generous with their help and encouragement. Jerry Grant shared his interest in Isaac and reinforced my determination to tell Isaac's story. Magda Gabor Hotchkiss and the late Bob Meader helped sift through manuscripts in the Hancock Shaker Village collection and pointed out other references. Andy Vadnais and Tom Donnelly guided me around Mount Lebanon as I tried to see it through Isaac's eyes. Sharon Koomler opened one of Isaac's clocks for me on a blistering hot summer day at Hancock Shaker Village. She also gently suggested that perhaps a decade of research was enough, a liberating comment. Christian Goodwillie shared information on clocks and songs, pointed out relevant artifacts, and found obscure references on delicate topics. Philip Adamo, M.D., helped me with the occupational health issues of Brother Isaac's final years.

I am also grateful to those who had a hand in polishing my manuscript.

Priscilla Brewer and Stephen Stein, the scholars who read it for University of Massachusetts Press, deserve special thanks for trying to save us all from the excesses of my writing, as does copy editor Deborah Stuart Smith, who made a valiant attempt to give my prose grace and style.

Gerry Wergland, my husband (like Isaac, an engineer), unflinchingly read countless pages and attended numerous Shaker talks. His support allowed me to return to school as a forty-year-old undergraduate, work straight through to a doctorate in history, and write full-time. I will be forever grateful.

Preface

ISAAC NEWTON YOUNGS is worthy of study for several reasons. His lifetime, from 1793 to 1865, spanned the rise and decline of the United Society of Believers in Christ's Second Appearing, the Shakers. Better yet, Brother Isaac documented Shaker history. His many manuscripts, preserved in accessible collections, provide insight into both the individual Shaker and the individual within the context of his society. And because he wrote in detail of his discontent, including his struggles with lust in a celibate society, yet remained a faithful Shaker, he shows how the sect succeeded and where it failed.

Isaac Newton Youngs lived at New Lebanon, New York, home of the Shakers' central Ministry. He was not an Elder, but he worked in close proximity to the society's leaders. As a member of the rank and file, Brother Isaac criticized the Ministry, sometimes in excruciating detail. The differences between his public and private journals can be illuminating because they reveal what he considered appropriate for public consumption (detailed record keeping and accurate information) and what was not (complaints about work, criticism of other Believers, and such matters as an operation on a brother's testicle). To protect himself, he encoded some comments and vented his frustrations in his journals. He compartmentalized his interior life, preserving some privacy in a society that allowed little. His writings therefore provide insight into his life as a Shaker seeking self-expression while living in a community that mandated conformity and stifled dissent.

Isaac Newton Youngs chronicled his struggles with lust in a celibate society. As a healthy young man, he was probably at his physical peak during the years when he wrote about battling his emerging sexuality. Few Shaker journals provide such intimate detail.[1] A case could be made for not including that information in his biography. Living Shakers might consider it too personal for publication. But Brother Isaac preserved that journal and later edited it, inserting words for clarification and heavily crossing out some passages, which I have not tried to bring to light. I have therefore included his problems with lust because it was a significant trial of celibacy.

Most Shaker scholarship focuses on special aspects of art, theology, or craftsmanship or provides a regional account or historical overview. And although biographical information on Shakers is embedded in many scholarly works, individual brethren have been generally neglected. An exception is Jerry Grant and Douglas Allen's excellent *Shaker Furniture Makers,* a meticulously researched set of short biographies. A full-length academic biography is overdue.[2]

Roughly four thousand attributed manuscript pages of Youngs's work as author, journalist, songwriter, scribe, and church historian have been preserved. His earliest journal began in 1815; his last ended in 1865, less than a month before his death. His Domestic Journal describes the village's daily life. His Personal Journal and Spiritual Autobiography trace his temporal frustrations and his progress in faith. His church history, A Concise View, is a highly detailed overview. Sketches of Visions, his first-hand account of the Era of Manifestations, is the benchmark against which other accounts can be evaluated. The Family and Meeting Journal that Brother Isaac wrote in his youth, along with the Personal Journal of his middle age, show the individual's problems in meeting the demands of his society.

Furthermore, Brother Isaac set a high standard for his writing. He even faulted other journal keepers for "not recording events more explicit, and intelligible to the unacquainted reader."[3] Other Shaker authors of the mid-1800s can be compared with Isaac Newton Youngs, but none matched his candor. When Elder Henry Blinn published a Shaker history with information from the various villages, he drew on Isaac's work but edited the life out of it. Youngs was evidently more forthright than Blinn thought appropriate. In many Shaker publications, individuals' personalities are thoroughly obscured. And though that may have been the Shakers' goal, it seems a shame to omit their personal stories from the history of their movement.

Believers' published autobiographies often submerged their personalities under their Shaker beliefs. Even in scholarly studies, many Shakers lack individuality.[4] Yet their religious life was not the sum of their character. There is no such thing as a generic Shaker any more than there is a generic American. And the details of their personalities, extracted from their writings, can be illuminating. Isaac commented, for instance, that Mother Lucy Wright, a forceful leader with a strong personality, was once "more stirred up than usually," that the New Lebanon tailor David Slosson was cranky, critical, and unpleasantly plain-spoken, and that Sister Clarissa Cogswell had a "courting disposition."[5] Each displayed characteristics inconsistent with Shaker ideals, yet all were Believers.

People keep diaries for many reasons: to help them recall the past, to work through problems or chart their progress, to express thoughts they cannot say aloud, to preserve something of themselves for posterity, or to record information for later reference. Isaac Newton Youngs kept journals for all these reasons. Some historians believe that diaries are the most truthful source available because of their immediacy and details. What is on the surface of each account, however, is rarely the whole story. By closely examining Youngs's writings, we can learn more about him. And he wanted us to do just that. He hoped that those who followed would be inspired by his accounts of Shaker life.

> I shall however leave a plain trace by my pen, which many will doubtless behold, & I hope with some satisfaction. . . . But whether or not, there be any trace left to my memory, or any solicitude be felt by those who follow me, whether I ever existed, or what I did—still to me, it is a matter of great concern that I be happy hereafter. For that reason, I spend much of my precious time, often out of my usual hours of sleep, writing to leave that which will shortly be of no use to me, but which I hope will edify those who follow after & be the means of encouraging them in the Gospel. If this be the case, when I am in Eternity, years & ages to come, I shall feel a happy reflection when I look thro the veil & see those on earth deriving a benefit from my labors; & when they come to join me in a blissful Eternity, our mutual happiness will be thereby increased. Isaac N. Youngs[6]

Brother Isaac's desire to be remembered was not unique. Others too wanted to leave a trace of themselves behind—a poignant hope for childless celibates. In defiance of their society's rules, craftsmen signed their work, sometimes dedicating a piece of furniture to the sister for whom it was made. Some Shakers left personal journals, poetry, songs, hymnals, and drawings with their names carefully inscribed. Isaac Newton Youngs preserved his manuscripts, some with entries addressed to you, the reader. He knew that many Shakers would be invisible to posterity, but he wanted those who followed, whether Shaker or worldling, to remember him and to consider what he had to say.

I first "met" Isaac Newton Youngs when I worked at Hancock Shaker Village, cataloguing the tool collection in storage. One of his handmade music pens, in a tiny rosewood case, caught my attention. Its design, its intended efficiency, its satin finish, even the printed, signed label on it—each detail revealed something about the man who made it. Though I did not yet realize that Brother Isaac was a perfectionist, that music pen was a clue.

After my stint at Hancock Shaker Village, I resumed my education at Mount Holyoke College, where I researched Brother Isaac for a paper in Jane Crosthwaite's Shaker seminar. Even today, I am not certain whether I chose him or he chose me. When I decided to do an honors thesis, his biography was my only choice. Because he has been quoted in numerous secondary sources, getting started was easy. Going on was not. His works are scattered through several states and twice as many accessible manuscript collections. But after several years of research, I can say for certain that Brother Isaac was both exceptional and ordinary, in ways that I hope I have made clear.

As I researched Isaac, I found more clues to his perfectionism. His music pen and its rosewood box were the first; his handwriting was the second. Though he did scrawl in his personal journals, he used a lovely, regular script in his official writings that he maintained almost to the end of his life. A third clue was his skill with words. His mastery of the challenge of rhyme and meter, revealed in the poetry he wrote and the hymns he composed, suggests a personality that derived satisfaction from getting it just right.

There was more to Brother Isaac, however, than the perfectionist. His work reveals that he was intelligent but also rebellious, showing disrespect by criticizing the Elders. Lucy Wright called him a ringleader, and that was not a compliment.[7] Perfection was the Shaker ideal; faultfinding was not. It made life difficult in a communal society where everyone had to try to live in union. A critic by implication sets himself above others. Thus, Brother Isaac, through his derogatory comments, provides evidence of his sense of superiority as well his need to work at humility.

Isaac misbehaved in many small ways. He did not comply with all orders. He could be cranky, self-centered, and disobedient. And he felt superior because of his intelligence and the privilege it brought.[8] But self-improvement was his ideal, and not just because he belonged to a society that required it. He expected as much of himself as the society demanded of him and was hard on himself when his own behavior did not reach the mark. Striving for perfection was the Shaker way, and his work had to serve his village.

Brother Isaac took his turn at farm chores. Even though he was clumsy enough to stick himself in the ankle with a pitchfork while moving barley, he was unafraid of heights and worked atop the highest roofs in the village until he was sixty-two years old.[9] Preventing leaks meant closing the seams in the tin roofs perfectly and completely, a job for which the careful, methodical Brother Isaac was well suited.

Brother Isaac was good with animals. He was a competent horseman and knew his way around livestock. He described himself as tender-hearted and expressed regret about the death of "a good old horse named Buck" who had to be put down "on account of his old age—being upwards of 31 years old." "Not many horses," he wrote, "have passed a more useful, honorable & good long life than old Buck—much loved by all."[10]

His tender-heartedness extended to children. He was kind to those who tried to be good, giving and receiving affection and sometimes toting little boys in his arms as he labored in worship.[11] Benny Gates called him "daddy Isaac" and Elisha Blakeman referred to him as his "gospel Parent."[12] But though Youngs was patient with children who tried to perfect their behavior, he had little patience with those who did not. He referred to one such child as "more fit for the company of pirates than here," and when he was assigned to correct another boy's discipline problem, he switched the lad, to "get it riveted in his mind." Yet his description of the episode shows that he was a reluctant disciplinarian, preferring to use firm government to win over a child.[13] As a good Shaker who practiced the Shaker motto, "Hands to work; hearts to God," Youngs despised laziness. A hard worker himself, perhaps compulsively so, he was disgusted with a 135-pound seven-year-old who would not move until bribed with sweets.[14]

Brother Isaac was not always serious. He made up rhymes and puns and shared word play with his friends. He whistled as he worked. A sense of humor shows up in his journals, where he recorded, in one entry, his amusement over the sight of several sisters chasing their wind-blown baskets about the dooryard and in another, the melee that ensued one morning at breakfast when a rat ran into the dining room and brethren chased it out. Brother Isaac was also a gifted mimic, whose skill inspired Giles Avery to remark, "I think he is nearly inspired to mimick for I never witnessed such scrutinizing mimickery before." In 1827, well after the death of Mother Lucy Wright, a sister noted that after he pitched a song, Brother Isaac "began to walk and motion like Mother." She recognized his impression of Mother Lucy Wright—someone he surely would not have imitated while she was alive![15] Though this image hardly fits our view of a nineteenth-century Shaker, Isaac may have practiced his imitations in front of a mirror. His success at mimicry, like his descriptions of people and events, showed the perfectionist's eye for detail.

Well into old age, Brother Isaac retained an almost childlike wonder about nature. But his appreciation was accompanied by the perfectionist's need to create order. In springtime, he noted when all the plants and trees came into bloom. He marked everything room by room that belonged in the Church Family dwelling, first numbering each room, then putting that number on each item that belonged there.[16] The Shaker desire for order and efficiency undoubtedly underlay the process. Anyone might have done that job, but Brother Isaac was the one who did it. The task fit the individual. Also, in keeping with his interest in scientific analysis, he measured everything—time, firewood, consumption of lamp oil, even his fellow Shakers, whose heights he recorded in an effort to determine whether there was any relationship between aging and shrinkage or "settling." "There appears to be much difference as to settling when old," he wrote. "For instance Henry Markham seems to have settled nearly 1¼ inches, while Stephen Munson seems not to have settled much if any. All were measured with shoes on. Brethren's shoes raise them ½ or ¾ of an inch & sisters' about 1¼." [17]

It would be nice to know what this interesting man looked like. But even though we have no photograph of him, we can deduce some details from other sources. Isaac Newton Youngs was 5 feet 8¼ inches tall (in his shoes), perhaps a little above average height for a man of his time. His weight was probably average, because he believed in moderation in diet ("I think temperance & a medium are the chief requisites"), despite his love for strawberries, watermelon, and apple pie. Like other Shaker brethren, he would have worn his hair long in back and cropped short on the sides, though by 1840 he was wearing a hair cap or wig to cover his baldness. The vanity that may have prompted his adopting the wig showed up as early as 1818 when he recorded in his journal that when his new roommate arrived he would have to govern himself with more caution in regard to vanity. [18]

On August 18, 1856, Youngs spent part of a day with Benson Lossing, who made drawings of several New Lebanon Shakers. Three of Lossing's drawings show a back view of a partly bald, gray-haired Shaker brother. In the heat of August, Brother Isaac would not have needed his hair cap. As one of two New Lebanon brethren known to be balding, he may well have been Lossing's model. [19]

Brother Isaac dressed in the outdated styles Shakers used as their uniform. The journal he kept as a tailor for the society records few new garments for himself, suggesting that his clothes may have been a little shabby. But we can assume that he dressed neatly, in keeping with the Shaker demands for neatness and cleanliness, and that his spare garments were sorted according to categories, folded precisely and stowed neatly, as were his other belongings. A visitor described Isaac's workshop as being in "perfect order." [20]

Brother Isaac was probably right handed. Although his left hand measured a quarter of an inch longer than his right in a tracing he made of his hands in his journal in 1854, decades of work as a tailor and scribe had probably drawn up and shortened the muscles in his dominant hand. [21] By then, his posture was probably stooped from bending over his work in writing, cutting fabric, and sewing. And he surely had calluses on his thumbs and fingers. He may have been nearsighted, too. Years of close work could have weakened his distance vision, and some of the spectacles he mended may have been his own. [22]

Even though this biography is entitled *One Shaker Life,* the chapters that follow, proceeding in overlapping chronological order, may at times seem to be describing different lives. This format is an artifact of Brother Isaac's journals. After completing his Family and Meeting Journal (1815–23), he no longer integrated all aspects of his life in one document. Instead, he kept separate journals on apostasy, tailoring, clockmaking, the Era of Manifestations, and personal matters, as well as the Church Family's Domestic Journal. The closest to an integrated account was his Personal Journal, where he touched on many topics. The rest of his journals compartmentalized his life. In this biography, I have respected his format, ordering chapters according to his concerns at different times, but I have tried to integrate material from all his writings to round out each topic.

In quotations, I have in most instances silently standardized spelling and added paragraph and sentence breaks for ease in reading. I have capitalized Elder and Brother (when used as a form of address), Elders (when referring to an official capacity) and Believers (when referring to Shakers), as well as the names of the families and orders constituting a Shaker community. In addition, I usually refer to individual Shakers as they called each other, either by first name or by their form of address, Brother or Sister. Some errors have probably crept into my text. I am sure Brother Isaac would not approve. But those mistakes, alas, are mine and mine alone.

Isaac Newton Youngs hoped for his writings to be a source of strength and faith to others, and so they have been for me. My thanks and blessings go to Brother Isaac and those who helped preserve his work for posterity. Because little is known about nineteenth-century Believers as individuals, a biography about one Shaker life, regardless of how representative it may or may not have been, must stand for those who remain obscure. In this way, perhaps Isaac Newton Youngs can serve his society one last time. This is his story.

One Shaker Life

1 Shaker Society
An Overview

THE SHAKERS, or United Society of Believers in Christ's Second Appearing, originated in Manchester, England, in the mid-1700s. They believed in divine revelation, celibacy, confession of sin, equality of the sexes, communal living, and separation from the world's people. "Shaking Quakers" were remarkable for the physical manifestations of their spiritual inspiration—dancing, shouting, shaking, and speaking in tongues—which attracted harassment. They held noisy services, invaded other denominations' worship, and clashed with townspeople. In 1772, the Manchester Shakers were arrested and fined for disturbing the Sabbath.[1] In 1774, after years of persecution, they emigrated to New York under the leadership of the charismatic Ann Lee. Known for her spiritual inspiration, Mother Ann prophesied, interpreted dreams, and healed the sick. Once she was said to have cast evil spirits out of a child. After she accused two women of sexual transgressions, one confessed and the other proved pregnant by a married man. Mother Ann's abilities were extraordinary, even among those whose worldview included communication with angels and spirits. Her followers considered her the second embodiment of Christ.[2]

The Shakers settled in Watervliet, New York, where they suffered persecution as religious radicals or as suspected British spies. But occasionally providence smiled on them. Paradoxically, what they later recorded as their first blessing was a 1779 Baptist revival near New Lebanon, New York. The meetings were characterized by extraordinary phenomena. Individuals "were fainting, crying out, falling down, and wallowing on the ground; whilst some were falling into trances, out of which they would emerge full of the spirit of prophecy." Many experienced strikingly personal revelations. Shaker witnesses recalled, "Vivid and intense were men's convictions for sin; cries for mercy rent the air; meetings were scenes of excitement, soul anguish, realistic portrayals of penalties about to come, as souls stood bare in their sins before the eye of God." Men and women of responsibility and position, church members of long standing, ministers and deacons realized their religion had failed and they were lost. "Conversions were swift and powerful; joy was felt as intense as the sorrow that had preceded. Visions of angels were seen; to some the heavens seemed opened." In the emotionally charged times of the American Revolution, the hopefuls had waited for the new epoch when Christ would reappear and warfare would end. But they had been disappointed. "Their emotions subsided; the meetings, so intense and absorbing, ceased; farmers and mechanics went about their work; the war went on." The stir died down, but it was not forgotten. The revival harrowed the soil for Ann Lee's planting.[3]

The Shakers' second boon was the famous "dark day" of May 19, 1780, which terrified many Yankees into giving their hearts to God. A morning thundershower, one observer recalled, was "followed by an uncommon darkness such as is not remembered . . . the night was [so] Extraordinary dark until one o'clock that a person could not see their hand when held up nor even a white sheet of paper . . . the cause was unknown." The gloom was so intense at noon that candles had to be lighted. In New England, "many families were in a perfect frenzy," fearing that Judgment Day had come. The phenomenon was so "very awful and surprising" that ministers preached on the coming judgment.[4] Ann Lee seized the opportunity to open her gospel to the public and plant her message in fertile soil. Building on potential proselytes' pre-existing evangelical beliefs, she used her own charismatic spirituality to attract converts. "The effects were surprising," according to one observer, who noted that the road to Watervliet was "instantly crouded." In June 1780, crowds were coming in droves to Shaker meeting.[5] By 1786, Ezra Stiles noted that the Shakers were "almost to a man Converts fr[om] . . . Baptists called there New Lights & Separates—accustomed in . . . Meetings to work themselves up to high Enthusiasm, so as in Worship all the Congregation to get to speak[g], pray[g] & singing all at the same time."[6] Ann Lee attracted Christians who sought religious ecstasy and a life without sin, even if it meant great personal sacrifice. Convert Daniel Moseley blessed Ann Lee for calling him "from Darkness to Light and from the power of Satan to God."[7]

Mother Ann was an astute evangelist, but she did not live to see her church fully established. She died in 1784, after suffering assaults by violent mobs on her evangelizing tour of New England. But after her death, her successors continued her work, gathering scattered Believers into orderly separatist communities. By 1800 the Shakers had colonies in New York, Massachusetts, Connecticut, New Hampshire, and Maine. In 1805, during the Second Great Awakening, they sent missionaries to evangelize the West and built more villages in Ohio and Kentucky.[8] By 1830, Believers were established, prosperous, and respected. The Shaker village at New Lebanon, New York, was the home of the central Ministry and repository of records, many compiled by Isaac Newton Youngs.[9]

Hard times drove some families into Shaker enclaves. Often, even when adults did not join, they bound out children as young as two years of age. Indentures signed at Watervliet, for instance, show that instead of the usual trickle of two to four children a year, eight families sent eleven children to that village in 1837. The Shakers counted on an influx of youngsters to ensure the perpetuation of the sect. Because they were celibate, they did not reproduce after becoming Shakers. Instead, they raised indentured children, hoping that they would join the sect as adults. Reciprocity between the generations was as essential to the Shakers as it was to all the world's people. The young depended on the adults for their upbringing and training in life skills, and the adults depended on the younger generations to care for them when they became too old or infirm to work. As long as the society attracted new members, the system was self-renewing. By the mid-nineteenth century, their population had grown to more than four thousand.[10]

The society was governed by a Ministry consisting of two Elders and two Eldresses. After 1796 the Lead, or head of the Shakers, was Mother Lucy Wright. Under the Ministry, two Elders and two Eldresses working in partnership ran each village. Theoretically, all were equal, but in practice, some derived the benefits of authority from their position as leaders. At the bottom of the hierarchy were most of the brethren and sisters, as many as five hundred adults and children in each village.[11] Larger communities were subdivided into at least three orders: the Church Family, for members who had risen through the lower orders into a state of spiritual purification and obedience, signed the covenant, and turned over their property; a junior order for those who had not yet made that commitment; and a novitiate or gathering order for those least advanced in the faith. Shakers held all property in common. Every village, though not entirely self-sufficient, was designed to be self-supporting.

Rules governed all aspects of daily life: travel, worship, reading, mealtimes, roommates, correspondence, work assignments, food and alcohol consumption, hours for rising and sleeping, and clothing. Shakers did not wear standardized garments at first. But about 1796, they adopted uniforms for the Sabbath. The identical clothing made their unity visible and identified them as a group apart from the world's people. The outdated styles they wore, described as "fossilized fashions," proclaimed their rejection of worldly craving and greed and showed that all were equal; no one had better or fancier clothing than anyone else. What one wore had to reflect humility, not "feed the pride and vanity of a fallen nature." [12]

Clothing was not the only aspect of Shaker life subjected to such scrutiny. Shaker furnishings and architecture were examined for modesty and efficiency. The goal was to minimize decoration that created unnecessary work, showed worldly pride, provoked lust of the eye, or promoted a craving spirit. Though the Shakers were tempted by superfluities, periodic purges eliminated items that Mother Ann warned them to give to the bats and moles of the earth. Overcoming lusts of all kinds was fundamental to Shakerism.[13]

Celibacy was a basic tenet of Shaker belief. Mother Ann Lee commanded her followers to take up the cross of celibacy against the lust of the flesh. Marriage, according to an Elder who spoke with the visiting François Marquis de Barbé-Marbois in 1784, was "contrary to the example of the Saviour who was never married,—to use his terms 'never had any carnal connection with a woman.' " From the start, Mother Ann told married people, as Lucy Wright later recalled, "You must forsake the marriage of the flesh, and travel out of it, in order to be married to the Lamb; which is to be married to Christ, or joined to the Lord in one spirit." To Believers, sex was "the principal seat of human depravity," or, as Elder Benjamin Seth Youngs put it, "the cause of all particular lusts and actual sins in our hearts and lives . . . the spawn which the great leviathan has left in the souls of man, from whence comes all the fry of actual sins and abominations." [14] Shakers believed that all humans were cursed by Adam's fall, which resulted from his disobedience in having sexual intercourse.[15] The only way, therefore, that Believers could purify themselves enough to get to heaven was to refrain from sex. So they tried to eradicate it from their utopian society.

The Shakers used poetry, hymns, sermons, and epigrams to drive the point home. The hymn "Rights of Conscience" advocated giving up lust and pride, calling on Believers to "Hate the flesh and sin no more." But celibacy was easier professed than practiced. Sexual suppression might have been facilitated by complete separation of brethren and sisters. Instead, men and women slept across the hall from each other, did chores for one another, saw each other at mealtimes and in worship, rode together to pick berries, and paired up for union meetings. The Shakers did not make celibacy easy, but self-mastery was a measure of commitment. They knew the volatile nature of sexual desire and counseled Believers to avoid temptation. "When you are obliged to be together at such times [as when sick or weak]," Brother Abijah Worster of Harvard wrote, "you ought to be as careful as you would be if you was at work among powder with fire." [16]

The Shaker system of incomplete separation created tension between lust and self-control, but rules regulated contact between Shaker men and women.

In 1818, Isaac Newton Youngs recorded some of the Elders' orders in his journal. A sister was not to mend clothing while a brother was wearing it. Sisters were not to go unaccompanied into the brethren's shops, or the reverse. Touching was not permitted except for medical treatment. When the Shakers codified their Millennial Laws, they devoted a section to regulating behavior between the sexes. Men and women could not be alone together for any longer than to do a "short and necessary errand." They worked together only by permission of the Elders. Brethren and sisters were not allowed to give presents to each other "in a private manner." Visiting in each other's apartments "without just and lawful occasion" was forbidden. When sisters cleaned the brethren's rooms, brethren were required to leave unless too weak or ill to move.[17]

The very existence of church orders, however, shows that some Shaker men and women did indeed share private union, did have intimate conversations, did visit each other unchaperoned, and did touch each other unnecessarily. Such misdeeds made rules necessary. And rules could be cited if a disorderly individual had to be expelled. But the Millennial Laws were not the only barriers to fraternization. Shaker convention and confession of sin, bolstered by the watchful eyes of peers whose surveillance made sexual pursuit difficult, also discouraged intimacy.

Nonetheless, some did fall from grace. Though many Believers mastered their sexual feelings and carried the cross of celibacy as a lifelong measure of their commitment to Shakerism, others could not. Enoch Jacobs, for instance, said he would "rather go to hell with Electa his wife than live among the Shakers without her."[18] John Deming admitted, a "vehement affection for Minerva has undone me." In some cases, the guilty parties were "shut out of union and not received again without confessions and professions of repentance and contrition similar as in other churches." But in other cases, the transgressors were expelled. Several instances of Shaker fornication have been documented, one resulting in pregnancy. "The most distressing thing was brought to light," New Lebanon's Eldress Betsy Bates wrote. "A young one made here in the Second Order by Theodore Long and Sally Thomas . . . Awful Awful Awful. Never did I think this would [have] been our disgrace." Long and Thomas were quickly exiled (and in opposite directions) before their lust could pollute others.[19]

Shakers who committed less egregious sins were expected to repent. The Apostles admonished their followers to confess so they could be forgiven, and Believers followed that model. They confessed their sin to one or two witnesses of the same sex, perhaps an Elder or Eldress or an older mentor.

Confession was essential to overpowering sin and a prerequisite to redemption. Confession also signaled humility and obedience; thus a reluctance to confess could be doubly damning. The unrepentant had to leave. Frequent admonitions made the point, "A scabby sheep affects the whole flock." Some couples "eloped" voluntarily; others were sent to another village or back into the world. Before 1812, "backsliding" Shakers were in and out of union repeatedly before they finally determined either to stay or to go, and their vacillation between the world and the cross must have made it difficult to enforce discipline on the remaining faithful. By August 1824, after several couples had defected, returned, confessed, then left again, the Ministry closed the door to apostates who wanted to return.[20] Such "scabby sheep" were more trouble than they were worth.

In addition to lust, conscientious individuals also confessed pride or noncompliance with Ministry edicts. Children were admonished, "If you have done wrong, confess it before you go to bed." A well-confessed Shaker could sleep with a clear conscience. The apostate David Lamson saw confession as the "secret lever" that gave the Elders such close acquaintance with Believers' psyches that they knew "exactly what influences to exert to keep them in subjection." He described the Elders' approach: "They are more lenient with young believers or new comers than with the old, and grant them many more privileges; and teach them doctrines and duties as they are able to receive them. As they often express themselves, the Shaker life is a *travel*. Every one is expected to make some 'travel in the gospel.' " Delinquency was soon exposed. The peace and quiet of a Shaker village meant that private conversations might be overheard and reported. Though the Millennial Laws prohibited "tattling, talebearing and backbiting," they also required anyone who saw misbehavior to "open it" by confession. In addition, the laws prohibited transgressors from trying to find out who told the Elders. Thus the Shakers policed each other. And some feared loss of union. Being cast out meant losing the protection—spiritual, emotional, and economic—of their community.[21]

Shaker society depended on Believers' conformity. Maintaining union in a communal society, however, was difficult. The Millennial Laws concerning union and divisiveness testify to the many and varied issues involved in bringing several hundred disparate individuals into a cohesive whole. And Mother Lucy Wright's preachings suggest that Shakers were often contrary. To help Believers adjust their attitudes, she admonished them to put away hard feelings and labor to be peacemakers. She worried about their anger and backbiting. They had to be humble and submissive to find favor with God. And she was more concerned about their unity than anything else. "You cannot go to heaven alone, but you can be lost alone," she said.[22]

Variations in outlook among Shaker villages also challenged the efforts to maintain union. In theory, brethren and sisters stood equal throughout Shakerdom. The society's balanced leadership was intended to maintain equality of the sexes. But that doctrine was marred by spotty compliance, and the Ministry could not enforce it in distant communities with contrary intentions. In 1816, Isaac Newton Youngs noted in his Family and Meeting Journal that the New Lebanon Shakers had been cautioned not to speak of "being placed in order, brother & sister in equality." Evidently the Ministry did not want the world to know that "there [was] not any family or order among believers, except Watervliet & this Church, that support that order." New Lebanon and Watervliet were the only villages that fully supported sexual equality, and Youngs recorded that fact for posterity, confirming what Shaker scholars have long suspected.[23]

Though Shakers had a well-defined set of beliefs, they did not publish a definitive creed. They focused on governing behavior rather than belief. But, as Daniel Patterson puts it, they agreed that mankind's downfall was lust of the flesh; that restoration could be attained through moral choices; that the first step in regeneration was to confess sin and renounce the world, the flesh, and the devil; that salvation was offered to all; that resurrection was of the spirit rather than the body, and that the fruits of this work could be enjoyed in the unity, love, and peace manifested by Believers.[24] Furthermore, their worship did not follow a set pattern. The absence of a written creed and liturgy meant that their beliefs could evolve with changing times.

In accordance with their ideals, Believers lived simple, orderly lives, and their simplicity and orderliness was visible in their villages. Though plain, their buildings were built to last. In 1790, a visitor gave his first impression of the New Lebanon Shaker settlement. The village, on the western slope of the Taconic ridge, was built along one street, he reported, "the houses neat and scattering, and all painted a dull yellow." Behind the buildings, orchards spread along the hillside. The meetinghouse was "a pure milk white, one story high." According to Mother Ann Lee, good spirits would not dwell where there was dirt; thus, Shaker villages were notable for their cleanliness. All things were in Shaker order. Such beliefs translated into landscapes that pleased the eye.[25] In 1819, a visitor wrote:

> The utmost neatness is conspicuous in their fields, gardens, court yards, out houses, and in the very road; not a weed, not a spot of filth, or any

nuisance is suffered to exist. Their wood is cut and piled, in the most exact order; their fences are perfect; even their stone walls are constructed with great regularity . . . instead of wooden posts for their gates, they have pillars of stone of one solid piece, and every thing bears the impress of labour, vigilance and skill, with such a share of taste, as is consistent with the austerities of their sect.[26]

Most New England farms evidently did not reach the same high standard that made Shaker establishments conspicuous. The neatness, the stone gate-posts, the perfectly stacked firewood—all were evidence of the Shakers' labor-intensive pursuit of perfection.

God, the Shakers believed, compensated a man according to his work, and work was sanctified by scripture. From 2 Thessalonians 3:10 they drew the lesson, "If anyone will not work, neither let him eat," and from Proverbs 10:4, "Poor is he who works with a negligent hand, but the hand of the diligent makes him rich." The Shakers expected to work with their hands six days a week and to labor in worship on the seventh. Children, too, were admonished to be diligent. "Improve all your time in something useful," and "Always be industrious for idleness is the parent of vice" were familiar to Shaker youth.[27]

Though they elevated work to the spiritual sphere, Believers also supported the occasional "winter Shaker," who arrived after harvest and stayed until the workload increased for spring planting. Despite—or because of—such transients and others who did not carry their full share of work, the Shakers derided laziness. Idle hands, they believed, do the devil's work, and the devil could not be permitted to gain a toehold, so laziness had to be discouraged. One Shaker song derides the "sluggard,"

> Whose object is to live at ease,
> And his own carnal nature please;
> Who always has some selfish quirk,
> In sleeping, eating, and at work.
> A lazy fellow it implies,
> Who in the morning hates to rise;
> When all the rest are up at four,
> He wants to sleep a little more.
> When others into meeting swarm,
> He keeps his nest so good and warm,
> That sometimes when sisters come
> To make the beds and sweep the room,
> Who do they find wrap'd up so snug?
> Ah! Who is it but Mr. Slug.

The sluggard rose late to shirk morning chores but appeared promptly at mealtimes. The kitchen sisters knew him well because he visited them often for snacks. But men like "Mr. Slug" were unlikely to remain in Shaker society because they were shamed for their idleness. The Millennial Laws warned, "Drones, sluggards, thieves and liars, or deceivers, do not belong among the people of God, and all such, together with the mocker and scoffer, will in no wise pass unpunished, in the final settlement with souls." [28] Shakers equated laziness with lying and theft. A sluggard stole other people's time and labor by not contributing his own.

Shakers who remained in union were supported all their lives with medical care, room and board, tools, and uniform clothing provided by the labor of the society's own doctor, nurses, cooks, farmers, mechanics, shoemakers, and tailors. Others worked at the society's lucrative businesses. At a time when the worldly elite considered labor degrading, Shaker men and women admired diligence and took pride in their work, striving to live up to Mother Ann's motto, "Hands to work; hearts to God." When Brother David Slosson died, Isaac Newton Youngs commended him for having been "very zealous at work" and for not having "left the earth in debt to it for his living." And of the aged Tabitha Babbitt, Brother Isaac wrote, "She was a remarkably useful woman—and very industrious—a specimen of which is that she has practiced knitting without light sitting up in her bed, before time of rising!" [29] Keeping the Shaker population fed, clothed, and solvent required everyone's effort. Reciprocity required it.

Shakers ran farms and businesses that produced goods for domestic consumption and for sale outside the community. Their industry made them self-sufficient and prosperous. By the 1840s, the New Lebanon society owned more than six thousand acres of land and several businesses. Their prosperity attracted comment. One worldly visitor described their buildings.

> They have more than one hundred large and substantial stone, brick, and wooden buildings, some of which are handsome. They have machine shops, sawing and carding mills, a tannery, workshops of various kinds, a large meeting-house, which cost at least twenty-eight thousand dollars, a large number of dwelling-houses of the most comfortable kind, together with herbal, vegetable and fruit gardens, laid out with great taste and order.
>
> Another large barn has recently been constructed 140 feet by 60, 3 stories high, and arranged for the accommodation of 70 or 80 head of cattle. The first story is built of solid stone, which protects the cattle from cold, and the stalls are so arranged as to feed them with great ease and without waste of fodder. Few of the barns in New York can compare with it for the saving of labor and protection of hay and cattle.[30]

The Shakers valued efficiency and, though they had a strong work ethic, they did not want to be overworked. Thus, they readily adopted labor-saving innovations. As a result, their barn was admired and their agriculture emulated.

Outside the Shaker communities, farmers made labor-saving changes in their barns while neglecting the woman's sphere. In fact, the image of the worn-out farmwife enslaved by toil was a staple of nineteenth-century literature, and farmwives testified to the truth of the matter. But Shakers lightened women's work too. The New Lebanon society's water-powered wash house was a model of efficiency that reduced the steps laundresses had to take and the loads they had to carry—a boon in a society that required cleanliness. The brethren built the machinery to make laundry easier for the sisters. They invested time, effort, and money in such conveniences—a wise move for men whose housekeeping was done by women. Each sex had to help the other if all were to prosper. Shaker union rested on a foundation of reciprocity.[31]

Notwithstanding all the work going on, a Shaker village was quiet and well-ordered, much more so than a worldly one. The occasional noisy child was "racketing" and considered disagreeable if not actually disorderly. Mother Ann had advocated going about in the fear of God, opening and shutting doors carefully, making no unnecessary noise, and Shakers aimed for that standard. A visitor described the peacefulness of the New Lebanon Shaker village.

> The streets are quiet; for here you have no grog-shop, no beer-house, no lock-up, no pound; of the dozen edifices rising around you—work-rooms, barns, tabernacle, stables, kitchens, schools, and dormitories—not one is either foul or noisy; and every building, whatever may be its use, has something of the air of a chapel. The paint is all fresh; the planks are all bright; the windows are all clean. A white sheen is on everything; a happy quiet reigns around.[32]

Even the individual Shakers were soft-spoken. They addressed each other with the Quaker pronouns thee and thou, and used "yea" and "nay" for yes and no. They stressed friendly and kind behavior in word and deed. Spiritual love was the ideal. Life moved "in an easy kind of rhythm," and for good reason. "Order, temperance, frugality, worship—these are the Shaker things which strike upon your senses first; the peace and innocence of Eden, when contrasted with the wrack and riot of New York," one visitor from the city wrote. "Every one seems busy, every one tranquil. No jerk, no strain, no menace is observed."[33] All appeared peaceful and life seemed to glide along without strife. Conflict was addressed in private.

Shaker children went to school seasonally, as was the custom of the time, boys in winter after harvest was over, and girls in summer. Children worked the rest of the year alongside the adults charged with overseeing them. Work, however, was not necessarily onerous. As Bruce Laurie shows in his study of artisans, the preindustrial craft system allowed time for "just plain fun" during the workday. Though Shaker craftsmen did not encourage the tippling the world's people enjoyed, they did allow their apprentices some simple pleasures. And though masters among the world's people could be cruel to apprentices, Shaker society regulated behavior. If a worldly master mistreated an apprentice, he rarely paid the consequences. But Shaker masters were encouraged to be kindly. Because they hoped to retain the children they raised, they were as indulgent as youths' behavior and the society's needs allowed. Inevitably, some found their assignments onerous. Elisha Blakeman, for example, disliked hauling wood in winter. Of the Shakers' logging camp he wrote, "Tegious! awful! desperate!" When he was told to care for the Ministry's horse, he wrote, "<u>No small cross</u>." But he did his duty.[34]

Children who grew up in Shaker communities were expected to do their duty and to show self-discipline. They were raised with a long list of duties to God, their superiors, each other, and themselves. But they were not perfect. "Now and then" in Sabbath services, one visitor observed of the boys, "I could detect a furtive smile and could see looks of merriment exchanged." The apostate Hervey Elkins reported that corporal punishment was forbidden, "except the use of small twigs applied to extremely contumacious children."[35] Competing elements created tension over child discipline. Believers had to retain children who would grow up to become Shakers themselves and keep the community alive, but also the individual had to make the effort to fit in. A Shaker village was no place for a nonconformist, whether child or adult.

Despite the steady schedule of work, Shakers had opportunities for recreation. Sometimes they "rode out" for an afternoon on horseback or in wagons in warm weather and sleighs in winter. Berry picking and, occasionally, swimming were summer diversions. Though Shakers were not allowed to go to worldly entertainments that would divert their attention from God, such as plays, circuses, and exhibitions, they did notice and discuss worldly novelties. Isaac Newton Youngs, for instance, in his Domestic Journal described, secondhand, an appearance by Tom Thumb in Albany in 1843. Another journal entry shows that he and others enjoyed the sight of a passing menagerie: "A caravan of wild beast went by here this forenoon, a great sight to us, altho' we could see but a small part, which was four Elephants & two camels. The rest were in [nineteen] covered carriages."[36]

Because a Shaker village operated on a schedule, however, daily life was predictable and such diversions were rare. Each household rose before dawn, adults and children alike. The brethren milked the cows while the sisters made beds and fixed breakfast, which they served an hour after the rising bell. Then everyone dispersed to do the work of the day, brethren to the farm and craft shops, sisters to their shops, laundry, and kitchen. The particularly onerous chores were rotated, laundry and cooking for the sisters and milking for the brethren. For harvest or spring cleaning, all turned to the task. The dinner bell rang a little before noon to call them from their labor. According to one who spent four months with the Watervliet Shakers, "Farmers then left the field and mechanics their shops, all washed their hands, and formed procession again and marched to dinner the same way as to breakfast." At mealtime they knelt in prayer by the tables, then ate silently, each in an assigned place, women seated apart from men. Each meal was consumed in about fifteen minutes. After dinner, they knelt and prayed, then returned to their labor and worked until supper.[37]

Shakers worked hard but could count on hearty meals with wholesome food. Every meal included about a dozen items. A typical breakfast, the lightest meal of the day, included meat, potatoes, wheat bread, rye-and-Indian bread, butter, pickles, applesauce, apple pie, salt, tea, milk, and water. One visitor reported enjoying a dinner of "very fine" ham, squash, potatoes, kidney beans, two kinds of beets, white and brown wheat bread, fruit pie, preserved fruit, Indian corn pudding, and "by far the finest butter" he had ever tasted. The good butter was evidence that the sisters took pride in their products, kept a clean dairy, and washed and stored their butter properly to keep it from turning rancid.[38]

Shakers ended their workday at eight o'clock and often devoted the evening to spiritual labor. After half an hour of retiring time to compose themselves spiritually, they joined in worship until bedtime. At least one evening a week, and twice on the Sabbath, they spent in supervised gatherings they called "union meeting." The union meeting was significant in Shaker society because it was a sanctioned opportunity for men and women to socialize. The society's early leaders, Isaac Newton Youngs explained, recognized that "male & female were so created that they would have a union together, and if it was not in the spirit, it would be in the flesh." The Ministry may also have seen that too much separation between the sexes could result in "party feeling" or divisiveness. Thus union meetings may have been intended to foster unity of interests as well as provide supervised socializing. So about 1793, the Ministry institutionalized union meetings, where all members of the society met in retiring rooms and sat in two ranks facing each other, about five feet apart.

In this position they entered into conversation on any familiar suitable subject, for information, edification, &c. Each brother and sister was obligated to converse more or less, with affability, observing the rules of good behavior in company and having no privacies.

As a general thing each brother and sister conversed with such as sat before them, observing not to be too profuse, contracted, or particular in their freedom & union with the opposite sex.

The order in which the brethren & sisters sat in their union meetings was directed by the Elders . . . such & such brethren facing such & such sisters. Also the sister, or sisters who sat facing a brother, for convenience sake . . . took care of his clothes, and did other kindnesses when necessary: and the brother or brethren in return did needful favors for the sisters.

Those who were most nearly associated in union meetings, were generally something of an age, and singers came together.

Union meetings continued for more than forty years. Children were not allowed to converse but sat quietly by the adults.

Brother Isaac believed that the system promoted "a chaste and orderly union." Outsiders saw union meetings differently. Some "evil-minded persons" construed the placing of certain brethren with certain sisters "as savoring of husband and wife" even though "private union" was prohibited. Nonetheless, some union partners did grow fond of one another and many were partnered for years, perhaps even decades. Union meeting partners remained linked until illness, removal to another dwelling, promotion, or death rendered a change necessary. But in 1841, in response to the suggestion of a visionist speaking in the name of Holy Mother Wisdom, Believers began rotating partners every other week, though only one sister remained responsible for each brother's clothing.[39]

A visitor described the conversation in an evening union meeting.

> Here, with their clean, checked, home-made pocket-handkerchiefs spread in their laps, and their spit-boxes standing in a row between them, they converse about raising sheep and kine, herbs and vegetables, building wall and raising corn, heating the oven and paring apples, killing rats and gathering nuts, spinning tow and weaving sieves, making preserves and mending the brethren's clothes—in short, every thing they do will afford some little conversation. But beyond their own little world, they do not appear to extend scarcely a thought. And why should they? Having so few sources of information, they know not what is passing beyond them. They however make the most of their own affairs, and seem to regret that they can converse no longer.[40]

The visitor was wrong about the Shakers' knowing little of what happened in the world beyond. On the contrary, they subscribed to periodicals and were informed about current events. Discussion of potentially divisive topics, however, such as religion, literature, and politics, was discouraged as contrary to union. As the brethren faced the sisters across the spit-boxes—the presence of which indicates that some chewed tobacco during the meetings—they made polite conversation without disorderly flirtation, complaint, or debate. And they had a good time, even if all they had to discuss was their latest meal. A Watervliet apostate later wrote that in one union meeting, a brother "eulogized" the sister who made the best johnnycake, adding, "by this means it might be said we enjoyed our dinner twice." In union meetings, according to Hervey Elkins, another apostate, Believers "converse simply, often facetiously, but rarely profoundly. In fact to say 'agreeable things about nothing,' when conversant with the other sex, is as common there as elsewhere." In Elkins's opinion, Shaker sociability differed little from that of the world, except perhaps for its ultimate goal.[41]

Some "real flesh hunters" Elkins reported, did sneak off on assignations during union meeting. Such regulated socializing was not meant to foster attraction.

> Nevertheless, an hour passes away very agreeably and even rapturously with those who there chance to meet with an especial favorite; succeeded soon however, when soft words, and kind, concentrated looks, become obvious to the jealous eye of a female espionage, by the agonies of a separation. For the tidings of such reciprocity, whether true or surmised, is sure before the lapse of too many hours, to reach the ears of the Elders; in which case, the one or the other party would be subsequently summoned to another circle of colloquy and union.

Shakers were closely monitored in "a constant system of *espionage*." In Elkins's view, the spies were all women. They were the arbiters of Shaker morality and their oversight was meant to stifle temptation.[42]

Shakers had little free time for pursuing the forbidden. Their lives were so closely scheduled that dalliance required determination. Indeed, brethren and sisters were under mutual surveillance even as they slept. At bedtime, men and women returned to their separate chambers and knelt in prayer before getting into bed. All were expected to retire and rise at the same times. Their day was typical of an agrarian society, scheduled according to cows' need to be milked and the daylight hours governing farm chores. Though Elders might give permission to sit up late to work, the need to ask discouraged the practice.[43]

That schedule of daytime work and evening union meetings or worship was followed six days a week. On Saturday before sundown, Believers prepared for the Sabbath by cleaning up and securing their shops and offices. Saturday evening, they held a special service of song and silent prayer. Alonzo Hollister described that meeting as "a time to shake off & break thru temporal care, bondage to pride, custom & material interests, that we might be free to worship God on the Sabbath." From sundown Saturday until sundown Sunday, all work was set aside except for essential chores that could not be neglected. Cows had to be milked twice a day, and livestock and Believers had to be fed. And if the Shakers were to uphold their high standards, beds had to be made and chamber pots emptied.[44]

The Shakers, always hoping for converts, welcomed the world's people to their meetinghouse for public worship on Sunday. One visitor described the Watervliet meetinghouse interior in the 1790s, about the time when the Youngs family began joining the Shakers. "The building was very light," she wrote, "and the walls, without being ornamented in any way, were perfectly smooth and painted a light blue." The "exquisitely clean" Shaker meetinghouse lacked "pulpit, pews, carpets, or any of the usual appendages of a church."[45] The setting exemplified Shaker simplicity, modesty, and humility. Elkanah Watson described Sabbath at New Lebanon in August 1790,

> The men advanced to the church in procession . . . all entered at the same door, and took their seats on the right side of the building. The women entered at another door, and occupied seats on the left side . . . they wore uniform simple dresses, with tight caps. There were about sixty of each sex.
>
> The spectators were arranged on benches against the wall, facing an open area appropriated to the dancing. At the word, the Shakers formed into solid masses, of a triangular form; the brethren in one column, and the sisters in another. One of the Elders then advancing to the front, addressed first the spectators, soliciting silence and decorum—and then the fraternity, exhorting them to keep in their own path, exhibiting the outer world as lost, but that the Shakers are sure of entering the straight and narrow way which led to life eternal.
>
> They all preserved a steadfast gaze upon the floor with their hands clenched, while every moment some individual would give a convulsive shake that agitated the whole frame. The discourse finished, the Elder ordered them 'to prepare to labor, in the name of the Lord.' At once they broke their ranks; the men stript off their coats, the women divested themselves of all superfluous articles of dress. They then re-formed in the same order with the celerity and exactness of a military column.
>
> Two or three Elders commenced a strange cadence, in hollow guttural

voices, rendered into a sort of dancing tune. The whole mass—men, women, and children, old and young, black and white, began to dance or rather move most awkwardly, raising their right knee high up, and dropping on the balls of their feet, the left foot performing a short up and down motion; all advancing and retiring three or four steps, and at every turn of the tune, whirling around with three steps. It seemed to me very like the movement of boys at school, in former days, when punished by stepping the bare feet upon a hot stove.[46]

Shaker services gradually changed, but during Isaac Newton Youngs's life, they were characterized by marching and dancing to unharmonized vocal accompaniment, with women and men on opposite sides of the meeting room or in separate lines, blacks side by side with whites, their racial equality unusual for their place and time. Less structured worship activities included gifts of divine inspiration, speaking in tongues, whirling, and other physical manifestations of the presence of God or divine spirits.

Many of the world's people respected the Shakers. Even Fanny Kemble, who derided Shaker religious practices, was impressed with them outside of the meetinghouse. "They are perfectly moral and exemplary in their lives and conduct," she wrote in 1835, "wonderfully industrious, miraculously clean and neat, and incredibly shrewd, thrifty and money-making." Horace Greeley, who also disparaged the Shakers' "singular worship," nevertheless commended the society's social welfare functions. "Here no widow clasps in anguish her shivering babes, and looks despairingly to her empty cupboard and fireless hearth."[47] Shakers took care of their own. And they were open to all who wanted to join. They set a high standard but were willing to rehabilitate anyone who sincerely wanted to convert. When a visitor in the early 1840s commented that many Believers undoubtedly had "contrary dispositions and habits," an Elder replied:

> You may say that there are rude materials of which to compose a church, and speak truly: but here (though strange it may seem) they are worked into a building, with no sound of axe or hammer. And however discordant they were in a state of nature, the square and the plumbline have been applied to them, and they now admirably fit the places which they were designed to fill. Here the idle become industrious, the prodigal contracts habits of frugality, the parsimonious become generous and liberal, the intemperate quit the tavern and the grog-shop, the debauchee forsakes the haunts of dissipation and infamy, the swearer leaves off his habits of profanity, the liar is changed into a person of truth, the thief becomes an honest man, and the sloven becomes neat and clean.

The Shakers' deportment, as far as the visitor could see, confirmed the Elder's words. Believers supported each other to become better people. But inability to conform meant expulsion; those who would not or could not adapt to the Shaker ideal either chose to leave or were cast out before they polluted others. As Isaac Newton Youngs wrote of one such person: "That one is void of simplicity & conformity, he is not worthy of the union of the people of God. He will not make a good Church member, unless he alters his course." [48] Remaining on the straight and narrow path to salvation was a lifelong effort that required commitment and self-discipline.

This, then, was the society that the Youngs family joined: spiritual, celibate, orderly, quiet, clean, prosperous, and committed to union, living their faith and working for perfection in temporal as well as spiritual labors. Believers' lives were not necessarily easy; human failings, disagreements and conflicts between personal needs and economic realities created conflict and stress. Isaac Newton Youngs found it difficult at times to live in union according to the Shakers' exacting standards of behavior. Beginning in his early childhood, he experienced both the benefits and the drawbacks of communitarian life.

2 Isaac Newton Youngs's Childhood and Youth, 1793–1807

ISAAC NEWTON YOUNGS was born to Martha (Farley) and Seth Youngs, Junior, in Johnstown, New York, on July 4, 1793. He was the last of ten children. The family moved from Schenectady to Stone Arabia to Johnstown in the two years before Isaac's birth. Seth Youngs did not own real estate. His unlanded status and apparent rootlessness suggest economic marginality, the sort of near-poverty that required moving to find a better situation.[1]

Isaac was christened in Johnstown's Methodist church. But Seth Youngs, Junior, sought a higher level of religious perfection than Methodism had to offer. In this, he may have been following in his own father's footsteps. Seth Youngs, Senior, had an "unorthodox turn of mind," and had been jailed in 1742 for "exhorting contrary to law." Also unorthodox, Seth Youngs, Junior, gravitated to the Shakers' radical views. A communitarian utopia had much to offer a man who sought religious perfectionism, especially if he had a large family in economic need.[2]

Some of Seth Youngs's kin were already Shakers at Watervliet, New York. Of twenty-six members of the extended Youngs-Wells family, at least twenty-four became Believers. Seth visited the Watervliet Shakers in November 1793 and returned to "open his mind" to the Elders in January 1794. Seth's wife, Martha, may have tried Shaker life but her son later mentioned that she had not "chosen to remain" with Believers. Some said that Martha deserted the family. By law, however, a husband held authority over his wife and children, and the legal system privileged the husband as the custodial parent. When Seth took the children, including six-month-old Isaac, to the Shakers, Martha's choices were to go along or to lose her family. Martha chose not to be a Shaker and had to fend for herself without the support of her family. Seth cast his lot with Believers and turned the nursling Isaac over to his brother and sister-in-law, Benjamin and Molly Youngs, who had also made a commitment to the Shakers.[3]

Isaac lived with his aunt and uncle for several years in a foster arrangement that was not unusual at the time. Children in Shaker settlements were separated from their parents at early ages, and so were children of the world. Being "put out" or sent to live with another family was an old Puritan custom designed to keep children from being spoiled. Though some resisted the move, children of any age were indentured to the Shakers.[4]

Though Isaac Newton Youngs would not have been in his mother's care even if she had signed the covenant and stayed with the Shakers, entries in his journals suggest that he resented her decision to leave the society, feeling perhaps that she had rejected him along with Shakerism. He later wrote of Shaker-raised children who were "hard to govern, and keep in good order, and apt to be fretful [and] cross." He wondered whether "[ev]il spirits did not strive more to work in them because they were cast out or rejected by those who were older."[5] Isaac knew that some children felt abandoned when their parents left them with Believers, perhaps because he felt that way himself.

Without family support, Martha Youngs was indigent, and so the town of Schenectady supported her as a pauper. Her caretaker, knowing the Shakers' prosperity, asked them for more money for her care. The Elders rejected the request. Isaac recorded their answer, showing little sympathy for his mother. Had she remained a Shaker, the society would have cared for her until she died, in keeping with the covenant between the society and its members. But she had to accept the consequences of her choice.

> If my mother had chosen to remain with our society in years past, she might unquestionably have enjoyed every needful comfort thro' life as well as myself, without experiencing any distressing dependence on others, but since it is as it is, I hope there will be wisdom & patience exercised towards her. It is true, on my personal account, I owe but little to her but my existence, as it is well known that I have been as an orphan, & brot up almost wholly among this society; & reason demands that I should repay my grateful services for the comfort of my aged & worthy Aunt & the aged & infirm of our society, from whom I have received nursing, favors & support in my infancy & childhood.[6]

In an era when children were parents' best hope for care in their later years, the Shakers shredded the security of nonmember parents whose children were Believers. Considering Mother Ann Lee's teachings on charity, including "Give unto him that asketh," the policy was punitive at best.[7] But the Elders may have feared the consequences of setting a precedent. If they assumed financial responsibility for Martha Youngs, they might have been forced to do the same for other apostates—a fiscal catastrophe that would yoke future Shakers to never-ending expense.

Despite the absence of the woman who had given him life, Isaac did not grow up motherless. His foster mother, Molly Youngs, filled the void, and Isaac loved her. He testified to his "esteem and thankfulness" for her early nurturing. When she was ailing, he wrote:

> I would assure you that I feel the tender feelings of sympathy for you, in your distress, and my heart is awakened to pity & sorrow, that one who has so often administered my comfort, should now be suffering. . . . I review with gratitude the days of my infancy . . . when you nursed me, as your own child. A tender & kind mother: and it seems as tho thru some means the honor & filial respect due to parents has rested upon you: I therefore renew my [love?] and gratitude to you, for all the favors you have bestowed.

Though Isaac may have felt abandoned by his biological parents, he had a warm relationship with Molly Youngs.[8]

Isaac's father had trouble sticking to his covenant. Seth Youngs, Junior, found the cross of celibacy heavy indeed. In 1800, he was a member of the "backsliding order" at Watervliet, living among those who had left the society, then returned. But despite his problems, he had spiritual gifts, including speaking in tongues, a supernatural ability the Shakers welcomed and valued. Seth Youngs was not an educated man but, according to anecdotes a kinsman related, he spoke Latin, Greek, "Indian," and French by divine inspiration, a manifestation of the power of God. Unfortunately, Youngs's spiritual gifts did not save him from a sorry fate. In 1815, he killed himself by cutting his throat.[9] Most of the Youngs family, however, prospered as Believers, becoming Elders, Deacons, and Trustees.[10]

Brother Isaac's Autobiography in Verse, a humorous retrospective view of his childhood and youth, provides more information on his early years, suggesting that he exercised initiative even as a small boy and that he was bright, creative, and lively.

> From birth to five or six years old
> I know not much but what I'm told.
> When under my Aunt Molly's care,
> Some dirty scrapes no doubt there were;
> But by the age of seven or eight,
> Some wondrous feats I could relate.
> My mighty scene (?) of Cat and sled,
> (Enough to rack a gen'ral's head!)
> My sermon to the wicked Len!
> Would make you stare, you may depend.[11]

Isaac thought himself better than his "wicked" contemporary at a very early age. And from age eight to ten, he had higher aspirations.

> And then to push the Capshief higher,
> My solemn trial of hell fire!
> Oh the deep views I witness'd then
> Can't be portrayed by Mortal's pen!
> To read in books I much desir'd,
> To skill in clocks I too aspir'd.
> In making dams and woodmills too,
> I often found much work to do
> But then I hastily skip o'er
> And pass to the age of ten or more.

Assessment of Isaac's "solemn trial of hell fire" is only speculative. He may have been referring to his removal from his aunt Molly's care, a change that did not suit him. A bright child who showed remarkable mechanical precocity, he could tell time before he "could talk plain," and he assembled a clock and tried to build a woodmill before he was ten.[12] But his life was unsettled after he left his aunt and uncle's home.

> My travel in back order times,
> Would greatly lengthen out my rhymes;
> My mountain scenes, also, alas!
> How glad I am those days are past.*
> A pleasant dream, I here could tell,
> How I, the mountain bade farewell.
> * Twas here that I did undertake
> A little wooden clock to make,
> But Abigail Richardson
> Burnt it all up—for her own fun.
> A flogging too she undertook
> To give to me (by hook or crook,)
> And for the same I ran away
> And told what had took place that day.

Had flogging children been common, Isaac probably would not have mentioned the incident with Abigail Richardson. But she may have been trying to break his spirit, to reduce his self-will to obedience and submission, which were, to the Shakers and other evangelicals, the only acceptable behavior for children.[13]

Though discipline was necessary, reprimands were not always so harsh.

Isaac's cousin Seth Youngs Wells wrote the model for governing Shaker children. (The fact that he had to write out instructions for child discipline suggests that punishment had to be regulated.) For a child of a tender disposition, he wrote, gentle admonition was sufficient, but if a child resisted chastisement, correction had to be proportionally more severe. A child "of lofty spirit" who disregarded reprimands might be ordered to kneel before the family as a lesson in humility. A badge of disgrace, such as the label "Bad Boy," was useful for shaming a miscreant. These punishments were gentler than those used among the world's people, where delinquent boys were strapped, whipped, or beaten by schoolmasters and parents alike. Public school teachers shamed unruly students with "whispering sticks" put into a talkative child's mouth like a horse's bit or a cleft stick pinched onto a culprit's nose while he stood before the class. Even comparatively mild schoolmasters were known to bag offenders in a sack for punishment. In Shaker society, only a stubborn and unrepentant child required the rod. To earn a whipping, Isaac may have pressed the limits. But the flogging did not work; he continued to misbehave.[14]

In 1800, Isaac moved to Watervliet's South Family, where he lived with Seth Youngs Wells, Benjamin Youngs, and four other men of the extended Wells-Youngs family. In 1803, he moved yet again, into Watervliet's Children's Order. Even so, he managed to get into trouble, as he related in his *Autobiography in Verse*.

> And how to Watervliet I went,
> And there 3 years or more I spent.
> At Watervliet time swiftly ran,
> Here I the taylor's trade began.
> And still my head was full of notions
> And oft bro't trouble for my portion,
> Machines and woodmills seemed so nice
> I would get caught in some device.
> One time a woodmill I erected
> Soon to be finish'd I expected—
> But O! I suffered the disgrace
> To see it burnt before my face!
> How oft I cut some silly caper
> Not fit to tell about, on paper!

Isaac's childhood was characterized by misbehavior. He expressed his anger. He pouted. He may have incited trouble. "I long was boyish," he wrote, "until I had full time to grow."[15]

Furthermore, he disliked work, which in Shaker thought made him a slug-gard. Children had to learn a good work ethic. Those as young as four or five were set to work, not just among Shakers, but among the world's people, as well. An indolent child reflected badly on his upbringing. One Yankee family taught their sons "that laziness was the worst form of original sin." Their children rose early and filled every hour with work appropriate to their age and ability. The Shakers did likewise. They reminded children, from an early age, "Improve all your time in something useful"; "Always be industrious, for idleness is the parent of vice"; "Never delay to tomorrow that which ought to be done today." [16]

When Isaac was assigned to tailoring at age ten, he would have preferred another trade, but the choice was not his. Despite lingering Puritan beliefs that each individual should choose his own calling between age ten and four-teen, the Shakers put the needs of the society first and made that decision unless an indenture specified otherwise.[17] Tailoring required self-discipline, which the boy sorely needed. His assignment to tailoring, which kept him under adult control through long workdays, may also have taught him humility.

Even though he became a diligent worker, Isaac Newton Youngs had a reputation for being "very forward." As an adult, he recalled his early years as "a pretty serious time" and excused some of his childish misbehaviors, noting that only "sober folks" thought him unusual for a boy his age. He was closely supervised and recalled, "I had disagreeable scenes to pass thro in learning my trade, conducting myself with superiors, grappling with the growing passions of nature, & labouring to go in union with my Elders, brethren and sisters." [18] Isaac had trouble settling down. Perhaps because he had been moved through several households, he lacked consistent discipline, though he later conjectured that evil spirits worked in children whose parents had cast them aside.

Despite his misbehavior, Isaac Newton Youngs took religion seriously even as a youth. In 1806, his commitment to Shakerism showed in a letter he wrote to his apostate brother James.

> If you ever want to be saved, the only way that you can be saved will be to confess and forsake your sins. He that covers his sins shall not prosper but he that confesseth and forsaketh them shall find mercy . . . you know not how soon you may be called out of this world to give an account for the things done here in the body—for every work shall be brought into judgment. . . . You have an immortal soul to save or lose. . . . I do not want to discourage you . . . I want to do you good and I hope you will receive it kindly.

Isaac invited his brother to return to the Shakers. "I believe you will be received with kindness," he wrote, "if you come with sincerity and set out again and take up your cross and confess." [19] Isaac's letter revealed his firm grip on Shaker beliefs. By age thirteen, he had internalized their concepts of godliness, covered or concealed sin, confession, redemption, the cross of celibacy, and eternal reward or damnation.

Isaac's childhood ended officially in 1807, when, at age thirteen, he moved to New Lebanon and signed the Shaker covenant. Shaker youth typically signed the covenant (or left the Shakers) at the age of twenty-one when their indentures expired, but Isaac was precocious. [20] His letter to his brother may have been considered among his qualifications for the faith. Signing the covenant was a serious commitment, but the Elders thought him conscientious enough to fulfill his side of the contract. His precocity made him an asset they did not want to lose. And he believed. He did not have to be convinced of the value of a Shaker life; he was already willing to devote himself to it, heart and hand. He also viewed his move as a great privilege. And it was indeed a privilege for a boy his age to live in the society that stood first among all Shaker orders; the Ministry's Church Family, at New Lebanon, was reserved for those who showed the most spiritual travel. Isaac later wrote that he did not have a real home until he arrived at New Lebanon. [21]

It is hard to imagine what must have gone through young Isaac's mind as he lifted his small bundle of belongings, climbed into a wagon with the North Family Elders to leave Watervliet on March 23, 1807, and headed east over the muddy roads of springtime. He may not have been eager to leave familiar surroundings, heading off on what was probably the longest trip he had ever taken.

The travelers crossed the Hudson River and wound their way up the rutted road into the Berkshire hills, leaving behind the river valley where spring had already arrived. The trip probably took most of the day through countryside Isaac had never seen before. New Lebanon was considered "beautiful in the extreme," with the Shaker village spread above it on the western lap of the Taconic ridge. Some hills were cultivated to the summit; others remained wooded. [22] At the New Lebanon Shaker village, trees had not yet budded out and the landscape was as bare as in winter. But in the mud month of March, the sap rose on soft spring days. And as Isaac ascended into the colder Berkshire hills, he may have seen thrifty Yankee farmers collecting maple sap to boil down to syrup or sugar.

The boy surely felt some trepidation as he approached New Lebanon, wondering whether or how he would fit in with the society's elite. He probably also had high expectations. Years later, when John Dean came to the

Church Family, Isaac expressed concern in his journal that the young man would be disappointed, perhaps reflecting the contrast between his own early expectations and his discovery that the Church Family was neither heaven on earth nor a place of perfect union, peace, and goodness.

> I feel some loth to have him come among us and see just how we get along, and meet with many disappointments, as I suppose he will, for I suppose (and have understood that he said) he thought he was coming to heaven and likely he thought the church were all perfection—no difficulties, nothing but union, peace and perfect goodness as it were. But he must find it quite different . . . & I fear his disappointment may be in such a manner as to hurt his faith for a spell.[23]

When Isaac arrived in late March 1807 with his expectations still untempered by reality, he would have found the New Lebanon Shaker village "remarkable neat and pretty," a balm to the eye. The world's people said that the Shakers there were "esteemed by their neighbors as an industrious, punctual, kind-hearted set of people." A boy far from familiar surroundings undoubtedly appreciated kindness. "I stayed that night at the north house," he recalled, "and in the morning about 8 oclock I . . . [was] left under the guardianship of Rufus Bishop to work with him at Tayloring." Elder Nicholas Bennet wrote, "Isaac Youngs comes into the church to work."[24] Not to live, but to work. At age thirteen, Isaac was considered a worker, an apprentice tailor with responsibilities, not a child. Thus on March 24, 1807, Isaac Newton Youngs entered his "settled home." Work and faith would dominate the rest of his life.

In New Lebanon, as in Watervliet, children's lives were intended to be stable and structured. They were well fed, clothed, and allowed some recreation. Childhood in the nineteenth century, however, was a chancy thing. Children were at the mercy of disease, and living in community meant that contagion spread in a flash. According to records kept by the New Lebanon Shakers, for instance, the settlement had an epidemic in January 1813. "The meazles prevail in the Church," wrote the scribe. "The fever has also come in among us & a number down with it." Twenty died before the end of February. And at Watervliet, Freegift Wells noted, "Such a distressing pestilence was never known in this part of the country; it seizes with great violence and takes people off in a short time."[25]

Such diseases meant that many children died young. As late as 1850, almost 50 percent of all U.S. children died before age fifteen. The prevailing view that death is always imminent shows up in a funeral sermon Timothy Dwight preached in 1803: "At every stage of their progress death ambushes their path, and unseen graves open to receive them . . . Infancy, Childhood, Youth, Manhood, and Age descend to the tomb." Survivors learned about mortality at a very early age, as did Isaac Newton Youngs. He lived though the epidemics and realized his good fortune. In 1807, he expressed his thankfulness that God had spared his life. He knew that he could not count on living into old age and the Shakers fostered that understanding to encourage children to work for salvation. A Believer's "chief duty while here on earth," Christian Goodwillie points out, was "to prepare correctly for eternity." Thus "We are Born to Die" and many other Shaker songs promoted the message that life was tenuous.[26]

Healthy or not, Isaac was usually under the oversight of concerned brethren who supervised boys to keep them on the straight and narrow path to salvation even when they deliberately strayed. And young Isaac must have stepped off the path often. But as Stephen Stein suggests, Shaker children were "integrated as much as possible into the life of the community." Isaac later described the boys' occupations.

> They are mostly employed on the farm in summer, at raising corn & potatoes &c, frequently engaged helping the brethren here & there, when needed.
> In winter they go to school, and when not in school they get in wood to the house & shop & various chores here & there. Boys in the boys' order seldom work at any particular branch of mechanical business.[27]

Isaac Newton Youngs's childhood resembled the upbringing of other Shaker-raised boys of his generation. He worked six days a week, learned to read and write, was apprenticed in a trade, and internalized Shaker ideals. Like other boys in an agrarian society, Shaker boys helped with all types of farm chores and unskilled labor. Two boys were considered able to do the work of one man. And work they did. Eggs had to be gathered, livestock herded and fed, and sheep washed and sheared. Boys cut, raked, stacked, and moved hay into the barn. They planted, harvested, threshed, and stored grain. Feeding the Church Family meant that boys milked cows, hilled and dug potatoes, and seeded, weeded, manured, cultivated, and harvested other crops. In fall, everyone picked apples and husked corn. They hauled and spread ashes and dung. Gangs of boys picked stones out of rocky fields, then carted them away. They planted fruit trees, boxed seeds, sorted broom corn, and made brooms and brushes for sale. Some braided straw for hats. Little boys were taught to knit and probably worked on the socks they wore out so fast. Older boys were given harder work, including logging, ditching, and plowing, the heavy labor that simultaneously exhausted them and lightened the load on the brethren.[28]

A farm village required year-round labor. Besides the work associated with crops and livestock, kindling had to be collected, and hundreds of cords of wood were cut, chopped, split, and stacked each year, then lugged to stoves and woodboxes. Much of that work was done by the village youths. A boy's indenture required that the Shakers teach him farming or a trade, as well as reading and writing, so some were apprenticed to the village craftsmen. But they helped with a variety of other jobs, as well. In one spring season, tailor's apprentices blasted stone, built fences, set onions, moved maple sugar, cleaned around the barns, raked the garden, and cleaned the village's dooryards, in addition to tailoring. A Shaker lad had as many chores as any other farm boy, and his work was both needed and valued.[29]

Sometimes the weather forced changes in their work. The cold year of 1816, for instance, brought more planting than usual, a smaller harvest, and increased need for firewood. The Year Without a Summer was an agricultural disaster. In the Berkshire uplands, at higher elevations where farming was touch and go in the good years, the cooler climate did not quite support agriculture. Many northeasterners commented on the phenomenon. Sarah Snell Bryant, a Berkshire resident, wrote in her diary, "Weather backward." Others elaborated. Samuel Griswold Goodrich said that the summer of 1816 in Connecticut was the coldest of the century. And it was worse in the Berkshire uplands. At the New Lebanon Church Family, Nicholas Bennet wrote on May 5, 1816, that "all was froze" a few days earlier, and the hills were "barren like winter." Temperatures went below freezing almost every day in May. The ground froze solid on June 9. On June 12, the Shakers had to re-plant crops destroyed by the cold. On July 7 it was so cold that everything had stopped growing. The Berkshires had frost again on August 23. A Massachusetts historian summed up the disaster.[30]

> Severe frosts occurred every month; June 7th and 8th snow fell, and it was so cold that crops were cut down, even freezing the roots. . . . In the early Autumn when corn was in the milk it was so thoroughly frozen that it never ripened and was scarcely worth harvesting. Breadstuffs were scarce and prices high and the poorer class of people were often in straits for want of food. It must be remembered that the granaries of the great west had not then been opened to us by railroad communication, and people were obliged to rely upon their own resources or upon others in their immediate locality.[31]

The weather in and of itself was not a hardship for hardy northerners accustomed to long winters. The real problem lay in the weather's effect on crops and thus on the local food supply. In 1816, the twenty-three-year-old Isaac probably had double the normal amount of farm work at planting time and less work in the fall when every crop ran short. The low temperatures meant that all able-bodied youth spent much more time than usual cutting, splitting, stacking, and hauling firewood. And the tailors may have had to expedite their work on winter clothing.

The following year brought extra help to the Shakers. In 1817, a tide of emigration flowed south and west. Many emigrants were impoverished and had to beg their way. But some went only as far as the nearest Shaker village. The population of the New Lebanon society rose from 317 in 1810 to 390 in 1820, a 23 percent increase. New England's Shaker societies also grew. During economic downturns, Shakerism's many temporal benefits, including lifetime support, attracted converts who were willing to work and needed room and board as much as they needed salvation.[32] The additional hands meant that Isaac Newton Youngs grew up with abundant help in his work.

Isaac's single most time-consuming job was tailoring. Apprenticed to the master tailor Rufus Bishop, he carried firewood, fed the stove, cleaned, ran errands, fetched whatever the senior tailors needed, and learned his trade. A tailoring apprenticeship followed predictable stages. A boy under twelve made the best beginner because he was still limber enough to sit all day in the tailor's squat. Isaac probably spent the first year practicing the simplest skills: learning how to use thread, needle, and thimble, working on scraps to master the different stitches. At that stage, he might have been entrusted with easy tasks, such as sorting and stringing buttons and sewing them on garments. Once he could handle a needle, he learned to hem trousers with a stitch strong enough to hold but invisible from the outside of the garment. When he was proficient at that, he began sewing the brethren's inner garments, then progressed to pressing seams and stitching more complicated apparel. After three years, he might have been taught to make and set in sleeves. In years four and five, an apprentice learned how to construct trousers and vests, and by his sixth year, he was expected to do the finishing touches on the most complex garments.

Only after he had mastered sewing was an apprentice taught how to measure the brethren, cut cloth, and fit garments. Cutting was hard to learn. As Isaac explained, it was "not reduced to rule . . . [and] the learner depended very much on the immediate instruction of an experienced workman." And since cutting mistakes were expensive because they wasted cloth, an error-prone apprentice could expect rebuke. Isaac spent his spring and fall tailoring seasons for six or more years learning the "art and mystery" of the trade before he reached journeyman status, when he could make garments on his own from start to finish. Not every apprentice moved up to journeyman and then master craftsman. Some proved incompetent or careless or were deemed unsuitable for other reasons.[33] But by the time Shaker-raised young men were twenty-one, they were supposed to be proficient enough at a trade or farming to contribute fully to their Shaker community or to make their own way in the world.

For Isaac, tailoring was filled with trials. The hardest thing for the boy may have been sitting still for most of the day. And the master tailor David Slosson was another cross to bear. Though Isaac was apprenticed to Rufus Bishop in 1807, Bishop was promoted to Elder in 1808, and his new job called him out of the tailors' shop. In Elder Rufus's absence, the hard-driving Brother David oversaw the apprentices' work. When Isaac arrived at New Lebanon, the boys were scattered among different caretakers, and he was under Slosson's care, rooming with him from 1806 to 1823. Being subject to him both in and out of the tailor's shop was difficult because the older man was critical and very "plain spoken." Part of Isaac's unhappiness in tailoring stemmed from Slosson's faultfinding. "I should be glad to get out of the shop on his account," Isaac later wrote, because "it seemed impossible to give him satisfaction."[34] Slosson's displeasure made the youth's apprenticeship a burden.

Another trial was the volume of brethren's clothing needed. To judge from a 1796 list of garments given to one brother, a Shaker man's wardrobe consisted of two coats, four vests, five pairs of britches or trousers, four pairs of stockings or socks, six pairs of footings, three work frocks, eight shirts, and other odds and ends—all of them made by hand, one stitch at a time. Clothing the village brethren was labor-intensive and time-consuming, requiring thousands of hours' work each year. And though their outfits were simple, the Shakers expected garments to be well-made and durable, which meant a lot of work for a boy who disliked bending over a hot tailor's goose, wielding needle and thread for ten hours a day, or addressing complaints about apparel he had spent hours making.[35]

In Shaker society, a tailoring apprenticeship was not year-round. The tailors generally began winter clothing in September by measuring brethren who needed garments. They cut and sewed through the winter. Their shop probably had windows on the south side, where the light would be unobstructed through the short winter days; good light was necessary for close work on dark cloth. In early spring, they began summer clothing. Farm work called them out of the shop in summer and early fall.[36]

Though boys had to be kept busy, their life was not all work. Isaac had a few friends his own age and enjoyed his time with them.

There were a number gather'd in
With whom I felt quite near akin.
Friend Garret Lawrence, (late deceas'd)
Among my mates was not the least,
Much real comfort we have taken,
If I am not a deal mistaken:
We loved to talk and make up rhymes
& have some simple sprees, sometimes.
And others I could mention, too,
Whose love was near, & friendship true.

Isaac Newton Youngs and Garret Lawrence were close friends. Because only six boys came into the New Lebanon Church Family between 1801 and 1810, Isaac and Garret had few age-mates, which made their friendship even more precious. They appreciated each other's sense of humor. They got into trouble together. They teased each other with the affection reserved for special friends. With "friendship true," they grew to manhood in the Church Family.[37]

The boys lived in the Church Family dwelling or "Great House," Isaac rooming with David Slosson. Garret was probably just down the hall, equally supervised. Though they later roomed together as adults, it is unlikely that the Elders would have permitted two such lively lads to share quarters before they were mature enough to settle down.[38]

The Church Family did not have a school when Isaac arrived, nor did they immediately make provisions for teaching him anything other than tailoring. Probably he had already learned to read and write at Watervliet, because the Shakers realized that their children needed the basic skills: reading, writing, and cyphering. But after the New Lebanon Church Family began taking in children, the village required a school. They began with a few boys reading in an evening class, and opened a day school in 1815. By then, Isaac was twenty-two and had made enough progress in his studies to teach.[39] But religion remained more important than education.

Isaac Newton Youngs and Garret Lawrence were educated beyond the average for the Shakers. Exactly where and how Isaac received additional schooling, other than the extra instruction in grammar he received at Watervliet (perhaps from Seth Youngs Wells) is unknown. Their schooling did not progress as far as it might have among the world's people because the Shakers believed that too much education was unnecessary, perhaps even dangerous. Learning hampered spiritual travel. Benjamin Seth Youngs, Isaac's older brother, mentioned the "prejudice of education" as a hindrance to faith, and he was not the only Elder with that view. As another Elder said, it was "easier to gain a thousand without it, than one with it" because learned people questioned, criticized, and raised objections rather than having faith. Mother Lucy Wright, the Ministry's Lead during most of Isaac's youth, continued the early doctrine of limited education.[40]

A visitor to the Shakers pointed out, "In a community it must be that the individual genius is largely sacrificed to the common purpose . . . and yet I believe that among the Shakers the sacrifice is compelled only by private conscience." He was partly correct. After Lucy Wright died, Isaac Newton Youngs sought out other means of educating himself, even discussing clockmaking with the editors of *Scientific American*. But Brother Isaac recognized the privilege as well as the pitfalls of education. He noted, "I mean to make use of my learning, as well as every other privilege which [I] enjoy. I intend that as far as it depends upon me, my learning shall not be a snare to me, or that the pursuit of it shall not [lead] me astray from my duty." [41]

As a good Believer, Isaac was committed to duty as a fundamental tenet of his religion. He later wrote that he did not have a conversion experience, but his faith grew as he did. Even in childhood, he wrote, he "felt a kind of disdain towards the wickedness & fashions of the world," because he thought he possessed something superior.[42] And he enjoyed worship. Believers had a full schedule of services and meetings. When Isaac arrived at the Church Family in 1807, Sabbath services lasted about three hours. A visitor described their meeting in 1805: "The chief elder, who seems to direct the whole ceremony, sat nearly in the centre. At first, the most profound silence was observed; when on a signal from the chief elder, all present rose from their seats, and the men and women formed two distinct rows opposite to each other, in form of a fan. They stood in this position a few minutes, when many of them began to shake and tremble." After the introductory shaking, the congregation chanted. Then the tempo of the service picked up. "A general shout now took place, followed by an odd kind of dance," the visitor wrote. When the dancers resumed their seats, two women came in with brooms and swept, first on the men's side and then on the women's, before the dancing continued.[43]

Shaker worship was not always the same. In 1807 the Church Family enjoyed a revival with "much awakening testimony." Spontaneous operations of the spirit included bowing, shaking, turning, speaking in tongues, and rolling. Believers were thrown to the floor and rolled like logs. New dances, marches, and songs were introduced "to enliven the sense, and make worship feel new and interesting." Isaac appreciated the enthusiasm and, having grown up believing in the validity of supernatural experiences, he was comforted by Shaker spirituality. A few years later, he wrote of Believers in worship: "O how happy they looked, how beautiful. Surely I said to myself, how mean are all earthly joys, how trifling are all the little trials which we have to pass thro in finding such spiritual comforts, such reviving glories which the gospel opens to our souls." [44] Even as a youth, Isaac Newton Youngs appreciated the benefits of his faith. And he took pleasure in spirituality for the rest of his life.

In 1823 or early 1824, at the end of his youth, Brother Isaac composed a song, poem, and prayer for the dedication of the Church Family's new meetinghouse. These texts, printed for such an important occasion, show that he was a trusted member of the New Lebanon Church Family. Having internalized the society's beliefs, he outlined the Shaker ideal in his poem, "Good Believers' Character," as a plan for achieving success as a Shaker.[45] He listed all the necessary character attributes. A good Believer could not be at peace with his own deficiencies; he had to put his own needs second to those of his society. No one could help slipping off the path of virtue occasionally, but Shakers had to confess their errors and make amends, striving for perfection, spiritual and temporal. Isaac's poem alluded to more Shaker ideals: obedience, virtue, truthfulness, thankfulness, humility, and kindness. All those qualities were essential for getting along in a communal society. To achieve salvation, Shakers had to "keep up a warfare within," against lust and sin. The cross was not only a biblical reference; the cross of celibacy was the burden Shakers picked up daily as long as they lived. Conquering sin and achieving salvation required it. Isaac Newton Youngs knew that Believers did not uphold these ideals perfectly, that they had human failings. His poetry is filled with admonitions to work for those qualities. But every Shaker was a Believer by choice. Brother Isaac chose that road to salvation when he was only a child. On the threshold of adolescence, he took a vow of celibacy that proved to be an overwhelming challenge in his twenties. And though he warred against his natural desires, his lust was very nearly his undoing.

Satan puts his paw on me, and I am captive led.

3 Youth and Lust

"A snare of satan to beguile the soul," 1818–1823

SEXUALITY WAS the cross of celibacy. Controlling sexual behavior was, therefore, one of a Believer's challenges. Mother Lucy Wright recognized that celibacy was a sacrifice. But she called on her followers not to flinch because the road to perfection was so straight and narrow. Taking an easier path would have meant living by worldly standards, rather than living up to the ideals of utopia. To promote their spiritual travel, therefore, they had to eradicate lust. As Isaac Newton Youngs wrote in his poem "Good Believers' Character," Shakers had to "feel it their duty to bear a full cross, and zealously run for the prize." Lustful impulses were a trial to be endured. The cross of celibacy was heavy and the prize could be elusive—and never more so than in youth.[1]

As a young man, Isaac Newton Youngs found self-control difficult. But nonetheless, the years between about age eighteen and age twenty-two, were good.

> I enjoyed myself the best that I ever did in my life, having gained a middling good degree of union, having freer access to Elders, coming some more forward in privilege, and having . . . more liberty of acting and speaking my reason. . . . I could go on and do the best that I know, feel safe in what I did, enjoy my union, and not trouble myself much about what was past, or what was to come.

The following years, however, were blighted by "the growing passions of nature." In his twenties, his disorderly behaviors—fueled by rebelliousness, lust, and affection for a Shaker sister—brought him repeated rebukes.[2] His writings show that he had moved, as he put it, from the "simple sprees" of childhood to more serious challenges. He alluded to those problems in his Autobiography in Verse. As manhood approached, "New cares arose, new billows roar, / New trials, I knew not before." Worse yet, he wrote, "Satan oft laid his tempting snare / & cross'd my track, most everywhere"; but God watched over him, and he never doubted his faith.[3]

In retrospect, Isaac Newton Youngs saw youth as a struggle, a constant battle against his own nature. In youth, the new trials that he "knew not before" interfered with his pursuit of the "golden prize" of salvation. And lust was foremost among those trials. In this, he differed little from other evangelical Christians who sought to keep themselves pure.

Isaac was unusual, however, in recording his struggle. Other Believers who kept journals shared the reticence of most nineteenth-century diarists on the subject of sex, rarely mentioning their personal difficulties with celibacy, despite their belief that lust was "the principal seat of human depravity." [4] Books in the New Lebanon Shakers' library suggest that the society did try to help its youth by providing literature on the issue of emerging sexuality, including practical aids to celibacy. Several works, for example, promoted chastity, including Sylvester Graham's *Lecture to Young Men,* published first in 1833. John Ware's 1850 *Relation of the Sexes,* which advises against masturbation, was on their shelves. And Dio Lewis's *Chastity, or, Our Secret Sins,* offered practical advice on stopping seminal losses. In all these works, clean thinking was the key to avoiding self-pollution; temperance and rigorous exercise promoted chastity. If a young man needed more help, he could wrap himself in a cold wet towel at night. [5]

And though Shaker youth must have had to cope with their own emerging lust, their journals include little explicit information about the onset of sexual maturity. As Stephen Stein points out, "physical changes within young men at puberty, the occurrence of nocturnal emissions, and other signs of physical maturation" are "notably absent in the written records." [6] The physical changes associated with puberty were veiled by discretion. But Isaac Newton Youngs, unlike other diarists, recorded some startlingly personal information. His frankness sets him apart from other Shakers. No one charted the personal problems or revealed the communal strength of celibacy as he did. [7]

Brother Isaac had been keeping the journal for three months when he wrote, "Some men & women come up from the hollow & go into the North family's pond together!!" The two exclamation points showed his shock; such emphasis was uncommon. Because the hollow was the home of apostates, former Shakers who had chosen to return to the world, the flesh, and the devil, their behavior was even more scandalous. Going into the pond together, in contrast to the Shaker brethren's chaste summer swims, was evidence of worldly depravity. That incident evidently jolted Isaac into sexual awareness, because thereafter, lust appeared with increasing frequency in his journal. He also saw the price a celibate Believer would have to pay if he succumbed to temptation. On the same day as the mixed swimming party at the pond, Bushnel Fitch left the Shakers, and Isaac noted, "I saw the danger &

vanity of youthful lusts (of any kind) which blind the senses with darkness & swiftly lead the soul to ruin." He knew he was not perfect, himself. Concerned for his own salvation, he wrote, "I must expect to have a grapple to get entirely out of the flesh." [8] He realized it would not be easy, and so he kept an account of his temptations.

Brother Isaac was dismayed by his own failings. "O how long! how long! shall I remain subjected to weakness, why is it!" he wrote. "Flesh is flesh . . . but O if I could once get . . . out, I would hate the flesh with all my feelings & never get catched with it again." [9] He did not explain how he got "catched with it," but we can imagine the evidence that might have accrued against a young man living in crowded quarters, his laundry done by the ever-watchful sisters.

The following week, Isaac sought help from the Elders, asking them to "labor for a gift for him." But the Elders told him he had to search for a solution himself. Undoubtedly they advocated praying; prayer was supposed to reduce sexual desire. The saying "Sinning will keep thee from praying, and praying will keep thee from sinning" was probably familiar to Isaac from early childhood. And he may have followed the advice to pray away his sin, because he felt steadier a week later. He had a clear idea of the strength of fleshly desires, however, when he wrote, "This is the gospel, that the spirit of a creature should govern the propensity of the body . . . like a gate to a pond of water [that] is the appetite which ever craves vent." Dammed-up desire was his problem. Despite the mandate of self-control, he was young, healthy, and interested in what healthy twenty-three-year-old men were usually interested in: sex. But, as Louis Kern points out, "For the Shakers, man's existence in this life, his hope for improvement, and his reward or punishment in the next life hung on his sexual conduct." [10] Though Brother Isaac hoped for salvation, he found it difficult to master his own nature.

The "secret and unaccountable evil" continued to assail him. He exerted his will but could not eradicate his libido. As he grew more desperate, his complaints became more specific. "If I am excited to evil," he wrote, "my mind is apt to run on it. The flesh is a deceivable nature. I have a struggle to keep it under. I can keep myself from willfully giving way, but it is harder to keep my sense and thoughts right." [11]

Trying not to think of sex, when Shaker exhortations continually reminded him of it, must have been difficult indeed. Songs they sang in worship dwelled on crucifying the flesh, denying the flesh, forsaking carnal pleasure, bidding carnal thoughts adieu, and variations on that theme. Some verses were colorful. Isaac himself wrote lyrics that included the lines, "Our fleshly natures we'll torture and vex," and "My old carnal nature I'll grind to the marrow." [12] Those lyrics affirmed the Shakers' cross of celibacy and served as psychosocial support, but the focus on lust also kept the topic fresh in a young man's mind.

Brother Isaac felt harassed by his own thoughts; every salacious fantasy was an invitation to ruin. But sexual desire was not the only problem. The other factor contributing to his misery was his quest for perfection. He wanted to be the best person he could be, according to Shaker standards. But his inability to control his lust meant that he was not living up to expectations—either his own or the society's. His deficiency was humiliating and frustrating.

Isaac unhappily continued his self-analysis through 1817. "If I had a real sense of the evil of the flesh, it would be impossible for me to be overcome in such ways that I am," he wrote. "I have in my choice & understanding re-nounced the flesh, with its affections & lusts: but these extend a great way, and I, unfortunately, have a great portion of them." Good intentions were not enough. Even so, his comment about having a "great portion" of affec-tions and lusts holds as much sheepish pride as it does humility. His words re-semble the confession of the sinner whose superlative is that he has sinned more than most. But lust spurred his creative writing and sharpened his ver-bal imagery.

> I think sometimes, O that I could dig to the bottom of my nature & pluck it up, as I would an evil plant, & sometimes I feel determined to stick to it with zeal—then again, becoming an old story, & looking forward & thinking what a long, slow & dubious work it will be, I feel slack, & would give out, were it not for fear of the consequences. So considering all things, I think it is best for me to keep on, for if I do not, it will be like entering a narrow passage where I must keep on & cannot turn back without certain destruction. [13]

That was the first occasion when Isaac discussed his fear of the consequences of giving way to his nature. He decided, with just a hint of reluctance, that it was best for him to try to stay in Shaker union, even though it would be a "long, slow & dubious work." His use of the supposition "I think it is best," rather than saying he knew it would be best, indicates some ambivalence. His curiosity could have been his undoing, but either his faith or fear of the consequences—or both—outweighed it. He may have been calibrating the society's standards, testing the limits, and looking for loopholes in church or-ders against sexuality.

Isaac Newton Youngs was not the only Believer struggling to bear the Shaker cross of celibacy. The Ministry reiterated the need for gospel order, and Mother Lucy preached, "They that will give way to fleshly thoughts, will give way to fleshly sensations & feelings, to wanton evil thoughts. . . . The soul that does such things should be shut off from God's people." [14] Knowing she was right and fearing the consequences of noncompliance, Isaac fought nature to keep his own thoughts pure. He had good reason to be afraid. One consequence of ungovernable nature was expulsion. For a youth who had been raised a Shaker and knew no other life, the possibility of being shut out of his society may have been frightening. (He saw the consequences for his peers who left the society and did not prosper; two months after Joel Wood departed with his union meeting partner, Clarissa Cogswell, Wood committed suicide.) [15] Pitfalls awaited the unwary. No wonder Isaac wrote, "This world is not a place of bliss," explaining in poetry,

> For flesh & blood, that's formed in sin,
> Involves the sense, impedes the way
> And mortal bonds, with lust within
> Forever tempt the soul to stray.
> & I must be on my guard
> Since I have undertook the race
> For it must go exceeding hard
> If I forsake the path of grace. [16]

Even in youth, Isaac had his eye on the better world to follow. Having made his commitment, he guarded against slipping; a lapse meant loss of salvation in the afterlife as well as loss of Shaker union in the mortal world.

By the spring of 1818, however, the twenty-five-year-old Believer was convinced that he was too shaky to succeed in self-control. He had been struggling against his sexual nature for three years with little relief, and he lamented his shortcomings.

> Instead of governing my nature, my nature governs me, and I have not
> the government over my own passions. I know that I intend to do right, to
> take up my cross against my ugly dispositions, but I fall short of what I
> ought to in this. That which I at one time, promise myself to forsake, at
> another, I indulge in. I feel spoilt, seeing I am so unsteady. [As for my near
> companions,] I cannot think they are so far from innocence as I am. So satan
> . . . puts his paw on me, and I am captive led! I may take up my cross against
> the flesh, but I am . . . unwillingly harassed with all the dirty thoughts that
> could be invented. [17]

Though he was ashamed of his lapses, he was continually beset by lustful thoughts. He had to do better. Conforming to Shakers' high standards of behavior required self-government, but controlling his own erotic fantasies was a trial of the highest order. Despite his good intentions, his mind kept veering toward the flesh.

Brother Isaac was clearly not the only Shaker stepping out of line in early 1818. The Elders found it necessary to warn the Church Family, particularly the brethren, about sexual misconduct. Unnecessary touching was forbidden and brethren and sisters were not to talk together in private; such behavior was disorderly. Believers probably received such reminders periodically, but that spring, they were repeatedly admonished. Evidently an epidemic of touching and private conversation had broken out; that deviance inspired a crackdown. Isaac wanted to prosper spiritually, and he knew he had to subdue his nature. Dismayed, he wrote:

> In the mean time my carnal nature was growing and making heavy progress over my youthful mind. The greatest and ruling tyrant of all the nations of evil was making strong invasions, and though I might have gained some over one enemy, so as to be able to take a little comfort, yet a greater and more secret enemy would beset me, & deprive me of what little comfort I felt.[18]

Brother Isaac felt that a carnal demon had invaded his mind and body. The constant struggle took its toll. And though he had not yet specified his particular problem, a subsequent entry sheds light on his dilemma. "Between flesh & spirit," he wrote, "the fleshly union must be forsaken, and the spiritual embraced. But in this separating work it is very difficult for the blinded soul to make the distinction." Then he described his disorderly feelings for a woman.

> I believe that the spirit of jealousy is very dangerous to a soul in the gospel. . . . When a male gathers a feeling of jealousy that a female is not so well affected to him as she ought to be, or that she is more sociable with another male or males, or that she slights him without occasion, & purposely too . . . I say let him or her, beware of where that spirit would lead to. . . . I believe it is a snare of satan to beguile the soul, and [lead] it into bondage to the flesh. Where this spirit exists in one, and it is countenanced in the other, there is a fearful path, whose directions point hellward.

Isaac would be tempted much longer than the forty days and forty nights that Jesus was tempted by Satan. Isaac's carnal wilderness lasted for years.[19] Worse yet, his attraction may have been reciprocated, or at least "countenanced," to the point of jealousy. Shaker doctrine maintained that nothing in the universe had "so quick and ravishing an operation, as a corresponding desire of the flesh in the different sexes," yet that was exactly Isaac's problem. He knew he was in jeopardy. He teetered over the abyss of romantic love through late 1818. In his journals he described the symptoms of infatuation as he agonized over his potential fall from grace. He wanted to please a woman and feared that she would not love him in return. His faith warred against lust and jealousy to foster misery.

> This is the c[ase] with me wherein my concerns respect the female—I know it is a nature in me that would lead me out of the gospel if I were to [follow] it—there is an acceptable union between male & female, but my nature would lead me out of the way to seek a disorderly union. My nature would delight in conversing with a pleasant female, whenever I could do it & not expose myself. It would seek for all necessary opportunities, and delight in making an excuse or errand at any kind of a convenient time [&] would natural seek for chores to please her, when the ground notion would be to please myself. And if at any time she was not as I wished, I would naturally be contrary & shun all opportunities possible, either for revenge or self will, or to see how she would feel.[20]

In the spirit of confession, Brother Isaac had analyzed his feelings earlier that fall, but analysis brought him neither comfort nor relief. He knew Believers' duty was "to live in perfect harmony and union, being careful in all they do and say, to conduct agreeably sociably with each other."

> But to always say something to attract the feelings of another, more than what is necessary for a sound union, or to . . . try to please every little fancy that may present itself, [for] fear that the other will not love me, or that the other [may] think that I do not love them, is not according to my faith. I know I cannot cherish the sensation without weakening my pure union . . . and I believe I have not that power over my secret enemies that I should have otherwise. I wish to shun it, and never give way to it.[21]

Isaac had seen enough apostates to know the road to ruin. He steered himself back onto the straight and narrow path instead, using his writing to reinforce his decision.

That decision, however, may not have been completely private or entirely voluntary. His feelings must have been evident to the Church Family's espionage system, which watched for misbehavior, because the Eldresses took him to task. In December 1818, they referred to his "change of late." They were worried about him. "They signified," he wrote, that "they did not desire me ever to go outside of good order to please any female. . . . Now from what they said to me about these things . . . I found there has a feeling got in that I have [been] partial, and some disorder perhaps as it respects my union."

Rufus Bishop also reprimanded him for making too many errands to the sisters' rooms. Isaac noted Elder Rufus' comment, "that I used to have a good name . . . but he was afraid I had been more loose than I ought to be." In a religious community with institutionalized peer surveillance, moral laxity was conspicuous and quickly challenged. Brother Isaac was ashamed of his shortcomings and humiliated by the criticism. The Elders must have been keeping an eye on him, afraid they might lose him to the world, the flesh, and the devil as they had lost other promising young brethren. The authorities' vigilance galled Isaac, but he knew he had to conform. Despite his shame at being caught and his desire to improve, he was realistic about his own nature. "If any one expects or desires me to conduct impartially, so wisely, and in such a manner as to not give any opportunity or pretext for others to judge me," Isaac concluded, "they look for something that I am not able to come to." [22] He knew he could not keep the orders of the church perfectly. But even though he intended to go no further with his "particular union" for a sister, he realized that he was unable to treat her as impartially as he did the others. His issues with the opposite sex were not easily solved.

In late December, Brother Isaac referred to his earlier tribulations as a hard lesson in humility.

> I have had considerable of labor in relation to my self since the 24th of
> October [when] I had a serious time, in attempting to free my mind from
> a burden with which I had been much troubled, and which has been a
> weakness to my confidence, zeal & strength in the gospel. I feared or dreaded
> to make my case known. . . . There is a kind of half way sinning, to give a
> little & would give way wholly if it were not for fear—this, my nature would
> tell me, I could possibly get by—because it did not amount to what I would
> call actual sin. . . . It was a serious matter to humble my self before the
> Elders and expose my ways, my little foolish tricks. . . . However I . . . found
> a measure of kindness & mercy yet left for me.[23]

Exactly what happened on Saturday, October 24, 1818, is not known. Saturday was the day of confession, for self-purification before the Sabbath. Perhaps Isaac humbled himself by confessing his half-way sin more completely to the Elders than he did to his journal. But on December 20, his resistance broke. His earlier defiance left, and he was grateful for the Elders' kindness, notwithstanding the fact that they were also the ones who had laden him with tension and shame. His fear suggests that he crumbled under the threat of losing union and possible exile. He evidently did what was necessary to remain in union with Believers. He wrote:

This is the nature of my fleshly mind, but I know this is not the straight &
narrow way—& I have [put] down my foot that I will not be governed by
this nature. I will take up my cross . . . [and] labor for a good union . . . I
will not seek to please anyone for the sake of pleasing myself. . . . I am
willing, yea, determined to sacrifice all that will retard my [pro]sperity in the
gospel. So far as I know my faith, this is it—& if this is not the straight and
narrow way, then I have not a right understanding.[24]

Setting aside lust in favor of spiritual love was the greatest trial of Isaac
Newton Youngs's youth. He had committed himself to celibacy when he was
far too young to truly realize what he was giving up. At age twenty-five, however, he had a better understanding of his sacrifice.

The Elders continued to crack down on unnecessary touching. On Christ-
mas morning, Isaac wrote of another sermon on the subject of brethren and
sisters touching each other, noting that the admonition was "quite crossing to
nature." Though he admitted that he "had an evil nature that needed to be
crossed," his temper flared. He had been further chided for visits to the sisters
and he resented the reprimand, evidently having decided for himself that his
visits to the sisters were within reason. "When the Elders remind me not to
be running any 'unnecessary frivolous errands,' " he fumed, "I feel a nature
in me that would tell them that . . . the Elders make unnecessary errands
enough."[25]

When Isaac Newton Youngs wrote those words, he was still a youth by
Shaker standards. In his twenties, he had trouble balancing his need for autonomy with his religious beliefs and the Elders' demands for submission.
And though his psyche may have been under the Elders' influence, his body
was not. In 1819, he analyzed his "weakness and depravity."

I find a continual war between flesh and spirit—but my nature is seldom
at rest, it must afflict me in some way or other. Though I may not feel
temptation, yet [I] am harassed with evil thoughts. . . . I know there is that
tie of a fleshly nature between the two sexes which renders this point an
object of much embarrassment to a Believer. Herein I discover a strong
evidence to [con]vict me that my inclinations & nature are corrupt. . . . My
nature will catch at every thing that seems to offer any opportunity [or]
possibility of pleasing its own corrupt self, nor is it disposed to look at the
righteousness of its desires.

Another thing that convinces me of my depravity . . . is that there is no
bounds to its ravings; and more than that after once seeing the folly and
suffering for the foolishness of its effects, I am not naturally disposed [to]
learn.[26]

Brother Isaac's carnal nature embarrassed him. Living in a community that associated sexuality with shame meant that he lacked alternative ways of viewing his own desire. In this sense, Shakers differed little from unmarried "self-suppressed" eighteenth-century evangelicals whose "remedies against uncleaness" included prayer and such practical tips as those offered by Nicholas Gilman:

1. When temptation assaults thee flee from it.
2. Avoid Idleness.
3. Give no entertainment to the beginnings of lust.
4. Fly all occasions of lust.
5. When assaulted [by lust], go into company.[27]

That advice might have been lifted directly from a Shaker prescriptive manual, had one existed. To a Shaker, as to an unmarried evangelical, lust was not a normal response accompanying physical maturity; lust was Satan's snare to entrap and pull him down to hell. Desire had to be fought and conquered, not channeled or accommodated. Gilman employed some of the same methods that Shakers advocated: avoiding temptation and idleness, repressing lewd thoughts and using social support (or peer surveillance) to avoid giving in. Isaac Newton Youngs used those techniques, as well. The lines of battle were clearly drawn in his personal war between the spirit and the flesh. He was dismayed by each small defeat and barely heartened by victory. He tried to be the best Shaker he could be, but he felt corrupt and was not optimistic about improving. Further entries were more than candid. In an enciphered entry, he confessed to his journal what he had previously spelled out only to the Elders. Though a young brother's confession to the Elders could not have been unusual, his confession in the Family and Meeting Journal was.

> E[lder] Br[other] says [no] one has a right or ought to attempt to unite in the worship that have [ma]rred their conscience or are under any defilement of the flesh. . . . Knowing that I have been some overcome, & given way some to the lust of the flesh, I have sometimes felt as though I was . . . not really fit to be among the faithful. I went out of the meeting and after the meeting made my case known to the Elders. E Br said . . . he felt there was new strength for me. I was kept [safe from lust] 3 nights & then twice overcome in the night! I know not what to say, I feel but little hopes of getting rid of this difficulty soon.[28]

Isaac had given way to lust on more than one occasion. He may have believed that his conscious mind was somehow inciting his body to misbehave. He felt guilt over the physical response he sought to master even while asleep.

Isaac Newton Youngs was frustrated on every level, intellectual, spiritual, and physical. His intellect told him that his will should govern his body, asleep as well as awake, but his physical response proved otherwise. His religion told him he must be doing something wrong to "give way" to the demands of lustful flesh. And at the same time, his body craved sexual release. Despite his efforts, Isaac's body continued to perform in a natural manner contrary to his religious beliefs. The Elder's encouragement toward "new strength" did not help much. Prayer provided insufficient control against a twenty-five-year-old man's biological imperative. And it was no consolation to know that other brethren had faced the same problem and conquered it.

Brother Isaac's desperation grew with his effort to suppress his sexual response; his encrypted journal entries became more graphic. Deciphered, another 1820 entry shows why he took precautions to conceal its content. He had succumbed to guilty pleasures.

> Having been overcome several times of late with the flesh in the night, [tak]ing hold of my member while asleep & once by giving way measurably while awake, I felt under considerable labor of mind, and it appeared very dark to me. I know my faith & intention have been to [follow] the gospel & gift, get the power over my lust & especially the trick of gratifying it w[hen] asleep; but it has appeared as though the power of evil was very subtle, & laying snares to overcome me in some way. . . . So I went to see the Elders, & [revealed] the foolish ways that I had to dally with the flesh. They said that they did not know but that I must [go] to Mother & Ruth! I replied I should not know how . . . to express my case, but said I would subject to every gift they felt for me.[29]

Conscientious in confessing, Isaac may have worn out the Elders with his continuing saga of lust. Elders John Farrington and Rufus Bishop had presumably already conquered their own desires of the flesh; they gave him the best advice they had to offer. Isaac's regular resurrection of the issue may have embarrassed or even annoyed them. Shakers had many socially constructed inhibitions against discussing sexuality, nocturnal emissions, and masturbation in ways that could have been helpful to Isaac Newton Youngs. Furthermore, their sanctions against conversation that excited lustful sensations meant that anyone who heard such talk was required to open it by confession before worship. Isaac's lust could have set off a chain of confession that might have overloaded the system. Out of answers, the Elders must have known that their suggestion that he share his dilemma with Mother Lucy Wright and Eldress Ruth Landon would squelch his enthusiasm for discussing it. And if Isaac did confess to the Eldresses, he did not detail that encounter in his journal. He merely ended the month of March 1820 by stating that "the flesh & my soul's happiness are opposed to each other." He added that when he gave way to the flesh, he felt a sting of conscience, which pricked him whenever he reflected on it.[30]

One of the problems of defining natural sexual response as contrary to social doctrine was that it absorbed massive amounts of attention and energy that might have been put to better use. The benefit to the organization, however, stemmed from two facts: lust is universal, and confession binds the individual more closely to the group. Confession affirmed the group's control or authority over the individual because it provided a venue for dispensing shame and forgiveness. According to one apostate, confession also told the Elders the "thoughts and feelings, purposes and propensities, character and condition" of every member, so the Elders knew "exactly what influences to exert to keep them in subjection."[31] Clearly that apostate believed the Elders used information obtained from confession to manipulate Shakers. Thus the guilt-ridden individual, by confessing the sin of the flesh, bound himself more tightly to the very organization that instilled guilt and shame. In self-control and community restraint, the Shakers succeeded better and longer than most.

The irony, as Louis Kern points out, was that Shakers invested so much energy in battling human nature that in denying sex, they became as obsessed with it as libertines were in attempting to enjoy it. Some nineteenth-century observers agreed. Ralph Waldo Emerson wrote of the Shakers, "When you come to talk with them of their topic, which they are very ready to do, you find such an exaggeration of the virtue of celibacy, that you might think you had come into a hospital-ward of invalids afflicted with priapism."[32]

Eventually, Isaac Newton Youngs may have come to the conclusion that he was putting too much energy into analyzing his sexual feelings. One of his last references to the perils of the flesh was encrypted in his December 4, 1820, journal entry: "For my part I feel the greatest trouble in relation to my falling, respecting the flesh in the night. Outward means seem but a poor security. I know I must yet get the victory over that, but I fear it will have to be through some serious tribulation."[33] He did not elaborate on what he meant by "outward means," but among Shakers, several were possible.

One possibility was dietary reform, but in 1820, when Isaac was considering outward means, the Shakers had not yet tried to eliminate meat from their diet in an effort to subdue their animal spirits. When they later tried to eliminate meat, opinion was so divided that they had to allow individuals to choose whether to be vegetarians or not. Brother Isaac may not have supported such reform. In an 1835 journal reference to Grahamism, he mentioned the "party feeling" that followed limited meat consumption. Party feeling, or a spirit of divisiveness, was strictly to be avoided.[34] Furthermore, dietary restriction was a touchy subject in a society where food was the only acceptable sensual pleasure.

Physical exhaustion may have helped some Shakers subdue lust. The apostate John Woods believed that Shaker dancing quelled their carnal nature and was designed specifically to mortify the flesh, though that sort of "outward means" had not worked for Brother Isaac, who had been dancing for years without relief. An 1823 visitor to the New Lebanon Shakers, identified as "S," reported that their "repeated exercises in singing and dancing, (or, if you will, shaking,)" were well known to "calm the passions, and exhaust the spirits of all people" and suggested that they might have "a tenfold effect when made a part of religious duty." Declaring, "What means they employ more privately to restrain rebellious emotions, and encourage that state of Platonism so much in repute among them, it would be unfair to imagine," "S" was disinclined to believe rumors that Shakers engaged in self-mortification as a means to subdue the flesh. Thomas Brown wrote, however, that they did dance to exhaustion, and in 1793, three young women were ordered to strip and whip each other as punishment for watching flies mating. But when Father Joseph Meacham heard of the incident, he decided that "the gift for stripping and labouring naked, and using corporeal punishment, had entirely run out: for they could not keep such conduct secreted from the world, the church had already suffered much persecution on account of it, therefore there must be no more such proceedings." Brown also refuted the rumor that the Elders ordered many brethren castrated. Those early practices, if indeed they ever occurred, probably ended long before Brother Isaac mentioned outward means. And Shaker brethren appeared too well-fed for anyone to have concluded that they ever mortified the flesh through starvation.[35]

By outward means, Brother Isaac could have been referring to some of the methods and devices mentioned in Dio Lewis's book on chastity. Lewis advocated the wet girdle treatment—wrapping up in a wet towel at night—but dismissed "spiked belts and spermatorrhoea rings" as "worthless." "It is not on any such mechanical devises or outward appliances," he wrote, "that you can depend for a radical cure." [36] Brother Isaac could also have been referring to castration, which had biblical precedents. Some of the world's people suspected Believers of using this means of eliminating lust; on one occasion, that suspicion sparked legal action against the society when outsiders reported seeing two Shaker boys skinny-dipping. The court exonerated the Shakers, however, after a doctor's examination proved that the boys had not been castrated.[37] Even so, though it seems improbable that many Shaker men would have chosen this solution, the rumors of castration bear scrutiny. Because an orchidectomy would have reduced testosterone level and with it, sexual response, such an operation could have been a boon to brethren.[38]

Beyond rumors, two pieces of evidence may support this possibility. First was the Shakers' use of the term *eunuch*. A eunuch by definition is a castrated male. The New Lebanon Shakers, like all farmers, knew the benefits of removing male livestock's testicles to reduce aggression and sexual pursuit. Also, they owned medical reference books that defined castratus and eunuchs, noting that eunuchs were entrusted with women because they could not perform sexual intercourse. Furthermore, according to the biblical book of Isaiah (56:5), devout eunuchs had God's promise of an everlasting name that would not be cut off, despite their inability to reproduce.[39] References to Shaker men as eunuchs are scattered through Shaker writings. Hervey Elkins, for instance, paraphrased a Bible verse, Matthew 19:12, to explain, "For there are some eunuchs, which were so from their mother's womb; and there are some eunuchs, which were made eunuchs of men; and there be eunuchs which have made themselves eunuchs for the kingdom of heaven's sake." The apostate Reuben Rathbun also wrote that he had labored "to become an Eunuch for the kingdom of heaven's sake." Neither explained how Shaker eunuchs made themselves so. But they were not the only ones who used the term. In verse and song, Shakers referred to themselves as eunuchs and virgins. John Hobart ended a letter to Isaac with a poem:

> For Christ in his Bride hath appeared
> To open the two leaved gate
> Where Eunuchs and Virgins rise perfect
> And enter the glorified state.[40]

Religious rhetoric, however, is something quite different from submitting to surgery. Elkins, Rathbun, and Hobart may have used the term in a metaphorical sense. Perhaps, in their view, voluntarily refraining from sexual activity made them equivalent to actual eunuchs who could not achieve intercourse.

A second piece of evidence is an encrypted entry from Isaac Newton Youngs's journal describing a Shaker brother's orchidectomy at New Lebanon in 1821. The encryption is the first clue that it holds sensitive information. Isaac wrote,

> Kpobuibo Xppd has again to come to the tfsjpvt pqqfsbujpo of having ijt other uftujdmf fyusbdufe, and what is xp[sf] the mjhbnvsf came pgg sometime after they had gotten uisp as they hoped: and the ~~seen~~ scene of taking vq the bsufsjft was much xptt the first pqqfsbujpo insomuch that

> Kpobuibo was resigned to ejf! and must inevitably, had it not been for the
> good exertions of those concerned.[41]

In the cipher, each letter represents the one immediately preceding it in the
alphabet. The translation shows why Brother Isaac took the trouble to en-
crypt it.

> Jonathan Wood has again come to the serious operation of having his other
> testicle extracted and what is wo[rse] the ligamure came off sometime after
> they had gotten thro as hoped: and the scene of taking up the arteries was
> much [worse] than the first operation insomuch that Jonathan was resigned
> to die! and must inevitably, had it not been for the good exertions of those
> concerned.

Isaac described the problem of a ligature coming loose and the attempted repair. In an era before anesthesia, the painful procedure must have tested a
man to his limit. And had such an operation become public knowledge, it
would probably have been misconstrued, regardless of the reason for it. But
one orchidectomy does not establish castration as an institutionalized
method of subduing Shaker lust. Brother Jonathan's surgery could have been
the result of an accident or an infection or testicular cancer.

Isaac, however, did not suggest any of these possibilities. And he did preserve this journal for the next forty years of his life, as part of his ongoing attempt to chronicle all things Shaker. So we must consider the possibility, at
least, that Shakers considered orchidectomy an option for reducing sexual desire. Reduced sexual function, including lowered interest in sex and difficulty
in getting an erection, would have been a desirable outcome. For a committed
Shaker, a reduction in sexual tension may well have been worth the risks of
surgery. But that particular method of controlling lust cannot be confirmed
as a practice of nineteenth-century Shakers unless more evidence comes to
light. As far as is definitely known, Shakers relied on what "S" reported as "a
constant system of espionage, strict discipline, example, sobriety, industry,
and regularity, added to a free scope in the unbounded regions of faith and
hope . . . to mortify the flesh, and mould men into true Shakers." [42]

Isaac Newton Youngs stopped discussing his lust in his journals when he
was in his thirties, but his concern did not end. He later wrote the poem "Dialogue Between the Flesh and Spirit" to show the battle of opposing forces, in
much the same way that Galatians 5:16–26 sets love, joy, peace, goodness,
and self-control against immorality, sensuality, strife, jealousy, envy, anger,
and dissention. In the struggle the Spirit asserts that it is "sure to conquer"
because it is "honest free and open, an enemy to lust." The Flesh replies, "But

since my doom is fixed, my life's a shortning span, I'll take my fill of pleasure, and get it as I can." The Spirit, then, vows to mortify the Flesh as long as it afflicts Believers. Brother Isaac's own personal war against the flesh plays out in that dialogue. The Flesh threatened, flattered and wheedled, seductively offering "golden treasures" of self-indulgence, an easy descent into eroticism. But the Shaker Spirit held out for a crown of glory and so did Isaac.[43] Though he might have secretly longed to take his fill of pleasure, he remained committed to celibacy. And through poetry, he bolstered his commitment and supported other Shakers who were bearing the cross.

When Brother Isaac wrote his Spiritual Autobiography in 1848 at age fifty-five, he had clearly stepped back from the abyss to preserve his union with the society, noting, "the pleasures of nature & the world look uninviting & finally disgusting." He touched on the topic of lust again in 1856, when he was sixty-three and in failing health. "I feel I have gained much victory over evil," he wrote, "& especially over the great ruling passion lust, for I feel that is pretty much gone & dead."[44]

According to Diane Sasson, sexual denial seems to have been less troublesome to many Shakers than foregoing the excitement and variety of life outside the Shaker community.[45] But bearing the cross of celibacy meant suppressing, not expressing, sexual desires. Thus Brother Isaac's account of his own struggle is even more compelling. By confiding his problem to his journals, he gave posterity a singular opportunity to understand the difficulties of celibate life. He could not have been unique in experiencing sexual frustration, but among Shaker diarists he was unique in discussing it. His conquest of sexual desire was a measure of his commitment to his faith. Brother Isaac may have felt that Satan put his paw on him, but he refused to be captive led.

This life is a state of trial, & not of rest.

4 Rebellion in Shaker Society
Learning Humility, 1818–1827

LUST OF THE flesh was not Isaac Newton Youngs's only problem. Other misdeeds of his youth involved pride, disobedience, "lust of the eye," and inappropriate initiative, which repeatedly antagonized Mother Lucy Wright and the Elders. And when they criticized him, he rebelled. Rebellious youths were unlikely to remain in a communal society, but Brother Isaac was and did. He tried to adjust his attitude even as he tested the limits of the Elders' authority. From a historian's point of view, his rebellion was a benefit to posterity because it illuminates points of conflict between society and individual and shows how a Believer responded to the demands of communal living.

Isaac appreciated his privilege in joining the New Lebanon Church Family, but living in the Ministry's order meant being subject to high expectations, including his own. In 1818, at age twenty-five, he explained:

> Although I have been pretty well prospered in my outward situations &
> circumstances, & have flattered myself with a hope that I should be able to
> prosper in spiritual things, yet I fear I shall not come out as well as I have
> hoped to. Since I came to the church I have passed through considerable
> to keep me down & to learn how to conduct myself towards others. . . .
> I have many times brought on myself tribulation & buffetings [& felt]
> discouragement; and though I might at times feel pretty well I would soon
> feel wholly spoilt, and lose my zeal to do well, and after being careless, I
> would begin to feel in danger, and then try [in] vain to do a little better.[1]

When Believers did not meet the society's standards, they were called to account for their actions. Some were rebuked after confessing to misbehavior. Others did not confess, but their misdeeds caught up with them anyway. Living a fully regulated communal life was hard. Despite their sincere intentions, Shakers were not saints, and some must have disliked aspects of the system they supported. But they found ways to cope that did not jeopardize their union. Isaac Newton Youngs found that if he complained discreetly in his journals, he could vent his feelings while maintaining outward humility. In 1817, for instance, he wrote:

> Elder B. said that <u>order</u> required us to get liberty of the Elders, when we want to set up out of season . . . I wish not to dispute the justice of it, but it is some crossing to me—& for this reason, many times I have a chore that I cannot find a convenient time to do . . . & I should be ashamed to ask for liberty to set up to do it, unless it was quite important—thus, perhaps, many things that I would do, will be left undone. But it is good to be under order, to help keep within bounds.

In this manner, Brother Isaac would complain for the rest of his life, stating the problem with the Elders' edict, explaining his objections to it, then closing with a remark designed to show his humble acceptance. Writing it out in the privacy of his journal was his way of expressing discontent while remaining in union as a Believer. He needed an outlet for socially unacceptable emotions because he could not afford too many messy confrontations.[2]

Brother Isaac complained when the Elders from time to time altered the color or pattern of the brethren's clothing, creating extra work for him and the other tailors. And he complained in 1816 when the Elders altered their worship exercise.

> The Elders speak considerable respecting our manner of laboring. . . . I should make a figure, if I should undertake to imitate all the odd motions of our assemblies: those of myself as well as others. It would fill a large place on my paper if I should insert all the teaching we have had. . . . Indeed the Elders have had a labour to gain the gift, and also to decide in all points what was just right.[3]

In an effort to promote union even in worship exercises, the Elders gave instructions to help their flock move as one. But Isaac, already showing signs of being a perfectionist, disparaged his fellow Believers' (and his own) unstandardized movements, the Elders' inability to agree, their inconsistent teaching, and his own lack of understanding. And when an Elder called him forward to demonstrate, he resented being used as an example. But a committed Shaker had to accede to his Elders' demands.

Moreover, he had to follow Shaker doctrine. Mother Ann had told her followers to reject the world and all things worldly. Her admonitions echoed 1 John 2:15–17, "For all that is in the world, the lust of the flesh and the lust of the eyes and the boastful pride of life, is not from the Father, but is from the world." Believers had to rise above worldly lust and pride and in doing so submit to the Elders' edicts. Isaac found submission difficult, however, and did not humble himself gracefully before his superiors. When they chided him, his response was to defend himself, rather than bow to their criticism.

One of Brother Isaac's conflicts began in 1818 with Mother Lucy Wright's inspiration to purge superfluities from Shaker life. Too many Believers wanted niceties, such as colored ink, gold earrings (thought to be a headache remedy), umbrellas, suspenders, and silver pens. They had gradually acquired all those items over the years despite Mother Ann's belief that her followers should "let all such things go to the moles and bats of the earth." Precious metals were evidence of pride and "lust of the eyes" and thus did not conform to Shaker standards of simplicity. Mother Lucy wanted them banned, so the Ministry proscribed them. "This was crossing to some," Isaac explained, "to give up such things when they had got them by liberty or counsel. But although these things had got in because some thought it would be healthy, or good on some account, yet it was the gift to reject them." [4] The edict annoyed Isaac. He had made and used red ink and silver pens and did not want to stop. He resented changes that cramped his creativity and limited his few liberties.

A dutiful Believer would have poured out his colored ink. But Isaac did not. Four days after Lucy Wright's doctrinal gift was announced, Elder Rufus Bishop asked Isaac whether he had "abolished" his red ink. The young man's truthful reply—that he had not—provoked a storm of disapproval. In the privacy of his journal, Isaac reported his conversation with Elder Rufus, rationalizing his own disobedience.

> I told him I was willing to give up all I had and though I had lately made a
> quantity, yet it was because I had been asked by some of the boys how it
> was made, and I thought it not proper to let them, for they might make great
> labor of it to no profit—so I thought best to make some and give them—and
> though I expected to use some myself, I had always been reserved in the use
> of it; not to write any sacred thing with it. But I have observed that there has
> been considerable of a use of it for fancy's sake; this is what Mother [Lucy]
> dislikes. And I think had it not been for such unsuitable treatment of ink, it
> would not have been rejected. [5]

He had evidently decided that the official edict did not apply to him.

Rufus Bishop must have reported the misbehavior to Mother Lucy Wright. Brother Isaac was evidently the subject of considerable discussion among the Elders that week, because Mother Lucy summoned him and Elder Rufus.

> Mother told me her object was to speak to me in behalf of the late gift.
> She said there was a gift of late respecting superfluities, that she supposed
> affected me some, but she was fearful that it did not work half so deep in me
> as it ought to. She had been fearful that I would run too far in curiosities and
> needless notions. "Why," says she, "I should by no means have dared to
> done as you have, in such things. You & Garret [Lawrence] & many of the
> young have been very forward. And I do not know but that you will be the
> ring leader and draw the rest on. . . ." She desired that I would take up a
> cross about such matters. "You may yet be called to be a help in keeping out
> [such] things, and if you do not, while you are young, set a good example . . .
> others can not have that faith in you that they might. If you get little nice
> notions, others will want them. You had better turn your genius to that
> which would be profitable. Needless things are a burden.[6]

Mother Lucy felt that Isaac and his friend Garret Lawrence, two of the New
Lebanon Church Family's gifted youth, had acted on their own initiative
rather more than Shaker society permitted, and she could not afford to let
them continue along those lines. And because the two were schoolteachers,
they influenced the Church Family's children. Undeterred, such forward
youth—even with the best intentions—might have raised havoc (at best) or
an insurrection (at worst) among the New Lebanon Shakers. Because the old-
age security of childless Shakers depended on the loyalty of younger Believers, such a division could not be tolerated. Their reciprocal obligations
required obedience.

Mother Lucy therefore asked Isaac to stop making silver pens and, he
recorded, she warned him to "remember what she had said, and be careful to
observe it; it made her feel exceeding ugly to see me running head long in such
things."[7] Mother Lucy addressed his rebellion through lecture and example,
without shaming him into leaving. She also gave him credit for his intelligence, even genius. But he had weaseled his way around her edict, so his in-
subordination had to be curtailed. And his self-serving rationalization
showed that his ego had to be checked, as well.

Isaac's response to Mother Lucy's lecture was more candid than politic.
When she asked him whether he was "thankful to have these notions rejected," he told her he had "not felt any particular feeling of thankfulness, but
felt reconciled to do according to the gift."[8] Though his answer was honest
and undoubtedly heartfelt, his candor verged on rudeness. Mother Lucy may
have despaired over the arrogance of such a promising youth. But Isaac was
not a hypocrite. He was honest enough to say exactly what he thought. Others might have told Mother Lucy whatever they thought she wanted to hear.

Isaac's journal entry the next day, however, shows his increasing maturity in accepting responsibility for his misdeeds. After contemplating Mother Lucy's advice he admitted, "I felt when she was speaking to me, as if I wanted to make many excuses, and tell her how free I have been in relation to having many curious things &c. . . . It is well for me that my circumstances have not admitted of gathering much," implying that if he had been able, he would have collected more. He realized that his acquisitiveness could threaten his union with Believers, and he closed, "So let me freely meet my fate, forsake [my] own pleasure, that, by the mercy of my Maker, I may obtain an abiding treasure!"[9] Forsaking his own desires was the recurring refrain of Isaac's life as a Believer.

Other issues followed the red ink incident. In 1820, Mother Lucy noticed that something had "gauled great I" in Isaac, and "she did not want to encourage great I" in him or anyone else. Mother Lucy was concerned that Isaac's self-will was getting the better of him, and she warned him to curb it. Believers had to put Shaker union ahead of their own wants and needs. What was best for the society, however, was not necessarily what was easiest for the individual. Mother Lucy recognized that young people in particular had wants that could not be satisfied. They "must not expect to please themselves with every fancy," she said, "or think to have every notion they would naturally want, or to have their own ways; but they must remember that they are called to be exemplary in all things." Isaac was evidently not the only young Believer who wanted his own way, and Mother Lucy countered their complaints. "Some think they have harder times than others, but such ought to consider whether there is not something in them which needs greater crosses to subdue."[10]

Many Believers, like Isaac, had human failings that created problems, and the Elders often had to preach on compliance with Shaker ideals. In his journal, Isaac commented on an address the Elders read to show how all the evil passions—anger, malice, envy, backbiting, unreconciliation, pride, and lust—led souls astray. Isaac thought every passion did not apply equally to everyone, but the message must have been uncomfortably specific.

> It was pretty plain and pointed, and tho' I believe [the] writing was not intended to point to any one in particular, I thot likely some might think you mean me now! & not relish [the message] quite as well; but I concluded that I should not [see] who it applied to, than to see one flounce or flutter at any particular part of it.[11]

Brother Isaac himself may have thought, "You mean me now!" Church Family Believers were not perfect; they needed admonition, even if it made them squirm.

Late June and July 1820 brought more trouble. Brother Isaac erred by painting two milking stools. He thought that because paint would protect the wood, and because milking stools were commonly painted, painting would be an acceptable way to finish them. He put the freshly painted stools to dry in a place where an Elder saw them and ordered him not to paint any more. The stools were taken to the deaconesses, presumably for sale. He soon found, however, "that the Ministry [was] stirred up about the matter and having found stools in general painted, ordered the paint to be scoured off every stool." The scouring order was punitive—a dubious lesson for a young Believer—and Isaac resented it.[12]

The Elders' response was significant in several ways. The exercise of power was (and is) generally fundamental to religion, which by its nature puts a boundary between the included and the excluded. Moreover, leadership implies authority to judge the boundary between acceptable and unacceptable. When Shaker authorities were empowered to run their followers' daily lives, every aspect of community life had to be judged accordingly, even material items as insignificant as a milking stool. Applying religious standards of perfectionism to all aspects of society meant making hundreds of decisions about what was right or wrong, even though some of those decisions seemed arbitrary to those on the receiving end of the edict. Furthermore, in this instance, the Elders' decision revealed their ignorance of that fact that milking stools were usually painted. Evidently, despite the society's philosophy of egalitarianism, the Elders, unlike other brethren, did not take turns at milking or doing other farm chores that would have brought them into regular contact with milking stools.[13]

Isaac vented his frustration in his journal, in ciphertext. The plaintext translation:

> It worked my feelings some . . . [to have] my stools taken away without my knowledge, & I could not help think that it was actuated more by zeal than by candor & fair dealing, & whether it was . . . wisdom to scour all the paint off, seeing the labor that it was to do it. . . . But I leave the matter. I believe doubtless it was right—it should be just as it was, as hard as it is to cut things off when we get going, unless something effectual is done.[14]

Isaac's response was fundamentally critical and therefore disorderly. Even in code, however, he had to be discreet to protect his place in the society and to protect his journal, which the Elders had the right to confiscate. Ending a complaint by noting that "doubtless it was right" to remove paint from milking stools may have been Isaac's insurance against having his journal taken away. He intended his writings to be his legacy to posterity. We must assume, however, that Isaac's bowing to the essential correctness of the Elders' action was genuine. Isaac's candor with Mother Lucy showed that he was honest about his feelings when he was asked for a response. But he had to address feelings before he could reconcile them, and because Shaker union required Believers to avoid discussing disorderly ideas, he may have felt safest confiding complaints to his journal. In writing, he worked through his negative emotions privately so he could remain outwardly in union.

Unfortunately, Isaac continued to exercise his aesthetic sense inappropriately and soon had another run-in with Lucy Wright. In late 1820 he finished a clock case with mahogany trim. Though mahogany had never been expressly prohibited, neither had it been deemed acceptable, and Mother Lucy's feelings, Isaac reported, were "more than usually stirred up." Evidently she was often annoyed, and Isaac annoyed her even more, perhaps in this instance because he had not considered the possibility that imported wood might be superfluous. After she denounced it, he noted hopefully, "She has not ordered it altered, so perhaps it will remain—but I must be careful in future." The incident, however, was not over. Before the end of the month, his hopes were scuttled.

> The feelings of the Elders . . . are so exercised about the mahogany clock
> door that I have at last painted it over. They thought Mother w[ould] feel
> better satisfied if there was something done about it. Thus . . . we have to be
> under much restraint, & [at] times do that which . . . is inconsistent, & a loss
> of labor & time.[15]

The inconsistencies were maddening. Paint was the remedy for hiding plain but overly rich wood such as mahogany, but paint was not acceptable for protecting a milking stool from splashes. The illogic of the authorities' decisions, as well as the inefficiency of the additional work required, disturbed the logical Isaac Newton Youngs. He was a perfectionist in his work habits as well as in his strivings for personal perfection. Shakerism satisfied his need for order and routine, but inconsistency and illogic distressed him. And when shifting views of paint created more work for him, he was furious. He may have been angered also by what appeared to be an arbitrary exercise of power. Two months later he was still smarting over the paint.

> I would observe some in relation to painting. There are very different
> opinions about the matter. . . . Some Elders I suppose think that it is
> necessary to paint milking stools . . . others think it quite unnecessary. . . .
> Indeed two persons of equal judgment would seldom be found to think alike
> [res]pecting it. [I do] not wish to borrow trouble in these matters, for I am

not able to know what is best in such things, & if those in care tell what is
best, so be it.[16]

The use of paint was a matter of personal opinion. The Elders may not have
agreed on it even among themselves. But Isaac had to work through the issue
before he could regain his sense of perspective. As a conscientious Shaker, he
would submit. Isaac did not want to "borrow trouble," but he did not have
to be happy about the new standards.

Brother Isaac then turned to the other irritating aspect of the issue: the expenditure of labor in carrying out the Ministry's edicts about paint. His detailed critique of their inconsistent standards sheds light on Shaker aesthetics
as well as Shaker union.

> I think sometimes there is a great . . . cost and labor laid out & perhaps little
> or no profit. . . . For a proof of the truth of my ideas, I refer to such things
> [as] has been common practice in painting floors. Many floors have been
> painted 2 & 3 times over with a nice coat of fine paint. Then the floor must
> not be used for several weeks, & when it comes to use, it must be covered
> over with nice sheets, washed & starched & ironed; these must be kept on
> several weeks more, and finally the floor must be pretty much covered over
> with a curious painted carpet so nice that delicacy forbids to walk on it
> without having a common carpet spread over it!!! Surely, I think the labor
> that is put on some of our floors, which in reason I must call lost, & so much
> worse than lost, it would paint over all the milking stools . . . that we could
> wish to paint from now to 50 years to come, thereby rendering them much
> prettier & in many cases more durable.

Isaac was baffled by inconsistent decisions that created additional (or in his
opinion, unnecessary) work. Ironically, other sources show that the Shakers
tried to reduce wear on their floors to reduce the expenditure of labor in up-
keep. In 1821, the new Millennial Laws admonished Believers to avoid pivot-
ing on their feet at the head and foot of the stairs, "lest they wear holes in the
floor," and that rule probably codified a reminder long used in the society.[17]
Isaac's indignation was fired by common sense as well as aesthetics. Why
paint floors and not milking stools—especially when paint rendered a floor
less durable and a stool more durable? And why paint a floor, which then had
to be covered with a painted carpet so delicate that a common carpet had to
be spread over it?

Brother Isaac had to contain his vexation. Anger was contrary to the
gospel. According to Mother Lucy, the spirit of Christ was meek, submissive,
and humble.[18] Neither Mother Ann nor Mother Lucy exemplified such qual-

ities, and all Believers did not exemplify them all of the time. But those attributes were nonetheless important to the smooth functioning of a communal society. So Isaac outwardly humbled himself and poured his anger into his journal. But criticism directed toward his superiors, even in his journal, hindered his advancement in his faith. In the end, Isaac realized that his disorderly feelings were unseemly. "I know there must be caution used, & especially in things of fancy," he wrote. "I sincerely do not wish to encourage fancy . . . and useless things but I would be glad some times more freely to enjoy things that are useful . . . especially in the mechanics' line." [19] Though he complained, he also hoped for union, perhaps realizing that his own attitude was divisive. At the same time, he longed for items that might have made his mechanical work easier. That craving would not be satisfied until after Mother Lucy's death.

The painted stool and mahogany clock door incidents took time to blow over, because Lucy Wright revisited the topic several weeks later. Isaac noted that when he

> was at Mother's shop on an errand, and conversed with her on several
> things, she spoke considerably against superfluities, & notions, & observed
> how natural it was to be running after the world & the things [such as]
> umbrellas, suspenders, &c. . . . She desired that I would be very careful to
> avoid labor for curiosity and said if ever I should be dbmmfe to tuboe [called
> to stand] as a ifmq [help] to others I should have to stand against such
> things.[20]

After reading Brother Isaac's earlier journal entries, it is not hard to imagine what went through his mind when Mother Lucy again advised him against superfluity. When she told him "to avoid labor for curiosity," she may have been warning him not to spend so much time experimenting with clocks and lamps, or measuring and recording information for posterity. She had already cautioned him against letting his mind run after unprofitable ideas such as a perpetual motion machine.[21] Trying to squelch the budding scientist, she kept her eye on him. And despite his impolitic response after the earlier episode, she may have been grooming Isaac Newton Youngs for a leadership position, perhaps even for the Ministry, because she alluded to his potential (as he wrote in cipher) for standing as a help to others. Encrypting those words shows that he meant to keep that information to himself.

The Shaker apostate Hervey Elkins further illuminated Isaac's problems and Mother Lucy's criticism, revealing that such treatment was institutionalized throughout the society.

> It is common for the leaders to crowd down, by humiliation, and withdraw patronage and attention from those whom they intend to ultimately promote to an official station. That such may learn how it seems to be slighted and humiliated, and how to stand upon their own basis, work spiritually for their own food without being dandled upon the soft lap of reflection.

The intent was "to see how much he can bear, without exploding by impatience, or faltering under trial." Brother Isaac knew he was being "crowded down" by one humiliation after another, as he had mentioned in 1818. He was under close scrutiny and surely did not feel he was being "dandled upon" anyone's "soft lap." [22] He might have been happier with less attention. But Mother Lucy's efforts to channel Isaac's ability in the right direction for the Shakers' benefit did not work as she might have hoped. Isaac continued to try new conveniences in his work as a mechanic and in doing so created work for himself. Trying to balance his need for autonomy against his society's demands, he vacillated between compliance and rebellion.

Even though Brother Isaac appeared to understand the Ministry's views, he continued to rationalize his own noncompliance with their edicts. Later in the fall of 1820, he ignored the Elders' demand that Believers surrender whatever they might have written about the orders handed down from the Ministry. Evidently some Shakers, including Isaac, wrote down rules as they were announced. "I was at a loss to know what to do," Brother Isaac wrote in a coded entry, "but seeing I had not written them . . . but merely for the sake of knowing what this one & that one said I thot to keep it to myself." His writing of the rules, if only for his own use, was a step toward codification of the Millennial Laws, which would not be done until the end of Mother Lucy's life.[23] But for Isaac, recording the church orders may have served another purpose. He may have wanted to get a grip on what must have seemed a distressingly fluid stream of rules.

Nevertheless, in a society that required confession and virtually eliminated privacy, Isaac's words, "I thot to keep it to myself," were disorderly, even tantamount to rebellion. He risked reprimand by refusing to comply. This episode shows the boundary that Brother Isaac, a conscientious Shaker, set between himself and the organization: he would do what he was told, as long as it did not affect the writing that helped him cope with communal life. His conformity had a limit. His personal writing was, in his view, beyond the Elders' authority.

Beset by the Elders, who had been riding him hard over every infraction, tormented by lust, and hounded by his own conscience, Isaac Newton Youngs addressed his ongoing struggles at age twenty-seven in a journal entry on his "church birthday" in March 1821, the anniversary of the date when he came to the New Lebanon Shaker village.

> The circumstances of our relation in the go[spel] . . . seem calculated to move every branch of an evil nature, to rouse every wicked disposition, and try [the] patience & fortitude of the soul to the last degree. . . . No one will ever overcome any evil passion without first being tempted. . . . This life is a state of trial, & not of rest. . . . I despair of ever finding any abiding satisfaction only in the things of the spirit & in doing the best that I [can.] [24]

Isaac realized that he had already lived the part of his life when he could enjoy himself without care or responsibility. Reaching maturity was a constant battle. But he was determined to maintain his union with Believers, and so he tackled the endless work of self-improvement, humbly admitting his failings and expressing willingness to work on his behavior. In April 1822, he wrote out a testimony to read in meeting.

> Kind Elders brethren and sisters, I am sensible that I am blest with a great privilege in this Church to learn the way of God and enjoy the blessings of the gospel and I feel thankful according to my measure. I kindly thank you for all your love and kindness to me. I know that without the help and kindness of those before me, I should be a poor creature. And I hope and pray that I may always keep the gospel, that I may stand faithful, if my life should be spared, when many old believers who have gone thro sorrow & tribulation, have left this world. And I hope never to disappoint any one, or be the means of your losing your labors for me. And tho' I suppose you chiefly know what my faith is, yet I believe it is my duty at this time to speak boldly of my faith & determination, which is to take up a square cross against the lust of the flesh, the lust of the eye, & the pride of my evil nature,
> To be subject to my Elders.
> If I get overcome with sin to confess it before I go to sleep.
> To show respect & give place to my superiors.
> To be . . . agreeable to my equals, and all my brethren & sisters.
> To be kind and exemplary to my youngers.
> To be strict to keep every order.
> To take up my cross against vanity & folly.
> To think less of myself & more of others.
> To fulfill all my duties with cheerfulness & punctuality.
> To strive to walk worthy of a good union with my brethren & sisters & not seek a disorderly union.
> And to treasure up & keep every gift of God that is given for us.

> And now I solemnly promise in the presence of God & his witnesses that I
> will keep this, my faith & determination so long as I live in this world:
> But if I forget this, then let my right hand forget her cunning; and let my
> tongue cleave to the roof of my mouth, if I prefer not the gospel above my
> chief joy.

The final lines paraphrase Psalm 137: 4–6: "How shall we sing the Lord's
song in a strange land? If I forget thee, O Jerusalem, let my right hand forget
her cunning. If I do not remember thee, let my tongue cleave to the roof of my
mouth; if I prefer not Jerusalem above my chief joy." [25] Believers would have
recognized the allusion in Isaac's intent to "sing the Lord's song," and to accept punishment if he did not.

Garret Lawrence was also having trouble reaching the ideal and set an example for Isaac, who noted that the gift to bear testimony originated when
Garret "wrote his determination & promised himself to read it aloud to himself every day through this year." Garret's public humbling, and possibly
Isaac's as well, may have been viewed as showing off, because Isaac wrote
that some people "rather reflected upon Garret." [26] And though a cynic might
suggest that Isaac's public testimony was just window dressing to compensate for his shortcomings, Isaac Newton Youngs truly was working to perfect
himself. As the Church Family's teacher and as a sincere Believer, he wanted
to set a good example. He worried about the society's youth because he saw
some, not much younger than himself, becoming arrogant.

> I see such a youth [as] being out of his place, having a high forward sense,
> pretending to know considerable, and being yet ignorant of his own
> folly. . . . He is at least destitute of <u>Humility</u>. When I see one arguing &
> disputing with his superiors, contradicting their opinions, setting up his own
> view, speaking loud & harsh & inconsiderately, [tell]ing them they have no
> more right to tell him what to do, or what is [right?] than he has to tell
> them—refusing their counsel, regardless of his union, telling them of their
> faults, & trying to keep up his side by . . . accusations, I say to myself, that
> one is void of simplicity & conformity, he is not worthy of the union of the
> people of God. He will not make a good Church member, unless he alters his
> course. [27]

But despite his own failings, Brother Isaac knew what it took to become a
good church member.

As Isaac Newton Youngs criticized, so was he criticized. During these
years, he had little respite from disparagement in his temporal labor or even in
his sleeping room, because he lived and worked under the thumb of the hyper-
critical older tailor David Slosson, whose faultfinding blighted Isaac's days

and nights. Isaac finally vented his feelings. He explained that the older tailor was "somewhat aged & broken," so it was "hard for him to endure those disturbances . . . that will naturally happen among so many as sleep in a room, for his turn is somewhat critical, & as he is awake, so is he when asleep, very easily disturbed." Isaac enciphered his assessment, which translates:

> I always considered him a small man [in] his creation, and a critical man to deal with. Quite disagreeable in his manners, and of [a] very uncomfortable manner of government over children. He is very critical in all his concern[s] and causes much trouble for himself and others. He's easily moved by what pleases him, is very plain spoken & is not endowed with as much wisdom as one might wish. But he has many good qualities. He is very spiritually minded . . . is a man of very clear & quick sight in spiritual things, has a great faculty of ministration; easy to flow with gifts . . . never holds a grudge nor seeks for failings in others (tho' very quick to see them & apt to speak of them). He was always remarkably zealous in his hand labor & zealous to do all he can for the support of the joint interest & his calling. I have been a great deal of, with & for David . . . and sought to make it as easy for him & others in with him as possible.

Unfortunately, Isaac went on to say, things had taken a turn for the worse because his work did not please Brother David. In early 1823, he "expressed great dissatisfaction" with Isaac for being negligent in his work and spending too much time away from the tailor shop. But Isaac was also making clocks; asked to build another one, he complained, "I have work enough to do." He could not satisfy everyone, and in desperation told the Elders that he could endure the situation no longer. Surprisingly, they agreed and even provided relief by relocating Slosson, signaling that individual needs could be accommodated. Though Isaac felt ashamed to have tattled, he was also profoundly relieved.[28] His gratitude, in fact, suggests not only that he was pleased to be out from under the "plain-spoken" Slosson's oversight but also that he was gratified to find that in some things he could have his own way.

Brother Isaac would later be described as a model of Shaker virtue. But his outward adherence to Shaker ideals rested on a foundation of privately disorderly thoughts confined to his journals, which he used to work through the problems of laboring under arbitrary and inconsistent authority. He tested the limits and pressed his luck, putting his own wants and needs first. When challenged, he preserved his position in the society by agreeing that his Elders were right in taking the action they did. There is no way to know how many other missteps Isaac may have gotten away with, mistakes he never bothered to describe because they provoked no conflict.

As Isaac Newton Youngs' experience shows, living in a communal society did not mean that nineteenth-century Shakers blindly accepted every doctrine or edict. Even the most dedicated Believer might doubt the Ministry's wisdom. But staying in Shaker union required outward adherence to the norm to avoid disrupting the society. Within that system, keeping a journal was perhaps the best way for a rebellious spirit to find expression without jeopardizing his union. Brother Isaac would spend his life as a valued member of Shaker society, and his long and useful service must be considered evidence of his sincerity and truthfulness as well as his conscientious struggle to control his own rebellion.

Isaac repented his own arrogance in questioning the Elders but had to do so repeatedly because he never stopped criticizing them. In a worship service in 1827, according to the Shaker sister Elizabeth Lovegrove, Brother Isaac

> expressed his feelings in relation to a haughty spirit and high mind. He said that he knew this was the greatest cause of his or any other souls being shut out of a blessing. He walked on his knees to a number of the Brethren and entreated their prayers. . . . Br. Rufus said it was a glorious work to confess sin & acknowledge our faults; [and] that he had often heard Mother [Lucy] say that it was a shame to commit sin, but no shame to confess it.[29]

Brother Isaac's effort to adjust his attitude was not entirely without humor. In late 1823, after several years in and out of trouble, he finished a self-deprecating six-stanza poem showing the irony of his situation as well as the problem of maintaining exemplary behavior. In "New Year's Thoughts," Brother Isaac thought that he might be able to be good one hour at a time. And if he could be good for several hours in succession, perhaps he could string together enough to be good throughout the year. (He would later elaborate on this poem and his experiment to carry out the plan.) But as in all Shaker hymnody, Isaac alluded to the danger lurking near. The struggle was exhausting, and he needed help to buoy up his spirits when they flagged. Such lyrics may have kept him focused on conquering evil nature and achieving grace. By keeping his eye on heavenly things, he could distract himself "from carnal joys and vain delight." [30]

Isaac Newton Youngs would bear the cross for the rest of his life, but it would never be easy. Much of his struggle was internal, involving mastery of his own passions and will. He was compelled by no outside force; he chose the straight and narrow path, and once his decision was made, he worked to stay on it. And by sharing his goals, he intended to empower others in the same effort, to validate the difficult choice, renewed daily, to be a good Shaker.

In addition to sharing his words, Brother Isaac lived his religion through his work. As an adult, he tried to perfect the products of his hand labor and left several material artifacts that show the result of his efforts. Second only to his journals, his clocks provide an enduring testament to his striving for perfection.

5 Clockmaking

The Youngs Family Traditions and Shaker Change, 1800–1840

ISAAC NEWTON YOUNGS was a mechanic at heart, fascinated by machines of all sorts, and foremost among his mechanical interests, from early childhood, was clockmaking. In his clocks, Brother Isaac aspired to the Shakers' material ideal, and his personality was well-suited to clockmaking. A perfectionist, he set high standards for his work; he was also analytical and orderly, interested in engineering and applied science. Determined to number, measure, and quantify all endeavors, he treated time and clocks no differently.[1]

Brother Isaac was a third-generation clockmaker. Two of his clockmaking relatives became Believers in adulthood, and their clocks show that the Shaker influence on design increased in proportion to their years in the society. Unlike his kinsmen, Brother Isaac was raised as a Believer from infancy and spent most of his youth under Mother Lucy Wright's scrutiny. Influenced by Shaker ideals from early childhood, he internalized the material standards of Shaker simplicity more than his older Shaker kinsmen did. And though he borrowed design elements from each of his mentors, he attained a purity of form that they did not.[2] Isaac Newton Youngs, last in the line, created an ideologically pure design that symbolizes Shaker simplicity and separation from the world. To understand the significance of his clocks, we must look at his predecessors' work in the context of Shaker ideology.

Shakers tried to live their faith in their daily labor. Their craftsmanship, Edward Deming Andrews explained, "reflected such principles as union (basic uniformity of design), the equality of the sexes (balance, proportion), utilitarianism (adaptation to needs, durability), honesty (mastery of techniques), humility and simplicity (absence of pretense or adornment), purity (a sense of pure form)."[3] "To satisfy Shaker ideals," Andrews also noted, objects had to "serve man's good and his needs *both temporal and spiritual.*"[4] Father Joseph Meacham, leader of the Shakers after Mother Ann Lee died, decreed, "All things must be well made and kept decent and in good order according to their order and use." Furthermore, he added, "All work done or things made in the church ought to be faithfully and well done, but plain and without superfluity."[5] *Well made, plain, and without superfluity.* In the early nineteenth century, Shaker custom allowed for nothing fancy just for the sake of decoration, nothing that would demonstrate pride or vanity. Whatever was the most simple and functional was best.

As Shakers aspired to spiritual perfection, they also aspired to perfection in their work. As communitarians, Shaker craftsmen were freed from the necessity of financially supporting themselves and their families so they could devote themselves to doing the best work possible. And they did. As June Sprigg points out, "The Shaker label became synonymous with excellence."[6] Perfectionists did not settle for shoddy workmanship. They were not supposed to waste time, materials, or effort on decoration, but they did invest in high-quality craftsmanship. Furthermore, they brought metaphor into their construction. "Straight" and "square" stood for honesty, fair dealing, and godliness, and in the Shaker context, they were also metaphors for perfection. Shaker sidewalks met at right angles; diagonal shortcuts were not allowed. The easy way was not necessarily the path of virtue, nor was the easiest mode of construction necessarily the most balanced, durable, or utilitarian. But though Shaker clockmakers worked hard to produce high-quality products, they were slow to eliminate superfluities. After 1800, the Youngs family clocks gradually evolved from worldly ornamentation to Shaker simplicity, embodied in Isaac Newton Youngs's 1840 clock (figs. 8–12).

The family tradition of clockmaking began with Seth Youngs Senior (1711–61), Isaac's grandfather, who began making clocks in Connecticut in the late 1730s. Because he was not a Shaker, his work is useful as the baseline against which later change can be measured. Seth Youngs Senior's 1740 clock (fig. 8) is an example of the worldly standards of his time and place, typical of the fashionable elite in the mid-eighteenth century.[7] His 1740 clock is a conventional tall clock, grandfather style, 86½ inches tall, with decorative turnings framing the bonnet, or hood, and moldings at the top and bottom of the bonnet and on the base. The impressively ornate brass and pewter face (signed S. Yongs) is shaped like a modified keyhole. The pendulum door has a small glass window so the pendulum is visible. The works are of brass and steel.[8] This design was intended to impress and thus, according to Shaker belief, denoted worldly pride and "lust of the eye."[9]

In the long-standing tradition of master craftsmen, Seth Youngs Senior passed his trade to the next generation, and when he made his will, he bequeathed his clockmaking tools to his sons, including Benjamin Youngs (1736–1818), Isaac's uncle and foster father. Benjamin Youngs's earliest known clock was one hundred inches tall, a case clock made in the Chippendale style. Benjamin Youngs probably built that clock before he became a Shaker, because it is the epitome of worldly display. Even fancier than Seth Youngs, Senior's Connecticut Valley clocks, it has an ornate face, a broken-scroll bonnet, and a delicate finial—a grandiose clock that towered over its owners.[10] But Benjamin Youngs's designs began to change after he joined the Shakers. He began removing superfluous decoration.

The Benjamin Youngs clock that appears in figure 9, with a case by Erastus Rude, shows that Shakers began simplifying their clock cases from earlier worldly designs. Gone are many labor-intensive details; the bonnet's curves have become Shaker-straight. The case retains other worldly stylistic devices, however, including the arch over the clock face. Seventeen inches shorter than his previous Chippendale-style clock, the case shows that he was scaling down. But it is more than eighty inches tall, with moldings on bonnet and base and turned columns framing the face. And the face is decorated with a painted floral motif that may have predated Benjamin's Shaker days.[11] All decorative details—arch, moldings, turned columns, and flowered face—are evidence of worldly pride. And some features added work for housekeepers. Horizontal moldings caught dust, so they had to be wiped regularly to maintain the Shaker standard of cleanliness. Ann Lee believed that good spirits would not dwell where there was dirt. "Where cobwebs and dust were permitted to accumulate," a visitor quoted an Elder, "there the evil spirits hide themselves." Accordingly, Believers kept their belongings spotless.[12] But the first Youngs family clocks required unnecessary labor in both construction and housekeeping. Even so, Shaker clock design was evolving.

The next in the Youngs family line of clockmakers was Benjamin Seth Youngs (1774–1855), Benjamin Youngs's nephew and Isaac Newton Youngs's brother. Though they had the same parents, Benjamin Seth was almost twenty years older than Isaac and grew to manhood among the world's people. He joined the Shakers when he was about twenty, so he had probably already learned clockmaking before he signed the covenant. Thus, he also had to make an effort to shift from worldly standards to Shaker ideals in his clocks. And though he tried to simplify his clock, he retained several conventional details (fig. 10).

Benjamin Seth Youngs's clock, believed to have been built between 1794, the year he joined the society, and 1805, when he began missionary work in the West, is a shelf clock about thirty-six inches tall.[13] It has decorative moldings atop the bonnet and at three levels of the case, as well as an oval cutout in the case door that was a throwback to his grandfather Seth's design.

Benjamin Seth gave his clock face a Shaker-square frame rather than the key-hole shape of the earlier Youngs family clocks and eliminated the turned columns on the bonnet, which also simplified the design and reduced labor. The overall appearance is understated because he sized it down to stand on a table or shelf. The smaller size was a move toward Shaker humility. But though Benjamin Seth's clock is harmoniously balanced, it is too worldly to be fully Shaker. Prideful moldings on the bonnet and base break the sweep of the vertical line and catch dust. Superfluous decoration meant extra and therefore wasted work, both in the manufacture of the piece and in its main-tenance. The lines of the mitered corners are diagonal, not square, so visible joints meet at forty-five-degree angles rather than at the ninety-degree angles that were ideologically "right." Furthermore, the works, like those of Seth Youngs, Senior and Benjamin Youngs, are worldly brass. These early Youngs family clocks do not therefore exemplify Shaker ideals of plainness and hu-mility. Even though both Benjamin Youngs and his nephew Benjamin Seth Youngs made progress by squaring off the cases and trimming some super-fluities, neither relinquished all aspects of worldly taste. Their clocks are hy-brids between worldly pride and Shaker humility.

Benjamin Youngs had changes yet to make, carrying Shaker clocks an-other step toward the ideal. Between 1806 and 1815, he shrank his clocks. At thirty-six to fifty-four inches in height, his wall clocks and dwarf tall clocks were less wasteful in labor and materials, as well as being less ostentatious.[14] He also eliminated the narrow middle of the case, as well as the profusion of decorative and dust-catching moldings. The design elements of these later clocks show his compromise between Shaker plainness and his earlier deco-ration. He was striving for humility and simplicity, but it did not come easily. Some of his clocks' faces had round frames, less appropriate than Benjamin Seth Youngs's Shaker square. And the slight taper to the base of this clock, though balanced, is not quite correct. The lines are straight, but they do not meet at right angles. Moreover, he continued to rely on the world for brass works. When Benjamin Youngs whittled away superfluity to better ap-proach the Shaker metaphor of straight and square, he achieved a transition piece. His shelf clock approached the ideal, but its simplicity is incomplete (fig. 11).

Having spent proportionately less of their clockmaking lives as Shakers, Benjamin Youngs and Benjamin Seth Youngs may not have been as con-strained by Shaker simplicity as Isaac Newton Youngs was. When Benjamin Youngs died in 1818, he had spent less than a quarter of his eighty-two years as a Shaker. For him, simplification required unlearning more than six decades of experience. Benjamin Seth Youngs did not become a Shaker until he was an adult, so he, too, had to adjust his views of clocks. Both found it difficult to discard design elements they had adopted early in their clockmaking careers. Perhaps they changed their clocks one step at a time to pare away superfluity, but neither had the luxury of time to perfect his design. And they were evidently so committed to brass works that they could not relinquish that dependence on the world. Nonetheless, the older Youngs family clocks show that their cases and faces continued to change. And those designs undoubtedly influenced Isaac Newton Youngs, the last of the Youngs family clockmakers, who lived the Shaker life nearly from birth.

Believers' clocks would reach the Shaker metaphor of straight and square only in the hands of Brother Isaac. Several factors contributed to his designs: his predecessors' simplifications, his increasing overwork, his own perfectionism, a second apprenticeship with a master clockmaker, and Lucy Wright's scolding. As a result, Isaac Newton Youngs set a new standard for mid-nineteenth-century Shaker clocks with his 1840 design (fig. 12). These clocks are Shaker ideals expressed in wood. But getting to that point required years of preparation, as well as other trials in addition to his run-in with Mother Lucy, and so an examination of his first experience in clockmaking may be in order. In his Clock Maker's Journal, Isaac described his earliest tutelage under Benjamin Youngs.

> When I was a child, I lived with my uncle, who was a clock maker—I used to be with him in his shop & watch his motions, learned the parts of a clock, & could put one together perhaps when 6 or 7 years old, & knew the time of day before I could talk plain. I had a relish for clocks & liked to be among them & to handle the tools, but as I left my uncle the spring before I was 10 years old, I did not arrive to much understanding or judgment in the business. I went where no such thing was carried on & clocks were scarce.
>
> I however retained some notion about them & wanted to be working at them, & in the fall after I was 10 I undertook to make one with a knife awl &c. but I had poor conveniences for it. Some time after I began it, my brother Benjamin [Seth] found it out & meeting me once, said, "Well. Isaac, how do you come on with your clock." I was a little confounded, but wishing to express in short my difficulties I replied, "Do you think I could make a clock go with a wooden wafer?" [15]

But the Shakers moved the precocious boy from his uncle's home to a family where clockmaking was discouraged, and when he built a little wooden clock, Abigail Richardson "burnt it all up." [16] Despite Richardson's cruelty, little Isaac did not stop thinking about clocks, nor did he forget what he had learned.

After Isaac moved to New Lebanon, he did no clockmaking until 1815, when he was twenty-one and was allowed to begin working with Brother Amos Jewett, who made clocks with wooden works. Isaac later wrote he was "pretty closely bound to tayloring" but he appreciated the privilege and liberty of working in Jewett's shop. Those key words, liberty and privilege, show that the young Shaker brother recognized his good fortune in being allowed to work with the older clockmaker. According to Isaac, Brother Amos was "very clever" with clocks.[17] That job was a labor of love. Over the course of his life, Isaac spent many more hours at tailoring than at clockmaking, but clocks fascinated him in ways that clothing did not.

In clockmaking, Brother Isaac borrowed design elements from all of his mentors. He further simplified his uncle Benjamin Youngs's design by paring away superfluous details and adopted Benjamin Seth Youngs's square clock face. Following their later examples, he made timepieces small and light enough to hang on a peg or stand on a shelf. He also adopted Amos Jewett's wooden works, reducing Shakers' dependence on the outside world as well as making the piece lighter. Though Isaac's work was the thematic descendant of his mentors' timepieces, it moved the Youngs family clocks further along the continuum of increasingly spare and square, incorporating his predecessors' "most Shaker" details to create a new design.

As his mentors had done, Brother Isaac put his name or initials on his work. When the Millennial Laws of 1845 ordered, "No one should write or print his name on any article of manufacture, that others may hereafter know the work of his hands," the Ministry institutionalized their disapproval of a longstanding practice. But Isaac Newton Youngs had done just that for years. He also numbered his clocks in chronological order, as Amos Jewett had done. He added instructions for their use and sometimes a short poem on the passing of time.[18]

Isaac spent years trying to improve his clocks before he was pleased with the results, systematically tracking what worked and what did not. His Clock Maker's Journal, begun under Brother Amos Jewett's tutelage, describes two decades of attempts to improve the works of his early clocks, No. 1 through No. 16, which he constructed between 1815 and 1835. In 1815, he described his first.

> Finished a little time piece, for the use of the Elders shop, & it being the first I have made of course it must be called No. 1. Remark. The first bob that I put to this seemed to be too heavy. I put a light-bob to it & the piece went much better—from which I inferred that a clock may sometimes go well with a lighter bob, when it would not with a heavy one.[19]

Under Brother Amos's oversight, Brother Isaac built the equipment he needed, including a "tooth engine" for the clockmaker's lathe, and continued his experiments. In 1835, he recorded:

> [I] undertook a new manner of making the wheels, i.e. to have wood cogs set in pewter rims. In that respect I succeeded pretty well. They look a little finer style than wood wheels, but I had a good deal of difficulty to make my work true—my pivots were very coarse & pinions not very true & it was some time before I could make it run well. I however succeeded so that with a very heavy weight it would go. I learned a good deal by this, found in particular that large pivots make a clock hard in preparation, also that the pinions had better be small than too large. This little rough production of my first fair attempts I called No. 1.

"After this," Isaac wrote, "I occasionally made timepieces & kept improving my knowledge, tools and conveniences, so that after making several I could make tolerable good ones." Twenty years of clock experiments, tinkering with pivots, pinions, cogs and bobs, brought satisfactory results. By 1835, he had built sixteen clocks, describing his findings with each improvement and failure and recording the amount of time he spent on each clock. Clock No. 2, "a cheap kind of timepiece," required thirty-two hours to construct in October 1816. Some of his innovations, however, did not meet his expectations. The size of pivots and weights was critical. And he was not pleased with the look of clocks Nos. 3 and 4 because the copal varnish he used on their faces turned them too yellow for his taste.[20]

According to his journal, Brother Isaac made no clocks in 1817, but in 1818, he made three. In January, he finished No. 5, with a "good cherry case," for the East house. In November, about the same time he was having trouble supporting a pure union with the opposite sex, he completed an "alarum timepiece" and also made a common timepiece with a case for the blacksmiths. In May 1819, he began No. 8, a striking clock, and worked on it a little at a time. He reckoned that it took him about forty days to make the clock and its case. "I put in iron boxes for the pivot holes," he wrote, "thinking this might perhaps do better than brass." He did not finish it until July 4, 1820, and that clock got him in trouble. Within four days of its completion, Isaac reported Mother Lucy's displeasure with the mahogany on the clock door. He had thoughtlessly slipped into unnecessary decoration and, he wrote, "I must be careful in future."[21] The incident nettled him, but he learned to avoid "fancy." And as if No. 8 had not already caused trouble enough, he found that the works were faulty. "The iron boxes [were] very poor things for pivots to run in," he concluded, "for they cut away the pivot very fast." He tried bushing the pivot hole with silver, an experiment he may well have kept to himself.[22]

Isaac's other work cut into his time for clockmaking. He had more to do than he could manage. In April 1820, he wrote:

> The 2d order have concluded to go without the larum made or bo't this season. They do not like to say much to the Deacons about buying one . . . but they will have to do a good while without if they wait till I make one, for I have work enough to do. I hope and trust they will buy one.[23]

I have work enough to do. Brother Isaac, who loved clockmaking, hoped the Second Order would buy a clock, because he was just too busy to build one. He had been tailoring almost full-time since he was ten years old, and other work assignments, such as teaching school, so filled his days and evenings by 1820 that he could not meet the village's demands for clocks. By 1821, he felt scattered because his different jobs often called him to two places at the same time.[24]

Despite his increasing workload, however, he finished No. 9 for the Elder Sisters' workshop in October 1821 and described it in his journal.

> The crown wheel of this is placed on the back side of the back plate & the plate has no shaft, but only operates on a short pin. For winding up the key passes thro' the face. One brass pinion, the rest english box. Pivots of steel knitting needles save the first & last wheels. I like the construction of it very well.

Isaac experimented with a variety of materials and tried to reduce his reliance on brass works. He also recorded his satisfaction—or dismay—with the results of his experiments.[25]

In August 1822, Isaac completed No. 10, "a rough cheap timepiece" without a case. He made it with "one pointer, to go round once in 6 hours, & having 2 rows of figures on the face or dial." He was still trying to simplify. In October, he finished a similar timepiece, No. 11, for the brethren at North Enfield, New Hampshire.[26] His building No. 11 for a distant society is a curious matter. Though he was so crowded with work that he hoped to avoid making a clock for New Lebanon's Second Order, he filled a request from another Shaker village. He did not explain why. But his clockmaker's journal shows little evidence of the heavy workload he recorded elsewhere. On the contrary, this account lists only his clocks and experiments as he tried to perfect his clockworks. Yet No. 11 marked the end of this phase of his clock making. Isaac did not record completion of another timepiece for eight years.

During those years, Isaac's heavy workload may have been exacerbated by a move to avoid New York state militia service and the resulting anxiety about the situation. The Hancock, Massachusetts, Shakers accepted Isaac Newton Youngs, Henry Youngs, Garret Lawrence, and twenty others into their society "for the express purpose of enjoying [their] civil and religious rights," freeing the New Lebanon Shakers from the financial burden of the fine that New York levied for noncompliance with militia duties. The move, however, was only on paper. Isaac and the other service-eligible brothers continued to work and worship in New Lebanon, spending only a few days a year on the Massachusetts side of the state line. Their pacifism came at a cost. For years, Isaac feared that the state of New York would investigate and jail the twenty-three brethren from New Lebanon for avoiding the muster.[27]

A Believer's day was to be filled with some productive activity every waking moment, and various journals suggest that Isaac Newton Youngs was indeed productive from 1821 to 1833. He spent part of every fall, winter, and spring in the tailor' shop and worked on the farm as well. He also went to the fledgling Shaker community at Savoy, visited his mother in Schenectady and his foster mother, Molly Youngs, at Watervliet, co-authored *A Juvenile Monitor,* helped build the new meetinghouse for the New Lebanon Church Family, wrote poems and a hymn for its dedication, and repeatedly repaired its tin roof. He built a table for the harness maker, traveled to Saybrook, Connecticut, and New York, taught school, transcribed hymnals by hand, helped build the brethren's workshop at New Lebanon, joined in the revival there, and attended a camp meeting. He kept at least two meeting journals for the Church Family from 1815 to 1828, composed his dialogue between the Flesh and the Spirit, repaired the Church Family's waterworks, built an arch in the sisters' weave shop, ran social meetings for the Children's Order, worked on the New Lebanon Church Family's dwelling or Great House in 1831, turned more than a thousand clothespins on his lathe, and laid a new floor in the dairy. He wrote *The Rudiments of Music Displayed and Explained* in 1833. Brother Isaac was one of the Church Family's leading singers, and he spent many evenings practicing or coaching the lower orders.[28] Demands on his time proliferated because of his versatility and his willingness to try to accommodate all requests.

For a while, however, Isaac was too ill to do any work at all. In March 1826, he went to Watervliet for several weeks "to recruit his health."[29] This may have been the Shaker version of a rest cure. Ordinarily, brethren sick with the usual late-winter illnesses recuperated in the Shakers' village infirmary. But Isaac had to leave home and go where fewer demands would be placed on him.

Despite his burgeoning workload, Brother Isaac resumed clockmaking in February 1830, when he finished No. 12 for the wash house and No. 13 for the machine shop. Of them he wrote, "These were a plain style, with tin front plates, pivot holes boxed with brass or silver, wheels of cherry, the pillars .screwed into the back plates. Made to hang on a pin, with no case but a boxing round the wheels." [30] His style was changing, not only in having cherrywood wheels in the works, but also by replacing the case with a box only around the wheels. Such a design probably eliminated hours of labor. The too-busy Brother Isaac may have been simplifying clock cases to reduce his workload as well as to meet the Shaker mandated standards of plainness and simplicity.

Isaac continued to experiment, even though such efforts meant additional work. Mother Lucy had cautioned him to avoid labor for the sake of curiosity, but she was gone and no one else oversaw him as she had. In 1831, he tested different metals' coefficient of friction, a subject that drew his interest for three decades.

> Made some experiment to prevent chafing on the foot of the hammer staff where the pins raise the hammer by putting on a facing of silver: burnished the pins & let them run without oil. I find after several months running that it does exceeding well, whereas formerly the bare iron coming in contact, it would run but a few weeks. Silver in such a case I believe is an excellent thing to prevent chafing by friction.

Though his experiment worked, Isaac did not make another clock until November 1832, when he finished No. 14 and No. 15 for the deaconesses and the physician sisters' shops. In 1833, he made a compound clock for the Church Family dwelling by putting clock faces in several rooms, all attached to gearing in the main clock located in the second loft. Such a design, in theory at least, standardized time throughout the Great House. The compound clock was a move toward unity and conformity. [31]

The last timepiece Isaac recorded in his Clock Maker's Journal was No. 16, finished in March 1835. It was a "different plan from any I have made—it has no pillars—is set in the case & has only one plate, easily taken out." He was pleased with the design. "I like the manner very well," he wrote. His most recent master in the trade, Amos Jewett, had died in March 1834, and after No. 16, Isaac discontinued his Clock Maker's Journal. But he was not finished with clockmaking. [32]

The clocks he made after 1835 are recorded in various other journals without extensive comments on experimentation. In July 1837, for instance, he made one for the Second Order's bonnet shop. Soon thereafter, unlike his predecessors (as far as is known), Isaac increased efficiency by making several similar pieces at one time. He inscribed at least three with the date May 12, 1840. That spring, he finished six new timepieces and carried three to the Second Order to set them up. But Brother Isaac's clock responsibilities did not end there. Every clock required attention to keep it running. From the late 1830s through the 1850s, Isaac reported such work, which included cleaning, repairs, and maintenance not only at home in the Church Family but also for the other Shaker families in New Lebanon and Canaan. And he repaired the world's people's clocks, too.[33]

Though he had been making clocks for more than thirty years, Isaac Newton Youngs retained his interest in innovations. In December 1848, he went to Albany to learn more about making spring clocks. But by January 1849, he was discouraged. "I have done a little, maybe 3 days work on a spring time piece that I began in 1840," he wrote. "I hope to finish it some time before I die—but it is doubtful. I can get but little time to work on it." [34] Isaac's other temporal responsibilities, especially tailoring, took precedence over clockmaking. And he was uncomfortably aware that time seemed to pass more quickly as he aged. Taking to heart Mother Ann's instruction, "You must not lose one moment of time, for you have none to spare," he wrote on No. 23:

> Behold! how swift the seasons roll!
> Time swiftly flies away!
> 'Tis blown away as fleety chaff
> Upon a windy summer's day.
> Then O improve it as it flies
> Eternal joys are for the wise.[35]

But Brother Isaac's 1840 design was ideal for Shaker purposes (fig. 12). Coming as it did during the Shakers' Era of Manifestations, when spiritual revelations made many changes in Shaker life, the design might have been considered a gift of inspiration.

Isaac Newton Youngs's 1840 wall clocks (about thirty-one inches tall and eleven inches wide) are the essence of Shaker simplicity. The clean, spare line sets them apart from earlier Youngs family clocks. The undecorated case is a square atop a rectangle, the base almost equal to two squares of the same size as the bonnet. Modest narrow moldings on the top and the bottom provide visual balance without breaking the strong vertical line. Isaac used no curved lines except in the round clock face, which is framed by a square window. The clock is plain and modest in size, thus efficient to build and light enough to hang on a peg. For the cases, Isaac used pine, sometimes combined with a light domestic hardwood, perhaps butternut, finished with a plain varnish. He applied a chrome yellow wash to the interior of his clock cases. No. 19 and No. 23 are almost identical.[36] No. 21, however, is walnut and the lower door is paneled with two glass windows separated by a thin strip of wood. The works appear to be made of cherry wood, or something equally dark and fine-grained.[37] By making wooden works, Brother Isaac reduced the Shakers' dependence on the world for clock parts. Even though the wooden works added to his workload, he evidently chose to sacrifice his own limited time to Shakers' separatist ideology. And perhaps he made wooden works because he preferred clockmaking to other tasks awaiting his attention.

One of Isaac's innovations in his 1840 wall clocks was to use the backboard of the clock case as the backplate of the movement, which made them lighter for hanging. No other clockmakers used that design, and Gibbs and Meader noted that "whatever Isaac had in mind, [he] verily produced a nightmare for future repairing" because they believed the clock case would have had to be disassembled to get at the works. But Sharon Koomler's minute examination of No. 23, the clock closest to the original condition, showed that the works could be accessed from both front and sides. Rather than closing off the works, Brother Isaac went to considerable effort not only to conserve weight by attaching the works to the back plate but also to make the works accessible for future adjustments and repairs.[38] That model appears to be almost a plain box, but it fits together like a Chinese puzzle, integrating works and case.

In his 1840 design, Brother Isaac eliminated superfluities both inside and out. He pared down the case to the spare, bare minimum. At the same time, he preserved harmony of line and form with attention to the Shaker ideals of balance, perfection, and straightness. Designing a case with straight lines and no superfluous decoration was, for Brother Isaac, a metaphor for the straight and narrow path to salvation.[39]

As the numbers of Shaker brethren dropped in the mid-nineteenth century, Isaac was diverted to other work. Furthermore, as he wrote in 1858, "The making of clocks among ourselves is now quite unprofitable, owing to the existence of so many factories in the world, where clocks are manufactured in immense quantities, and sold for a trifle—even down to one dollar apiece!"[40] He may have been thankful that he was not trying to support himself among the world's people, where talented artisans were sometimes hard pressed to make a living. Though he built no more clocks, he remained responsible for clock adjustments and repairs—not a trivial matter, because by 1860, the New Lebanon community had ninety-six clocks. An inoperative clock was worse than no clock at all. Its silence contradicted union and punctuality and contributed to disorder, a reproach to the very ideals that inspired its presence in the first place. When Isaac was unavailable, the village missed his clock maintenance. During one of his absences, Giles Avery wrote, "The old clock in the house hall, the old standby, is in want of a doctor and loudly calls for br Isaac to come home again, notwithstanding our mortification being so illiterate in clockquackery."[41]

The Shakers' demand for clocks must be considered in several ways to show the trade's importance to Isaac Newton Youngs, the interplay between Believers' ideals and their temporal labor, and the significance of clock time in nineteenth-century Shaker society. First, Brother Isaac appreciated being allowed to pursue his own interest—an opportunity that was not to be taken for granted. His interest, in turn, served the Shakers. Isaac was one of the few who understood the complicated engineering of a clock and who could build a working clock and also keep it running. His work, therefore, contributed to Shaker union and conformity by helping to keep Believers on time.

Second, the Shaker ideal of simplicity, reinforced by Lucy Wright's mandate to avoid superfluity, found expression in wood and metal under Isaac's hands. Ironically, Mother Lucy's attention to the details of his work in his twenties may have freed him from over-reliance on his predecessors' standards. Without her close scrutiny and his own burgeoning workload, Isaac might not have felt such a pressing need to simplify.

Third, Isaac's perfectionism shaped his clocks. Clockmaking, like the work done by a scribe or a tailor, required close attention, steady hands and good eyesight, hours of precise work with little tolerance for error, and technical knowledge, whether it involved the best recipe for ink or varnish or the friction coefficients of various metals. Isaac preferred consistency, as is evident from his mass production of the 1840 design. His consistency served the Shakers, who were already attuned to uniformity and punctuality. And his perfectionism turned material ideals—square, straight and plumb—into physical reality.

And fourth, during the years Isaac was making clocks, from 1815 into the 1840s, clock time was increasingly important to Shakers; they wanted more and more clocks. Ironically, Isaac was alarmed by their proliferation in the New Lebanon Church Family. He saw the desire for clocks as a symptom of worldly acquisitiveness that was inappropriate among Believers.

> What are we coming to about clocks? How much I have felt my soul vexed at hearing folks say "others can have clocks to themselves—one in such a place—& such a place—why can't I have one—We need one in our room—

or our shop as much as such or such a one"—I don't see as there is any stopping till we get a clock in every room & shop.[42]

What Isaac did not realize was that the spreading demand for clocks and concern for clock time was less a sign of acquisitiveness than a harbinger of change. Shaker values were changing, and not just because Shakers occasionally had to catch a stagecoach or train. Clock time had even invaded Shaker farming practices. When Isaac made clock No. 23 in 1847 for the Second Order's barn, he was dubious. "It is rather a new idea to have clocks in barns," he wrote, "but they seem to be needful & admissible, under suitable restraint." According to a visitor in 1846, the Shakers milked their cows "exactly at fixed times." He added, "So punctual are the attendants to this, that a clock is kept in the apartment, and the herdsman told us at what moment the cows would be in their places." [43] A clock in the barn was evidently a novelty for dairy farmers in the 1840s. Whether the Shakers adhered to the cows' schedule or not, the cows told time by their udders' fullness, not by a timepiece. The Shakers were applying a new standard of time and labor not to their cows but to their herdsmen.

Clocks were more than just a way to tell time. Though their use in standardizing behavior and increasing efficiency was consistent with Shaker values, they were also symptomatic of a move to manage work, to assign a "reasonable"—or profitable—amount of time to any task, as factory operatives well knew. Applying clock time to the Church Family's daily schedule meant that the industrial "time is money" values of the world's people were seeping into Shakers' daily lives. When the seasons and hours of daylight no longer constituted the smallest units of time necessary for doing business, clock time was essential for getting the most out of workers, even among the Shakers of the 1840s and 1850s.

Brother Isaac himself moved from his earlier artisanal values, which involved working just to complete a task, and implemented the time values associated with industry when he began timing his tailoring work to determine how long he took to make garments and buttons and recording the number of hours required to build a clock. He set time-oriented goals and worked by the clock. Unfortunately, setting a goal based on optimum conditions often meant frustration for a perfectionist like Isaac Newton Youngs because the inevitable hindrances of real life meant he could not always reach his goal. Brother Isaac would find himself increasingly frustrated as the years passed and he tried to cram more and more labor into his workdays.

Furthermore, Isaac was not the only Shaker who counted the precious hours. He made clocks for the Elders' and Eldresses' shops, the blacksmith's shop, the wash house, the machine shop, the deaconesses' shop, physician sisters' shop, the bonnet shop, and the barn, where Shaker brethren and sisters evidently felt they had to be mindful of the time as they worked. By 1840, time had indeed become "the task-master of toil." [44] Shaker society had evolved far from its origins as a group who banded together to serve God and support one another. They were slipping away from the preindustrial agrarian way of life of Mother Ann's day. Though the New Lebanon Shaker village remained outwardly serene by all accounts, Believers' work was increasingly done by clock time. And clock time meant that Shakers were applying the world's industrial standards of time to utopia.

A most surprising & interesting sight to behold.

6 Journey to the Western Societies

A Respite from Work, 1834

IN 1834, Isaac Newton Youngs, who had never traveled widely, accompanied Elder Rufus Bishop on a tour of the western Shaker communities, a journey of more than two thousand miles. The journal Isaac kept on the trip resembles the published travel journals that were a staple of nineteenth-century literature. He was an excellent observer with a good sense of humor; he collected information, sizing up people and places as naturally as he drew breath. His attention to detail, so evident in his work as clockmaker and scribe, is revealed in his vivid descriptions. The trip journal also reveals new facets of Isaac's personality, including the anxiety that would plague him in later life.

The trip west was a political necessity. Trouble was brewing among the western Shakers; their distance from the New Lebanon Ministry had become an issue. Fearing that the westerners were becoming too independent, the Ministry decided to send a two-man delegation to investigate. "Brothers Rufus Bishop & Isaac N. Youngs," Seth Youngs Wells wrote, "were selected as the missionaries." The Ministry had full confidence in their tact and judgment as well as the examples they set as models of Shaker faith. Their assignment was to evaluate the western communities, confer with the Elders at Union Village, and report back to the Ministry. The journey was long, expensive, politically sensitive, and fraught with hazards. But for Isaac, it was a once-in-a-lifetime opportunity.[1]

Isaac's journal served several purposes. He used it to preserve memories for himself and to help his homebound friends "see" what he had seen. He used it as a report for the Ministry, writing down his observations on each Shaker community and augmenting them with maps he drew of the western villages. The maps were invaluable to the Ministry in their efforts to assess the state of those societies and probably also helped to jog the travelers' memories when they presented their report to the Ministry. Finally, because the Elders required traveling Shakers to relate all that transpired on their journeys, the journal fulfilled that function, as well.[2] Isaac opened the journal with a

disclaimer to excuse his poor handwriting—yet another example of his frustrated perfectionism.

On June 3, Elder Rufus and Brother Isaac traveled first to Watervliet,
where Believers held a farewell ceremony and sang, "O take our love with
you," while Rufus and Isaac held out a handkerchief by its four corners "in
token of receiving a bountiful store of love and blessing." Isaac reported, "I
felt a forcible impression that no Antichristian minister ever took up such a
bountiful and precious collection." Blessings were a boon to carry them
down the road. On June 4, they went to Schenectady so Isaac could visit his
mother. She had long suffered from mental infirmity; in the bitter weather of
February 1817, she had been found wandering "quite deranged and unable
to give any account of how she came there." When Isaac saw her in 1834, his
mother was "rather wild & unwilling to notice me. She did not at first know
me, but after some consideration and conversation she became more conversant and showed a good deal of memory; . . . [she] said I was born on the 4th
of July . . . christened in the old Methodist Church at Johnstown." [3] Isaac did
not have to visit her; no one would have thought less of him had he omitted
that call. And he was patient with her infirmity. In fact, her mind had so deteriorated that the visit may have meant more to him than it did to her.

The next morning, June 5, Brother Rufus and Isaac boarded the packet
boat *Warren* on the Troy and Erie Canal line, part of the network of internal
improvements that facilitated transportation between the Northeast and
Midwest. Although boat travel was easier than stagecoach or horseback, the
canal boat also carried the world's people. Most of them, Isaac reported,
were "tolerable civil company—Some of them, however, were rude, & one or
two of the females were real brawlers at politics, & much was said about
[President Andrew] Jackson." Political debates were rare among Shakers,
who discouraged topics that aroused contention or "party feeling." And
though Isaac knew strong-minded women, he viewed those who publicly expressed their opinions as a novelty worth recording. [4]

When the boat stopped at Syracuse on June 7, Isaac went ashore to explore and do some shopping. On his return, he wrote, "I met with some bad
luck." The boat was gone. He took off down the tow path hoping to catch up
to it. The boat he overtook was not his own, so he boarded to ask advice.
"Here the captain told me he was certain that our boat Warren had not gone
by—so I rode on to Canton, [where] I concluded I would wait . . . till our
boat came up which I did & after awhile our boat came up & there was much
rejoicing." Elder Rufus chided him, but Isaac added, "& I am not sorry."
When Isaac recopied the journal, he did not excise that remark, with the pro-

noun underlined for emphasis. He concluded his record of the incident with the comment, "After this, matters went on well for some time."

Isaac continued describing the sights and sounds along the way, including the "constant roar" of bull frogs in the great marsh near Montezuma and the excitement one morning around two o'clock when a horse fell off the tow path into the canal. All hands had "quite a bustle" to get him out so they could go on.[5] The first leg of their journey then proceeded without further mishap, and on Wednesday, June 11, the brethren left the canal and rode north to the Shaker community at Sodus, on Lake Ontario, a convenient stop for Believers traveling farther west. The brief visit was a model for those that followed. The brethren toured the community and visited the schoolhouse; Isaac mapped the village and saw the local sights.[6] After four uneventful days, they resumed their journey by packet boat. Farther west at Lockport, where the canal dropped sixty feet, the stone locks were (by all accounts) magnificent. The capital and labor required to create the canal and the locks were almost as interesting as the engineering. Isaac also noted the lamps suspended over the locks. He wondered who kept them lit in bad weather, adding, "I should not like to cross it in a high wind." [7] Isaac was not acrophobic; he worked on the New Lebanon meetinghouse roof, thirty feet up. But the lock's lamps were so exposed that the idea of crawling out to light them in a storm gave him the shivers.

Brother Isaac enjoyed the sights but the Shaker brethren themselves were as much a novelty as the scenery was. One evening aboard the boat, they sang a few Shaker songs for the other passengers. Isaac's voice, perhaps the best at New Lebanon, must have made a good impression, because their music was well received and made a good end to the day. "After this, all hands cleared out of the cabin to give place to make up the beds," Isaac wrote, "& we generally laid down to rest about 9 ocl. I slept very well & did not wake up more than once or twice till about 4 ocl." He woke rested. "Not one bump all night," he added.[8] A good night's sleep while traveling with strangers was unusual. Aside from the lurches of boat travel, Isaac was unaccustomed to such close company with the world's people, who often violated Shaker social norms. Furthermore, travelers had to be vigilant against theft. Outside of Shaker communities, the brethren could rarely let down their guard.

At the end of the canal, the brethren changed boats for the voyage down Lake Erie. The trip across the lake was "wearisome," Isaac wrote, because their boat was overloaded, with "scarcely a decent place to sit down long at a time—no chance to write, & there being nothing to do, it made one feel dull & weary." Brother Isaac did not like being crowded, he was uncomfortable cooped up, and he was not accustomed to idleness. But he made the best of the situation. "By walking about & getting into various positions & sometimes getting into conversation with some one, viewing the sloops sailing around on the Lake I could enjoy a tolerable comfortable feeling," he wrote.[9]

On June 16, the brethren reached North Union, Ohio, where they stayed for six days. Isaac could relax in the safety of a Shaker enclave. He was also pleased to attend worship. The Ohioans' fervor thrilled him; they shouted and clapped so loud, Isaac reported, that his "hair almost stood up on end!" "And still," he added, "I could hardly forbear smiling at their engagedness."[10] Though their zeal pleased him, his effort to keep a straight face indicated that he thought their response excessive even by Shaker standards of religious enthusiasm. Western Believers' fervor far exceeded that at New Lebanon in 1834.

He also enjoyed North Union's excellent food, remarking on the "high dish of chicken, warm cake and butter," and the wonderful strawberries they had for supper. But he was critical of the primitive conditions. Their log buildings were roughly built. The kitchen lacked the conveniences that the sisters at New Lebanon enjoyed, and the schoolhouse had a ladder rather than stairs to the upper level. As a master builder, Isaac had high standards; he expected buildings to have solid walls and satin-smooth floors. "Here," he noted, amazed that the schoolhouse was neither weather-tight nor vermin-proof, "we can occasionally take a peep outdoors between the logs." Furthermore, "by being pretty careful, one could walk across the floor without stubbing his toes very badly!"[11]

By June 24, Brothers Rufus and Isaac were on a canal in Ohio, enroute to Union Village. Brother Isaac was again impressed with the canal as an engineering achievement, noting that some locks were blasted through hills sixty feet high, a massive undertaking. But the tow horses again caused a problem. When the boat tied up to take on water, Isaac wrote,

> [the] horses, being left by their driver, took it into their heads to move on, and the rope began to pull on the water-post, the hands began to fly about to save the post & the Captain cried "ho" to the horses; "Where's that fool of a driver?" &c when out pops the poor blundering lame boy from the cabin with a great hunk of bread butter in his hand. He tried to get at his horses but the boat was off from shore & he had to hobble across the bridge; & finally got at his horses, which had stopped after the Capt. had called to them long enough & swore a little so after quite a bustle we got regulated & went on again.[12]

Isaac empathized with the hungry boy, cursed for leaving his horses for a snack. He knew what it was like to be called to task for an unintentional mistake. But farther along, he met another unfortunate boy who, in contrast, prompted only disgust. Isaac, whose journal entries were mostly straightforward descriptions, tinged sometimes with humor, was uncharacteristically derogatory in his description of the boy.

> Here I saw a sight, full as remarkable as any that I have seen.—viz: a boy
> 7 years old next Sept. [who] weighs 135 lbs! Is about 4 feet tall. His name
> is Luke Medcalf. He was on board the boat Utica which we met. I stepped
> aboard to get a sight at him; he sat in the gang-way so that I could not well
> see him. I took some sugarplums & held out to him; he said he could not
> reach them! I told him he could get up & come to me. So he got up &
> waddled along, so that I had a chance to view him!!! A real squaddy heap! [13]

Brother Isaac viewed the overweight Luke Medcalf as a phenomenon as interesting as Lake Erie and canals blasted through sixty-foot hills. He was not accustomed to obese or lazy children. Children in the Shaker villages were well-fed, though not overfed; nor were they allowed to be so physically inert that they built up the amount of flesh Medcalf carried. They worked and they exercised in worship. Medcalf, who tried to avoid moving but could be enticed with sugarplums, was by Shaker standards a sluggard, whose appearance and behavior prompted Isaac's disdain.

Medcalf was the high point of the journey from North Union to Union Village, Ohio. Isaac reported few oddities except for a remarkable lack of kindness along the route their stagecoach took after they left the canal. When they were traveling one evening after dark, the stagecoach driver stopped at several houses asking for a candle for his lantern; at each, he was denied.[14] For Isaac, coming from a hospitable Shaker village, the worldly Ohioans' stinginess was astounding. On this trip, he would find over and over again that the world held little charm.

The brethren arrived at Union Village, the largest of the western Shaker societies, on June 29. The *Ohio Gazetteer* described the place as a handsome community whose hospitality made it "a pleasant retreat from the bustle of the world." After they were received and fed, they were "way-layd by a number of brethren, who stood showing their teeth, waiting for the chance to get hold of us." Isaac's imagery connotes aggression, but it is hard to say whether he meant only to be funny or was deliberately comparing the Ohioans to territorial dogs warning them off. Considering that the purpose of their visit was to assert the Ministry's authority over the western Shakers, he may have

dreaded a confrontation. But the Ohioans welcomed the travelers enthusias-
tically and even, Isaac joked, feted him on his birthday, the Fourth of July.
"The much celebrated day of <u>Independence</u> has again arrived, big with event!
The cannons roaring just as they do down east . . . but I don't know as the
Ohio-ites . . . should make such a fuss for me! But however, the folks here at
Union Village know it, & as a proof they gave me a new pair of trowsers this
morning." [15]

Among the Believers at Union Village was Andrew Houston, who had visited New Lebanon in August 1826 when the Ministry was considering removing Shakers from Indiana. He renewed his friendship with Brother Isaac
in 1834, and, despite the sensitive nature of the visit, appreciated the brethren's mission. He later wrote to the Ministry, "We have no doubt but you sent
the best fruits of Lebanon . . . in whom there is no guile and in whom is
found no occasion of stumbling." Brothers Rufus and Isaac impressed him
with their "meekness & humility, deeply interested in the upbuilding of the
gospel, able and willing to encourage and strengthen the weak, sociable and
easy of access." [16]

At Union Village, Isaac met Daniel Stag, a "blind man, a sound believer;
much pleased to feel us." Brother Daniel earned his keep spinning mop yarn
and working in the kitchen. He showed the visitors "how he went about with
his little dog, with a strap around his neck." [17] Isaac also enjoyed worship at
Union Village. On the Sabbath, July 6, "a number of songs were sung," he reported, "& then they had some exercise in the quick circular & finally, nothing would do but that I must lead the ring." He was pleased by the honor.
"We had a real high," he added. After dancing they sang and "the animation
grew higher & higher, & shouting & clapping of hands ensued, with much
hopping & skipping like so many new lights that seemed at a loss for ways to
express themselves—It was enough to fill one with surprise, And make one
stare, And set erect one's hair." He compared the uninhibited Ohioans to
"new lights" at a camp meeting. The New Lebanon Church Family had not
been that fervent since the revival of 1827. [18]

On July 10 the brethren made a brief side trip to Watervliet, Ohio, where
they saw the gristmill, wagon shop, and carding machine. [19] When they returned to Union Village, Isaac watched several brethren and a dog finish a rat
hunt; they had killed thirty-four rats in an hour and a half. "This is a tolerable
good specimen of the rat concern in this place," Isaac wrote. "There is a very
great abundance of rats here, not only in the buildings, but in the fields &
barns & they devour much corn." Each bite the rats ate was unavailable for
livestock or humans. Every farm supported a rat population, but dogs, cats,
and traps could minimize their numbers. At New Lebanon, the Church Fam-

ily typically kept up to a dozen cats for just that purpose. In Ohio, however, where the rats were winning, the Believers did not seem to be sufficiently concerned with rat control.[20]

Rats were not the only drawback to Ohio. July was high summer, and hot. After touring Union Village, inspecting twelve-foot-tall corn, visiting the pottery, looking at silkworms, Isaac checked the thermometer and found it was 103 degrees—much hotter than a typical summer in the Berkshire hills above New York's Hudson River. Isaac "sweat a good deal" and "slept but little" in the heat. After a sweltering sleepless night on July 24, the brethren arose at three in the morning to leave for Whitewater in a covered wagon.[21]

At Whitewater, the brethren met Allen Agnew, who had lost his right hand and half of his forearm in an accident with a buzz saw. Isaac was impressed with the man's ingenuity as well as his determination to work despite his handicap. He described Brother Allen's prosthesis, a "tin socket which he fixes on his arm, in which he attaches some kind of tools, can work at turning lathe, can do various jobs of wood work, can write with his left hand." The brethren also visited the brewery at Whitewater.

> They make considerable extensive business at brewing malt beer, generally about fourteen barrels a week; here is a pack of rude fellows of the world who had got together in the shade of the brewery house, & were shooting a mark, & said "they were shooting for beer;" one of them came in & told aged Joseph, they wanted a gallon of beer; but I did not stay to see whether they got any or not.[22]

The brew house attracted loungers too lazy to work, rude and potentially dangerous. But Brother Isaac merely described the scene and marked the brewery on his map.[23]

Outside of Union Village, Isaac disliked southern Ohio. He rode through a spot called Hell's Half Acre, a "scrandy place." Further along, he saw a log barn where "two bears were chained for good behavior—hideous looking things." And in Harrison, "there was nothing very inviting," he wrote, "for it was quite an insignificant looking place, small & dirty and stinking enough, I should think, to breed the Cholera." [24]

Kentucky was worse. Brothers Rufus and Isaac crossed the Ohio River on July 30, heading to the Shaker community at Pleasant Hill, about twenty-five miles southwest of Lexington.

> About 11 ocl crossed the Ohio in a little sort of scow, just big enough to hold us—got across safe, and landed at a dreadful rough steep place one would hardly think of its being a ferry any more than if there were a brush fence

there—paid 75 cts ferriage. . . . So much for a beginning in Kentucky, a pretty fair specimen. And now for a ramble over the hills, along the runs & stony bottoms of dried up water courses, thro the desolate regions of a slave state.

This was Brother Isaac's first commentary on slave society, and Kentucky did not impress him anyway. When they came to a fork in the road near a village school, "I stepped in to enquire the way," Isaac wrote, "& the gazing rustics ranged around, viewed me with surprise. The [school]master said he did not know the way; but one of the boys told me." [25] A Shaker was a novelty in Kentucky, and local etiquette permitted staring at strangers, which was considered rude at New Lebanon. [26]

The following day, the road was worse. "As far as we could see to the right & left," Isaac wrote, "the earth seemed to be nothing but one continued roll of ridge & hollow, hill & gulf." He had never seen such wild country or such narrow, rough roads. "Not a single dwelling house have I seen today fit for any decent people to inhabit & not much wonder at that, for I know not that I have seen a half acre of level land today." The few people lived in squalor and looked as miserable as their patches of corn. The brethren passed at least 250 ridges that day on the road along the "backbone of Kentucky." Isaac added, "I think too that the ribs show pretty plain!" [27]

The towns were no better. Georgetown looked good from a distance, he observed, but close up, "it was a poor old, mean, dirty-looking place, & some of the buildings being whitewashed outside made me think of painted sepulchers, & 'dead men's bones.' " And Lexington was "not elegant—not very clean—the inhabitants not very enterprizing." Even the county seats did not meet Northeastern expectations. Many other visitors to the slave South made similar comments. Slavery, heat, illness, or all three combined, induced lassitude in whites, even those who did not own slaves. And Southern cleanliness was not up to the standards of a Northern Shaker whose home village was notable for being spotless. Isaac was happy to get to Pleasant Hill safe and sound, and to be among Believers again. Three years earlier, Robert Wickliffe had written, "Let a stranger visit your country, and enquire at Danville, Harrodsburg or Lexington, for your best specimens of agriculture, mechanics and architecture, [and] . . . he is directed to visit the society of Shakers at Pleasant Hill." [28] The visiting brethren undoubtedly concurred.

Among Pleasant Hill's attractions were watermelons, which the visitors "devoured without much delay or remorse" daily. In fact, they feasted on watermelons. One day, they "had to attend 3 or 4 times to eating watermelons, & these being pretty good hinder[ed] us a good deal." The following day, they were "several times much hindered in attending to watermelons, a duty which was difficult to get by!" Pleasant Hill also offered Brother Isaac opportunities to play. The conscientious Shaker who filled every moment at home with work or worship and who fulfilled his western mission by touring villages, keeping careful records, and offering advice on music, teaching school, tailoring, and clocks and other mechanical matters, "had some diversion with a large mud turtle" at Pleasant Hill's dam. And once, in the cool of the evening, they took a walk to the cliffs above the river. "We came to the mighty brink where we could look down more than 300 feet below us to the Kentucky river," Isaac wrote. "The point terminates in a rocky precipice perpendicular for nearly 200 feet! It was a sublime sight, but we dare not approach near enough to look perpendicularly down." They climbed higher. "Here we amused ourselves like boys, in rolling down stones over the edge of the precipice, & witnessing the wonderful cracking, threshing, & bouncing along down. . . . Thus we worked perhaps half an hour," Isaac wrote, "& it being very warm, we sweat profusely, like we had been pitching hay!"[29] The contrast between his simple pleasures at Pleasant Hill and his increasing labor at New Lebanon shows how completely the middle-aged Shaker had invested himself in his work.

At a farewell ceremony Isaac "spoke some of [his] feelings," thanking the Kentucky Shakers for their kindnesses and also for keeping the gospel. Then everyone knelt to covenant that they would always do so. This ritual suggests that the Believers at Pleasant Hill, far from the Ministry's control, may have needed a reminder of their covenant. On August 20, their farewells complete, the brethren left. Isaac described their departure.

> Here were perhaps 100 of the brethren and sisters, who came here to see us for the last time in this world & to express their unfeigned feelings of love & respect. So we mutually wished each other a kind farewell, and future prospering, hardened our hearts, and turned our faces and rode off with speed.[30]

Isaac was sorry to leave. But they had to keep moving to finish their tour before winter. A seven-mile ride took them back to Harrodsburg.

> While waiting [for the stagecoach, Isaac wrote,] I took some time to view matters and surely the more I looked the more I was disgusted. The back yard of the tavern where we stopped was the most disgraceful scene of filth. Here was a poor old duck, with both wings broken, went humbly crouching along paddling in the mud for a morsel to eat. The hogs, the hens &c were strolling about seeking what they could find. All these creatures had politely

left their manners just as happened, and I should suppose that the beasts in human shape had also contributed a portion! I do not know where to go to find a stink that was not there.[31]

Isaac Newton Youngs had been raised around barnyards. As a boy, he had hauled his share of manure. He used an outhouse. He could not have been too prissy. But in Shaker villages, dung was not left lying around, going to waste. It was gathered, carted, and spread on gardens or fields. Only slovenly or wasteful people left it where it fell unless it was in a field that needed fertilizer. Worse yet, he wrote,

> In this yard also was the common place for drawing water for common use. It was a large sort of well dug out of the rock into which they descended by steps. In the bottom of this, the water being shallow, there set what I took to be milk pans, butter vessels and a variety of things to be kept cool. This vault about 20 ft. deep was loosely covered over with planks with spaces big enough to let a Negro thro!!

The water "looked muddy like as if dirty potatoes had been washed in it"— unlike the scrupulously clean Shakers' spring house or dairy. Kentuckians were either unaware of the most basic principles of public sanitation or did not care. Isaac had worked on drainage projects, an aqueduct, and waterworks, so he knew about public sanitation. But much of the west was devoid of such amenities.[32]

Kentucky had little to recommend it. Poverty and ignorance were everywhere visible. Isaac observed that the "Negroes," whether free or slaves, were dressed in rags and even the buildings looked shabby. "On one of the houses I heard a miserable bell, ringing," he wrote, "I supposed, to call boarders in to dinner, and I thot by the sound of it rather than go to it, my first thot would be to run the other way." Even the bell was a sorry thing. Lest anyone at home think he was exaggerating, Isaac concluded, "This is an honest statement of Harrodsburg & it is too applicable to a great part of common towns in Kentucky." And yet Harrodsburg was a county seat and a market center with two of the finest spas in the South.[33]

Slavery and filth were bad enough, but the brethren also encountered violence. At Saunders' tavern, a stagecoach stop, a fracas erupted. One passenger struck another with a stick and bloodied his head; the victim, determined to get revenge, picked up a large stone to throw but a great stout man held him back. Isaac wrote, "Surely thot I this is raw head and bloody bones!"[34]

Fortunately, pleasant times lay ahead. At South Union they were met by "perhaps 50 or 60" smiling Believers, who Isaac wrote, seized "hold of your hand or handkerchief or clothes as if they would pull you to pieces for mere joy with every expression of love & respect." Once again, Isaac, evidently accustomed to more reserve, may have been intimidated by the western Shakers' fervent greetings. But he enjoyed the role of the visiting celebrity, ate watermelon, talked with Sister Nancy Moore about her songbooks, and recorded information about John Smith's round bee house two stories high, the fulling mill, and Jasper Spring. The visitors had some excitement when a chimney caught fire and all hands rallied to put it out by forming a bucket brigade. They saved the building, but it was "a narrow escape," Isaac noted, because water was scarce. Isaac also collected a story about Gensy Dillon that he recorded without comment, though its inclusion, like the story of the worldly women who were "real brawlers at politics," suggests he was unaccustomed to aggressive women. When a worldly visitor, determined to sleep with his wife, climbed into her bedroom through a window, Sister Gensy, set on enforcing Shaker rules on their guests, pushed her way into the room and removed him.[35] Gensy Dillon preserved Shaker standards by physical force, and her community preserved the memory in their oral history.

In Kentucky, Isaac relished his meals as he had in Ohio. Mimicking the local accent, he also noted that they were served with unaccustomed elegance. "About 4 we took supper in their great dining room," he wrote. "Here we had matters in rale ginerwine style. Every fly was scared away; we were waited upon to all intents and every dish on the table was handed to us in the most polite manner." At home, each Shaker served himself from platters on the table, and so, lest his readers to think that his hosts were adopting worldly airs, Isaac added, "and yet I must say it was in simplicity." After supper, Isaac collected more anecdotes as he sat on the piazza in the cooling evening air. He heard about his older brother Benjamin Seth Youngs's early missionary work and "how a great many in these western parts thot he was a boy and pitied him when he stepped out to preach." As at other Shaker communities, the local brethren showed the visitors the sites of interest and took them on an outing to the Nob, a "cobble hill" that rose about 175 feet above Jasper Valley, and to explore a nearby cave and Jasper Spring. Isaac noted that he found "no lack of employ every moment," with writing and running errands about the village as he prepared for the trip home.[36]

Brothers Rufus and Isaac left on September 11 in a wagon and went thirty-eight miles toward Louisville. The following day, they stopped at Cold Spring Cave so Isaac could get some "petrifaction," a souvenir to show to the homefolks. He still collected curiosities that Mother Lucy would have thought superfluous and Rufus Bishop no longer enforced her demands. Near Green River, the brethren met some teamsters, "a rough set of Kentuckians, very swearish!" Isaac wrote that they would "damn their horses' souls to everlasting fire and brimstone, their hoofs, &c. to hell flames forever!! & I should think the rough roads & heavy loads was enough already to torment any poor Sinner. We however got by them safe without being damned ourselves." [37] Shakers were not allowed to swear or even to use relatively mild expressions such as "My stars!" So the teamsters' profanity was remarkable to brethren unaccustomed to such rough language. But the day improved after that encounter. At night, they were pleased to have "pretty middling accommodations for Kentucky," but Isaac noted that their hosts were Yankees, not Southerners. When they could, they picnicked along the road. After one such stop, they left the crumbs "to a crew of long snouted, lean lank sided, picked rumpd Hogs, such as generally run loose in the woods of Kentucky." Even Kentucky hogs were sorry critters. [38]

The longer he was in Kentucky, the more Isaac noted the effects of slavery. The next night, he commented on how their host ordered a black servant out of bed to make the fire before dawn. "This is no uncommon thing in Kentucky," Isaac noted. "Poor Sambo . . . has to crawl out long before Massa, & . . . cut the firewood, dark as it is." He empathized with the black workers, slave and free, who supported whites. But the incident showed the master's poor planning; Shakers would have had their firewood cut and stacked close at hand before they went to bed at night. When the brethren reached Louisville, Kentucky, "a pretty flourishing place," they noted "many fine buildings & elegant stations belonging to rich people—nabobs of Louisville who doubtless felt mighty big and grand." According to Basil Hall, who visited there in 1828, the city was large and handsome; he mentioned the slaves only in passing, evidently feeling no empathy with them. Isaac Newton Youngs likewise observed the city's wealth, but to him it rankled. Isaac, an abolitionist like most Shakers, concluded that Louisville's prosperity was "fettered by the bands of slavery." [39]

The brethren left Kentucky on September 15, and when they arrived in Cincinnati, they went to a barbershop to be shaved. Their barber was a "wooly headed yellow man" of singular appearance. Isaac did not speculate about the parentage of such a light-skinned man of African ancestry. But for a Shaker, analysis would have been disorderly if it touched on whites' sexual exploitation of blacks. From Cincinnati, the brethren returned to Union Village, Ohio. The brethren were "glad to get once more among good folks where [they] could feel at home." [40]

On September 26, Rufus Bishop sent a letter from Union Village to New Lebanon to describe their return itinerary. "The Ohio river being too low for boating," he wrote, "we must take the stage to Fredericktown, then the railroad to Baltimore, & if we could do without sleep, we should probably be home soon but not without writing from Baltimore or Philadelphia when we may be at Hudson." Isaac added a note to say how much they looked forward to being home again. Sister Sarah (probably Sarah Bates, his counterpart in teaching and tailoring) had written to the travelers, and Isaac replied, "We love to hear about the school . . . I can almost see the girls all in a nettle coming up to Sarah . . . and vexing her almost out of patience, and I hope . . . that we shall find her bright and lively as ever." [41] Isaac's side of the correspondence shows that though Shakers supposedly had no "particular" friendships, neither were they "out of sight, out of mind." Brother Isaac longed for the comforts of home.

Isaac, however, still had business in Ohio. At Union Village, he talked with the brethren about "building ovens, joiner work and such like," spent time with Andrew Houston, and finished a map of the New Lebanon community for him. On October 1, Isaac recorded, "We arise this morning having prepared our things and fixed our feelings for setting out this day for home." But he added, "It was really touching and affecting to the tender heart to have . . . to part and perhaps never again to see one of those lovely faces again nor hear those voices any more while on this mortal shore." [42] Isaac was probably sad to say goodbye to his friend Andrew Houston, who also described their departure. "Some burst into tears; others look thoughtful and sorrowful—some ask when we ever shall see any of them again?" [43] But the brethren had to go.

Elder Rufus and Brother Isaac met with trouble right at the start. When they arrived at the stage station, the stagecoach was already full, and those aboard had "but little feeling to accommodate" the Shakers. None of the other passengers "would yield a hair," Isaac wrote. "One evil eyed man went so far as to say that he would lose his life, before he would give up his seat!" But sixty-year-old Rufus Bishop pushed his way aboard the stagecoach anyhow. The less-assertive Isaac described the scene.

> Br. Rufus stood up in the stage perhaps 5 minutes and could hardly stir. At last with the advice of the manager, one passenger gave up his seat & to make out the rest I offered to ride on the outside. Thus with a man and his 4 children, 4 women, 2 other men & Br. Rufus inside and the driver and myself and another man on the outside, we were jammed in smack full. Now cracks the whip and off we go, leaving our good brethren in much anxiety; they will doubtless long remember how they last saw us. Now we must take our fortune good or bad & make the best of it. Our load is heavy, our road is muddy, our skies are lowery, our weather some rainy, our companions poor sinners & the young ones are cross and the little dirty things sometimes smell rather Rank.

Rufus Bishop prevailed by making the other passengers so uncomfortable that one gave way. Though he was a Shaker and a pacifist, he was not meek, and he did not permit the world's people to bully him. As a Ministry Elder, the older man was accustomed to getting his way. Isaac, however, tried to be accommodating.

Stuffed aboard the stage with surly sinners and cross, smelly children, they got under way. Brother Isaac enjoyed the view from his precarious perch atop the stage. Just past Warnersville, he remarked on "a curious mound of earth—the work of ancients, say 10 ft. high & 40 ft. wide." About dusk, it rained, and on the slick road, the stage nearly tipped over. Some passengers— perhaps including Isaac—had to jump off and got "very much muddied." And after dark, stage travel on bad roads became unpleasant, even terrifying.

> Now on we go thro the dark wilds over tremendous hills . . . with only the light of the stage lanterns. Our road went winding along on the sides of high hills, with steep & high banks above us on one side and high precipices on the other below us where we could see by the glimmer of our light the tops of high trees on a level with us here. For a long time we would be crawling slowly up a long hill, and reaching the top, would descend with great rapid[ity] that it would almost alarm one when a small accident, the stumbling of a horse or the like might have pitched us off the brink and landed us all in eternity. Had not the roads been pretty good down these hills, it would have been really fearful, for the horses never slack from a swift pace, till they reach the bottom of the hill.[44]

Despite Isaac's anxiety, they made it into Maryland without mishap, arriving on election day, when folks were in town "thick as maggots in a cheese." "They seem to be very talkative," he wrote, and "seem to entertain a slight variation of opinion so much that I fear they will get to deciding it by hard knocks before they get thro!" And, indeed, at Middletown, "one fellow had already got a bloody blow, in his eyes or just below."[45]

By October 8, they were in Baltimore amid the commotion of city life. Awakened at three in the morning by fire engines, Isaac got out of bed and walked several blocks to see the conflagration. "They conquered the fire finally," he wrote. "I left the noisy rabble and returned to rest, and dreamed of being home." The next day, they boarded the steamboat *George Washington* for the voyage up the Chesapeake Bay to Philadelphia. Aboard the boat, Isaac described another perplexity of travel. Mealtime was an ordeal. When the breakfast bell rang, the brethren had to step lively. Isaac described the scene.

Now the nimblest Hog is the luckiest fellow! Each one rushes almost squealing for his mess. This is nothing uncommon however at tavern or on steamboats for it is the general practice for all. As quick as the bell rings, then every one springs; then all that are lucky enough to get there, pounce down upon their seats the best chance they can get and seize hold of what they like best and no matter if they leave on their plate half of what they took off while others go without.

Isaac added, however, that the food was "generally tolerably good." But Shakers' table manners were better than the common travelers', perhaps to their own detriment.[46]

On October 9, Elder Rufus and Brother Isaac were in Philadelphia. Isaac rose at dawn to see the city's waterworks, reckoned among the principle attractions. Isaac found them "an admirable display of neatness and elegance, & mechanical performance enough to astonish the beholder." After breakfast, he toured the U.S. Mint. He described the entire process: melting, molding, rolling, annealing, brightening, die-punching, edging, and pressing. "The machinery is chiefly driven by a magnificent steam engine and were I to describe this exquisite workmanship, its excellence, high finish and expense, it would be incredible."[47] Such sights were not idle entertainment; they might provide new ideas to benefit Shakers.

On October 10, the two brethren were in New York City aboard the steamboat *DeWitt Clinton* for the trip up the Hudson. The boat carried more passengers than beds for the overnight trip, "so they took the settees and placed them in order and laid on them table leaves & then spread on the beds," Isaac wrote, and "100 were accommodated in this way." He secured sleeping space in the crowded cabin, and "slept pretty well for awhile" but woke to see a man hurrying out with a pair of boots. Afraid the boots were his own, Isaac jumped up to check, found one boot but not the other, and thought "O boderation! Can't a body get along thro the troubles of human life without losing a boot?" Eventually he found his boot. But "boderation" may have been swearish for a Shaker. Brother Isaac was cranky and tired of travel.[48]

Brothers Rufus and Isaac arrived at Hudson, New York, on October 11, sent their baggage back to New Lebanon by teamster's wagon, and took the Pittsfield stage to speed their return. They were in New Lebanon within an hour and a half by the stage—only to find that two brethren and two sisters including Sarah Bates had gone to meet them at Hudson. But they received a hearty welcome nonetheless and were glad to return safely.[49] By the time Rufus Bishop and Isaac Newton Youngs washed off the dust of the road, they had traveled at least twenty-one hundred miles as the crow flies.

The inspection tour must have borne fruit, because changes were made in the western villages. Union Village broke up its North Family and dispersed those Believers among other orders.[50] At Pleasant Hill, Kentucky, Elder Samuel Turner was forced to resign after the rank and file complained about him to Rufus Bishop, who had a low opinion of Turner already. But Isaac's journal did not allude to these problems.[51]

As Isaac traveled, he compared Shaker life with worldly life and invariably found, as he may have anticipated before setting out on his journey, that the world fell below Shaker standards in manners, cleanliness, industry, thrift, education, temperance, and civility. Raised a Shaker, Isaac Newton Youngs was not cut out for life in the world. When he finally returned to New Lebanon, he was happy to be back home. Travel helped him appreciate the peace and quiet of a Shaker village and the love and friendship of his intimate friends. He had missed them while he was away, and they had missed him, too.

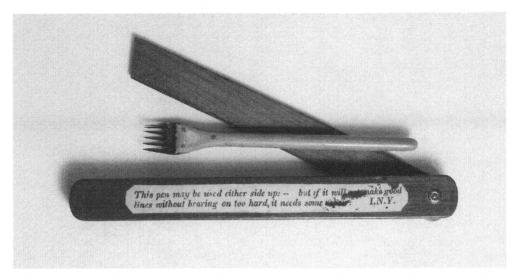

Fig. 1. Isaac Newton Youngs's music pen and case, an example of his meticulous work. Hancock Shaker Village, Pittsfield, Massachusetts. Photo by author.

Fig. 2. Isaac Newton Youngs may have been the model for the balding brother in Benson Lossing's drawing of several New Lebanon Shakers in August 1856. *Harper's New Monthly Magazine*, July 1857.

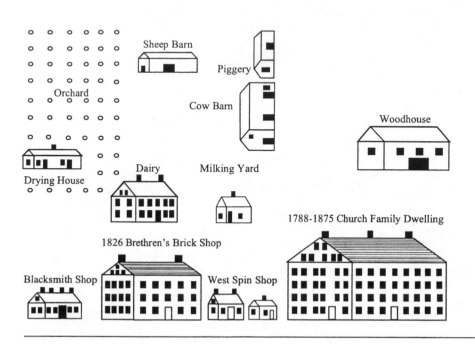

Sheep Barn

Piggery

Orchard

Cow Barn

Woodhouse

Drying House

Dairy

Milking Yard

1788-1875 Church Family Dwelling

1826 Brethren's Brick Shop

Blacksmith Shop

West Spin Shop

←——South

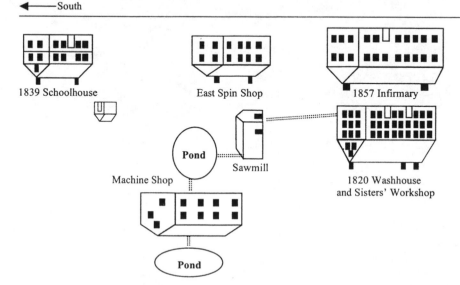

1839 Schoolhouse

East Spin Shop

1857 Infirmary

Pond

Sawmill

Machine Shop

1820 Washhouse
and Sisters' Workshop

Pond

Fig 3. New Lebanon Church Family, 1820–75. Drawing by the author, 2005, in the manner of Isaac Newton Youngs. Buildings not to scale; smaller buildings, some ells, privies, barns, and sheds not shown. Note that the New Lebanon Church Family's appearance changed from year to year, and it never looked exactly like this because the first Great House, as shown, burned in 1875 before the brick Ministry Shop was built; the first meetinghouse was reoriented when it was moved, and several other buildings were built or demolished. My thanks to Tom Donnelly and Jerry Grant for information on the physical layout of the village. Sources: INY map circa 1827–39 and Henry Blinn map circa 1842–48 in Robert P. Emlen, *Shaker Village Views* (Hanover, N.H.: University Press of New England, 1987); INY, Concise View, 1860 map, 498, WM 861.

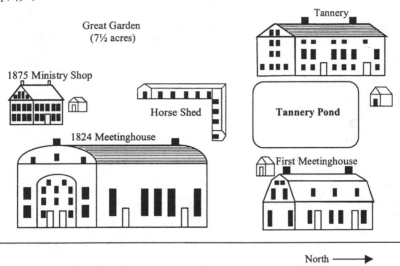

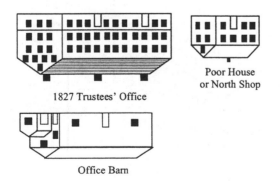

Fig 4. The New Lebanon North Family dining room, with Isaac Newton Youngs's 1840 clock hanging between the windows. *Frank Leslie's Illustrated Newspaper*, September 1873. Shaker Museum and Library, Old Chatham, New York.

Fig. 5. Shakers worshiping, 1830s, George Gilbert. Shaker Museum and Library, Old Chatham, New York.

Fig. 6. New Lebanon Church Family dwelling and meetinghouse, 1830s, where Isaac Newton Youngs lived and worshiped. John W. Barber and Henry Howe, *Historical Collections of the State of New York* (New York: S. Tuttle, 1842).

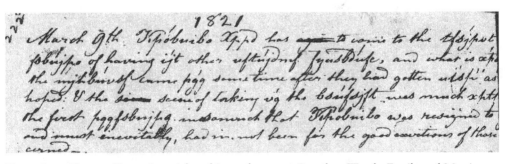

Fig. 7. Isaac Newton Youngs's enciphered journal entry on Jonathan Woods. Family and Meeting Journal, March 9, 1821, Library of Congress Shaker manuscript 42.

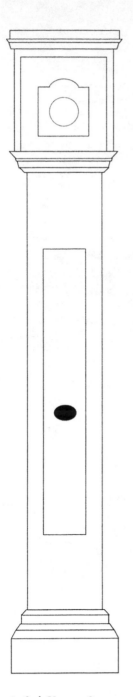

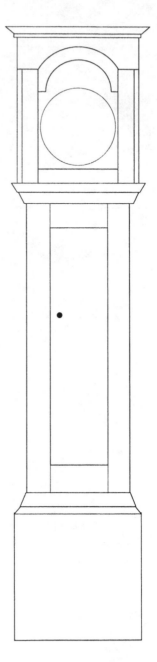

Fig. 8. Seth Youngs Sr., 1740
grandfather clock, 86 inches tall.
Historic Deerfield, Massachusetts.

Fig. 9. Benjamin Youngs's
tall clock, circa 1790–1805,
83 inches tall, case by Erastus
Rude, 1811. Shaker Museum,
Old Chatham, New York.

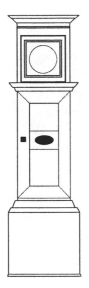

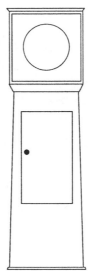

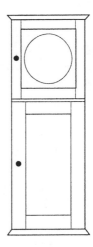

Fig. 10. Benjamin Seth
Youngs's shelf clock, circa
1794–1805, 36 inches
tall. Henry Ford Museum,
Dearborn, Michigan.

Fig. 11. Benjamin
Youngs's later shelf clock,
circa 1810–15, 36 inches
tall. Henry Ford Museum,
Dearborn, Michigan.

Fig. 12. Isaac Newton
Youngs's 1840 clock,
31 inches tall. Hancock
Shaker Village, Pittsfield,
Massachusetts.

Fig. 13. The whirling gift. David R. Lamson, *Two Years' Experience Among the Shakers* (West Boylston, Mass., 1848).

Fig. 14. Shakers' Square Order March, probably in the New Lebanon meetinghouse where public worship services were held on the Sabbath. Drawing by Benson J. Lossing. Lossing illustrated the Shakers' return to regimented choreography and the absence of spontaneity in worship. *Harper's New Monthly Magazine*, July 1857.

Fig. 15. New Lebanon Shakers' 1839 schoolhouse. Isaac Newton Youngs was master workman for construction of their new schoolhouse. Photo by Jack E. Boucher, June 1962. Historic American Buildings Survey, Library of Congress Prints and Photographs Division, HABS, NY,11-NELEB.V,10-3.

Fig. 16. Shop with lathe in Brethren's brick workshop as it existed in the 1920s. According to Jerry Grant and Douglas Allen (*Shaker Furniture Makers* [Hanover, N.H.: Published for HSV by University Press of New England, 1989], twentieth-century Shakers remembered that Orren Haskins (1815–92) used this shop in the late nineteenth century. In earlier decades, however, another brother, perhaps Isaac Newton Youngs, must have used this shop and its "pretty little lathe." Photo by William F. Winter, Jr., Historic American Buildings Survey, Library of Congress Prints and Photographs Division, HABS, NY,11-NELEB.V,4-5.

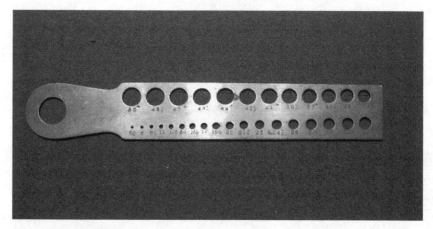

Fig. 17. One of Isaac Newton Youngs's specialty tools, a brass gauge for measuring the diameter of metal rods for mechanical work, such as clockmaking, or for making sisters' tools, such as bodkins and knitting needles. Private collection.

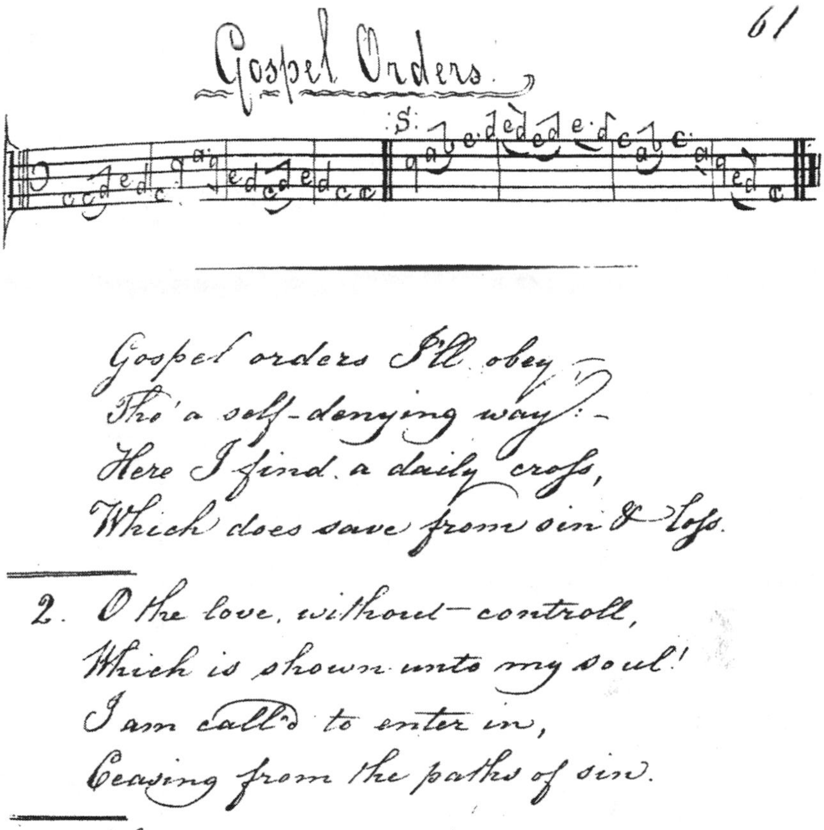

Gospel Orders

Gospel orders I'll obey
Tho' a self-denying way; —
Here I find a daily cross,
Which does save from sin & loss.

2. O the love, without controll,
Which is shown unto my soul!
I am call'd to enter in,
Ceasing from the paths of sin.

3. What a priv'lege I possess,
In mount Zion to be bless'd!
O how thankful I should be,
That my soul can now be free.

4. Free from sin's unlawful claims,
Free from nature's gauling chains: —
I will be a subject child,
Keep a spirit meek & mild.

Fig. 18. Music and words to Isaac Newton Youngs's hit song "Gospel Orders." H. L. Eades, *A Collection of Hymns, Anthems & Tunes, Adapted to the Worship. By the Singers at South Union, Ky. April 4, 1835*, 93. Library Collection, Shaker Museum at South Union, Kentucky.

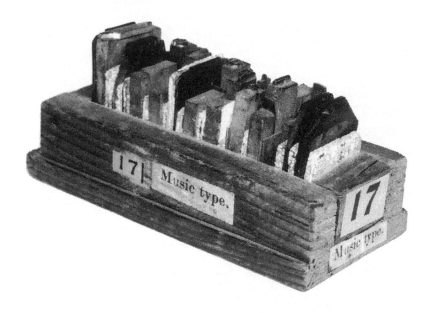

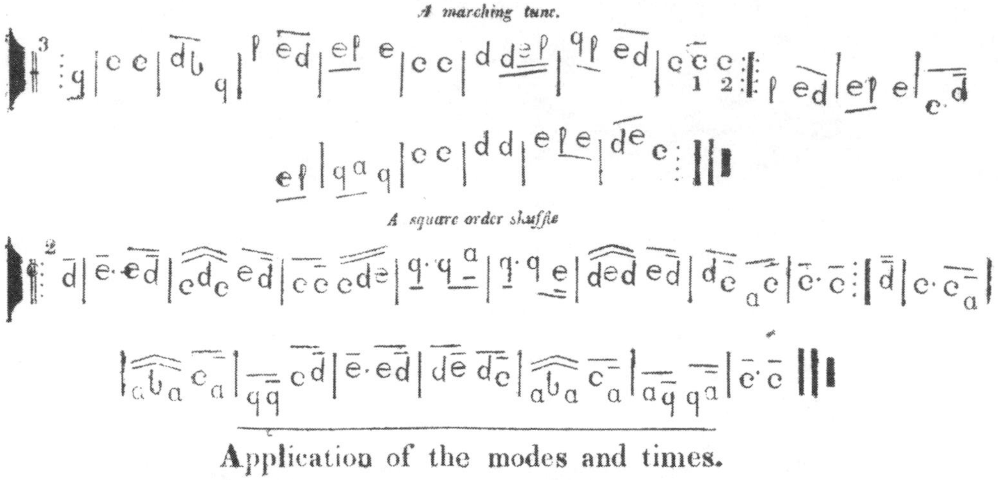
A marching tune.
A square order shuffle
Application of the modes and times.

Fig. 19. Isaac Newton Youngs, *Short Abridgement of the Rules of Music*, 1846. Hancock Shaker Village, Pittsfield, Massachusetts.

17
Music type.
17
Music type.

Fig. 20. Lead music type, possibly that which Isaac Newton Youngs hand-cut in the 1840s. Hancock Shaker Village, Pittsfield, Massachusetts. Photo by author.

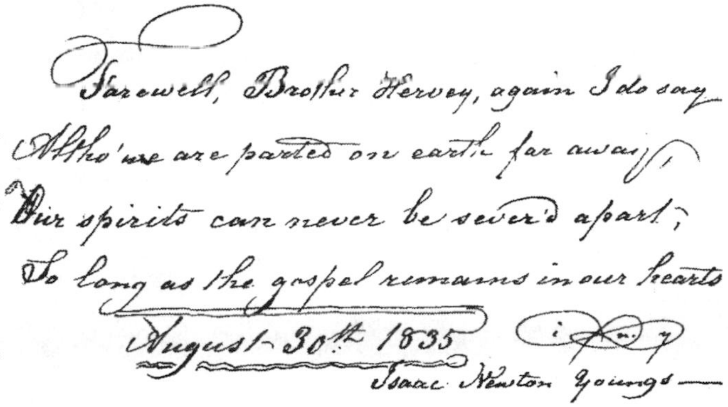

Farewell, Brother Hervey, again I do say
Altho' we are parted on earth far away,
Our spirits can never be sever'd apart;
So long as the gospel remains in our hearts
August 30th 1835
Isaac Newton Youngs —

Fig. 21. Isaac Newton Youngs monogram in Eades, *A Collection of Hymns*, 93. Library Collection, Shaker Museum at South Union, Kentucky.

A
Day Book or Journal
Of Work and Various things
Kept by
Benjamin Gates.
Beginning October 1st
1827.

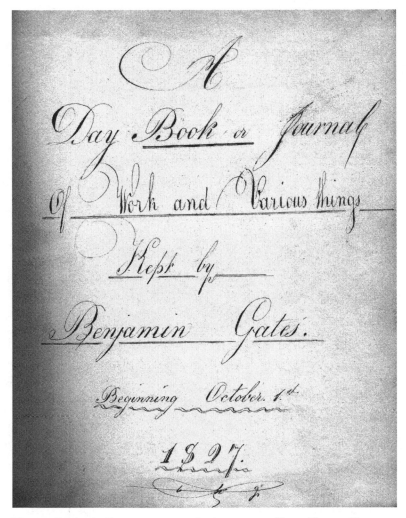

Fig. 22. Benjamin Gates monogram, in the manner of Isaac Newton Youngs, 1827. Winterthur Museum Library, Andrews Shaker Collection.

Fig. 23. The 1826 Brethren's Workshop, New Lebanon Church Family, housed tailor, clockmaker, shoemaker, cooper, and carpenter shops, as well as Isaac Newton Youngs's mechanical shop in the south garret. Isaac moved into that shop November 27, 1827, with Benjamin Gates's help. In 1846, the tailors' shop was over the Elders' room. Sources: Benjamin Gates Day Book, WM 819; Thomas Hammond, Trip Journal (1816–53), 102, WRHS 30, V:B-36; Daniel Myrick Trip Journal, 1846, Williams College. Photo by author.

Fig. 24. New Lebanon Church Family circa 1870, looking north, with Sabbath visitors' carriages. The dwelling or Great House where Isaac lived and died is at center. Author photo of stereopticon by Irving of Troy, New York. Hancock Shaker Village, Pittsfield, Massachusetts.

There were a number gather'd in
With whom I felt right near akin.

7 Intimacy between Men in Shaker Society

ISAAC NEWTON YOUNGS's friendships show how nineteenth-century Shaker society fostered attachments between men. As Priscilla Brewer points out, Believers' closest friendships were with the same sex.[1] Shaker brethren spent most of their time in the company of men. Celibacy, a burden they all shared, drew them together; their letters show that they encouraged one another in bearing the cross. Moreover, Shaker society promoted same-sex relationships by providing mentors who acted almost as parents for youngsters. Isaac Newton Youngs helped raise boys who loved him; several viewed him as a father. Under those conditions, Brother Isaac formed intimate friendships. He loved, and he was loved in return.[2]

Professions of affection between Shaker men have raised eyebrows as well as questions. Some scholars view their flowery sentiments as evidence of homosexuality rather than as chaste homosocial friendship. But such a conclusion is faulty. Flowery language was common in nineteenth-century men's correspondence, as Donald Yacovone has shown. Men used expressions of fraternal love that today would mean something else entirely, and so we cannot apply today's standards to nineteenth-century men.[3] Furthermore, if all Shaker men who used terms of endearment in their correspondence had been homosexual, the society would not have had to separate the sexes.

One must concede, however, that some Shaker brethren probably were homosexual. It is unlikely that several thousand men could have been drawn from the U.S. population without including some whose sexual preference was for men. Homosexuality is even mentioned in the Bible among early Christians (Romans 1:26–27), who believed in the Old Testament sanctions against it (Leviticus 18:22). The nature of Shaker life promoted emotional attachments between men (and between women), rather than with the opposite sex, and if homosexuality is broadly defined as same-sex emotional intimacy, then many Shakers could have been thus categorized.

Regardless of sexual preference, however, Shakers banned sexual activity of any kind. Conversation that excited lust was contrary to gospel order and required confession. Sexual feelings were disorderly. As discussed in Chapter 3, Brother Isaac confessed even his involuntary self-gratification. If any Believer knew of another's sin, he was supposed to reveal it to the Elders. Thus the society policed itself. In theory, at least, a Shaker brother's sexual preference was irrelevant, because he was not supposed to act on it. Those caught in sexual acts had to leave.[4]

Isaac Newton Youngs's own writings support the conclusion that he was probably not homosexual. We know, for example, that he was attracted to at least one woman. In his twenties he showed attachment to a Shaker sister that can be construed as evidence of heterosexuality. Also, when Isaac heard that the apostates Thomas Munson and Alex McArthur were "very much married together," he was horrified. His response, written in a private journal where it would serve no purpose as disinformation, suggests that he disapproved of homosexuality.[5]

Shaker celibacy meant conquering lust—perhaps the hardest cross men had to bear if they were to remain in orderly union with Believers. And since most of the brethren here examined did remain Believers throughout their lives, they probably did not pursue secret alliances or dally in private. Thus it is unlikely that all those who sent hugs and kisses to other brethren wanted them as sexual partners. But because brethren's correspondence with men included expressions of love, their letters have been quoted out of context to suggest they were homosexual.[6] Further analysis, however, shows that brethren were writing creatively to affirm gospel love rather than to express feelings motivated by lust.

Donald Yacovone found a culturally pervasive and "remarkably constant language of fraternal love" in his study of American men's correspondence before the twentieth century. The same language pervades Shaker brethren's letters.[7] By looking closely at the correspondence of Isaac Newton Youngs and his friends, then widening our view to include that of other Shaker men, we can see the overall pattern and context of the brethren's loving words.

Unfortunately, little of Isaac Newton Youngs's writing survives from his childhood. But we do know that several friends were gathered in about the time he came to New Lebanon, and he felt "right near akin" to Garret K. Lawrence, the only friend named in Isaac's "Autobiography in Verse." Isaac may have welcomed Garret into the New Lebanon Church Family when he arrived in 1808. Garret became his best friend and Isaac loved him.[8]

As adults, Isaac and Garret often worked together. They taught the Church Family boys' school beginning in the late 1810s. During the winter of

1829–30, Brothers Isaac and Garret, with Sisters Olive Spencer and Sarah Bates, held social meetings in the children's order. The objective was for the children to learn scripture, while "those who presided gave instruction, and explanations, and answered questions," Isaac recalled, "to enlighten the understanding and promote the principles of virtue and morality." Isaac and Garret collaborated on other projects, as well. They aspired to perfection in song and must have been proficient because they were consistently among the leaders in the Church Family choir.[9] The Elders seem to have trusted their judgment. In January 1834, for instance, when the Elders realized reading materials had to be better regulated, they assigned Rufus Bishop, Seth Youngs Wells, Isaac Newton Youngs, and Garret Lawrence to purge books "not fit for Believers to use" and to create a library so all would "have an equal chance to get useful knowledge." [10]

Isaac Newton Youngs and Garret Lawrence were best friends; they were like-minded and spent much time together. They were roommates for years.[11] Their affection showed in their correspondence, beginning with a letter Garret sent to Isaac in 1826 when Isaac was in Watervliet recuperating from illness. Garret wrote about temporal matters, such as the firewood, "pretty much sawed," the newly plastered cheese house, new window blinds the brethren were making for the Meetinghouse, and "a large heap of lambs at the barn, and an April fool bull calf which weighed 130# when only 6 hours old." He gossiped about Joseph Babe, a new Believer fleeing his debts in Boston. He touched on spiritual life, knowing that Isaac would want to hear of the "awakening" in the Church Family. Garret also wrote about his own problems, as any friend might do with his intimates. Garret suffered from lustful feelings and wrote of his effort to overcome them, using nautical metaphors from hymns such as "Vain World," which compares life to sailing a tempestuous sea, and "Gospel Honesty," which refers to the compass of the soul, fatal shoals, and the wrecks of lust and pride.

> Now dear Brother, I suppose that the sun shines bright, the sky looks blue, and the waters run clear with you; and that every now and then you receive a kiss of charity; while with a fair wind, smooth sea, flowing sails and streaming colors, you are sweetly and swiftly sailing for the celestial land. While poor me is a beating the briny billows against wind and tide, enveloped in fog and roaring for life. But I am not discouraged at all. If you will take up your spying glass and look <u>away</u> back, and listen with both ears, you may perhaps hear the splash of my oar as I tug at the midnight hour, and perhaps see the surge beat beat upon the bow of my little bark, while I perseveringly stem the tide of nature. I shall fetch it by and by. I have a good compass firmly placed in the binnacle, and the needle has lately been touched

> with the heavenly magnet, and feels the invisible attractions of gospel love; and though it may sometimes vary, when passing over extensive beds of <u>natural</u> & <u>attracting</u> ore, yet in the main it points toward the true polar star.

By sharing problems with trusted friends, brethren established emotional intimacy. When they drew on imagery from Shaker songs, they reinforced their faith.[12]

Isaac returned his friend's affection. His letters to Garret were warmer than either his journals or his official writings. In August 1833, he wrote to "Inexpressibly Beloved" Garret:

> Having now a good chance, I undertake to roll out a few ideas from the point of my pen. And first, as to a certain scrap that I received this morn . . . I was well pleased with it . . . coming from the poor exiled Garret. Now beloved as to certain queries in your letter . . . I have in fact but little hand in state affairs. I can say but little: I don't know but they thought you had such fine times there you would hardly perceive a sweet cake from here. . . . I hope however we shall have <u>a chance</u> before long to settle this difficulty.
>
> As to the mighty threat you made that you wouldn't say a <u>word</u> about your journey, & about Saratoga, the foaming steam boats, swift cars, steam horses &c. I don't want you to say a word about them, I'd a great deal rather see them, or have you see them, and you may scratch out all you have wrote about it as soon as you have a mind to! But in return you may depend you will have to come home, before <u>I'll</u> tell you a syllable about our affairs; how we are feet, head & ears in hay, oats, pease, beans & barley O!

In the nineteenth century, Shaker brethren commonly used "Beloved" in their salutations and good friends might logically embellish it further. The letter may have approximated Brother Isaac's conversation with Brother Garret, livelier than official correspondence, teasing, affectionate, occasionally sarcastic. In some respects, however, this personal note circumvented Shaker order. The comment, "I don't know but they thought" shows that Isaac considered Garret his ally against "them," probably the Elders or the Ministry who dealt with "state affairs." This "us versus them" reference is problematic because it indicates what Shakers called "party spirit," the divisiveness contrary to union. Furthermore, Brother Isaac closed with "Keep this scrall to yourself, & not let even your left hand see It."[13] This warning was also disorderly. Outgoing correspondence was supposed to be approved by an Elder, and when mail was received, unopened letters were to be shown to the Elders, then opened and read in their presence.[14] But in this instance, Isaac may have used his position as scribe to skip the approval process and wanted to make sure that Garret did not give him away. This collusion, unique among Isaac's correspondents, suggests a high level of trust as well as emotional intimacy between the two men.

Other letters between Isaac and Garret evidently were approved by the Elders and show no evidence of Isaac's us-versus-them attitude, but the warmth of their friendship still flows through the rhetoric. From Ohio in 1834, Isaac and Rufus Bishop wrote home to the Ministry, and Isaac directed part of the letter to Garret. Isaac was constantly in company with others, but he missed his closest confidante. And though the tone of this letter was less casual (probably because the Ministry would also read it) Brother Isaac still called Garret "my dearly beloved friend." [15] Such a sentiment could not have been considered disorderly, much less sexual, if he included it in a letter that he knew the Ministry would read. And Isaac repeatedly addressed his friend in such terms.

In a letter dated 1835, Isaac sent Garret love from all, "especially your old companions in Nos. 7 & 8," which included the sisters who lived just across the hall. Then he added "a double portion of mine, warm & fresh from my heart" and closed, "I still remain your constant and prayerful friend." Constancy was a virtue, and their friendship was a constant in their lives. Over three decades, these two men grew up together, taught school together, led songs together, wrote prescriptive works together, worked together, roomed together, and resisted the Elders' edicts together. Their correspondence shows that they shared emotional intimacy, as well. But their intimacy was not necessarily sexual. Despite their expressions of love, the evidence does not support the conclusion that the two men had a physical relationship. [16]

Letters document Isaac's friendships with other brethren with whom he was even less likely to have had physical relationships. In 1840 when he wrote to all the societies about music, he addressed at least one brother as beloved and routinely sent his best love. He also sent gospel love to Andrew Houston at Union Village, describing their friendship with flowery rhetoric.

> Your memory still glows with warmth in my breast. Never, I trust will be untied that knot of love, which we tied together, in the summer of 1826; never will be cut asunder those silken cords of union, which grew with our first acquaintance, & have strengthened with succeeding communications. [17]

He signed the letter, "From your lover, Isaac N. Youngs." Knots of love, silken cords, and the term *lover* collectively suggest sexuality to the twenty-first-century mind. In context, however, the reference probably meant gospel love holding them in Shaker union. And silken cords of union were drawn directly from Shaker hymns, such as "Diadem." Reminding Believers to "let no inferior passion rise," the hymn exhorts,

> Keep in your hand the leading clew
> The silken cord, the golden chain,
> The union of the happy few
> Who do a daily cross maintain.

Silken cords of union held Believers together not as lovers but as celibates resisting passion. "Protecting Chain," like other hymns, was intended to promote celibacy, not lust, and also to invoke "a cord to unite us in bands of pure love." [18]

Another Andrew Houston letter sets the brethren's metaphors of love into the context of Shaker life. From Union Village in June 1829, Andrew wrote to his "Dearly Beloved Brother Isaac," saying that he was standing up snugly under the cross, cheered by Isaac's epistle of August 18, 1827, which he had read over and over again.

> When ever I look over it, streams of love and warm sensation are the consequences. I am inclined to think that if we could actually meet we could now take one real talk; love you know is of a growing nature; and pen & ink is not equal to seeing, hearing, & feeling—but for the present I must content myself with the former expedient.

Andrew assured Isaac that keeping Mother Ann's gospel was his ambition, despite "the little crosses, trials & tribulation that the death of the old man costs . . . for even in this life I receive an hundred fold and feel well rewarded for my labor." He added, "In short I fear not missing the road so long as I am attentive to the guide boards, the way is plain and well mark'd." He asked Isaac to "be so kind as to tell my good friends that my love to them has not diminished aught, but rather increased; the visit I had with you has ever since been a source of consolation." He went on to explain how important Isaac's spiritual support was.

> And the conversation that passed between us on matters of eternal worth is not quickly forgotten by me, it was what my soul desired and that which filled it: If I am not mistaken there was something like or as good as a stipulated agreement between I.N.Y. & a.c.h. to stick to the cross forever, and as I have no doubts on your part, it remains for me to prove by my works & words as near as possible that I have at least the same determination.

The rest of Brother Andrew's letter included the village news: their hard winter, late spring, prospects for good peaches, and hot summer weather. He ruminated over his map of Union Village and enclosed a "small receipt to make a lacker for drying paint," explaining its use at length. He requested seeds or grafts of "a very smooth, shin'd, plump, rich, delicious pear" he had tasted at New Lebanon. Then he returned to spiritual matters.

> I had like to have used up all my paper on temporal things. I must at least keep enough to send my love on for I know I have much love for you and many others at Lebanon. We have not lost our love in the West for our good friends in the East, Nay by no means, but look up to them as spiritual parents whom we delight to love. It is true, as you said in your letter, "Satan works, but God works to the best advantage," this is happily true in all places & cases where God works, God is always at least seven while Satan is six.

He reported the news of all the Elders and Eldresses and wrote, "Now be so kind as to accept my best & everlasting love, and in a particular manner I wish you to be so good as to give the same to ours & our—Beloved Ministry—To your good kind Elders & Elder Sisters, to Joana our good Sister, & to good Br. Hiram, in short to all inquiring friends." His love was meant for everyone, not just his correspondent. He ended, "I have written in union. So farewell from your friend and lover, Andrew C. Houston." In the context of the whole long, newsy letter, love played a much smaller part than temporal matters and discussion of all things Shaker. Moreover, he referred to the death of "the old man," a biblical metaphor for sexual sin, including "fornication, uncleanness, inordinate affection, evil concupiscence, and covetousness," which invite the wrath of God, as well as that of Shaker Elders.[19] Furthermore, Brother Andrew made a point of noting that he had written "in union," that is, with the knowledge and permission of the Elders, evidence that he was most likely not Isaac's physical lover despite the term used in his closing. Finally, Andrew's letter and Isaac's answer three months later show that the brethren were encouraging each other in their commitment to bearing the cross of celibacy.

Isaac replied in September 1829 to his "Dearly beloved brother Andrew" in a long discourse "concerning our union, & love to each other."

> I read your last communication to me, of June 4th, with much satisfaction. Joy, I dare say, sparkled in my eyes, & cheering glows flushed over my countenance, as I traced the ~~thots~~ feelings of my distant friend. To find you "well & hearty" & not only so, but "standing up snugly under the cross," I must own, came up to the point.

Isaac focused on spiritual matters, including his own "ardent desire" to be "Attentive to the guide boards." He explained, "And I think it is right that those who are bent upon being good, should strengthen each other. This is certainly much better than to be stumbling blocks to each other; and as you hinted in your last letter of the agreement between you & me, 'to stick to the cross forever.' " He also thanked Andrew for the "very nice & intelligible map," as well as the lacquer recipe, and apologized for his inability to send pear seeds or grafts. "So here I be, in debt, amidst plenty!" Isaac wrote. "I must beg you not to think me guilty of willing neglect, for as true as Jonathan ever loved David, I would go to the extent of my abilities to do any friend a favor, & you in particular." He closed with "a fresh store of good love from your gospel relations in this place . . . who still remember you in pure love; for love has not diminished with us, but glows to every Believer, far & near." [20]

Such was the context of brethren's expressions of love. These brethren had business to conduct, and, in most instances, they were careful to remain in union as they corresponded. The biblical reference to Jonathan's love for David might be construed as a reference to sexual love, though it is unlikely that these two nineteenth-century Shakers thought of Jonathan and David's relationship beyond that of one friend doing a favor for another. Furthermore, the allusion was a longstanding, even historical, convention for expressing fraternal love, used, for instance, by John Winthrop, one of the Puritan founders of Plymouth colony, in a letter he wrote to a friend in the 1600s: "my soule is knit to you, as the soule of Jonathan to David." [21]

Andrew Houston's friends at New Lebanon included Garret Lawrence. Andrew and Garret also wrote to each other about diet and medical matters and exchanged news about Isaac. In November 1835, Andrew sent an embrace and kiss to Garret and asked him to "Thank & kiss Br. I.N.Y. (if you love him well enough) for me." [22] And in May 1836, Andrew apologized to Isaac for not writing sooner to "one who knows that if I could get in reach of him he would not only get well hugged & kissed but well pinched into the bargain." [23] In a letter to Garret the following September, Andrew sent kisses to all the brethren he knew, adding, "Give my best love to that good Brother who has lost his pen and writes with his pencil, and begs room of you in your letter at that, tell him I sincerely love him & thank him for past favors." [24] Many brethren sent love to distant friends, but Brother Andrew was the only one so generous with his kisses. Isaac replied to him with good humor.

> Beloved, ah much beloved,
>   I never want to begin two letters alike, nor need I at this time, for I have a brand new article to begin with. In perusing a letter you lately sent to Garret,

I perceive a hint that somebody had lost his pen, & I felt some hit, for I had written a little with a pencil, & therefore supposed you meant me.

   Lost my pen! awful thought; not I. I have pens & ink enough to employ ten men, certainly if they were as much pushed for time as you & I are. Lost my pen? nay, I would not lose that for a great deal. But as much as I set by my pen, I would lose a corn basket full of them, rather than my love, my love to the gospel, to my Elders, my brethren & sisters. I trust I shall keep my love till long after goose quills & silver pens are out of date. But enough of this. I suppose you believe me.[25]

Isaac and Andrew continued to exchange affectionate messages through the 1830s, and they continued to tease each other; Andrew's next letter referred to Isaac's "profusion of pen & ink."[26] These men could have had sexual relations, but it seems unlikely, given their respected roles in their distant villages, as well as their lifelong commitment to celibacy. Furthermore, though Isaac addressed Andrew as "much beloved," he also extended his love to the gospel, Elders, brethren, and sisters in a manner that hardly seems sexual.

   The brethren's three-way correspondence ended with the death of Garret Lawrence, who had been in ill health for years. During the summer of 1833, his rheumatism was so bad that Brother Henry DeWitt, the New Lebanon Shaker shoemaker, feared for his life.[27] Garret seemed to recover from that episode, but his health took a turn for the worse. His medical treatment may have created tension between Isaac and Andrew. At the end of an otherwise affectionate letter to Andrew in 1836, Isaac's tone shifted. He wrote, "As to matters between Garret and you, your sickening drugs, & meaner things, your plants, hepaticas, trilobas &c . . . & all your flowery tit for tats, I shall not interfere much. Br. Garret wishes me to send you his best love."[28] Isaac worried about Garret; he disapproved of the treatment Andrew advocated, and he meant to interfere, perhaps believing that his love for Garret gave him the right to do so.

   Garret continued to fail. He tried different treatments and remained "able to keep about and do much good" but was still "quite out of health." In mid-December 1836 he began having "hard turns of pain about the stomach and bowels." On January 22, 1837, Garret was at the point of death, and a Ministry sister wrote, Garret "said his faith was in the increasing work of God [and that he] wanted his love given to all at his funeral." His last words were "Stick close."[29] And then Garret Lawrence, Isaac's closest friend and confidante for three decades, died. He was forty-two years old.[30]

   After Garret died, Isaac changed. His later writings show little evidence of close personal relationships because he seemed to have no extended correspondence or special friends. He may have drawn into himself, cut back on letter writing, or stopped saving his letters. In 1838, Andrew Houston mentioned that he had not heard from Isaac. "I wonder if you have forgotten me entirely," he wrote to his "beloved good old friend Isaac." Andrew missed their goose quill chats, despite "the limited intercourse allowed us by the clay or case of this earthly tabernacle" and hoped nothing would impede their union. Perhaps Garret Lawrence had been key to the correspondence between Andrew and Isaac. Or Isaac may have offended Andrew with his comment about "sickening drugs and meaner things," when Garret was dying. Andrew closed with his "unfeigned love & respect;" even so, his letters lacked their earlier warmth.[31]

We are left, however, to consider the significance of these Shaker men's expressions of affection and metaphors for love. A small sampling shows that Isaac Newton Youngs, Garret Lawrence, and Andrew Houston were not the only ones who wrote in such terms; similar phrases were common in other brethren's writings. Thomas Hammond of Harvard listed in his journal thirteen brethren he loved, including Isaac Newton Youngs, Henry Youngs, and another brother he had just met for the first time at New Lebanon. Henry Bennett, a wheelwright in his sixties, called forty-one-year-old John Dean "beloved" and closed with "take a large portion of my best love." Giles Avery, age twenty-two, mentored the younger Franklin Barber and they exchanged "the warmest emotions of love." Seventy-year-old Seth Youngs Wells closed a letter to Rufus Bryant with "accept my love with the rest, and make as free use of it as you think proper." R. W. Pelham opened a letter to the New Lebanon Elders "Much Beloved," ended with, "Accept of my best gospel love," and asked that it be passed along to his friends.[32] According to Priscilla Brewer, Elders Grove Wright and Grove Blanchard shared a close and warm friendship. And when Elder Hervey Eads sent his love to Isaac Newton Youngs, he also used vivid imagery.

> I must think now of closing, but I wish I could kiss you first. This thing of meeting and parting, contains both sweet and bitter. How shall I make you feel the warmth of my love? I'm afraid I can't do it. Will it do to say I love you from the bottom of my heart? This don't near satisfy <u>me</u>. Let us take hold of the silken cords & draw a <u>double</u> knot—I love you with that love that surpasses all natural love.[33]

Other brethren, old and young, some in positions of authority, sent love and kisses and used colorful metaphors. To judge from their words of love, these men cared for each other. But Hervey Eads made clear what others did not: that his love went beyond "natural" love. To Shakers, the love beyond natural love was gospel love, a sentiment on a higher plane. Thus their words should not be interpreted as sexual. They probably reflected the bonds of gospel love, tied by the same cords of union that Shaker songs invoked.

References to kissing raise additional questions. A letter Andrew Houston sent to the Ministry at the end of Rufus Bishop and Isaac Newton Youngs's 1834 visit is larded with flowery compliments, such as, "We <u>cannot</u> say too much good of them," and refers to the hugging and "even kissing" among the brethren at departure.[34] The expression "*even* kissing" [emphasis added] suggests that kissing was somewhat beyond the norm, but it must have been acceptable behavior for brethren under such circumstances; otherwise, Houston would not have mentioned it to the Ministry.

Other writings reveal that hugging and kissing were frequent in and out of Shaker worship. During inspired meetings in early 1840, Derobigne Bennet wrote, "We loved, blessed, hugged & kissed each other," adding that Barnabas Hinckley "exhibited considerable simplicity & freedom in speaking and hugging and kissing the Brethren." Diane Sasson reports that the Shaker James Wilson's autobiography recounts a spiritual "hugging match" and describes the "hugging gift." And David Lamson describes another mass hug: "The Elder says, 'I feel as though I wanted a little gift of hugging.' The brethren then gather up into one clump, and the sisters into another, and have a general embrace." And when Brothers Rufus and Isaac arrived at one Shaker village in Ohio, the Elders hugged and kissed them both and "said they had orders to do so, right from Lebanon." [35] Such displays must have been sanctioned by custom, because they were reported openly. Had the brethren feared censure, they would never have written about hugging and kissing to the New Lebanon Elders, nor would the Elders have preserved those letters. Likewise, if an Elder had thought hugging a dubious activity, he probably would not have shared the gift in worship. As Carroll Smith-Rosenberg points out, if the authors of words of love also expressed guilt, remorse, or the need for secrecy, we might construe their love as self-conscious homosexuality. But nothing of the sort appears. (The note Isaac ended with the words "Keep this scrall to yourself, & not let even your left hand see it" lacks a sexual reference.) Without further evidence, we must conclude that the brethren's love was probably platonic.[36]

Pure or platonic love, as opposed to lust, is a concept difficult to grasp in today's world, when sexuality streams from all media. But in the nineteenth century, many Shakers used flowery words of love in their letters to each other, echoing lyrics from the society's hymns, where knots of love and silken cords of union were probably not evidence of sexual innuendo. If they had been sexual references, as John Kirk suggests, then many male Believers could have been homosexual.[37] Yet it seems unlikely that Shaker society was a hotbed of homosexuality. Confession, lack of privacy, and constant surveil-lance militated against sexual contact. Certainly these men's exchanges were affectionate and sometimes surprisingly physical. Celibacy did not mean that Shaker men lost their ability to feel love or their need for emotional intimacy or physical affection. Quite the contrary: the brethren directed their love to those deemed acceptable—other brethren. They gave and received within the limits Shakerism permitted, using conventional expressions of love to show spiritual love for each other, not lust.

Read as excerpts and out of context, the comments of the eleven brethren quoted here might resemble sexual innuendo or evidence of illicit love affairs. But it is unlikely that these responsible Shaker brethren, including Elders, Deacons and other authorities, all had ongoing sexual liaisons and remained in Shaker union. A Believer caught in such a relationship would have been shut out of union with Believers and forced to leave. And some brethren may have feared loss of union more than anything else. Part of what bound a Shaker to the Society of Believers was fear of losing economic and emotional support, as well as the hope of going to heaven, if he left his community.[38]

As for Isaac Newton Youngs, he was horrified when Samuel Copley was caught in a sexual act and heaped opprobrium on him. "He has been ad-dicted to it both before & since he came here," Isaac wrote in a passage with details that were later heavily crossed out. "I see where a fleshly nature may lead me, and what are its final effects." His response to "fleshmonger" Thomas Munson's homosexuality was similar.[39] Shakers had too little pri-vacy to carry on sexually for very long without being caught. Bearing the cross of celibacy meant fighting off nature, battling temptation, and staying pure to remain in gospel order. Lustful thoughts incited guilt, as Brother Isaac's early journal entries reveal. It is therefore unlikely that he would have engaged in extensive sexual contact with anyone, much less multiple partners over decades.

Nonsexual love, however, was important, and some Shaker brethren did love others. Though Mother Lucy may have promoted "emotional celibacy," that effort failed utterly. Attachment is so fundamental to human nature that the attempt to stamp it out was futile. Letters to and about Isaac Newton Youngs from younger brethren that he mentored speak of their admiration and their love in terms much like those that appear in the correspondence be-tween Isaac and his friends. These young men felt free to explain in writing why they loved Isaac. Elisha Blakeman wrote of his former mentor, "I first made his happy acquaintance, in the year 1827, and tho' I have no claims to favoritism, on his part, yet I have been so far an object of his interest and at-tention, that in him I found a Father and friend, and can rise up and call him blessed." Benjamin Gates, as a child, wrote to "daddy Isaac" because he loved and missed him and wanted to stroke his head and kiss him.[40] Franklin Barber, another of the rising generation, recalled Isaac's telling the school-children on March 16, 1837 that "the reward of all [one's] toils & labors [came] <u>after</u> the toil." Barber felt he had "gained good" from Isaac's remarks, though, he said, that one incident was "but a little grain of corn on the long full ear of good things that I have received from you." He loved Isaac for ex-emplifying Shaker virtues.

> Dear Brother, how I love you, the constancy of your Soul in the cause of goodness & Truth, demand or excite, both love & respect. Your zeal & perseverance in the way of God . . . are a bright pattern I consider, for me to follow after. Yea, your speaking in meeting, your zeal & simplicity also, make me to love you, & excite me to have more of the same myself; it is a strength & encouragement to me. I observed your course at the time of sacrificing Journals &c. & I admired the readiness with which you supported the good side & complied with the gift. The thankfulness you so often express for the late spiritual gifts & manifestation, are another evidence of your constancy on the good side. For these bright examples I love & respect you, & also for your good kind feelings for the young, & the interestedness you ever manifest for their welfare.[41]

Brother Isaac lived his religion daily and the young brother wanted to grow up just like him, and not just because he feared eventual punishment if he did otherwise. Giles Avery read Barber's letter and concurred. To "Beloved Brother Isaac," Avery wrote, "I thank you heartily for the perusal of this let-ter, it has done me good; &, by the way, I would beg leave to bestow upon you my thanks for the full ears <u>I</u> have received from thee <u>also</u>; &, be assured they never shall want a crib, or the increase of the tilled kernel lack a place." [42]

Those letters show that younger Shakers such as Barber and Avery had good reasons for loving Isaac Newton Youngs. He was kind. He encouraged them to bear the cross. He set a good example. But theirs was gospel or spiri-tual love, not lust. Back in 1818, Brother Isaac had written a verse describing the love of one Shaker brother for another.

> My love you'll find of that pure kind
>   Which cannot fade nor die;
> Nor have I found that it is bound
>   By any fleshly tie.[43]

That could have been window dressing designed to conceal Brother Isaac's true nature, expressing what the Elders wanted to hear rather than what he really felt. But his long and respected tenure as a Shaker suggests that he was sincere in his faith and committed to living without sex in a celibate society. New evidence could come to light to prove otherwise, but until it does, Brother Isaac's journals documenting his efforts to quell his own lust, along with the brethren's rhetoric of pure love, suggest that he conscientiously carried the cross of celibacy to the end of his days. Despite his collusion with Garret Lawrence in small things, Brother Isaac was in accord with the larger principles of Shakerism. But celibacy did not preclude either gospel love or intimate emotional attachments.

Shaker brethren were committed to spiritual love. They showed their devotion to their religion by worshipping in union and supporting the society with heart and hands. And at intervals, their faith was refreshed by revivals of gifts of the spirit that spread through the society. One of those revivals included inspiration far beyond Shakers' common expressions of gospel love and thankfulness.

To render the veil between time and eternity almost transparent.

8 Shaker Worship, Isaac Newton Youngs, and the Era of Manifestations

ISAAC NEWTON YOUNGS played several roles in Church Family worship. As early as 1815, he recorded Mother Lucy Wright's discourses, adding his own comments and thus shedding light on how the rank and file responded to her messages.[1] He composed new songs and transcribed hymnals. In 1819, in an effort to standardize Shaker worship, he began "getting hold of singing," which included his setting the pitch for the Church Family choir so everyone could start off on the same note. One visitor described it as "an astounding yell . . . uttered by the strongest voice of the center band [of singers], which was immediately caught up by all." Isaac, according to Elisha Blakeman, was "worthy of imitation," "beautiful and exact in exercise, [and] zealous and devoted in singing; in which for many years, he occupied the leading gift." As Richard Nunley points out, "singing together brings disparate individuals together as one," so Brother Isaac brought the singers into union—a Shaker ideal.[2]

Isaac also coached the lower orders in singing, dancing, and marching, practicing for perfection in an apparent effort to bring worship up to his own standards. We can measure his success not only in Elisha Blakeman's (perhaps biased) testimony but also in visitors' comments on the precision of New Lebanon Shakers' music. One visitor said their singing had "no false notes or slips of time," and another said of their dancing, "Their evolutions must have been well practiced, for they were as perfect as those of dancing on a stage."[3] Indeed, Shakers' public services were performances that attracted curious outsiders. But when their worship grew more dramatic, it drew more criticism. An examination of Shaker worship before and after 1837 reveals Isaac's part in the change as well as the tension between Shakers' spiritual enthusiasm and their need for acceptance by the world's people.

Religious performance was as regular as the seasons in the Berkshire hills in the early nineteenth century. Itinerant evangelists held camp meetings and exhorted anyone who would listen, including Shakers. Elizabeth Lovegrove wrote in May 1827 that a new minister was preaching hellfire and damnation in the hollow at night, sometimes until dawn, and that Isaac Newton Youngs and Garret Lawrence attended.[4] A camp meeting could be spiritually invigorating, and Believers might recruit converts there. Nonbelievers also attended, if only for the excitement of seeing others in the throes of religious ecstasy.

Outsiders visited Shaker services for much the same reason. They were fascinated by Shaker celibacy and their focus on sex. Sermons and songs dwelt on crucifying the flesh, quelling lust, and forsaking carnal pleasure. The world's people were also drawn to Shakers' physical worship, a radical divergence from mainstream religious practice. Congregationalists did not dance in Sunday services. Shakers, however, performed in choreographed Sabbath marches and dances, taking their authority from the Bible. According to scripture, anyone can praise the Lord with dancing.[5]

Early visitors remarked on Shakers' dance and convulsive shaking.[6] Descriptions of dancing and shaking in worship, as well as what the Shakers interpreted as demonstrations of divine power, appear throughout Isaac Newton Youngs's journals. In an 1815 entry, Isaac wrote, Mother Lucy Wright started a service at New Lebanon by suggesting that "each one might shake a little, so," he recalled, "we all shook. Then we labored [by dancing], two ranks facing each other." To that point, the service was highly structured, but then, Isaac wrote, Samuel Spier was "taken with operations of power, . . . [knelt] down, [and spoke] in an unknown tongue, very loud & powerfully. [He] walked around in deep distress; fell onto the floor, in apparent agony, turned black in his face; & one might think he was dying." Brother Samuel recovered, Isaac explained, when the spirits released him.[7] Most other Protestant worship was less dynamic. But Shakers were committed evangelicals, unbound by mainstream religious mores, and their dramatically unconventional services made them a tourist attraction.

Shakers tolerated outsiders because they hoped to attract converts, and because they wanted to dispel persistent rumors that they danced naked or sacrificed children in their rites.[8] Shakers could not afford to live completely separate from the world. And visitors flocked to Shaker Sabbath. In 1836, Giles Avery, a New Lebanon Shaker, estimated the Sunday crowd to be one thousand. Six hundred curious strangers watched another service. Sometimes spectators outnumbered Believers and sat in the Shakers' seats; the overflow stood outdoors and peered in the meetinghouse windows.[9]

At the beginning of a public worship service, brethren and sisters filed in separately and sat on opposite sides of the room. A brief welcome to the spectators was usually followed by a sermon on separation of the sexes. And then the dance began. A visitor wrote of an 1820 Sabbath that, compared with what would follow, was fairly staid:

> After the sermon the people rose, the men and women . . . three deep, on the opposite sides of the room; a person then stepped in front of each company, and they joined in singing a hymn in a lively tune, swinging from side to side, and beating their feet alternately, with perfect regularity. [I] have been informed that, upon some occasions, the dance is more active.

Worship was "seldom, if ever, twice the same." [10] Occasionally individuals, "taken with operations of power," like Samuel Spier, pulled away from the orderly ranks. Shakers also varied their songs and changed their manner of laboring in marches and dances. In 1827, for instance, Isaac was inspired to improve their circle dance; he asked "to have the inside rank of the circle turn their faces the other way, for he wanted to see the faces of the brethren and sisters as he was going round." They complied with his gift and redirected the concentric circles to turn in opposite directions so "every wheel was in motion." Innovation invigorated worship. [11] And Isaac Newton Youngs aspired to perfection in Sabbath performance.

Perfection required practice. On weeknights, Isaac rehearsed dances and marches, often going to the lower orders to teach new songs. [12] Such drills were necessary if all were to perform in unison—and their synchrony was a metaphor for their union as Believers. Isaac's concern with perfection began early. On one occasion, in 1816, an Elder called him forward to show how he had done the march with two steps rather than the three they had been told to take. He was embarrassed and later grumbled, "I put off my coat & made my self a publick sight for all. I hope I shall get the matter right before long." [13]

Despite Shakers' striving for perfection, some services were uninspiring. In October 1828, when enthusiasm was at a low ebb, Isaac wrote that the Elders "endeavoured to excite us to wake us up & be more zealous." They failed. The New Lebanon Church Family entered a period of bland worship that dragged on for years. That was why Isaac was so startled by the Ohio Believers' excitement in 1834. [14] By 1835, Giles Avery complained that Church Family worship was "so dull that one would scarcely know whether we were trying to serve God or something else." [15]

Change, however, was imminent. Brother Isaac later wrote, "The Chh went on several years, without much change, or any essential addition of new forms of worship, but resorting occasionally to some variety, to promote life and zeal, not to become formal: until the year 1837, when there commenced a new era." [16] That period in Shaker history has become known as the Era of

Manifestations, or Mother Ann's Work, and it included events that are not yet fully understood.

In the fall of 1837, several girls in Watervliet's Second Order reported having visions. Rufus Bishop counseled the girls; such gifts, he said, were from God, "given for the purpose of strengthening their faith" and showing them the certainty of "rewards and punishment beyond the grave." Those visions prompted an outbreak of shaking, turning, bowing, and speaking in tongues. But Elder Rufus evidently felt uneasy about their enthusiasm, because he added, "to be honest about the matter, I think there was rather too much of the wind, fire & earthquake to satisfy Believers who have had a long & fruitful travel." [17]

Many Shakers welcomed the new gifts of divine power, but the girls' behavior was so singular, even for Shakers, that the Ministry had doubts. To corroborate the initial reports, they sent Isaac Newton Youngs to Watervliet to observe and write an account of the manifestations. They told him how to treat the girls who were acting as instruments of the spirits. "You doubtless know that it is the Ministry's feelings not to have much made of the visions in the presence of the visionists, or in any way that they would be likely to know it, fearing that it might exalt them." [18] Exalting individuals was to be avoided in an egalitarian society.

Isaac was in an uncomfortable position. As a schoolteacher, he knew that children might collude in mischief. But he was the right man for the job because he was a smart and detail-oriented observer, he knew children, and he was willing to consider all possibilities. He was open to scientific investigation of natural phenomena and had a critical eye. He analyzed evidence and drew conclusions accordingly. At the same time, he believed in the spirit world and appreciated the value of spiritual manifestations in stimulating faith.

Even so, Isaac may have gone to Watervliet thinking that if the girls had hoodwinked an entire village of Believers, he might have to contradict his mentor, Rufus Bishop—a disagreeable prospect. And the Ministry trusted him to render an accurate report. But when Isaac reached Watervliet, he was amazed at what he found. He described the visionists as

> two persons with closed eyes, unaffected by any thing which may be done to
> them, yet [synchronized] in a great variety of exercise . . . singing songs
> never before heard, in unknown tongues and oft times in English, with
> beautiful, intricate & graceful motions, both perfectly [in unison] . . .
> keeping perfect time & performing all the peculiar motions . . . turn and
> bow & pass swiftly about the room without stumbling.

Brother Isaac, however, was not just an observer; he did not take the visions—or the visionists—at face value. He experimented to determine whether the girls' spiritual gifts were genuine by placing obstacles "in their way on purpose." [19] He went to Watervliet not only to observe but also to test the youngsters. Over seventeen days, he observed fifteen manifestations and noted that they were increasing. He reported that the girls talked with the souls of departed friends. Some showed ecstasies of joy and love. Others were with the damned. They writhed and twisted in agony, groaning with heart-rending anguish. They bowed and shook. All, according to Isaac, were open and unembarrassed about their experiences in the spirit land.

After testing the visionists and weighing the evidence, Isaac was convinced that what he saw were true and valid spiritual gifts. "In all these," he wrote, "I saw the same marks of divine manifestations." The evidence was enough, he wrote, "to convince any rational person that there were living intelligent beings invisible [but] in a state of conscious existence," and that those beings communicated through visions. He confirmed that the girls were in contact with "spirits who did not inhabit bodies of flesh & blood." As a Believer, he was awestruck. "All this seemed to bring a spiritual world very near to my senses," he wrote, "& to render the veil between time and eternity almost transparent." The manifestations were consistent with Shakers' worldview, based on Mother Ann's example as well as scripture, that visions are divinely inspired and are proof of messianistic times. "Your sons and daughters will prophesy, your old men will dream dreams, your young men will see visions," Joel prophesied when he predicted the coming of the Lord (Joel 2:28). "I can boldly testify," Brother Isaac reported, "that it is a wonderful manifestation of divine power of an invisible agency operating on & in the mind, soul or spirit of an individual, in a manner positive, real & intelligent." With this declaration, Isaac Newton Youngs became a pivotal figure in the Era of Manifestations. Had he not validated the visionists' spiritual gifts, the subsequent years of Shaker life and worship might have been quite different.[20]

When Isaac returned to New Lebanon with his written report, he demonstrated the visionists' actions so the Church Family could have a better sense of what he had seen. Aaron Bill described Brother Isaac's imitations as "very interesting & remarkable," and so skillfully done that Giles Avery said, "I think he is nearly inspired to mimick for I never witnessed such scrutinizing mimickery before." [21] Isaac's mimicry may well have provided a script for others to follow. Displays of spiritual power required not only religious faith and belief in communication between spirits and mortals but also an understanding of what constituted acceptable behavior. And to spread, they required validation from earthly authorities, including peer support. Brother Isaac provided that validation, and the Ministry confirmed it.

In early 1838, visions cropped up in other Shaker villages. To track the phenomenon, Isaac began a new journal that showed how the Era of Manifestations unfolded. While monitoring reports of visions elsewhere, the New Lebanon Church Family waited for some of their own. They waited. And waited. Brother Isaac was uneasy because by March 1838, none had appeared there. "Surely it is a day of wonders," he wrote, "—I hope we shall not be neglected." For the Church Family to be spiritually inadequate was unthinkable because it was home to the Ministry and Believers most advanced in spiritual travel. And others commented on this deficiency in the society's leading order. Isaac heard that "Some one at the 2d family at Watervliet said the Chh had not traveled to visions yet, signifying they were behind the 2d family, & others that had visions." He thought it "no sign that they are any better for having visions—but why is it that we & the Chh at Watervliet have no visions. . . . I can't think it is because we are all so good that we need nothing to wake us up." Isaac knew the Church Family was not perfect.[22] But the Ministry's community needed spiritual gifts, and the sooner, the better.

With such expectations, someone was bound to act, and someone did. In late April 1838, Philemon Stewart brought a spirit message from the highest Shaker authority to fulfill the Church Family's longing for divine recognition. His inspiration was visible in his physical operations, groaning, head in constant motion from side to side, barely able to walk with the support of two brethren. The first and second orders assembled to hear what he had to say. "The scene was solemn, and awful, and filled the whole assembly with great fear of God," the scribe reported.[23] The New Lebanon Shakers validated Philemon Stewart's gift before he said a word; they assembled to hear him. If they had ignored him, his performance might have ended there. But union required unanimity and the Church Family needed manifestations.

Brother Philemon augmented his theatrical entrance by assuming Ann Lee's authority. And when he delivered her message, he took the Ministry to task. A Believer could have done so only by acting as a proxy for a recognized authority such as Mother Ann.[24] Brother Philemon said that she was appalled at the village's appearance. "It makes her feel tribulation to see the old rubbish lying about, gates swinging, latches off, fences & walls down, boards off from the fences," he said. "Such things, she says, impede the spiritual travel and bring darkness." The New Lebanon Shakers had slipped from Ann Lee's standards of perfection. And there was much, much more, all critical. Mother Ann ordered them to purge superfluities, "for if we gather that which is needless, it will be a clog to our souls, and engage our minds to no profit."

Over the next two months, Mother Ann delivered forty-eight pages of messages through Philemon Stewart to the Church Family, including, Isaac noted, a warning to not discuss her messages among themselves—a canny way to stave off second-guessing. Among other targets, her admonitions attacked what Isaac held dear, including the curiosities he collected and the knowledge he admired. Nevertheless, Brother Isaac thought the evidence of supernatural agency was indisputable.[25]

The village took Mother Ann's admonitions seriously; within a few days, Isaac helped straighten the fence around the meetinghouse and the rest of the society spruced up the village beyond the usual spring cleaning. Furthermore, Philemon's spirit message opened the floodgates of manifestations at New Lebanon. By May, the Church Family showed an unusual spiritual liveliness. Isaac described one gift that shows how individual Believers longed for divine notice. He reported that "among the rest," Sally had brought "very comforting words" to Rufus Bishop, from Mother and the spirits. "This was in answer to a request that [he] made on his knees," Isaac wrote, "that he might feel one gift of God tho ever so small, that he might know whether he was accepted." [26]

Like spirit messages, physical operations also began proliferating in 1838. Isaac noted several on May 14: "Mary Wicks was taken with shaking this afternoon, while opening her mind. She continued shaking & bowing all the time, both in meeting & out"; "Eleanor & Semantha had a wonderful time of shaking, bowing, talking & various exercises till past 11 ocl at night—others considerably exercised"; and, "Elisha Blakeman was moved by power at the table, first of the kind I have seen among the brethren." By late May, the Church Family dwelling seemed "alive with new lights, or such as are wro't upon," Isaac reported, adding, "It really looked wonderful to see 5 or 6 sisters & 3 brethren all in motion, coming from the east house to meeting & then going home." Better yet, he wrote, "The motions in meeting exceeded by far any thing of the kind witnessed before. . . . It is beautiful to see such life in so many." [27] Isaac preserved visionists' names for posterity, showing who did what, when, and where—a practice soon ended, perhaps to avoid exaltedness.

Brother Isaac's journal also explains how important spiritual manifestations were to Believers. "No comparison has ever been seen among us before," he wrote. "It is very different from the dark times of '35 & '36. I truly feel my soul filled with thankfulness, it is what I have long desired but never expected to see the like by a great deal." [28] *It is what I have long desired but never expected to see.* In those words lies the paradox of the Era of Manifestations: the Shakers' desire for spontaneous operations of the spirit along with the expectation that widespread manifestations were unlikely. Such a dramatic change was unexpected, but it was welcomed.

The phenomenon, however, required management. Brother Isaac later alluded to the Shakers' attempt to regulate the gifts when he wrote that the initial operations were performed in public but soon "were confined more to hours of worship." Those gifts were evidently under conscious control. Some visionists, however, were clearly beyond self-discipline. A visitor to New Lebanon in September 1837 described what was evidently considered excessive behavior even before the new manifestations appeared there: "Several of the women appeared to be thrown into violent hystericks, and in particular, one girl of seventeen threw up her handkerchief into the air, tore off her cap, and required the care of two or three of the older women to hold her down." The sister's behavior evidently exceeded what Shakers considered acceptable for public worship.[29]

Indeed, some Shakers were embarrassed by uninhibited behavior in front of outsiders. "Much wisdom was needed," Brother Isaac later wrote, "for the protection of the gifted ones, & to prevent those gifts from tending to wildness." The Shakers tried to keep the phenomenon within acceptable bounds, which showed ongoing tension between inspiration and the daily requirements of their communal society, or as Stephen Stein puts it, between Shaker gift and Shaker order. There was, indeed, an appropriate time for everything under heaven.[30]

Other gifts of inspiration at New Lebanon included new songs, dances, and marches, with bowing, jerking, and turning. Alonzo Hollister said that turning showed Believers' willingness to turn out of their old ways; thus some whirled until they dropped. Worship became chaotic, even hazardous, as Hervey Elkins observed: "Amidst so many arms, legs, and bodies, revolving, oscillating, staggering and tripping, it is not remarkable that a few should be thrown prostrate . . . upon the floor." [31] Eventually manifestations spilled over into Shakers' temporal lives, as an 1838 entry in Isaac's journal indicates: "I don't know what our hired workmen think to see so much going on," he wrote, "as they must see in our door yards!" [32]

When the public heard the news of spiritual whirlwind, earthquake, and fire, crowds flocked to Shaker services. After visiting Watervliet, Horace Greeley said Shaker worship resembled a camp meeting—a homely, unsophisticated event irresistible for its ardor. Though the worldly elite had long derided Shaker worship, they had rarely compared it to a revival. Shaker worship had changed. The occasional individual in the throes of inspiration had been supplanted by the contagious frenzy characteristic of camp meetings, a triumph of enthusiasm over reason and order. Believers' increasing spontaneity had some negative effects. As worship grew wilder, outsiders were less respectful, and some seem to have attended only to find fault. Greeley suggested that a cynic might see Shaker worship as "a handful of miserable fools and bedlamites making themselves ridiculous." And in September 1839, Fanny Appleton Longfellow visited a crowded New Lebanon service and criticized mercilessly, comparing the singers who pitched the song (probably including Isaac Newton Youngs) to "so many old witches or enchanters." One Shaker sister particularly horrified her. "She wrenched her head nearly over her shoulder on one side and the other, and then jerked it nearly to her knee," Longfellow wrote. "She stopped at the end and varied it by spinning like a dervish, twisting her arms round her head like snakes. Doubtless they regard her as a saint, for I saw a faint imitation of it in others."[33] Longfellow's vivid description illustrates exactly the spontaneity that Brother Isaac found so spiritually refreshing. That others imitated the dancer's gyrations shows the social nature of the phenomenon, which was spiritual balm to Believers united with the gift.

Other observers corroborated reports of increased enthusiasm in New Lebanon's Shaker worship. Some Believers "seemed writhing in agony," visitor Lawrence Pitkethly wrote. "The head, in particular, as well as the whole body, was kept in a sort of rolling motion." If Believers felt inspired to whirl, shriek, bark, or throw themselves on the floor, they did so with affirmation from their peers. In a society where self-expression was stifled and creative energy was absorbed by hard work, Shakers could give their creativity free rein in worship. In addition, the exertion may have quelled lust and provided an enhanced sense of well-being. But from 1838 into the early 1840s, Shakers' enthusiasm exceeded their recent tradition that was based on choreographed performance; many Believers revived the individual inspiration of Mother Ann's day and updated it to include new forms of spiritual expression. The Ministry were both pleased and alarmed; they worried that such gifts might degenerate into disorder.[34]

Brother Isaac's journal shows that by mid-1838, the New Lebanon Church Family was literally awhirl with spiritual inspiration. He happily described the manifestations he saw on Saturday, May 19.

> I saw passing here & there outdoor under motions, Felix at work. Lucy Gates, wonderfully shook about . . . Matilda R very powerful as she went round Miranda Barber at a surprising rate, she said she never felt so till last night. Abigail Hathaway jerking round—Elizabeth Lovegrove beat everything for motion. Elizabeth Sidle much wro't upon; Sarah Ann Lewis in bowing, motion[ing] & sing[ing]. Sally Dean, flying about, under

operations. Samantha—John Dean & others at the office in much distress, & I don't know how many more.[35]

At Sunday services on May 20, Isaac counted fourteen brethren and sisters and every boy but one "under operations." Anyone could be moved by the spirit. The next week, Isaac listed more.

> Miranda B. has kept going a good deal of the time from Friday night 25th to this time, tho with some cessation, but I believe she is constantly in motion thro' every meeting. . . . Elisha B[lakeman] & Felix [Robert] have it about them I believe about all the time, jerking & motioning with hands & arms— I don't think they have been still any meal time since the 25th.

Alonzo Hollister recalled, "In our family of fifty adults, there was, I think, as many as fifteen or twenty that were used by the spirits, as Instruments, more or less—more of the sisters' side than on the brethren's." [36] By June 1838, manifestations disrupted daily life throughout New Lebanon's Shaker society, which was previously notable for being calm, serene, and orderly.

This is not to suggest that Shaker communities became chaotic. On the contrary, with fewer than half of the adults overcome by the spirit, they managed to cook meals, do laundry, milk cows, feed chickens, tend livestock, plant, cultivate, and harvest crops, and run businesses. But in the next few years, some spiritual gifts became remarkably inconvenient because the instruments had the power to order the actions of the entire village. The "Midnight Cry," for instance, began with a dozen Shakers marching through every room in every building, a two-week process. On the third night, everyone was awakened between midnight and four a.m. to gather for an hour of "active worship." And in February 1843, the Church Family's brethren had to leave their warm beds at 3:30 a.m. to climb Holy Mount. Giles Avery noted that the outside temperature was only twelve degrees.[37] But the frigid night hike showed the brethren's commitment not only to the manifestations overall, and to that particular gift, but also to Shaker union.

Some Shakers implied that things were out of hand because a few instruments did nothing but receive visions. One brother complained, "They shake wherever they go; whether at work or at table! and sometimes their shaking is so violent that it is nearly impossible to get any food into their mouths, and they have to leave the table without eating." Spiritual gifts stole time from Shakers' temporal labor as visionists whirled and jerked through their chores. Philemon Stewart received so many spirit messages that he had little time left for his usual duties. Such excesses had to be discouraged. One girl, for instance, was told "not to have any more visions till she worked & gained time" for inspiration.[38]

Sometimes entire days were spent working through gifts. On Tuesday, November 23, 1841, the Church Family rose at 4:00 a.m. to hear an inspired writing. Isaac recorded the scene: "I can state but little of their solemn words, but they brot us into wailing & tears!" The quiet halls of their dwelling became bedlam. "While going to breakfast it was the most solemn scene I ever witnessed," Isaac wrote. "Many were so wrought upon with the spirit of lamentation, weeping & wailing, that they cried out aloud as a little child under correction, and in the 2ᵈ hall, the floor a great part of it covered by the many that lay prostrate at their length! and the house resounded with a heavy roar!" The noise must have been deafening. Afterward, the Church Family spent the morning in retiring rooms, then ate lunch "in great solemnity," and went to the meeting room for worship. Again they were laid low. "Yea we lay prostrate on the floor & cried aloud in vocal prayer," Isaac wrote, "& for a long time it was a continued loud roar of intermingling voices, bursting forth in fervent supplication, imploring the mercy of God, that he would not cast us off." Finally the instrument responded, "I delight not in the distress of any souls—had ye taken warning when I called to you, this need not have been. Signified we must learn, & keep humble."[39] One instrument could thus rule the movements of dozens of Believers who would have otherwise spent that Tuesday working. Isaac Newton Youngs recorded the details for posterity.

As manifestations continued to evolve, the peculiar nature of many gifts raised doubts about their authenticity. Shakers drunk on spiritual wine and visitations by ghostly menageries or spirits of howling Indians proved too much; inspiration crossed the line of acceptability.[40] Derobigne Bennet, who kept the Church Family Journal of Inspirational Meetings in early 1840, may have had doubts. He described a "very good meeting" where they drove off four evil spirits with "hot warfare," commenting, "Many were wrought upon . . . voluntarily I suppose." Though he enjoyed lively worship, he suspected that gifts could be intentionally created.[41] Soon after that entry, the Ministry replaced Bennet with Isaac Newton Youngs as journal keeper. Bennet's comment and his subsequent replacement suggest that the Elders may have acted to quell questioning of the phenomenon they had validated.

Certainly some spiritual gifts were falsified. Isaac reported that one girl, Ann E., augmented a gift, then had an attack of conscience. "In the morning at the school house when dancing," he wrote, "she went beyond her gift & danced of her own accord & made her operations at that time, & that was very wicked; she should never give a morsel beyond the gift that was given her at such times & pretend more than there was &c." Her spirit guide told her not to "act any thing . . . of her own accord . . . under the appearance of being inspired," so the girl confessed her misdeed, but Isaac was furious. Feigning or augmenting a gift was fraud. Even so, it was better to learn of the deception and set the little forger back on the straight and narrow path. Isaac summed up:

> I do not want to be deceived & imposed upon, & believe this & that to be a gift, a vision &c &c which is only made. It would disgust me very much to have any one old or young take the advantage & mix in their own stuff & pretend to some gift or to alter or fix the matter at all to suit themselves or others; and tho' it would not alter my confidence in visions or real gifts of God, yet there are many among Believers that would make a dreadful work of it, if they found one instance they knew was made, they would be ready enough to deny the whole, tho' perhaps ever so true & evident in the sight of others.

Brother Isaac was concerned that a gift found to be fraudulent would prompt many Believers to question the validity of all manifestations. He evidently knew some individuals who were already dubious and wanted to avoid giving them further cause for skepticism, and so he may have kept the fraud to himself. Furthermore, having validated the early visionists, he may have been reluctant to challenge gifts himself. Others who harbored doubts seem merely to have gone along with the phenomenon to remain in union. Shaker customs that stressed uniting with every gift, as well as peer pressure to conform, discouraged questioning. Even so, Isaac continued to watch for forgery. Indeed, some had been exposed. "I have watched these gifts and operations . . . closely to see if any pretence went undetected," he wrote. "There have been I learn some cases of pretence or overstepping of the real gift, but as far as I know any thing, it has been severely reproved and exposed by a true gift." He concluded, "And this is my confidence in the present manifestations, that no imposition or forgery will be suffered to pass." [42] Thus Isaac Newton Youngs assured posterity that Shakers did not automatically accept every gift. They policed the phenomenon to discourage pretenders, but the policing effort revealed tension between visionists and those who wished to control them.

More doubts surely arose with what appeared to be power struggles between visionists whose spirit messages pushed competing agendas. In 1838, Philemon Stewart's communication from Mother Ann called for limiting education and superfluous reading. That gift was affirmed by another instrument, perhaps Elisha Blakeman, who said that the spirit of Garret Lawrence brought a message of humility.

> It was in the line of retracting his errors in the example he had set in seeking worldly knowledge & fame. That he had spent much precious time in reading & writing that which was worse than nothing, when it would have been much better for him to have been gathering up sand & throwing it into the street & then throwing it back.[43]

But in January 1842, other instruments brought spiritual "books in abundance."[44] Those gifts were contradictory, and the contradictions could not necessarily be reconciled.

Moreover, gifts could be remarkably personal; one may have been aimed at Brother Isaac, who whistled as he worked. An instrument reproved whistling the songs of Zion as "a grief to the spirits."[45] Isaac worked "with many a whistle" and his tunes may have exasperated someone. A spirit message may have been a painless way for a spirit to address mortal aggravation. Much worse, however, were the spirit messages that resulted in Believers' expulsion from the society. Instruments' spirit-instigated accusations sent committed, lifelong Believers into exile.[46]

Other gifts, clearly inspired by Believers' concerns, may have been useful for forestalling trouble. When the spirits, as interpreted by a visionist in 1840, warned the New Lebanon Church Family "to come more together & not be so scattered" in their sleeping rooms, the Elders moved many Believers into new chambers, effectively increasing peer surveillance. Some did not want to move. Isaac had lived in room #7 for many years, and he had trouble accepting change. Also, in response to other messages reported from the spirits, union meetings were more closely regulated. "It was now the gift for us to come more into order, & be more together, and not to divide in the rooms," Isaac wrote, "but for all that live in two rooms to come into one—& to have a Godly union, in order, nothing private." Consolidating Believers into larger union meetings provided better oversight to forestall temptation. Isaac later spoke in meeting of his feelings about the gift. He said that "he felt determined to take hold heart and hand to keep every order & to be united in every gift," and though "he <u>had</u> felt as tho he should feel sober about it . . . he now felt resolved not to give way to any hard feelings, but be cheerful." He added, "so far as any cross was required, the tighter it was to an evil nature, the quicker we should gain the victory." And then he exhorted the younger brethren and sisters to take hold of the gift cheerfully. Resentment was contrary to union.[47]

In retrospect, however, Brother Isaac believed that certain manifestations were disruptive. Visionists were overcome at inconvenient or indiscreet times and places, sometimes in front of the world's people. He noted that such operations were "not in private nor confined to hours of worship, but in common view, in the house, at the table, in the shops door yards & even the fields; jerking, bowing, shaking, arms flying in all directions, whether in sight of Believers or unbelievers." [48] Though he validated gifts of inspiration and appreciated the spiritual refreshment, he thought that they should be restricted to worship or private times. Other Believers evidently also felt that their heightened religious enthusiasm had become incompatible with public display, and, in the early 1840s, they closed worship to the public. [49]

Despite the enthusiasm he described, Brother Isaac did not feel that his writings did justice to all that he had seen. "O would that I were able to give a full, just & expressive statement of these things," he wrote, "but Mortals' pen will never do it. But tho' I can retain but a shadow, & record but a faint glimpse of these things, yet O may I treasure in my heart the true spirit thereof." [50] Many spiritual gifts were evanescent, living only in memory. But others were not, including the drawings visionists began making in the 1840s to illustrate spiritual gifts. The drawings may have been inspired by the imagery in Shaker hymns, including flowers, living vines, celestial doves, streams of love, the tree of life, an arbor of love, an eternal fountain, and golden chains and harps—all images that Isaac Newton Youngs penned in lyrics before the Era of Manifestations began in 1837. [51] Some images came full circle when visionists gave Brother Isaac spirit messages on paper.

Polly Reed, for instance, made spiritual valentines for everyone in the Church Family. On June 2, 1844, Isaac wrote, "A singular circumstance occurred in the morning meeting. . . . A heart was given us with a promise that we should yet know what was written on them—the writing was now accomplished—& the presents were ready to be given out. The brethren & sisters then came forward, kneeling down & receiving the papers, in the form of a heart; beautifully written over with words of blessing in the name of the Father." [52] Brother Isaac's heart of blessing calls him "a peace maker within Zion's Holy Temple," as well as "a scribe in Israel, and a faithful soldier of the Lord." On the heart were drawn a clock, a lyre, and an open book, representing Brother Isaac's labors as clockmaker, musician, and scribe. [53] Sister Polly used her spiritual message to commend him for skills that served the Shakers. She appreciated his work and told him so. And he in turn cherished the gift, preserving it for posterity.

The Era of Manifestations could not last indefinitely. Eventually Isaac recorded a meeting that "seemed silent & indifferent." Perhaps fatigue set in. As Isaac put it, "There has been an astonishing and almost constant exertion of the spirits & the united efforts of the visible lead & also the labor & exertion of the body more or less universally, all tending to keep the sense, faith & zeal awake." After instruments spent a week writing by inspiration, Isaac observed, "It appears that this kind of manifestation is drawing near to a close, & what will come next besides tribulation we know not." In January 1841, Brother Isaac was assigned to preserve inspired messages for posterity. "It will doubtless require more than a year to do it," he wrote. Because hundreds of messages had been "written promiscuously" in books and on scraps of paper, he organized them chronologically for "order & convenience" and recopied them. For months he worked almost full-time, collecting and transcribing. The assignment was daunting, but it dovetailed with his interests. He undoubtedly put his own slant on some accounts of spiritual gifts, visions, and physical manifestations because he was the gatekeeper, deciding which gifts were significant enough to be recorded and which were not; thus, through his own writing and others' messages that he chose to preserve, Isaac shaped posterity's view of the manifestations at New Lebanon. He wrote:

> The writing of these things has caused me many hours labor and close
> attention; and never would I be willing to perform such a task, were it not
> for my love to those spiritual manifestations, which form a principle feature
> in our religious worship. I have written in the best manner I was able, &
> have endeavoured to confine myself to the most important parts, while a
> great portion of that of less importance must pass off, unrecorded. How long
> before I pass off from the stage & leave all below, I know not; but those who
> come after, may perhaps feel thankful for my labors.[54]

Brother Isaac was sad to think that the era was ending. He felt a letdown after a long and arduous project was finished. But in April 1841, he led a ritual of thankfulness in worship, bowing to the Shakers' heavenly parents in gratitude for the spiritual operations.[55] Brother Isaac affirmed his Shaker faith as well as the manifestations.

Elisha Blakeman praised Isaac Newton Youngs's hard work in preserving the Era of Manifestations. "He entered into the spirit of it, with heart, soul and body," Blakeman wrote. "Volumes were filled with long and precious messages; delivered thro' instruments from our heavenly parents, thro' no other medium than the memory of our Brother . . . grasping all that nothing be lost; the smallest song did not escape his vigilant eye and his industrious pen."[56] When the writing was finished, however, Isaac noted that he was "thankful to get thro." In his personal journal, he was more candid. "It has seemed like a long and wearisome work," he confessed.[57]

Dwindling fervor meant that by the mid-1840s, Shaker worship had normalized enough to admit the public again. In 1847, John Dwight, a visitor, described Sabbath at the New Lebanon Church Family meetinghouse, which was again filled with curious spectators.

> First came a spiritual hymn or chant, sung standing, to a very homely, humdrum, secular sort of tune, with a brisk, jig-like motion. It was sung in unison, all the voices on one part, from grandest bass to shrillest treble; the very plainest, baldest thing that could be called music, having a rhythm and a melody, but rigorously rejecting all unnecessary wealth and coloring of harmony. The close of every song was marked by a sepulchral lengthening out of the last note. There reigned the same neatness and correctness in this performance, as in their costume and their clean floor; no false notes or slips of time.

They swung into their choreographed dance, brethren and sisters moving two by two to "the jig-like hymn of their own chanting, both hands dangling loose and fin-like before the breast, . . . journeying round the room in circles, with strange limping step." Occasionally they paused while someone testified to their faith. Dwight observed:

> The most singular thing about their singularities was the absence of all fanatical intoxication. In the songs and dances we saw nothing of that violence and frenzy which have been reported of them; all was moderate, deliberate and self-possessed; no distortions, whirlings round on tip-toe, groans or frantic shouts. The Spirit did not seem to wrestle with them, but to descend upon them soothingly.[58]

Dwight expected fanaticism; instead, he saw a well-rehearsed performance. In the 1850s, other visitors observed that extraordinary phenomena such as spinning and convulsive ecstasies had ceased. "Such exhibitions are of rare occurrence now," Frederika Bremer wrote, "or care is taken that they do not occur in public."[59] And whatever they did in family worship remained private.

Isaac Newton Youngs may have missed the excitement; he appreciated spiritual gifts that kept faith and zeal awake. The manifestations so stimulated his faith that he later wrote that his "real travel heavenward" began in 1837. And he played important roles in the era, validating the early gifts at Watervliet, policing visionists for fraud, describing instruments in the throes of inspiration, and recording the sacred writings for posterity. His manuscripts illuminate the changes in daily life and worship. Shakers deemed his records "a strength to any class or age"; they appreciated Brother Isaac's long and wearisome work. By the 1840s, he had already left a "plain trace by [his] pen." [60]

9 Spiritual Autobiography

The Journey of Life, 1848

ISAAC NEWTON YOUNGS'S spiritual life neither began nor ended with the Era of Manifestations. His commitment to his faith lasted for the rest of his life, and he showed it by persisting as a Believer, contributing to worship, living and working by Shaker values. But he rarely wrote about his own spiritual experiences. Some of his spiritual gifts, in fact, were preserved only in other Shakers' writings, such as Sarah Bates's record of Isaac's gift of music from the spirit of Garret Lawrence.[1] On only one occasion did Isaac elaborate on his personal progress in faith, and that was in his Spiritual Autobiography, which he wrote in 1848. Much has been written about Shaker doctrine, but little has been forthcoming on individual Shakers' spiritual lives; thus this document is worth examination.

At age fifty-five, Isaac looked back on his life and evaluated his spiritual progress in a letter to Brother Oliver Hampton. Exactly what prompted this endeavor is unknown. Isaac evaluated all things, and so it is not surprising that he would also examine his own spirituality. Shaker beliefs supported him in assessing his spiritual state, because Believers were supposed to strive for perfection. Scripture drove the point home; "Be ye therefore perfect, even as your heavenly Father is perfect," was surely a verse that Shakers meant to heed.[2]

Putting a lengthy self-assessment in writing was atypical, however, even for Isaac. He was not reluctant to discuss spirituality; in fact, he welcomed the opportunity to cheer, enlighten, strengthen, and encourage others. But he rarely wrote of his inner spiritual life before or after the Era of Manifestations. Though he may have discussed it with his peers, in union meetings or worship, he gave the topic little attention in his journals. But perhaps his faith was so settled that he felt no need to put it in writing before 1848. It seems reasonable, therefore, to infer that something inspired him to take up his pen. Any or all of several factors could have prompted him to write this manuscript. One possibility is that Oliver Hampton requested an account of Isaac's spiritual travel. Though the formal tone of this work is inconsistent with the easy familiarity of Isaac's earlier correspondence, suggesting that it was not originally written to be included in a personal letter, Isaac may have altered his tone to fit the seriousness of the subject.

Another possibility, which could also account for the formal tone of the Spiritual Autobiography, is that the New Lebanon Church Family received a spirit message suggesting self-evaluation. But if that were true, surely more spiritual autobiographies would have survived. The Shakers preserved an abundance of sacred writings and it seems likely that they would have given the same attention to spiritual autobiographies. The scarcity of such personal retrospectives suggests that this exercise was uncommon and that Isaac wrote his Spiritual Autobiography on his own initiative as he did the pledge he made in meeting in April 1821 when he examined his behavior and listed the traits he had to improve. That pledge also had a formal tone resembling public language suitable for a presentation to a group on an official occasion. But the public language did not detract from either message. Despite their formality, both were personally revealing.[3]

The most likely possibility is that Isaac's motivation for writing his Spiritual Autobiography came from within. The passing of time may have prompted Isaac to take up his pen. He surely realized that he had crossed the meridian of life, commonly supposed to be about age forty-five in the nineteenth century.[4] That passage in itself could provoke self-examination. And to judge from his personal papers, Isaac was more introspective than most Believers. He may have wanted to reassure himself that he had, indeed, made progress in his faith.

A spiritual autobiography could be useful in other ways, as well. If he shared it, Isaac's story could benefit others. By showing that he had met the enemy, endured the struggle, and overcome nature, he could hearten younger brethren battling the same foes. And if he presented himself as imperfect, he could reassure others that they, too, could rise to the challenge. Isaac reflected on subjects that were perhaps more revealing than he intended, but in doing so he provided information on how he addressed his defects, mapping out a practical plan of applied faith to help others succeed as Shakers.

Isaac may have hoped that his account would help the society retain young brethren who were deserting in droves. By the 1840s, it was clear that Shakerism attracted and retained fewer adult men than women. As for the children Shakers fostered, a lower percentage of boys remained among the faithful in adulthood. Shaker-raised girls were evidently more willing to live celibate as women.[5] The loss of able-bodied young brethren was such a concern that Isaac had written extensively about raising children to become lifelong Believers. His prescriptive guide for youth, *Juvenile Monitor*, for instance, provides, along with advice on good manners, advice on how to live in union with Believers. In other genres, Isaac's poetry and songs also promoted Shaker values.[6] In his Spiritual Autobiography, he may have been sharing his strategies out of self-interest, in an attempt to forestall male apostasy. If he could "sell" his methods of rising above personal imperfection, he could encourage others to stay in the faith. Aging Believers needed the assistance of the younger generation of brethren.

In addition, Brother Isaac wanted his writings to encourage others in the gospel, and he may have meant his Spiritual Autobiography to be as much a part of his written legacy as his journals and his church history. Though some of his writings may have served as a coping mechanism in venting anger and frustration, his Spiritual Autobiography did not. This account served a different purpose. Isaac not only wanted to be remembered; he wanted to be remembered as a righteous Believer, however flawed. He wanted others to know that he had to work to remain in union, and that it was not easy, even for one whose faith was strong. He wanted posterity to know that the rewards were worth the struggle.

Isaac was honest in his self-presentation, as far as it went. He was not, however, entirely forthcoming. He did not include all of his problems, nor did he mention his objections to Shaker doctrine. And he did take exception to certain beliefs. In the early 1820s, for instance, when the Ministry was considering publishing an argument on the existence of the devil, Isaac, with his scientific mind, wanted proof and commented, "For my part I think it unprofitable to meddle very f[ar] with such secret matters; indeed I think it impossible for any man living on earth to know, or that no one [has] sufficient substantial evidence of the origin of the D[evil]." The problem could be summed up in the question: If God is all-powerful, and if God is good, then why does evil exist? The debate continued to percolate through the Church Family. Almost two years later, Isaac, aware that his disagreement was disorderly, encoded another journal entry about the origin of the devil. "I cannot alter my sentiment that good & evil never were united," he wrote, "that no evil ever flowed from God."[7] As he showed during the Era of Manifestations when he tested the visionists at Watervliet, Isaac questioned and examined evidence before making up his mind about spiritual things. He confirmed that approach in his Spiritual Autobiography. But he did not mention his doubts or question the Ministry in this document. It was a model of Shaker union.

Isaac's account of his own spirituality was not, therefore, quite complete. Nonetheless, this retrospective view is a boon to the biographer. Its focus on Brother Isaac's inner life affirms some of the conclusions we have already drawn and provides additional material that we could not otherwise hope to discern.

Brother Isaac often used scriptural allusions in his writings, secular as well as religious. His poem for May 1862, for instance, mentions the new spring grass as a carpet for the naked soil, "with flowers inwoven without toil," a reference to the biblical lilies of the field that toil not. And his comments about "the lust of the flesh and the lust of the eye" echo the gospel of John as well as Mother Ann's teachings. Brother Isaac also cited scripture in his Spiritual Autobiography. In a discussion about the futility of acquiring earthly wealth, he drew on Jesus's words in Matthew 6:19–21, "for where the treasure is, there will your heart be also." And Isaac described his youth as a journey resembling the Israelites' wanderings through the wilderness. He assumed that his readers would be familiar with the story from the book of Numbers: God provided the Israelites with manna and water, but also sent a plague to punish the greedy. They lost on one hand what they had gained by the other.[8] Despite his extensive knowledge of scripture, however, he did not base his Spiritual Autobiography on it. He took a pragmatic approach, instead, revealing how he succeeded in bearing the cross throughout the journey of life.

The Spiritual Autobiography reexamines, in vivid metaphor, several subjects Brother Isaac had already examined. He recalled his childhood and his growing conviction in faith, as well as his childish disdain for the world. Well before adulthood, he felt that the Shaker life was better than any alternative. But growing up brought tribulations that a young person could not have foreseen. This account updates several of Isaac's youthful struggles to 1848, adding information on his fear of falling from grace, his relief in subduing his passions, his confidence in the power of prayer, and his rejection of "letter learning," which, as the autobiography shows and Isaac admitted, was "imperfect at best." Isaac continued to be more candid than many Shaker diarists in inventorying his own problems and faults. But here we see a shift in his candor. Rather than directly naming sexuality, he resorted to euphemism—perhaps necessary if he planned to use this document to support other brethren. He focused instead on humility and self-denial while also accepting human frailty in pursuit of faith. Isaac must have made his point, and made it effectively, because he remained a role model for others, including Oliver Hampton, the recipient of this spiritual autobiography.

❖   *The Spiritual Autobiography of*
      Isaac Newton Youngs, 1848[9]

I TAKE MUCH delight in reciprocal communications. I love to
exchange sentiments particularly on spiritual subjects, & on things that
respect our future welfare, beyond the things of time; when it can be done
in a way to cheer, to enlighten to strengthen & encourage each other in the
great & trying work of self-denial, & to ameliorate the rigors & toils of
our hazardous journey thro this world. Some characters despise religious
conversation & are disgusted with any one's being what they call religious,
I consider such as being natural or carnally minded. "Where the treasure
is, there the heart will be" & out of the abundance of the heart the mouth
speaketh.[10]

We universally find that people, old and young, are free to converse
about matters that they feel interested in. Why then should we be silent
about matters that concern our spiritual welfare? Matters of the deepest
interest & of the most momentous importance. What does such silence
bespeak? We read that "They that feared the Lord spoke often to one
another" & it is reasonable to suppose it was about spiritual things that
they conversed. I would not recommend a seeming to be religious, or
much talkativeness about religion in times & places calculated to lessen
the solemnity & dignity of divine things—nor the life & character not
sincerely corresponding with heavenly sentiments. But I do think that a
freedom in speaking on spiritual things is necessary, both in meeting &
out of meeting, at all suitable times & places.

I cordially acquiesce in the sentiments expressed in your letter, & find
much in it to confirm mine, & to assimilate your Spirit with mine. This
will tend to increase the bonds of our faith & obedience. I suppose it may
be some interesting to you, to have sketched a little outline of the history
of my Journey thus far thro' time—touching my spiritual travel.

By the turn of the wheel of Providence my lot was cast among believers
when I was about 6 months old, where I have thus far spent my life, pretty
much secluded from the bustling throng. Of course I know but very little
by personal experience, of this vain world or the ways of men. I have
known no such thing as passing any particular crisis, or turning point of

conviction, or when I first received faith in any particular degree. My faith grew with mind. It grew with my growth & strengthened with my strength.

In my childhood, I felt a kind of disdain towards the wickedness & fashions of the world, as thinking I possessed something superior. I was very much secluded from other children, so that I almost entirely escaped getting into mischief & learning evil in that way. In my advanced years I have been very thankful that such was the case with me. As I grew into youth, I became some more associated with other youth whereby I was more exposed, yet but little to what some are. Thro this I learned the great necessity of youth being watched & protected concerning their company with others.

I have also been exempt from harassing relatives, to entice me with them to enjoy the world. And this I have learned is a great blessing. Situated as I was, I knew no way but to submit to what was for me, without expecting or even wishing in my better judgment & prevailing feelings, for any other ways, or change in my condition. I have never yet indulged one feeling of regret that I was not left to experience an unrestrained course in the wide world of sinful pleasure.

From my earliest recollection, I was always devoted according to my sense, to spend my days in the faith & Society of Believers—making no provision for what might come—that I would endure if matters went thus & thus favorable, or that I would flinch at such & such trials. And this has been a great anchor to me in the trials I have met.

Now, from the foregoing, some person perhaps might suppose I had a very easy row, and thot myself pretty good, but let them not judge hastily. I have had my struggles. My lost nature grew with manhood. My pride, self will, & passions increased with my body & mind. I had my own cross to bear, or suffer the goadings of conscience. I had to be tutored & trained out of my own ways. There was no peace unless I toed the mark. I had my own choice to make. It was not suddenly made at any one time, it had to be seriously done over & over, continually setting out anew; altho I never once turned my mind to meditate on any other determination.

The pleasures of this world & my own will, were as a mysterious treasure hidden in a box. An insatiable desire would harass & prompt me to want to know what it was. I had not become bound with vicious habits, nor my passions inflamed by indulgence like an old sinner's, yet my ignorance of the effects of sin was as great a snare to me, as Adam & Eve's ignorance of the tree of knowledge was to them. I will here insert a few lines from a little poem I wrote a few years ago relating to my progress in life.

As I grew up to reason's age
More serious thots my mind engaged,
The childish season was exchanged
For scenes of manhood, new & strange.
New scenes arose, new billows roar
New trials I knew not before.
Satan oft laid his tempting snares
And crossed my track most everywhere.
I passed thro many sober times
Which I shall not put into rhymes.
Religious things I here might mention
Which claimed good share of my attention.
The Lord beheld me, night & day
The Devil watched me for his prey.
And conscience hanging round about me
All seemed to try my courage stoutly.
I've been perplexed all round about
But still did never yield to doubt
About the truth of sacred things
Or what to souls, true comfort brings.
And still I hold my courage fast
The Golden Prize I'll gain at last.[11]

As I grew in body & mind, my love for self increased. My faith in God & love to virtue also increased, so as to keep the balance on the right side in a general sense. I gave my mind to understand the principles of the gospel, & searched for evidence in favor of my faith, in the Bible & in every thing that met my view. This continually increased my confidence in the faith, & outweighed my natural reasoning in favor of my passions. And I may say this was one of the flukes to the anchor that held me.

Another was, that inward principle of faith & conscience, seemingly created with me, not derived at all from reason, but entirely beyond it. Something I could not get by. The third fluke was a firm confidence in future reward, which brot a remedy for all present difficulties.

This may serve as an outline of my spiritual condition until the year 1837, at which period I date the beginnings of my real travel heavenward, for I do not think that before this, I ever gained anything that amounted to gain upon the whole. I had as it were, but been preparing materials for my journey. For tho I did the best I knew most of the time, & gained much good in many things, yet on the other hand my struggles were increasing, so that I lost by one crook what I gained by another. I own this is something like the old Israelites in the wilderness, & my sentiment in this matter may appear singular & doubtful, but I think were it not for multiplying words too much for this time, it might be satisfactorily explained.

Before this, while nature was on the increase, I wondered how souls could get so in this world, that the pleasures of nature & self would not appear enticing, supposing they could indulge in them. I thot it hard if one must always be harassed thro a long life, as I was, & always feel themselves in jeopardy—& how there would be anything but the same kind of cross so long as any nature remained, I could not well understand. For a number of years, I felt as tho I was on a needle's point, not feeling certain how it would turn with me; viewing it a dreadful thing to fall, & yet hard to stand, fearing lest some unfortunate turn might prove my destruction. Yet I did not feel discouraged, or turn in my mind to flinch in case it came tighter thus, or so.

Thus I continued struggling along, uphill & down, through sloughs & mudholes, coming in contact with stumps and stones & rocks of offense— thro dark night & cloudy days—passing once in a while over a short piece of good road —then over waters of affliction, the tempest raging & angry billows roaring & beating against my poor little boat. Then would come a calm, with clear skies & shining sun, at which times I would find my latitude & longitude, set my compass & sail on well, awhile. Next, perhaps, I & my companions would have a wilderness to go thro, where the enemy lay in ambush. There we encountered skirmishes & were often fired upon, & some times, alas! some fell by my side, one here & another there, but thanks to the captain of our band, this never did any more than alarm me a little. It never disheartened me, as I for one, was determined to see the matter thro. At length I began to feel a little foothold, in which I gained some assurance of final success.

From this time I could perceive that the pleasures of the world began to lose a little of their charm. This was about the beginning of the late manifestations of visions, inspirations, &c. Here I began to travel perceptibly without crooking much or losing time. Here I experienced an establishment of faith that nothing I have since met has shaken in the least. I soon felt that I had obtained a degree of victory that I never found before. It was easy for me to bear my cross & not feel much inclined to evil in any way. I soon began to feel a settled assurance that I should endure to the end, & it appeared clear to me that I might yet reach that state, where no temptations could allure me, & no trials overthrow me. At times, I could see the travel of my soul & feel satisfied for the time.

In the course of a few years, I gained that I had never expected to gain in this world. This may seem like saying a good deal, but do not mistake me & think that I mean to boast of my goodness or perfection. I feel far from that. I speak freely in recommend[ation] of what the gospel will do for those that desire it.

From my experience thus far, I draw the conclusion concerning the travel of souls, that in the commencement of their rising from a fallen state, they are first convicted of their loss, receive faith & begin to bear the cross thro fear of hell or condemnation, having to exert themselves against the alluring charms of nature. After struggling awhile in this way, those charms begin to lessen & the cross feels less severe. After awhile these charms lose much of their force. The cross grows less & less in proportion as the passions & will are subdued, until the pleasures of nature & the world look uninviting & finally disgusting. When every principle of nature is crucified & extinguished from the soul, it is beyond the reach of temptation, & it serves God out of pure love.

Here I will digress a little & relate a little experience I had about 24 years ago, to show that one may live a perfect upright life, if he really wills to do so.

Our Elder John Farrington, speaking in meeting, once said that any one might be just as good & perfect as he or she was a mind to be. I rather disputed it in my mind & thot it a hard saying, but finally determined to try. It was about the time for general opening of our minds. I endeavored to be pretty honest & so set out to be perfect for a time, for experiment's sake. I was sincere, & found in truth I was able to walk perfectly blameless, according to the strictest dictates of my conscience in thot, word & deed & without knowing an instance wherein any other one saw aught in me that was amiss. My sensations in this time, I cannot well describe.

I felt especially guided by some soft & gentle influence, ever ready to apprize me when danger was near. I felt no underhanded, mean excitements around to ensnare me, nor did I feel a slavish fear, nor a rigid superstitious nicety about what I said or did. All I had to do, was to be strictly watchful, not voluntarily to meditate on any evil thot, & not to speak or act anything that upon reflection I knew to be wrong, or would have a tendency to evil. I enjoyed my reward for this, almost continually, as I went along. I felt a peculiar sense of cleanness as if I had just been washed all over, & had put on a clean dress.

I kept this state about six weeks, & then fell back & became more careless & indifferent, not feeling really willing to practice so strict self

denial. This experience was always a lesson to me. I have often thot, &
do now, that if believers would all unite as a body to live in this way, we
should be as Angels of bliss & enjoy no small degree of Heaven on Earth. I
feel that my life and character has been very far from this. I feel unworthy,
& tho in the eye of the laws of men, I never committed a crime in my life,
yet I feel so full of humiliating insignificance & petty errors, that I have
nothing to boast of. I feel dependent on God & his people for mercy, &
hope that I may yet be found worthy to inherit a place among God's
justified & accepted creatures. One thing I know. I have devoted myself
& am consecrated to God & his people.

There is no subject that I contemplate with more pleasure than that of a
future existence. I look forward with great anxiety to that day when I shall
launch from the shores of time into the broad ocean of Eternity, praying
that it may be in peace & justification. O Eternity! Never ending existence!
How magnificent & sublime the thot! It is the most consoling—the most
animating & auspicious Idea that I can conceive. The thot of existing
Eternally, with the prospect of endless happiness & glory, peace &
righteousness unceasing, with a full enjoyment of the infinite goodness
& blessing of God, our Great Creator.

The prospect of becoming acquainted with the numerous spirits who
existed of old, & with the events that have transpired in the works of
God—the attainment of unbounded wisdom & knowledge of what was &
is & is to come, is a most transcending & sublime reflection. How can the
mind realize it or comprehend the thousandth part thereof? It is enough to
shame the atheist & to cause infidelity to shrink into contempt.

Surely this is worth our greatest exertions—an incomparable reward for
any sacrifice the gospel requires. Why then should we not be encouraged
to persevere in good works? How can we fail of receiving our just reward,
when each good deed will weigh in the balance, & be attended with an
eternal happifying consequence, the effect of which will never cease. A
good deed is aptly likened to a pebble, thrown into the still waters of a
pond, which causes them to vibrate until a ripple expands over the whole
surface.

Even such I consider is the consequence of our actions good or evil.
They will never cease to affect our conditions, & not only us, but those of
other souls whether near or remote, in proportion as we are connected
with them. Therefore we are greatly accountable for our deeds, on account
of their effect upon others & will have to suffer so far as they injure others
& vice versa.

I want to say a little on the subject of Prayer. I have great faith in the overruling Providence of God, & I believe he will exercise his power & influence greatly in condescension to the requests of his dependent creatures. I think our prayers to God for each other, have a very salutary effect to draw the attention of guardian angels & to increase their exertions in our behalf, for our protection.

As to prayer in general I would say much, but in short, I believe prayer to be of unspeakable worth & importance to us, for it places the mind in an attitude that of itself, is a great safeguard against evil. It renders the spirit less liable to temptation, awakens the sympathy of guardian spirits, & renders us accessible to them. Abundantly do I think of that ancient saying, "Praying will keep thee from sinning, & sinning will keep thee from praying."

Mistaken mortals sometimes get their affections placed on human learning & education to refine them & elevate them . . . out of a degraded state of ignorance. They think & argue it is necessary to render them useful &c. But I think if they would go in private & stand on their knees five minutes in sincere prayer to God, or labor till they feel one gift of repentance, it would do more towards refining & elevating them, than reading or studying a fortnight. Indeed, the more one reads or studies in the sense that I have reference to, the worse it is. I speak of aspiring after refinement & elevation by mere human learning, derived from books, or the study of Science & art, beyond what real duty requires. I do not write this from any suspicion of yourself, but merely to express my sentiments on Prayer.

As to letter learning, I once had great lust for it, but now I feel but little anxiety about it. It is imperfect at best, & the acquisition of it would prevent my doing my duty, & doing more good other ways. It would also absorb attention from the less pleasing but indispensable work of self-denial. Where the tree of knowledge grows, it must absorb the vital principle of the soil of the mind & rob the more delicate plants of virtue. It is foolish for us to toil for more than we really need here of that which we cannot carry with us, or that will be of no use to us in a future state.

The principle of intelligence will doubtless be unfolded to perfection in the future state of the righteous. The means to obtain the true knowledge that will be useful there, will doubtless be manifold superior to any means here, therefore I feel to wait patiently & be satisfied with a small portion here.

IN 1848 WHEN Isaac Newton Youngs wrote his Spiritual Autobiography, he was at the pinnacle of his temporal abilities, secure in his faith, and optimistic about his eternal reward. He had traveled far from the lusts and rebellion of his youth and knew that with persistence, the struggles of life's journey could be overcome. His description of life as spiritual travel may well have been modeled on John Bunyan's *Pilgrim's Progress* (1684), which had inspired many Christians to view life as a pilgrimage past temptation, sin, and despair, slogging through the putrid mire of the Slough of Despond, avoiding vanity, error, and doubt. Though Bunyan's tale was a relic of the embattled Puritan, its imagery persisted into the nineteenth century in the concept of life as a quest for salvation.[12]

Just as Hopeful did in Bunyan's book, Isaac tried to "ameliorate the rigors and toils" of the journey for his fellow travelers. His desire to encourage others is evident in the fact that he sent the Spiritual Autobiography to Brother Oliver, and he may have read it aloud in meeting, as well. His encouragement evidently worked, because Alonzo Hollister transcribed this message for posterity.[13] His willingness to spend precious time copying it out indicates the personal regard he felt for Isaac, as well as his respect for the older brother's wisdom and experience. And for Isaac, sharing a good deed was, as he put it, like dropping a pebble into a still pond and watching the ripples widen out to every shore. He hoped that the benefits would spread far beyond their initial point of impact.

Brother Isaac's dismissal of "carnally minded" Believers who "despise religious conversation" reveals once again that the Shaker community was not a homogeneous group, despite their shared faith. Considering that Shakers had to open their minds to the Elders before signing the covenant, it seems curious that some were uncomfortable discussing their beliefs; it does not fit the evangelical model.

Evangelicals tend to judge things as right or wrong, either white as an angel's wing or black as sin, often without addressing the shades of gray that might lie between. By creating a dichotomy between those who were willing to discuss spiritual matters and those who were not, Isaac was making a similar sort of judgment. Though he was not always so quick to condemn those who disagreed with him, he did believe that spiritual conversation was necessary "both in meeting & out of meeting, at all suitable times & places." His scriptural reference, "Where the treasure is, there the heart will be," suggests that he considered religious conversation a route to heavenly riches.[14] To Isaac, religion was a constant concern, and his spiritual life was not relegated to the meetinghouse; it imbued all things Shaker, temporal matters as well as church, daily life as well as worship. And though worship was an important part of his life, he knew that spiritual travel took place outside of the meeting-house as well as within.

In this document, Isaac confirmed that his spiritual growth, or "real travel heavenward," began with the Era of Manifestations. Though his religious conviction grew with maturity, the manifestations speeded his spiritual journey, invigorated his faith, and gave him a "settled assurance" that he could endure to the end.

Before his faith matured, however, Brother Isaac traveled through a dangerous wilderness of temptation and sin; there lurked Satan's minions to ambush the unwary. Isaac, like Christian in *Pilgrim's Progress,* was saddened to see some of his peers fall in skirmishes with Satan. His other writings show that he thought apostates received exactly what they deserved: a quick descent to hell through the world and the flesh.[15] In his Spiritual Autobiography, however, he regretted their loss.

Long before 1848, Isaac had examined his own behavior and worked at his faith. As a young man, he had looked for loopholes in the Elders' edicts and defied orders to turn over his writings, though he usually knuckled under to preserve his union. And when Elder John Farrington challenged him, saying that anyone could be as good as he had a mind to be, Isaac at first "rather disputed" the idea, calling it "a hard saying," perhaps because it reflected badly on him. In the end, however, he decided to test himself against Elder John's premise. He wrote about his test of personal perfection in "New Year's Thoughts."

> I often have set out anew,
> To take my cross and travel through,
> More zealously to watch and pray,
> And keep within the narrow way.

Isaac's poem shows that his greatest challenges lay within himself. So he tested himself against Elder John Farrington's premise. He designed an experiment in self-government to try to improve himself just as he did his clocks. His goal was to be as perfect as possible. He wrote his rationale into his 1824 poem with good humor and no little irony.

> It surely is within my pow'r
> To be quite perfect one whole hour;
> No better one than twenty-four,
> And just as well two days or more.
> And if I'm good three days or four,

Why not as well a hundred more?
And if so long I wisely stear
Why not be good throughout the year?

All things considered, the experiment sounded like a great idea. He tried to be perfectly good, one hour at a time—a measurable goal characteristic of his temporal labor, here extended to his spiritual labor, as well. Optimistic about his quest for virtue, he wrote,

I know I can be perfect too,
In all I think and say and do;
By a continual careful mind,
Which, like a watchman, ever kind,
Will fill my soul with Godly fear,
And teach me when there's danger near.[16]

Twenty-four years later, when Isaac Newton Youngs wrote his Spiritual Autobiography, he described the result of his experiment in self-perfection. Over and over again, he chose to be good, one hour at a time, but goodness required constant vigilance. He worked on his thoughts and actions and reported that he managed to be perfectly good for about six weeks. But he was not apologetic about ending the endeavor. Despite the limited success of his experiment in self-improvement, when he was especially good, Brother Isaac felt "a peculiar sense of cleanness" that was a reward in itself.

Isaac's admission that he could not sustain the effort seems unusual. As a man who wanted to leave a record for posterity, he might have presented himself as more perfect than he truly was. But his decision to be candid about his experiment and its ultimate failure shows he believed that trying to be good was worthwhile regardless of the end result. He wanted to show younger brethren that they did not have to fear imperfection as long as they made a genuine effort at self-improvement. In fact, like Christian in *Pilgrim's Progress*, Isaac may not have been able to reach his final destination without testing himself. Spiritual travel required it. Furthermore, coming to terms with his own imperfection may have been a rite of passage in reaching maturity.

Isaac may have gone beyond the Shaker norm once again, in making the effort as well as describing it for posterity. Deliberate self-assessment, whether it resulted in marked improvement or not, was one more stage of the journey toward salvation.

Isaac's experiment revealed that living as a celibate separatist did not require perfect behavior. Though self-improvement may have been the ideal, perfection was not attainable. If (as he said) all Believers could be perfectly good all the time, they would truly enjoy heaven on earth. Alas, they did not. Strict self-control of thoughts and deeds evidently was not as perfectly practiced among Shakers as even the best Believer might have wished—thus the need for Mother Lucy's admonitions against hard feelings or chafing and galling one another, as well as the Millennial Laws against superfluities, anger, vulgar expressions, filthy stories, lying, backbiting, and tattling.[17] But surely no Shakers, from the Ministry down to the sloppiest backslider, ever believed they were truly perfect. Such an assessment would have negated humility. All Believers knew in their hearts just how deficient they were. The key to living as a good Believer may have been making a conscientious effort at self-government and recognizing when danger was near. No one could avoid all temptation, but they could control how they responded to it.

Moreover, Isaac's suggestion that prayer would help in the effort to be good may have been the Shaker version of Jesus's words on the Mount of Olives, "Pray that you may not enter into temptation." [18] Isaac believed that prayers drew the attention of guardian spirits and increased their exertions on his behalf. He felt that he was supported in goodness, not only by scriptural example and mortal Shakers, but also by angels. His welfare was a concern of divine beings—a special boon at times when he needed strength or consolation.

Though Isaac had not attained the level of perfection he desired, some issues of his youth, including the cross of celibacy, seemed less problematic in his middle age. By 1848, as he wrote in his Spiritual Autobiography, "the pleasures of nature & the world look uninviting & finally disgusting." In his fifties, he might have been ashamed of the indiscretions of his youth, but he did not withhold information on his earlier interest in natural pleasures; in fact, he wanted his readers to know that such yearnings are typical and can be overcome.

Even though some of Brother Isaac's lusts had diminished, one desire had only been suppressed. The length of his commentary on education suggests that he was still struggling with the issue despite his protests to the contrary. However indispensable self-denial may have been to a conscientious Believer, it was less pleasing than "letter learning." And though Isaac felt "little anxiety" about acquiring more education, those words indicate that he did, indeed, still want it. A few years later, he would visit the New York State Library in Albany and write wistfully, "Any one can look around, or read what he pleases." [19] Significantly, he wrote that in his personal journal; he held that information close.

In his Spiritual Autobiography, however, Isaac upheld Shaker values. The tree of knowledge could prove poisonous. Therein lay the serpent of temptation.[20] Isaac had been taught since childhood that learning could divert attention from spirituality until even the most devout Believer might favor education over faith, and he upheld that view. Better to avoid temptation by refusing the forbidden. And as Isaac approached old age, he believed it foolish to toil on earth for that which he could not carry into a future state of existence. Though he may have longed for learning in his mortal life, he accommodated himself to Shaker beliefs to live in union with his society, and he passed that message on to other brethren.

Even so, Isaac ended those paragraphs with the hope for superior means to obtain true knowledge in the afterlife. His anticipation of omniscience at his "launch from the shores of time into the broad ocean of Eternity" is further evidence of his faith, as well as his desire to know all things. Though he looked forward to the great beyond, while he still lived on earth, his advancement in self-discipline gave him a sense of satisfaction. He could see his progress. And if the tree is known by its fruit, then Isaac Newton Youngs reflected credit on Mother Ann Lee and the religion she planted in American soil.[21] Though he never found it easy, he continued to live by the admonition in Proverbs 1:8 to follow his mother's teachings. Brother Isaac may not have been the typical Shaker brother, but his experience stands for every Believer's effort to bear the cross. His struggles as well as his successes must speak for others who remain mute to history.

After penning his Spiritual Autobiography, Isaac dropped the subject of his spirituality. As far as we know, he never again described his spiritual life in writing, even though he lived until 1865. In March 1857, he made a passing comment on what he called his church birthday, the anniversary of the date when he arrived at New Lebanon in March 1807. He noted that his journals would show what his temporal employments had been. "But as to the spiritual part," he added, "that must remain with the inner memory."[22]

Brother Isaac's temporal life, however, was another story. Considering the Shaker link between work and worship, it is interesting that Isaac Newton Youngs's Spiritual Autobiography included nothing about labor. Though Isaac had clearly applied Shakers' spiritual values to his 1840 clock designs, showing his faith by his works, he did not refer to work in this account of his spiritual travel.[23] That omission suggests that he had compartmentalized his views on work and religion by 1848. He did, after all, keep separate journals for work and religious matters. In this respect he resembled other brethren who wrote journals for years with hardly a mention of anything spiritual.[24] Isaac's omission could also have stemmed from the fact that his work life was sailing along on an even keel in November 1848. But ahead lay a fundamental problem that would blight the rest of his life: overwork. Changes in Shaker society, the loss of temporal support, and the passage of time afflicted the aging brother until work because a source of tribulation rather than satisfaction. Brother Isaac's spiritual path aimed for heaven, but his temporal life was headed for purgatory.

The more I gather upon me, the more perplexity it will be.

10 Perfectionism and Overwork in Middle Age

WHEN ISAAC NEWTON YOUNGS noted the passing of time in 1840 with the inscription on his clock, "Behold! how swift the seasons roll! / Time swiftly flies away!"[1] he also noted the effects of age. To cap off the rest, Brother Isaac was losing his hair.[2] But he did not have time to dwell on baldness or aging. He had too much work to do.

Work was fundamental to Shaker success. As Suzanne Thurman points out, Believers were industrious because they inherited the eighteenth-century Yankee work ethic. The local population equated work with virtue, and they brought that view into Shaker society. Moreover, Ann Lee left Believers with the credo "Hands to work, hearts to God." Like other communitarians, Shakers institutionalized their values about work. Accordingly, their Millennial Laws directed that "every one should work diligently with their hands, according to their strength, for the public good of the society." Everyone worked for economic security and also "to build community, identity, and equality." In addition to being a test of character, work was, according to E. D. Andrews and Faith Andrews, "the root of achievement." Shakers ate not "the bread of idleness."[3] Individually and collectively, they could demonstrate competence, mastery, and success through their work and perhaps attain a measure of grace by investing Mother Ann's ideals in the products of their hands.

The result was visible. The world's people commented on Believers' industriousness as well as their spotless buildings, well-built barns, fertile fields, and fat cattle. Benson Lossing observed in 1856, "No idle hands are seen." But he thought Shakers were contented as they labored for the general good. In this he was mistaken. Personal and economic factors generated so much work that temporal labor, which can be a fundamental satisfaction in life, could become something else entirely. And though Lossing spent time with Isaac Newton Youngs at New Lebanon, he did not see the workload that plagued the good brother.[4]

In theory, Shakers were expected to work steadily but moderately. The Elders may have counted on labor to keep Believers too busy for disorderly behavior, but no one was supposed to be overworked. One visitor compared Shakers to "culprits confined in a house of correction and condemned to hard labour for the sake of improving their morals," but Shakers were so socialized to duty and industry that they did not have to be compelled to work; they did so voluntarily.[5] A Believer could achieve success in temporal labor. Isaac Newton Youngs did just that, but the burden overwhelmed him, and though he seemed to relish being in demand, he complained for years that he had too much to do. In fact, Brother Isaac may have needed to overwork himself to fulfill emotional or psychosocial needs. His versatility and competence could have brought praise and satisfaction, feeding his ego in a way Shaker society permitted. And perhaps being in demand made him feel wanted and needed. As long as he reaped those benefits, he was unlikely to cut back on his work.

From the 1820s on, Isaac Newton Youngs was short on time. He forfeited rest and fretted over tasks left undone. Nonetheless, he was often good-humored about being busy, as he was in this 1833 note, a masterpiece of brevity, written before dawn.

> If convenient I should delight in repaying the many notices I rec from you in writing while over at Wvlt but as nobody can do anything without a chance I hope you will accept the will for the deed. This much must suffice.
> In boundless love, farewell.   i.n.y.
> (in the dark of the morning)

Sometimes Isaac was unable to finish everything he had to do during the usual fifteen-hour workday and stayed up late, or "set up out of season" to finish a task, such as the Autobiography in Verse, which he completed at midnight. He was vexed when the Elders required Believers to ask permission to work after bedtime because Shakers' labor was not supposed to invade their sleep.[6]

Other New Lebanon brethren were also too busy. Henry DeWitt, for instance, complained in 1836, "With busy hands can't work so fast, But what there's more to do."[7] Isaac equated temporal labor with doing good but he believed his workload was beyond his control and he rarely felt relaxed about it. "For I am that kind of folk that is wanted in several places at once," he wrote, "& besides being needed in all general & important calls, in my leisure hours (if such a thing be possible) there are many greedy wants, ready to swallow me alive."[8] His skills were so much in demand that work became another cross for him to bear. Furthermore, his drive to complete all assignments to his own exacting standards invited frustration. As early as 1821, he revealed the toll his workload was taking.

> I have been more scattered, and have . . . been more depended upon by others, & consequently met with many cases wherein I could not give satisfaction on all hands. I have had to feel care & concern in whatever I undertook . . . or lose the approbation of others. I have found it true that the more I gather upon me, the more perplexity it will be to me; for if it be an addition of work, it renders it more difficult to do all that is necessary in its proper time, and to the satisfaction of all concerned: different branches will unavoidably clash, and require one's attention at the same time in different places.

Isaac concluded, "I am harassed on every side." This passage outlines the problem that hounded Brother Isaac for the rest of his life. Work tugged him hither and yon, but he knew he "gathered upon" himself more than he could handle and spent too much time on the "naturally agreeable" jobs.[9]

Despite the demands on his time in 1837, Isaac penned the long Autobiography in Verse, using several verses to describe his work. Making light of his employments, he addressed his overload.

> Forty-four years now since my birth,
> And I'm still living on the earth,
> And full of bus'ness night and day;
> With scarce a moment's time to play;
> I've work enough, that's now on hand
> For 15 years, for any man.
> I'm overrun with work and chores
> Upon the farm or within doors.
>
> Which ever way I turn my eyes;
> Enough to fill me with surprise.
> How can I bear with such a plan?
> No time to be a gentleman!
> All work-work-work, still rushing on,
> And *conscience* too still pushing on:
> When will this working all be done?
> When will this lengthy thread be spun?
>
> As long as *working* is the cry.
> How can I e'er find time to die?
> Must I be sick to get away?
> O that is harder yet, I say!

> But still at work I won't complain,
> Upon the whole I think 'tis gain.
> It's none too bad for any man
> To do what little good he can.
>
> Be sure the Devil will have to flee,
> And seek some other place but me
> To find a workshop to his crook
> 'Mongst idle brains, or I've mistook.
> I don't pretend I've done too much,
> I don't a single stroke begrutch.
>
> .　.　.　.　.　.　.　.
>
> Of various kinds of work I've had
> Enough to make me sour or sad,
> Of taylr'ing, Join'ring, farming too,
> Almost all kinds that are to do,
> Blacksmithing, Tinkering, Mason work,
> When could I find a time to shurk?
> Clock work, Jenny work, keeping school
> Enough to puzzle any fool!
> An endless list of chores & notions,
> To keep me in <u>perpetual motion</u>.
>
> .　.　.　.　.　.　.　.
>
> And by the time I'm 45
> If I should be well, & alive
> I hope some better times to see—
> For that is just the way with me,
> To always look for better days
> With brighter sun, more cheering rays
> Yet ne'er to slight my pleasant bliss
> Nor present happiness to miss;—
> But make the best of everything,
> And let each day its fortune bring.

Brother Isaac tried to view his situation as better than it actually was. Had it been ideal, he would not have needed to put a good face on things. The fact that Isaac wrote a long, rhymed poem in meter—a time-consuming project that he completed at midnight—shows how he spread himself too thin by doing an optional but agreeable task.[10]

Without corroboration of Isaac's self-serving comments about the demands on his time, we might view him as a whiner who wanted to do less or a braggart who thought a lot of himself. But he was neither. In fact, others recognized that he was exceptional. Lucy Wright mentioned his "genius," and the Elders remarked on his "many abilities" and "good understanding." Elisha Blakeman, in his eulogy to Isaac, was more specific. He wrote that Isaac Newton Youngs's "mechanical genius was remarkable," adding that he "could turn machinist, mason or any thing that could promote the general good. Very many of our little conveniences, which added so much to our domestic happiness," Blakeman concluded, "owe their origin to Br. Isaac."[11] He was a tailor, clockmaker, mapmaker, mechanic, inventor (of a metronome, toneometer, leveling instrument, and five-pointed pen for drawing music staffs), lens-grinder, stonecutter, button maker, bookkeeper, tinsmith, printer, pipe fitter, joiner, and blacksmith. He built a sundial, made tools including a weaver's reed, turned clothespins, and laid floors. He was the master builder for the New Lebanon Church Family's 1839 schoolhouse and designed a new teacher's desk, as well. He also may have had a hand in the ingenious water-powered machinery in the wash house, which lifted wet laundry into the attic to dry.[12] Except on Fridays, when he was scribe, he also joined the common work. Isaac turned his hands to whatever needed doing.

In the year 1837, for instance, the year he wrote the Autobiography in Verse, he also wrote the Domestic Journal, one of his daily tasks from 1834 to 1865, started a diary for remarks he did not wish to record in "more public journals," built a sounding board for the meetinghouse, calculated the hours of work the Church Family lost to illness, death, and funerals at 1,750 days, replastered the shoe shop ceiling (a "nasty job"), oversaw cutting timber for the new wood house and supervised the raising of it, worked on the road, made a clock for the Second Family, taught singing, and turned out with the other brethren for milking cows, haying, and cutting corn stalks. He tinned the meetinghouse roof, nailed rafters, shingled the wood house roof, gathered information about Watervliet's visions, and wrote up his findings. He tailored, as well, keeping two hundred men and boys clothed winter and summer.[13] And even though he had help, he felt the pressure of responsibility for bringing many projects to fruition.

Why did Isaac do so much? Several factors account for his workload. All Shakers expected to work from dawn almost until bedtime. Furthermore, versatility was an economic necessity. In this modern age of specialization, it is hard to imagine the many skills that nineteenth-century men in rural society had to master. Many farmers did a little of everything.[14] In that respect, the New Lebanon Shakers resembled other Yankees. Even so, versatility does not have to create a heavy workload. Isaac's sense of duty, however, made it hard for him to decline an assignment. He could not make the Elders understand he was overloaded. Also, he was a perfectionist. His neat handwriting makes most of his journals a pleasure to read. The tiny rosewood case he made for his music pen was precisely cut and finished satin smooth. His meticulous, even picky, habits meant that each job might take more time than anticipated.

Isaac Newton Youngs also created additional work for himself through his writing. He wrote at least four thousand manuscript pages, and that total does not include the sacred writings of the 1840s. "I have written journals a good many years, beginning in the year 1815," he reported. "I wrote 14 volumes of general & religious matters—also wrote the Domestic Family Journal since 1834—and more than a dozen various journals of my own labor, my journies . . . perhaps this is enough." [15] In addition to his desire to leave a trace of himself for posterity, Brother Isaac had good reason for putting pen to paper. "I spend much of my precious time, often out of my usual hours of sleep, writing to leave that which will shortly be of no use to me, but which I hope will edify those who follow after & be the means of encouraging them in the Gospel." From the afterlife, he hoped to "look thro the veil & see those on earth deriving a benefit" from his labors. He also wrote directly to "you," the reader. In his Personal Journal, he closed an entry, "So reader you have my history of the matter." [16] Isaac Newton Youngs hoped that others would gain from his words, but the time he spent writing exacerbated his overload.

Brother Isaac ratcheted up his workload in other ways, as well. He wanted conformity and order. Much of his temporal labor involved standardization, tailoring uniform clothing and making clocks to standardize time across the village. He also numbered rooms, as well as the furniture, chairs, and brooms that went in them, showing that he was, as Jerry Grant suggests, a compulsive categorizer. The numbering project increased efficiency and union and reduced conflict over borrowed or misplaced belongings. But it took time, as did his quantification tasks. For the census, he collected more information than the government required. He measured Shakers' heights. He weighed the East House cat. He studied the family's labor needs. He calculated the labor for getting the Church Family's firewood to be about 38 hours to a cord, including cutting, drawing, splitting, and hauling. Another year, he figured that cutting their 250 cords of wood took seventy-two ten-hour mandays. [17] He did not indicate that he was assigned to make those measurements, so he may have quantified firewood, Shakers, and cat to satisfy his own curiosity. And when he built conveniences such as the new teacher's desk, those boons soaked up time that Isaac could ill afford to give. [18]

Isaac's workshops showed his versatility and his commitment to order. In the autumn of 1846, a Harvard Shaker named Daniel Myrick visited New Lebanon. In his trip journal, he described Isaac's two spaces in the brick brethren's shop. First, he saw the tailors' room, where he remarked on Isaac's "curious contrivance for a tailor's seat." Isaac, who had sciatica, probably designed the seat for his own comfort. To Myrick, Isaac's other workplace was also revealing.

> After a little stop here [in the tailors' shop] he goes with us to the south garret where he does all kinds of curious work. Here was the greatest variety of tools I ever saw in one shop. He had a pretty little lathe where he turned buttons and he showed us how he did it. He has also a soldering furnace. Notwithstanding his various tools and his varied work, everything was in as perfect order as tho but one kind of business was done.[19]

This description of Isaac's workplaces is particularly significant. Though he was in the tailors' shop when Myrick arrived, Isaac took the visitor upstairs to his mechanic's shop. Isaac was not so much leading a tour of his shop as showing it off—evidence, perhaps, of his pride in his work. Furthermore, his tools—more than Myrick had ever seen in one shop—provided evidence of Brother Isaac's versatility. They also suggest that Isaac had slipped from Mother Lucy's standards. In 1820, when she raged against superfluities, he had written, "I would be glad some times more freely to enjoy things that are useful . . . especially in the mechanics' line."[20] By 1846, he may have acquired all that he wanted. Myrick's comment on the number of tools suggests that Isaac owned many more than other brethren had, and his comment about neatness, which he did not mention in other shops, suggests that Isaac was measurably neater than his peers.

Button making illustrates how Shaker thrift and Isaac's perfectionism added to his workload. Rather than purchase buttons from the world, Believers made their own. In May 1820, the Church Family made nearly 28,000 buttons, and that spring Isaac wrote, "I have work enough to do."[21] When buttons were needed in 1835, Isaac was "very urgent" to get them made and set his apprentice Benjamin Gates to work "at the buttons night & day." The two brethren made two thousand dozen buttons of bone, coconut, and horn.[22] In 1840, Isaac described button making in detail. He spent a week fixing a machine to saw bone and more than another week sawing. He recorded the results. He could cut "the first side of the buttons 200 in 10 minutes & of the 2$^\text{d}$ side 200 in 15 minutes . . . drill 200 in 10 minutes & smooth 200 in 20 minutes, which was about 28 minutes to every 100."[23] In 1851 and 1853 he made buttons again. He could smooth and polish one per minute, "tho' pretty close work."[24] He tried to better his time even when he was competing only against the clock, applying industrial values of efficiency to his work almost as if he had to meet a quota or make a profit. Isaac took satisfaction in the work. Making buttons gave him a sense of accomplishment. He may have made buttons because he could turn out a superior product for less money, and he must have preferred the buttons he made to his own high standards. Thrift was a virtue and the savings benefited the society.

Isaac gave other jobs the same close attention. He often saved or made money for the society, but each responsibility added to his overload. Teaching is a case in point. Isaac began teaching school in 1816 with a short-term commitment to supervise five boys allowed to read in the evenings. By December 1817, his class had grown to forty-five boys aged four to twenty-two. The job gave him opportunities to buy books, but the drawbacks of teaching sometimes outweighed the benefits. In 1819 Isaac wrote, "I feel some releasement, and glad to have the time come when I need not be bound to attend to the school, for it is quite a burden, & a hard matter to give satisfaction either to [my] self or others." The next year he wrote, "Today there came eight of the world to see the school, to see if we brought up our children in ignorance as they had heard reported." The state school inspectors had also visited. Even though Isaac noted, "they appeared well satisfied," he felt pressured to make the school a success. And he had to avoid ideological straying. "I intend that as far as it depends upon me," he wrote, "my learning shall not be a snare to me, or that the pursuit of it shall not [lead] me astray from my duty." [25] Education had to benefit the Shakers; knowledge was a means to an end, not a goal in itself. Furthermore, teaching incurred additional problems.

> I feel some straitened in my conduct, [Isaac wrote,] lest others mar[k] me pretty close, and I betray some marks of exaltedness, or lest I take delight in being some thing, or striving to be greater. . . . I labour to keep [my] place, and not feel or act above the others on account of any of my activities. . . . The Elders tell me sometimes that [I] have so many abilities & have so good understanding & faith that I must expect some buffetings and trials, lest I be exalted. [26]

A teacher, by virtue of his own authority in the classroom, provoked jealousy among students only a few years younger than he. Being elevated meant paying a price for achievement.

Isaac Newton Youngs, however, put his learning to good use. In 1820 he and three others received teaching certificates from the state of New York; their certification meant that the Shakers could receive public monies for their school. The school inspectors acknowledged the Shaker school was "equal if not superior to any they ever saw of common schools." Brother Isaac appreciated the state's validation of Shaker education, though the Shakers' public school brought them closer to the world's people. "I do not wish to attract the world among us by our school . . . yet, for our honour & the honour of the gos[pel] I wish to have the world see cause of commending us, & I think it is as right for us to have our school money, as to take money for our prod[ucts] or manufacture." [27] Isaac wanted the Shaker school's quality recognized just as the excellence of Shaker seeds and chairs were admired. And the school was profitable when the state paid them for educating children. In fact, revenue may have driven school certification.

Teaching led to more work, including the job as master builder of the new schoolhouse in 1839, a four-month assignment that overlapped his busy season in the tailor's shop. Moreover, children created work beyond the school. After a trip to Watervliet, Isaac wrote,

> There were a number of children & youth there, whom I viewed with pity, knowing what they must yet go thro' if they ever kept the way of God, and much more, if they did not. I perceived some of the children there had a hard row to go in. And I felt sorry in behalf of the children, that their . . . government was not such as might be desired. And where there is not a regular, firm government, and such as will attract [the] love and faith of children, it . . . gives but little encouragement for a boy that has a bad disposition to try to reform.

Some children were hopeless, such as the small arsonist who set fire to the Second house "for the sake of seeing it burnt," or the boy "more fit for the company of pirates than here," both expelled without regret. A boy might be redeemable, or not. "When I look at the young," Isaac wrote, "& consider that these are they who must come forward & stand as the Church of God, when those who are now advanced in years are gone off the stage, I cannot forbear thinking of the serious consequences." Good Believers had to have "the fruits of <u>righteousness</u>, <u>peace</u>, <u>humility</u>, <u>conformity</u>, <u>brotherly love</u>, <u>simplicity</u>, <u>industry</u> . . . <u>cleanliness</u>, having a feeling to be <u>helpful</u>, and not make unnecessary labor or trouble for others." Unfortunately, many children lacked those qualities. Their disrespect was distressing. Some boys hung around the shop and argued when told to leave. "Such, if they harbor such a spirit, & grow up in it, will be a trouble wherever they go & will many times blast the fruit of a good spirit [in] others." [28] Isaac himself had been a forward youth and often in trouble, but when challenged, he had gone along with the gift. The new generation, however, seemed less tractable.

Thus, youthful misbehavior prompted another job. In 1823, Isaac Newton Youngs, Rufus Bishop, and Garret Lawrence wrote *A Juvenile Monitor: containing instructions for youth and children; pointing out ill manners and showing them how to behave in the various conditions of childhood and youth.* The first edition included twenty pages of admonitions, with Shakers' need for conformity, humility, and obedience evident on every page. "Never play mean, dirty tricks," the brethren advised. When in company, they wrote, "Be careful not to talk too loud, nor too much." Cleanliness is important because "filthiness of person and purity of mind can never agree." They addressed table manners. "It shows low breeding and selfishness," the brethren commented, "to pick out the best of the victuals." Scratching, picking the nose, ears, or teeth, belching, or smacking the lips were also impolite. Eavesdropping, prying into others' belongings, entering shops without permission, cutting words into furniture, and damaging books were prohibited. Each admonition reveals how Shaker-raised children misbehaved, from grubbiness to vandalism. If all Shaker children had been good, instruction would have been unnecessary.[29] But however valuable the message, writing a book was time-consuming.

Isaac's concern about children did not abate as he aged. In 1851, he began writing a lengthy tirade against boys' misbehavior: loitering, wasting time, questioning and rebellion, rowdyism, "laughing, cant phrases and silly byewords." He derided those who "want to read poetry, history, biography, romance—or any thing, if only it is <u>interesting</u>" and who waste lamplight in "broad day light . . . [when] they ought to be to work with their hands." Reading made boys lazy—a failing that the industrious brother could not abide.[30] Having sidestepped that trap, he felt he had to warn the next generation, an effort that added to his workload.

Brother Isaac volunteered for other jobs, as well. A prolific composer, he wrote dozens of marches, quick tunes, and shuffling tunes. His hymns and marches appear in many Shaker songbooks. His song "Gospel Orders" was a hit; it appeared in most manuscript hymnals.

> Gospel Orders I'll obey,
> Though a self denying way.
> Here I find a daily cross
> Which does save from sin and loss.

The lyrics cover "nature's galling chains," the need for "a spirit meek and mild, gospel works and pure desires" for the "meek and upright soul."[31]

Isaac Newton Youngs also tried to standardize Shaker music. In *Rudiments of Music,* published in 1833, he noted that some singers "crowd in trills & apoggiaturas, slides, shakes & slurrs as thick as they can get them!"[32] Frustrated when others did not meet his exacting standards, Isaac used his music book to adjust others' singing to his own aesthetic sense. Even though the changes were consistent with Shaker conformity, they were based on

Isaac's belief that his way was best. In 1840, he began corresponding with singers throughout the society to standardize music notation. According to Daniel Patterson, Brother Isaac's persistence and tact were responsible for their success.[33] But though music may have been a labor of love, it was also extra work when he was already busy.

The job did not end with the new music notation. When the Shakers published the next book, Isaac cut his own type, set it, and did the printing himself. Because "many little jobs & calls" hindered him, he wrote, it required "much perseverance in my situation to go thro with such an undertaking, having but little experience in printing & a poor press, poor supply of common types, &c."[34] But Isaac was willing to try almost anything, and that attribute, so useful to his community, increased his workload. In *A Short Abridgement of the Rules of Music,* he advocated "patience and perseverance" because "practice makes perfect." He specified how to sing the notes, with "a uniform & fair tone on the key note, without suffering [the] voice to run down, or alter the pitch . . . to give stability & correctness to the air of the notes."[35] Stability and correctness were metaphors for Isaac's Shaker life, but the underlying issue was perfectionism. He tried to standardize all things, and every job took precious time.

In the 1840s, Isaac's complaints increased with the "abundance of calls & jobs which naturally fall to me to do." He was ailing and annoyed by demands on his time. Late in 1843 he worked on a roof, and in January 1844, he wrote, "I have been confined a fortnight in the 2d house, with sciatica, which I suppose was bro't on me by working on the barn roof in cold windy weather."[36] The sciatica was the first of the physical complaints that impeded his work.

In 1846, when Isaac returned to the tailors' shop full time, his two apprentices did much of the work and all went well for some months.[37] But the village's supply of laborers and apprentices shrank when six decamped in 1847. In his private journal, he agonized,

> Is there none of the younger part that will abide & be good for something? Must they & will they all drop off, & prove abortive, like the rotten potatoes of late years? It is truly sickening & heart rending to see what a failure & destruction there is of late among us—how many have turned their backs, & those too who might have been of great use & a great help among us—those who filled important places & whose services were greatly needed.[38]

The society was hemorrhaging workers. In 1845, the New Lebanon Church Family had housed only nine young men aged seventeen to twenty-five, so the loss of six was a blow from which they would not soon recover. A farm succeeded (or failed) on the strength of its young men. Many young brethren departed before they were mature enough to ease the brethren's load. Who would care for Isaac and his contemporaries when they were too old to work? In this respect, the Shakers resembled other Yankees whose offspring abandoned them to seek their fortune elsewhere. Many feared that the "choice spirits" of the rising generation were leaving, draining away population and strength. Dissatisfied with northeastern farm life, young men scattered. By mid-century, the western Massachusetts minister Orville Dewey cried, "Is our life going out of us to enrich the great West?" It was indeed. The older population who stayed behind, including the New Lebanon Shakers, felt both fear and sorrow as the younger generation left.[39] If all Shaker youth went to the world, aged Believers could have ended up as destitute of elder care as some of the world's people.

Isaac continued to be overrun by work. "My time has been occupied in a very broken way," he wrote in 1853, "which I could not help, though very disagreeable to me." He added,

> O my time is so filled up with little choars & jobs that I am almost out of patience. It seems almost as if I bro't nothing to pass, and can hardly tell what I have done & still feel in a hurry & sometimes in a worry I have so much to do & cannot get time to do it—as soon as I get one choar done, another is wanted.[40]

By age sixty, Brother Isaac was overwhelmed by his workload, anxious, ill, rushed, and impatient with his own inability to meet all demands. But he confined his despair primarily to his personal journals. Perhaps he thought such complaints were best kept to himself. Even in old age, Brother Isaac still carved out a niche of privacy where he could. Perhaps if he had expressed his dissatisfaction to the Elders, he would have received relief in his temporal labor. His reticence may have been his undoing.

The Elders and Deacons could have hired out some of Isaac's work by purchasing buttons, clothing, and clocks from the world. But these things were not done, and the resulting workload wore down an aging brother. To ensure fiscal solvency, the Elder and Deacons hired as little outside help as possible, and because they did not pay competitive wages, they had trouble getting help. In 1837, when Isaac noted, "many thousands are thrown out of employment" and cheap labor was plentiful, the New Lebanon Church Family still was short on help. In the 1830s, local farmers paid from sixty-three cents to a dollar a day to farmhands who planted, spread manure, hoed, or harvested. The Shakers paid nineteen to thirty-eight cents a day. And though they did give one painter eighty-seven cents, most of their hired help did not receive premium pay.[41] By offering such low wages, the Shakers signaled that they were more concerned about solvency than they were about brethren's workloads. Rather than hire outside help, they overworked the faithful.

Another factor in Isaac's overwork was that some brethren were unwilling to volunteer in times of need. They, too, may have been overloaded. In October 1837, Isaac described the Church Family's backlog. Several problems had arisen simultaneously: their gristmill was running behind; the canal had to be re-dug; the wood house was unfinished, leaving their firewood uncovered; and farm labor was scarce. Everything had to be done before the Berkshire winter complicated outdoor work, and few brethren would work beyond their own concerns. Isaac complained that it was like pulling teeth to get help. Because he tried to accommodate all demands, he was shocked when other brethren did not. Reciprocity, fundamental to Shaker union, evidently suffered in times of stress.[42]

As a result, Brother Isaac felt harassed by the demands of some jobs, and in the early 1850s, none roused his indignation as much as repairing the Church Family's tin roofs. Tailoring also became a cross to bear. Both jobs nettled him; they were never-ending, so he could not get a sense of satisfaction from either one.[43] Isaac's work on the tin roofs shows how his skills, humility, and readiness to learn a new trade, along with the Elders' unwillingness to hire help, created a temporal nightmare for the dutiful brother. Rather than a source of satisfaction, tin work became a trial that made him almost despair of life.

Isaac Newton Youngs began working on tin roofs when the New Lebanon Church Family built the 1823 meetinghouse. Tin was fireproof and lighter than slate. When the first tin roof leaked in 1830, they had to replace it. The job took two months with the help of many hands. Unfortunately, a violent storm wrecked the roof. "A portion of the old tin not yet taken off, was exposed to the wind; & was blown up, rolled, twisted & torn in a terrible manner," Isaac recalled. "It cost us many days labor to get it taken apart, and prepared for use again—and considerable of it was wasted." Waste meant lost time and money, but tin remained the material of choice, and in 1831, Isaac readied more tin for the Church Family dwelling. Preparations took nearly two months and roofing employed four brethren for two weeks. But again the tin did not stay put. In December 1834, a piece blew off. Working when weather permitted, they were still trying to secure the tin in late January when another windstorm attacked the roof. Isaac pounded more nails into the tin and soldered the nail heads to stop leaks. In October 1837, Isaac and his apprentice, Benjamin Gates, were atop the meetinghouse again, nailing down the tin roof, "the first fastening not being sufficient." By then, Isaac had only one helper, and the burden rested most heavily on him. That burden was the Elders' doing. Professional tin-roofers were available nearby, but except for the herb house roof, installed by "Crego and Company," the Elders employed their own brethren. Domestic labor was cheaper than hired help. Furthermore, the Elders viewed tinning as a potential source of revenue, because they hired out Benjamin Gates to do roofs for the world's people.[44]

Isaac was not bothered by tin again until 1848, when he helped raise Watervliet's new meetinghouse and worked on its roof. By then, he detested the work. At Watervliet, he wrote a song called "Trying Day." The first line, "Lord, give me pow'r to stand in the trying day at hand, for I know tribulation is near," may have reflected his feelings about a day spent on a tin roof.[45] In 1850, despite the drawbacks of tin roofs, the Elders demanded more, so Isaac improved his tinning tools, bought new shears, and made a clinching machine. In September, he and Amos Stewart spent days repairing the meetinghouse roof. In 1851, they roofed the new wash house with forty-three hundred running feet of tin, all requiring soldering. They also began covering the office barn roof with tin. Tin roofs were installed on the dairy house, herb house, and privy. But tin continued to loosen in storms. A heavy northwest wind nearly blew off the tannery roof twice, raising it in places so it flapped up and down.[46]

In September 1855, Isaac was on the roof again. "I have this week been at work on the Great House roof, closely examining it, putting in some more nails where some had worked loose or other places where it seemed necessary, & soldering the heads," he wrote. "My object is to do this thoroughly at this time, to make it secure & prepare it for pai[nt]ing, to fill the joints, to fortify it against storms." He had the assistance of one apprentice, but the sixty-two-year-old brother needed more help. Isaac had not always borne the load of the tin roofs. "At the first I was merely a workman, without much knowledge or influence," he wrote. "Nicholas Bennet was foremost in the business & Joseph Hawkins took an active part & the work went on as we could best agree among us." But finally the tin roofs became Isaac's by default. He complained,

> There have been a good many (a dozen or more) different persons that have worked at it more or less, & but a few of them have ever borne any real burden or responsibility about it. They have nearly all died or absconded— & what are left have slipped out of it & left me to bear it. And now at this last labor, I feel as tho it was the closing of my labor about these tin roofs. I am getting too old and lame. This last job has nearly used me up. . . . I now resign the whole burden & responsibility—Somebody else must take it.[47]

Isaac wrote much more than appears here. Furthermore, at least one page was cut from his journal at this point, so either Isaac or someone else thought his comments disorderly enough to remove them from posterity's view. The remaining text shows that in 1855, the conscientious Shaker revolted against his temporal labor. That entry, however, was in his personal journal, not necessarily seen by anyone else.

Isaac's comments were not the worst part of his tinsmithing. By the time he finished soldering leaks on Church Family roofs in 1855, he had soldered hundreds, perhaps thousands of feet of tin roofing, and it had indeed nearly used him up. He had spent 120 days preparing tin, plus more than 230 days on the roof, and his humility in accepting roofing assignments had only brought him more tinsmithing work. Just a few days after he finished repairing the dwelling roof, he suffered "an attack of nervous weakness" and went to the infirmary. His health had been precarious for at least two years. His disposition had clouded over until he rarely recorded a sunny thought.

Brother Isaac was angry for several reasons. Those who made the decisions about tin roofs neither shared in the work nor provided him with adequate assistance. Also, because his peers had "slipped out" of roofing when he needed help, Isaac was angry about the loss of labor and by the failure of reciprocity essential to communal life. Furthermore, as a Shaker, though he did not expect to retire from work, he did expect his duties to lighten after he turned sixty, and he may have felt that working high above the ground was dangerous when he was in poor health. He could not get beyond his resentment. Two weeks after the outburst in his Personal Journal, he penned a second tirade, this time in the New Lebanon Church Family's Domestic Journal, which everyone consulted. "Here I wish to make some remarks concerning this roof," he wrote.

> I wish to have it understood by all concerned, [he continued, addressing in particular the Elders,] that I consider this last fixing of the roof, & painting it, to be the close of my labor & responsibility in behalf of those two tin roofs, the Meeting house and Great House. . . .
>
> After it became evident that the tin was not sufficiently secured, I bore a serious burden & suffered much about it in my feelings, until it was secured; nights & nights have I lain in bed, all of a sweat, with fear that it would blow off! And it was by close watch that I at several times detected it in beginning to work loose, in time to secure it by nailing. Thro' all this I have borne the chief burden & responsibility, & have spent much time on the roofs with no one to help me, except in the first work of preparing the tin & putting it on, in that there was first & last perhaps more than a dozen different hands.

These have all in one way & another dropped out of the concern, & left the whole burden to me.

Isaac had snapped. "I do now & hereby resign all care, duty, or responsibility therein, to whomever it may most properly belong," Isaac vowed. "I think I am getting too old, & have already borne a sufficient burden." [48]

Even though Brother Isaac resigned from roofing, he remained over-worked for the rest of his life, perhaps by his own doing. Good work resulted in a sense of personal satisfaction at a job well done and may have attracted attention and praise—rewards that could be equated with love. Furthermore, deliberate overwork is symptomatic of an obsessive-compulsive personality, including a drive for orderliness, perfection, and control—traits that Isaac Newton Youngs exhibited. Staying too busy can also help in coping with anxiety and depression, and by the time he was middle-aged, Isaac tended to look on the dark side of things and had to make an effort to be upbeat. Per-haps work served as a coping mechanism, as did the complaints he recorded in his journals. [49]

Regardless of the causes of Isaac's workload, his diligence served the society. Shaker ideals fostered perfectionism, which flowered in a man who craved order, union, and a settled home. Paradoxically, considering the Shaker ideal of humility, Isaac's drive for perfection must have been attended by ego. A bright, ambitious Believer might have used his versatility to lever-age mastery of a new trade that could give him more choice over how he spent his time, even when time ran short. And Isaac may have been as ambi-tious as Shaker society allowed. Despite their institutionalized views of hu-mility and obedience, some Shakers did want to shine. Even outsiders noticed that some brethren looked particularly forward. One visitor wrote of the New Lebanon brethren in 1847, "Most of them were gentle and mechanical looking persons; but here and there was one more imposing and ambitious looking figure, who seemed as if he should have passions, and whose exis-tence amid that monotonous, tame life we could not so readily account for." [50] Isaac Newton Youngs described himself as forward and his work showed that he wanted to excel. His versatility gave him confidence in ac-cepting new jobs, but the Shaker work ethic, his sense of duty, and his effort to humble himself meant that he could not decline work until he felt desper-ate. And the Elders continued to give more and more work to a gifted and competent individual until it became a burden. Worse yet, the tin roofs were not an isolated problem. Isaac's responsibility for tin roofs was mirrored in his primary trade of tailoring, and from tailoring he could not resign.

I very much begrutch the time I take at tayloring.

11 Tailoring

A Burden for Six Decades

ISAAC NEWTON YOUNGS'S complaints about work exposed interrelated tensions within Shaker society, including apostasy and the resulting labor shortage, issues of economics and separation from the world, and the personal ramifications of Shaker virtues such as obedience, humility, and duty. And though Isaac had resigned from roofing by 1855, he had another source of temporal despair: tailoring. Worse yet, the tailors' shop was often shorthanded.

Isaac Newton Youngs was apprenticed to master tailor Rufus Bishop when he entered the New Lebanon Church Family.[1] "I worked at it about 16 years (from 1804 to 1820,)" he recalled, "before I began to bear much burden about it, there being others older than I, who bore the chief burden or responsibility." In one sentence, Isaac twice called tailoring a burden. "I was put to the business before I was 11 years old," he wrote, "tho' disagreeable to my choice." He would have preferred different work; furthermore, the critical master tailor David Slosson made workdays a trial.[2] Isaac's trade was another cross to bear.

When Isaac began tailoring, the brethren wore blue for the Sabbath. "The men were dressed in blue coats, blue and white spotted pantaloons, and black waistcoats," a visitor wrote.[3] In 1805, those garments were their Sunday best, made in uniform patterns by village tailors. The Ministry set standards for Sabbath clothing, periodically decreeing new colors and designs.[4] Such regulation seems like something Isaac Newton Youngs would have appreciated as he tried to bring all things into Shaker order, but changing clothing standards created extra work for Shaker tailors.

Clothing Shakers was a tedious process. Every garment was hand-sewn. The simplest piece of clothing, a pair of drawers, took six hours to make. One pair of trousers required ten hours and a jacket, sixteen. A vest might have taken eight hours. Though sisters did the mending and may have made the brethren's shirts and work frocks (which did not appear in most New Lebanon tailors' journals), the tailors spent several thousand hours a year cutting, fitting, and constructing brethren's garments. In 1835, forty-three brethren in the Second Family alone required thirty jackets, four surtouts or overcoats, nine coats, twenty-five frocks, thirty pairs of trousers, and seven pairs of drawers, about sixteen hundred hours of work, or twenty-seven weeks' labor for one hand working sixty hours a week. In 1839, the construction of 316 garments for the village took more than thirty-six hundred hours' labor.[5]

Tailoring was attended by tribulations. Isaac found fitting difficult and was disconcerted when he could not perfect a garment. Furthermore, the work was never-ending, so he rarely felt a sense of completion. Another hardship was customer relations. In 1820, when Isaac took more responsibility for the tailor's shop, he was annoyed by complaints. The society's youth disliked the Shakers' antiquated fashions, and their criticism nettled the tailor. Long hours of hand labor gave Isaac ample opportunity for reflection, and he compiled a litany of discontent.

> When I see any dissatisfied about their clothes, their conveniences . . .
> showing dissatisfaction with some little thing [tha]t is not worth minding,
> complaining their garment is too long waisted [or] is not a nice color—they
> never can have like their equals—and as they [can]not complain of not
> having enough, they must dislike the quality or shape of something. Such
> as give way to such discontented feelings, and . . . ponder upon it & plainly
> show it in their deportment, [they are not likely to make] good Church
> members. . . . When I see those that are careless with the temporal blessings
> they possess, putting them to unsuitable use . . . and not [bei]ng cautious [to]
> save & preserve what they are blest with . . . and even willingly wear out,
> waste or destroy [some]thing because it does not suit them quite so well as
> they wish, I think [they] are inconsiderate . . . to cause unnecessary labor for
> others.

Isaac bristled at the destruction of his handiwork. And some individuals evidently tried to give away garments they disliked, so the Millennial Laws prohibited disposing of clothes unless done "in union with the Taylors."[6] Self-centered and inconsiderate behavior meant that the Shakers' investment of time in those children was worse than lost because they intentionally created work for already-overworked adults.

Despite his criticism of the society's youth, Isaac was dependent on boy apprentices for help in tailoring because the brethren's wardrobes were too much work for one person. As a master tailor, Isaac had the help of apprentices from fall until spring. In late September, after summer farm work was done, the tailors returned to the shop. Everyone who needed a garment was measured. Isaac cut the cloth. He assigned the easiest garments, drawers, to the newest apprentice to stitch together and gave harder jobs to those with more experience. After a break for winter school, they tried to finish summer clothing before warm weather, when they returned to farm work. Brother Isaac described how he selected one promising apprentice.

> Rufus Hinkley comes into the Taylors' shop, to learn the trade of me. I had a feeling to him the first time I saw him, & spoke to the Elders for him, if he should ever come here to Live. As far as we have seen of his conduct & appearance, I like him much, & now I hope to be prospered with him & h[ope] he will prosper & make a good believer, & a profitable Chh member.[7]

Isaac may have been recruited the same way. But most apprentices did not remain with the Shakers. Rufus Hinkley apostatized in August 1835; he had completed his apprenticeship and by age twenty-five wanted to make his own way in the world. Others followed. Isaac was distressed by the many assistants that he trained and lost. "This produces serious feelings," he wrote, "when I reflect back on the number that have been at this business since I began to bear some burden in it."

> Out of 15 that have worked at it . . . there is now none but myself left in the business. Those 15 were David Slosson, Rufus Bishop & myself, Rufus Hinkley, Joseph Tearney, Benjamin Gates, Cyrus Wilson, Charles Smith, Charles Knight, Kimbal & Charles Bruce, Norman Traver, Charles M. Sears, John Bruce & Wm. Pillow. Of these none are living among us but Benjamin & he is closely engaged at other business.

Older tailors died or were diverted to other jobs. Most of the younger men left the society by age twenty-five. As Isaac put it, "Children brot up among us, when they grow up to choose for themselves . . . turn their backs on the way of God." Despite the turnover, Isaac had at least one co-worker and one or two apprentices until 1853.[8] Only one apprentice, Benjamin Gates, remained with the Shakers. And when Brother Isaac had Benjamin's help, he rarely complained about tailoring. Thus their relationship is worth examination.

In 1821, three-year-old Benjamin Gates was the youngest boy in Isaac's school. He must have been a promising prospect, because Isaac chose him for a tailoring apprenticeship in November 1823. Benjamin's earliest letter, one of the few extant missives from Shaker children, went to "Beloved Brother Isaac" when the schoolmaster was recuperating at Watervliet in 1826.

I want to see you so very much that I am in hopes if you get any better you
will come home and see me so that I can stroke your head and kiss you once
more as I used to. I believe that the time seems longer to a little boy than it
does to a man for it feels like a great while to me now. But I mean to be a
good boy so that you will love me and take care [of] me when you come
home. . . . Sarah says if I do so well all the time you will love and bless me.
Be so kind as to give my love to William B. and to all the little boys and to
daddy Isaac every day. Farewell from little Benny.

Isaac had been gone for fifteen days and Benny missed him.[9] He loved Isaac as
a father, and he expected to be loved in return. And the boy was not shy with
physical caresses. Like other youngsters, Shaker-raised children needed love
and affection. Brother Isaac probably responded to the boy's sweet and loving ways. Indeed, Benjamin Gates may have been the son that Isaac Newton
Youngs would never have. And though some scholars suggest that Shakers
did not foster familial attachments, such was not the case with "little Benny"
and "daddy Isaac."[10] The boy looked up to Isaac not only as a father and
teacher but also as his master in the tailoring trade. In 1827, Benjamin Gates
began a journal that preserves evidence of his respect. On the title page, he
wrote his initials as Isaac wrote his own, creating a monogram that probably
required practice to perfect. As a nine-year-old, Benjamin deliberately and
consciously patterned himself after his mentor.

    Benjamin helped Isaac build a forge in the brethren's new brick shop gar-
ret where they did mechanical work. When they moved into the new shop, he
composed a verse that suggests a happy relationship:

> Joy to Isaac he this day
> From his old shop does move away
> And in his new one goes to work
> With many a whistle & many a jerk![11]

Benjamin's rhyming couplets resemble Isaac's own poetry—another example
of the apprentice imitating his master. The boy also went to Isaac's school,
helped make buttons and nails, and scoured the shop's new lathe. Sometimes
Isaac provided a special treat (beyond the sweets he bought for his students),
such as an overnight trip to the city—a rare diversion. "I go to Albany with
Isaac Youngs," Benjamin wrote, "& take much pleasure." Mostly, however,
they worked. The lad helped Isaac on the waterworks, in carpentry, and, at
age twelve, on tin roofs, suggesting that he was fearless or that he would do
anything for "daddy Isaac."[12]

    Though Isaac surely kept a close eye on his apprentices, he probably was not an exacting taskmaster who criticized as mercilessly as David Slosson had done. Benjamin Gates generally found the master tailor's company a pleasure. When Isaac was away in 1837, Benjamin wrote to Isaac, describing him as "good company, that felt zealous & interested in work, and had an anxious desire for my prosperity and welfare, all of which gave me much courage & caused the time to pass very happily with me. But the lonely lonesome hours that I have passed thro' in your absence," Benjamin wrote, "have not been very few I assure you." Signing himself the "lonesome apprentice," he closed with his best love and also sent love from the brethren and sisters in rooms No. 7 and 8.[13] Benjamin Gates's loving, even filial relationship with Isaac Newton Youngs shows some youngsters adopted fictive kin when natural relatives were unavailable. And Brother Isaac seemed relatively satisfied with life as long as Benjamin worked with him.

Tailoring, however, may not have been Benjamin's ideal job. In 1833, when he went back into the tailor shop after a summer at farm work, he wrote, "Rather dull times, to be so still." He felt the same way at summer's end in 1846. But by the 1840s, Benjamin Gates was a master tailor teaching the trade to the apprentices John Bruce, Cyrus Wilson, and Norman Traver.[14] Brother Benjamin was a blessing to Isaac. A competent tailor who would persist as a Believer was what the society—and Isaac Newton Youngs—needed.

Despite his good help, Isaac continued to resent the Ministry's wardrobe changes. In 1839, they considered new summer coats. And if so, should they be red, blue or drab? "There are different opinions about this," he wrote, "& the matter will be likely to rest for awhile." He noted, "I feel very much averse to changing colors & forms & introducing new things in clothing. It adds greatly to our affliction & expense."[15] Isaac's concerns reveal an underlying tension in the society between thriftily retaining old outfits emblematic of humility and separation from the world and satisfying those who craved change regardless of the work it piled on the tailors. And his complaints spiked with every modification of brethren's apparel.

Isaac was relieved when he was excused from tailoring. As the Era of Manifestations ebbed, he was set to work on the sacred writings. "After the year 1840, for about 6 years I was pretty much exempted from the business," he recalled, "& Benjamin Gates, my apprentice had the principle charge of the work." Though Isaac called the sacred writings "a long and wearisome work," he felt they had lasting value. The brethren's clothing, however, did not. Garments frayed, tore, and wore out. Buttons were lost. Boys destroyed or outgrew their apparel. Tailoring never ended. Unfortunately, Isaac's exemption from tailoring was not permanent and worse was to come.[16]

After Isaac returned to the tailors' shop, Benjamin Gates, evidently tired of tailoring, too, was transferred elsewhere. On September 14, 1846, he wrote, "This day I am entirely released from the Tayloring Business. It will be 23 long years the 15 of November next since I commenced learning the Trade." His use of the words "released," and "long years," suggest that Benjamin was glad to move on. Except for making an occasional garment for himself, he would never return to tailoring. For Isaac Newton Youngs, the loss was incalculable. But he did his duty in the tailors' shop, aided occasionally by Elders Rufus Bishop and Amos Stewart and a series of apprentices.[17]

By 1850, the New Lebanon Shakers clothed 216 men and boys, many of whom were hard on their apparel. In one fall season, Isaac cut 102 new winter garments, including 53 pairs of trousers, 18 jackets, 5 surtouts, and at least 7 coats, as well as 19 pairs of flannel drawers. Thriftily recycling fabric, he "cut over" (or cut from old clothes) 7 trousers, 7 surtouts, 3 jackets, and a coat. The next spring, he cut 145 summer trousers, plus vests, drawers, jackets, and coats as needed. As the master tailor, Isaac had to do the expert work of cutting and fitting, as well as making the most complicated outerwear. With tailoring as with button making, he quantified his time, and in one instance tracked the hours needed to make one surtout:

> 1st day, began at 8 oclock—Got all the stitching done & the facings done on in 5 hours. The button holes done in 2½ hours more: got the linings out, & the back & back lining sewed in ¾ths more. All by day light. Worked 7¾ hours.
> 2d day—Began at 9 ocl. Made the back, was two hours in doing the whole (reckoning the ¾ths last night;) Sewed the inside seams to Sleeves & linings. P.M. Put in the side pocket—put on the buttons, put in the linings & got the surtout tried on & trimmed by day light. Worked 6½ hours.
> 3d day. Began 8 ocl A.M. Put on the cuffs & sewed the outside seams to the sleeves & linings in just 1½ hour, and joined the surtout, & got it pressed before dinner. P.M. put in the pockets, got the collar on, and the linings joined. & bottoms trimmed by day light. Worked 7¾ hours.
> 4th day: began ½ past 7 ocl. Got ready to fit in the sleeves before noon. Finished about 4 ocl. Worked 7½ hours. . . . In all—29½ hours[18]

A surtout required four days to make after buttons were made, cloth was purchased, sponged and pressed, the recipient was measured and the garment, lining, and facings were cut. The exercise was useful only if he had to assess labor costs or set a standard for his help to meet.

Isaac was fortunate to have adequate assistance for several years after Benjamin Gates left tailoring. Both Charles Sears and John Bruce progressed in competence until they could make the most complex garments. Isaac still did most cutting, but the apprentices did so much of the other work that he was free to putter, making drawers, doing alterations, keeping records, and writing on Fridays as usual. In February 1851, he taught Charles how to cut, and Charles began cutting out the brethren's summer clothing. A week later, Isaac wrote, "This week I have cut out a white flannel waistcoat for Nicholas Bennet—chief of my time I have spent writing . . . lined some thimbles &c." The tailors began the summer jackets at the end of the month. In March, Isaac handed off the work to his subordinates and the sisters who stitched twenty-two pairs of trousers and thirty jackets. He fitted the brethren's jackets. In April, he cut out garments, brought his accounts up to date, and did "various jobs too small to mention." Most of the sewing was done by April, when his apprentices were diverted to outdoor work. Benjamin Gates came into the shop once or twice to cut clothes for himself. Amos Stewart made a pair of trousers and some drawers and Rufus Bishop made up the white waistcoat and four pairs of drawers, including Isaac's.[19]

The tailors' shop in early 1851 was a well-oiled machine, with Isaac feeding cloth into one end and greasing the cogs to keep it running smoothly, providing intermittent oversight to make sure that nothing stalled the works. With two apprentices or journeymen, the shop might have operated indefinitely without causing him concern. He might even have been able to turn the trade over to the next-junior tailor. But that was not to be.

A cascade of disaster began with Rufus Bishop's death in August 1852, a turning point for Isaac Newton Youngs. With that "heart-rending" news, Isaac lost his mentor as well as Elder Rufus's occasional help.[20] Bishop's death foreshadowed further problems. The year 1853 began with Benjamin Seth Youngs's injury in a fall. Benjamin never fully recovered, so Isaac had to assist his older brother with changes in the book he was writing. Isaac's time that spring was "very broken."[21] A third blow followed. In May 1853, Isaac's two well-trained apprentices, Charles Sears and John Bruce, both absconded within a week, leaving before they finished the brethren's summer clothes. Isaac was livid. In the Domestic Journal, he noted that the Shakers paid Bruce's railroad fare "to Satan." In his Private Journal, Isaac erupted, "O the generation of vipers! How can they escape the damnation of Hell—I am willing to see them suffer till they are humbled, till the sorrow they have made for others, falls on their own heads." He was especially irate because one of the "vipers" returned to entice others away. Isaac lamented, "If such wretched apostacy continues—what will become of Believers, when there is so little ingathering . . . seldom any one is willing to take the cross: & it really seems that it is impossible to save any children that we gather In—or but one of many." Isaac felt "borne down in sorrow & almost bereaved of hope." But he continued alone, cutting the brethren's summer trousers well into July.[22] His prospects were bleak.

> How the business will be supported I know not. . . . I do not feel able to do it all—and as to taking another boy to learn I feel but little courage for that; there seems to be but little hope of success with any boy. As for me, I feel I am getting too old to learn another boy. And it seems to me high time that I was entirely released from the business—there is more than I can do at other mechanical work.

With that, Isaac began a series of tirades about his labor problems. He tried to be philosophical. "I do not want to borrow needless trouble," he wrote. "I shall endeavor to be reconciled to whatever I find to be my duty—that is the way I have done so far & I expect always to do so. I can do the best I can while I live & when I am done with time, those who follow after may do as they can." [23] Isaac's emotional state was fragile, but his problems were real. By late 1853, he was sixty years old and pessimistic about getting an apprentice who would stick with the trade and stay with the Shakers. His best prospect, Amos Stewart, began tailoring at age forty-seven when he joined the Ministry in 1849, but other duties limited his work. So when Isaac's apprentices went "to Satan," their tasks fell into his lap. Losing his help was a terrible hardship; Isaac could not hope to divest himself of tailoring until he had a fully trained successor.

When Isaac returned to the tailor's shop that fall, he had too little assistance and no prospects of better times. He poured his worries onto the pages of his journal. "I can but feel sorrow & alarm at our precarious condition," Isaac wrote. "It seems we are driven to extremes of distress. There is scarce a brother among us who is not deficient in help & strength. More to do than we can do—scarcely any thing can be done in season. No help or hands to call out, without distress, at common jobs. None is willing to turn out & help, out of their immediate branch because they already have more than they can do, in proper season." Reciprocity, fundamental to the success of Shaker society, fell short. Shakers were not supposed to be overworked, but the aging Isaac Newton Youngs had more than he could do. He no longer joked about his workload; he agonized over it and blamed it on apostasy.

> Think once what should we have been now, as a society, if all that have been gathered in had been faithful & truly interested in the gospel! We should . . . [have] had abundance & to spare. . . . But alas! How different—a few determined souls persevere through trials and dark scenes—while the greater part drop away, like blasted fruit! [24]

Despite the reduced number of hands, the society's Elders and Deacons did not hire tailors or buy clothing, and Isaac's labor shortage continued. In his Tailor's Journal in September 1853, Isaac recorded his efforts to keep up, despite the departure of his apprentices.

> I made a beginning, alone, this morning to examine into the boys' clothes, to make the necessary changes, & ascertain what will need to be made for them. But where am I? How is it? Alas! Solitary, alone! Bereft of friend & assistance! Surrounded by a gang of 18 boys who wear & tear clothes sufficient for twice that number of men! All these are to be taken care of & done for, by somebody.

After "serious reflection," he calculated that the boys' clothes would take eight weeks' work. Though doing the work without help was a daunting prospect, when he finished inventorying their garments, he acknowledged, "I have done this day's work with much less confusion than generally, when I have had one or two to assist, whose manner & conduct only tended to keep the boys in a nettle & uproar." [25] Nonetheless, he continued,

> there is the cutting & making for all the rest of the Church. And who is going to do it? An echo answers, who?! As it is, all this tayloring for the males cannot be supported by male taylors. They who should have borne this burden & done the work, are gone, absconded, basely deserted!—and perhaps fiend-like are rejoicing at the sorrows they have left behind for others.

He had, he said, "tasted of sorrow & disappointment, in endeavoring to obtain some successor who could be relied on to take the burden of this business" before he was too old. Shaker-raised youth served out their apprenticeships according to their indentures, then left. "My temporal condition is very disheartening," he lamented. "I am now entirely alone in the tayloring. I am bound to it . . . no one else feels that it belongs to them. If I take a boy to learn, it is ten chances to one whether he abides & does well. It would be 5 or 6 years before he could bear the burden & release me." [26] He felt imprisoned in the tailor's shop and recorded his woes in every journal he kept.

Though Isaac had swallowed his frustrations for years, this time he must have made his feelings known. Or perhaps brethren without winter clothing complained to the Elders. With no one but Isaac left to do the cutting, "the burden of making fell on the sisters," he recalled a decade later, "& a sorrowful burden it was to them." Sisters had occasionally stitched some of the brethren's summer clothing but not their heavy outerwear. In 1853, however, the sisters were forced to help, and Isaac, dismayed, wrote in his Private Journal, "If the sisters take hold to help for the present—they are resolved not to gather the business upon themselves—there's the pinch. They are only possibly willing or consent to do what I cannot do. But the question is, how much can I do? That depends on how much I distress myself in undertaking to do."[27] Brother Isaac did not want to exploit the sisters any more than he wanted to overwork himself. But as Shaker brethren declined in number, no one was left to do the sewing but the sisters. Isaac was worried.

> The work must of course be done by somebody; and there seems no possible way but that it must fall upon the sisters, all that I do not do—& that is a sore trial to them. They feel as tho they are already drove out of reason with their work; & to think of taking the burden of the tayloring, that properly belongs to the brethren, feels more than they can patiently bear. The sisters as a body are extremely industrious—and to have to suffer under an unreasonable burden because of the evil doings or failure of others, feel hard.[28]

This passage is significant for its implications about relationships between Shaker men and women, as well as between Elders and the rank and file. Brother Isaac implied that he had discussed the subject with tailoresses who told him exactly what they thought. When he wrote, "they are already drove out of reason with their work," he may have been quoting them directly. Moreover, the tailoresses resisted filling the men's labor gap, revealing an unseemly (for Shakers) "us versus them" attitude, or "party spirit." Shaker union had limits. They realized that once they took the brethren's sewing, they would become permanently responsible for it. Nonetheless, they agreed to help. They may have empathized with Brother Isaac, who repaired machinery and made knitting needles and bodkins for them.

The passage also shows that the Elders and Deacons knew that Isaac had too much work but were unwilling to resort to other expedients, such as paying a tailor of the world's people to make the brethren's clothing. They could not hire an outsider for a service that required such close physical contact. Fitting trousers on Jonathan Wood, for instance, a tailor would have noticed evidence of his orchidectomy—an undesirable prospect with potentially devastating consequences. Even so, the brethren's sewing, if not the fitting, could have been hired out, and was not.

The Elders, Trustees, and Deacons did business with the world's people in many other lines of work. Though they believed that hired help was undesirable, they paid hundreds of dollars a year to outside workers for wood chopping, farm labor, tending the gristmill, painting, and building stone wall. And though the society must have been financially secure by the 1850s, they did not divert cash or personnel from their lucrative businesses into tailoring. Isaac understood that the profitable herb and seed business was also short-handed. Otherwise, he explained, "perhaps Benjamin [Gates] might take the burden of the tailoring . . . but as things are now, that seems out of the question." Profits took precedence. Even if Benjamin Gates had wanted to return to tailoring, his labor had to go to making money rather than keeping the brethren clad. Unfortunately, the pursuit of profit came at the expense of the faithful. So Isaac was stuck. He keenly felt the "disagreeable obligation," but he had to accept the sisters' help.[29] The Elders and Deacons, however, did take one significant step toward providing relief to those who made their clothes: they bought sewing machines. By autumn 1853, the machines were a benefit. But the sisters did not make brethren's garments until the Elders and Deacons ordered them to.[30]

In his usual methodical manner, Brother Isaac figured out how much time was needed to make each garment. "I think the following to be about correct for garments of medium size and quality," he wrote in his "Tailor's Journal." He estimated that a pair of drawers would take six hours, trousers ten, a jacket eighteen, a coat thirty-six, a surtout forty, and a great coat, forty-two hours. Though tracking the time required to make each garment was an exercise typical of Isaac Newton Youngs, it was also characteristic of industrial production among the world's people, where time standards were used to assess a worker's value. Isaac may have been establishing a baseline for comparing hand sewing to machine stitching, because he noted that the sewing machine saved the sisters 8¼ days when they made cloaks. He expected a surtout to take more time than the 29¼-hour garment he made in 1846, but in 1853 he had less help in the tailor's shop than he had in 1846. But Isaac later figured that machine stitching reduced construction time by a third, and simple sewing of straight seams was "nearly or ten times as fast as by hand." Even so, the sisters did not finish the brethren's winter garments until February, late in the winter season.[31]

The tailoresses may have protested the assignment to make brethren's clothing by taking their time to do the work. They had little free time, themselves, and perhaps they balked at sewing the men's heavy garments, which had previously been considered the brethren's responsibility. The men may have grumbled, but a garment received late was better than none at all. And none of them volunteered to help with tailoring. Brethren were overworked, as well, and were not inclined to sew as long as the sisters could be induced to do it.

Though the Elders did help by buying sewing machines and assigning sewing to the sisters, they were less helpful in another respect. They changed the color of the brethren's Sabbath uniform again. In January 1855 Isaac wrote,

> Cut out three fine blue broadcloth jackets. . . . You may think strange of this, since it was decided some years ago, never to have any more Blue jackets! But the Rulers of the land of Zion have repealed the decision & concluded to have Blue jackets again, which of course pleases the fancy of many—but I guess it won't fill the money-purse much nor make any less labor.

As had been his habit for decades, Isaac derided the Ministry for wasting money and creating work. Furthermore, cravings for new fashions were proliferating. In July 1855, Isaac cut out trousers of bought linen and sniped that when one brother learned another had a pair, the first also wanted something very nice. Isaac exclaimed, "Such are the freaks of fancy!" Like new blue jackets, the bought-linen trousers incurred expense and extra labor. But Isaac was not above making a pointed reference to himself because he noted, "I cut over an old blue jacket for my self—INY—indeed!" Fortunately, the tailoresses remained helpful. Isaac praised them for making drugget trousers, coats, and jackets. "They are all certainly very worthy of credit, for their faithfulness & industry," he wrote.[32]

In 1855, Isaac was sick on and off all year. In September, after he resigned from roofing, he resumed tailoring. In late October, he complained that there was "so much to do & so many calls here & there" that he could not work steadily at anything. He wrote,

> Very much crowded with work—enough to discourage us. I do not know how the work is going to be done. Those that are able and <u>know how</u> to bear a burden are very scarce. Every one feels as if he, or she, has twice as much to do as they are able to. So many have died—so many gone off—so many too young & so many too old to bear much burden in work.[33]

Many Believers were overworked, the result of dropping membership. The Elders continued to overload Isaac, who expressed his increasing desperation about tailoring.

> And what seems strange is that it seems hard to make any one take the hint of the state of the work. There is so much to do that requires all the strength to do it, and those in care seem not to realize it; they almost think it strange if I am not out at gathering apples &c. They seem insensible of what confusion will follow if the work is not done soon. I never met with such a time of

affliction about my work. O I hope these matters are not going to grow worse as I grow older, if they do, farewell to peace & comfort.

The Elders and Deacons were men in their thirties and forties whose perceptions of Isaac's workload evidently did not match his perception of overwork. Brother Isaac was unable to make them understand that he could not keep up with measuring, cutting, and fitting the brethren's clothes even with the sisters' help in sewing. The trials of tailoring worsened as he aged. Isaac would not have a comfortable retirement. In the nineteenth century, most people worked until they wore out, but they expected their workload to diminish in old age as the younger generation took over. The idea was thoroughly ingrained in Americans' worldview; they assumed that the aged had "old heads to contrive and devise," while younger hands did the physical labor. But too few young hands were available to carry Isaac's burdens.[34]

Isaac had a break from tailoring in November 1855, when he went to Albany to shop. His wistful description of wandering freely in the library after he finished his errands is a poignant reminder that he still appreciated books and learning even though he had willingly limited his opportunities for more education and had helped purge the Church Family's books.

> I went awhile to the state library, free for the public—looked round—and was much edified with the wonderful collection of books, maps, &c—much art & expense is displayed there. Any one can look around, or read what he pleases—by only calling for what book he wants. I sat & talked awhile with the Librarian, & then came on to the RailRoad office—and among the rest, saw a ludicrous scrape, of a drunken fellow that took some chestnuts from a pedler's stand and tried to get them into his pocket![35]

Isaac was well entertained by the time he left Albany, not only by the state library but also by the drunken shoplifter. Such diversions were all the more remarkable because they were not Shaker. They symbolized both the drawbacks and the benefits of Shaker society, the loss as well as the gain.

Isaac was in no rush to return home. He rode the train to Pittsfield, Massachusetts, where he stayed overnight with John Campbell, who "was extremely kind & had very good accommodations & his wife was very kind." After breakfast, his host knelt and prayed—an act of piety rare among the world's people who hosted him. The hospitality was pleasant and satisfying, and Isaac was not rushed or harried.[36] Beset by the Church Family's demands, he appreciated the kindness he received from the world's people, including the librarian and the Campbells. His "settl'd home" was not the haven it once had been.

By the time Isaac returned to the Church Family, he had stretched what was ordinarily an overnight trip into four days away from home and work. Whether his delayed return was a deliberate and therefore disorderly effort to avoid work or a sanctioned respite for the worn-out old tailor, somehow he achieved the desired result. Later that fall, whether because of Isaac's health or because winter garments were not ready when the brethren needed them, the Elders belatedly realized the state of the tailoring business and assigned him a new apprentice. "Horatio Stone came into the taylor's shop to learn the trade," Isaac reported and added, "I hope & trust he will prosper here better than most of those who have heretofore been here." [37] Even though it would take years of training before the apprentice could take over, Isaac was heartened.

The work proceeded. Isaac measured, cut, and fitted while Horatio and the sisters sewed. Then Isaac pressed the garments and made the final adjustments. But despite the help, he felt "Very much drove to keep the work along, to cut out & fix, as fast as wanted." He was "very much <u>here</u> & <u>there</u>" about his work. In December he wrote, "And so ends the Old worn out, dreary year of 1855." He felt old, worn, and dreary himself. He also noted "the same old round of drive-drive at work—I have so many ways to go and am so unsteady about my work that it seems to me that I bring to pass but little." [38] But that could not be helped. Precarious health was interfering with Isaac's labor. Like one of his clocks, he was losing time as he ran down.

Isaac was ill through 1856, and his condition undoubtedly interfered with his work. The perfectionist who timed his own labor was frustrated at his inability to do all that was needed. And in 1857, he was again annoyed by change. The Elders, he reported, had just introduced "fine fulled cloth blue jackets for Sabbath day—a great expense." He reiterated: "I think we make ourselves much unnecessary labor and expense by being so nice . . . & by having so many sorts & so frequently changing our uniform." Furthermore, he wrote,

> Also this year we have abandoned our cotton striped trowsers, & substituted worsted, & for that reason have to get something for the boys. We have tried alpaca for this year but that is too outrageous frail & wretched bad to make—and so we keep tormenting ourselves just to please the fancy when other things in which we suffer shame & disgrace, have to go without time & means to keep them in order—as our farm fences & buildings.

Isaac was dismayed by the Elders' priorities, which favored superfluity over substance. In addition, the flimsy alpaca added work not only in the making but also in the maintenance of clothing. His peers' desire for nice clothing upset him, as well. "It seems impossible to satisfy that craving sense—wanting something different—nicer—something that someone else has," he wrote, "& if we get something very nice [then we] want something not so nice, to save the nicest." Isaac concluded, "My soul is many times vexed in me." He may have felt like a relic of Mother Lucy's beliefs, one voice crying for simplicity, humility, and conformity, while others promoted more worldly values. And uniforms were unsuccessful as a social statement if everyone wanted something better or different. Human nature seemed determined to undermine equality despite Shaker intentions. And finally, his comment about deteriorating buildings and fences suggests that the manpower shortage meant that Shakers could no longer maintain their infrastructure, which showed the same decrepitude that Isaac felt. In 1856, Benson Lossing wrote after a visit to the New Lebanon Church Family, "Order and Neatness there held high court with a majesty I had never before seen," but Isaac noticed the difference.[39]

By 1860, though Isaac did the measuring, Horatio Stone had taken over most of the tailoring. Isaac wrote, "He gradually came into the cutting and for two or three years [did] the principle part so as to release me considerably from the burden; and I have been fondly hoping that I should never have to bear much more burden about [it]: tho I have never, from first to last felt entirely free from a burden or concern in the matter."[40] Despite the lightened load, Isaac's health was so precarious that it took a toll on his work.

Brother Isaac's problems were multiplying and his record keeping shows his decline. In 1858, his entries in his tailor's journal dwindled. Journals that he began in neat, inked script deteriorated in the late 1850s. He must have noticed the change because he switched over to pencil. By 1860, however, some entries were faint, as if he lacked enough strength to press the pencil point down on the page. By the end of 1860, though his official writings remained neat, his book of tailor's measures was a mess. In 1862, fabrics were noted under the column for dates and his writing was even sloppier. Though the disorganization may have reflected his feelings about tailoring, his difficulty exceeded anything previously evident. Others noticed his decline. A Shaker Deaconess commented on Brother Isaac's feebleness in 1861, and word of his disability must have spread, because Isaac received a letter from a Shaker brother who tried to console him. Isaac suspected his time was short. By the time he finished his tailoring in May 1862, he thought he would not live long enough to return to the tailor's shop to do the following season's work, because he wrote in his tailor's journal, "Anon, Farewell—I.N.Y."[41]

He did, however, return to the shop. In early 1863, to Isaac's dismay, Horatio Stone was reassigned to be a herdsman. Isaac was left to "shoulder the pack, & tug along, as best I can!" He called it "the most trying cross I have ever met in my life, about my work, being nearly 70 years old & under bodily infirmity." By February, when Horatio was transferred, most of the brethren's winter clothes must have been finished, but summer clothing should have been in production. Isaac had to forge on alone, measuring and cutting. "But I have never heretofore neglected anything I believed to be my duty because it was disagreeable," he wrote, "and I shall still try to do my duty." Isaac squared himself to the work, but he was bitter. "I have been bound, & felt bound to the business for nearly 59 years, with occasionally a spell of releasement," he wrote. "I have never felt free from it, well knowing that if all others failed, the burden would fall right on me. And so it has proved, to the present time." He continued, "It is true, it is designed for Elder Giles [Avery] to assist me in cutting, but as he has never learned the rules, it will take him some time to learn. . . . And even then I do not see how he can be relied on to take the whole charge of the business, consistent with his calling in the Ministry." Isaac explained, "I should feel very different, if I were young & in health." But he dreaded the work. Worse yet, the brethren's styles were changing again, "as to form, color & kind of cloth." He was confounded by such a decision. "This is very contrary to my judgment to introduce this additional expense," he wrote, "just now, in time of a lamentable war, when nearly everything is outrageous high priced." Brother Isaac did note that news of the Civil War had reached their peaceful village, but he wrote little of it.[42] He had more pressing personal concerns, and in 1863, tailoring was uppermost in his mind.

"We are slaving ourselves to please our fancy," he concluded. "If those who are the means of it, could bear it, it would seem more fair." Brother Isaac actually meant that he himself was being enslaved by the Elders' decisions, just as he had been with tin roofs. The change infuriated him not only because it meant additional work and expense for the society but also because fancy fabric showed a lack of humility. The new clothing offended him both spiritually and temporally. And it was easier for the Elders to decree the change than it was for others to carry it out, so he railed against that injustice. He also dreaded the work because he found it hard to fit anyone to his own standards. Considering his perfectionism, fitting must have been a trial in itself. Isaac's anger rose until he used language bordering on profanity.

I have been, for a little while past taking a little comfort, hoping that I had got pretty much released from the vexation of Tayloring, when lo! all of a sudden, I was requested to take hold of it again!! O Botheration, I cannot forbear exclaiming, Away with it, I can hardly consent to meddle with the

dirty business! I very much begrutch the time I take at tayloring, tor there
is more that naturally falls to me to do, and at which I have a better faculty
than tayloring.

By confining his pique to his journal, he remained outwardly in union but he
had to vent his frustrations. Then he resumed the humble tone that had followed his outbursts for forty years. "But still," he wrote, "I do not mean to be
rebellious if the general good requires me at tayloring. I am willing to do
what I can consistently. I have not long to live, & these . . . perplexities will
soon be past." [43] As usual, he did his duty. But he was so dispirited that he almost longed for death.

Isaac tailored through 1863, "quite out of health," cutting and fitting
forty garments, a fraction of his previous work. His strength ebbed, but he
carried on. "It is very contrary to my feelings to be bound to this business,"
he wrote. "But circumstances require that I should bear the burden a while
longer, if possible—so, for the general good, I am willing to try to do it. But,
the time is short that I shall be here, I think . . . but a few days or weeks??" [44]
He was old, tired, and overworked, and his emotional state was increasingly
precarious. By 1864, Brother Isaac was miserable, indeed. He dreaded death
less than tailoring. "Thankful shall I be when I get entirely free from it," he
wrote, "but what a sorrowful scene I shall have to pass, before that day
comes. O I dread it! Not <u>death</u> do I mean, but the sufferings. No one knows
my feelings, [and if they] could realize them, they would sympathize with me
more than they do." Brother Isaac was desperate. "O merciful Father," he
cried, "help us in the days of trial." He could only hope that God would grant
him more comfort than the Elders provided. The old tailor was weakening.
"O I feel as tho' I should never do much more," he observed in his taylor's
journal. "I can hardly write." Despite his anxiety and sorrow, he held fast to
his faith and closed, "Let each one strive to set a good example." [45]

Since 1853 Isaac had been slipping deeper into anxiety and depression.
Giles Avery may have gone into the tailor's shop as much to keep an eye on
the old tailor as to help him. By the spring of 1864, Isaac knew he would not
live much longer. "It is probable to me that I may never do much more cutting
in this shop," he wrote. "My health is gone, & it is not likely it will ever return. I suffer much from nervous distress." As he had done for several years,
Brother Isaac once again wrote "Farewell" in the tailor's journal, and that
was his last entry. [46] He slipped out of tailoring and was forever freed from the
work he hated.

I think it is about time to call myself an old man.

12 The Final Years, 1853–1865

THE LAST YEARS of Isaac Newton Youngs's life were not a time of ease and comfort, though age brought relief from some chores. On July 4, 1853, Isaac wrote, "This is my birth day—60 years old. I went to milking for the last time this morning. . . . I think it is about time to call myself an old man. How many years I shall have yet to live, I know not—but I hope what few I do live, I may spend in doing some good." Most Americans in the nineteenth century did not live to age sixty, the age when Yankee farmers and craftsmen often handed the farm or business over to a son in exchange for lifetime support. Even when they did not retire, such men could slow their pace as the younger generation shouldered the load. Isaac, however, did not have the option of retiring. He would work until he wore out.[1]

And Isaac was indeed wearing out, mentally as well as physically. His attitude plummeted in 1853; his worries extended beyond the trials of tailoring and working on tin roofs. He had ample cause for low spirits. In addition to his physical problems, his closest kin were declining and dying. In January 1853, his older brother, Benjamin Seth Youngs, was badly hurt. The day before Benjamin died in 1855, Isaac reported the death of another brother, Wilson Youngs, who had "lost his senses." His next-older brother had also become mentally unstable. "Henry Youngs is suffering infirmity," Isaac reported, "which affects his mental faculties, to which he has been subject more or less heretofore." And before Isaac's sister Elizabeth Youngs died, she suffered at least two strokes and became "somewhat insane." The family history of mental instability, seen earlier in Seth and Martha Youngs, extended into their children's generation, and that boded ill for Isaac.[2] The afflictions and deaths of his natural relatives bore him down. So too did the deaths of mentors and friends. Rufus Bishop was gone. David Rowley, a "beloved friend," who may have taught Isaac woodworking, died in 1855. "O it is a sorrowful thing," Isaac mourned, "to part with such a one."[3]

Though Isaac's outlook darkened in the 1850s, he was not always angry or depressed. He did have good days when he reported small pleasures or expressed satisfaction in his work. He delighted in a trip to New York to shop for sewing machines. When he finished his shopping, he strolled along Broadway, seeing the sights. He stopped at the offices of *Scientific American* and chatted with the editors, then visited James Rogers, a clock maker working on "a curious contrivance . . . a head fixed so that the cap of hair ran up once in a few minutes, clear of the head!" At home, Isaac probably enjoyed working on his toneometer, a device of his own invention for defining music scales, and a sundial for the medical garden. He made bone buttons, a satisfying job. He posted books and wrote on Fridays, as usual, and spent some summer weekdays haying. He mended spectacles and built a new button machine.[4] He still relished mechanical work and created new jobs on his own initiative.

Emotionally, however, Isaac was slipping. He had included an illuminating comment in an 1830 letter. "I will always look a little on the dark side," he wrote—and then he crossed it out, perhaps thinking pessimism was amiss.[5] By the 1850s, however, his tendency to look on the darker side seemed to overshadow his efforts at optimism. His anxiety appeared in small ways at first. For instance, he made an offhand comment in his journal about the river railroad on his trip to New York in June 1853. Though he thought the train a marvelous way to travel—all the way to the city in only three and a half hours—he added, "A very pleasant route, but it really seemed serious to think how small an accident would have landed us all in shocking destruction!"[6] He had recorded a similar fear on his trip to Ohio but such commentary did not proliferate until the 1850s. At the same time, his work anxieties increased. The number and extent of his fears, as well as the fury of his outbursts, were unprecedented. His darkening views marked a major change in his thought processes.[7]

Furthermore, a new emotion crept into his commentary. In April 1854, Isaac wrote a long assessment of the Elders' decision to tear down the old Second house. He inserted his usual disclaimer: "I do not pretend to decide in my feelings positively whether it is right or wrong to tear the building down." Then he added, "But still, were I to make no allowance for the opinions of others whose judgment may perhaps be better than mine, I should not think it right to do it." He elaborated with a scathing critique of the waste, expense, and inconvenience of the demolition. His assessment resembled what he had been saying about the Elders for forty years, but this time he incorporated something new. Isaac was saddened beyond reason at the destruction. "It has really seemed mournful to me this week to see & hear the destruction going on—tearing & rending—what a waste of stuff!" he wrote. He closed, "Farewell old 2d house, you are left unto us desolate . . . the spot where you stood looks solitary & bereft!"[8] Isaac's uncharacteristically mourning the loss of the building as an old friend shows that something was amiss. Perhaps he viewed the destruction of the old building as symbolic of his own deterioration. He knew he was wearing out, too. Health problems major and minor provoked him to prepare for death.

On his birthday in 1855, he wrote, "I am 62 years old today—feel myself approaching to the closing period of life. I want to be prepared for I know not what will come. I feel very anxious that when I leave this world, all my concerns may be in order & my work properly done." He chose two songs, "Vain World" and "Happy Change," to be sung at his funeral.[9] In one sense, choosing funeral hymns was characteristic of Isaac Newton Youngs, who prepared thoroughly and wanted to leave his work properly done. But it also heralded his increasingly morbid turn of mind. Death could indeed be a happy change if it ended suffering. The lyrics of "Happy Change" suggest that Isaac was ready to shed his aged body, cease his manual labor, drop his earthly cares, and let angels guide him to a peaceful realm beyond physical pain and suffering.[10] Isaac was ready to retire—not from work, but from life. His other choice, "Vain World," was a bitter goodbye.

> Farewell! Farewell! vain world farewell!
>   I find no rest in thee.
> Thy greatest pleasures form a hell
>   Too dark and sad for me.[11]

His apprentices' apostasy, tailoring, and tin roofs sapped the pleasure from his temporal life so that work, formerly a source of satisfaction, approached perdition. His world had become dark and sad, indeed.

Beyond work, Isaac had additional reasons for the downturn in his mood. He was increasingly infirm, literally afflicted from head to toe. As David Hackett Fischer explains, being old meant being racked by illness, living in physical misery with pain a constant companion. To paraphrase an early description of geriatric decline: the memory fell short; the brain ran dry; and the back began to bow. Teeth fell out; eyesight dimmed; hearing, appetite, and strength diminished. Even the sense of smell deteriorated. Legs stiffened until once-nimble limbs could barely creep along. Long life in the nineteenth century, according to Rev. Eliab Stone, was "not so properly called living, as dying a lingering death." [12] As Isaac deteriorated, he may well have anticipated death as a welcome relief from suffering.

A year-by-year examination of Isaac's infirmities shows how he declined. Physical illness was not the worst of his troubles. His fears proliferated with age. After reading about fires in 1855, he wrote, "I never felt so fearful—sensing the danger & dependence of poor mortals." This level of anxiety was unusual for Isaac, and he evidently realized it when he wrote that he had never felt so fearful. After 1853, fear stalked him until it shook his faith. "Where is our safety or hope," he wondered, "if we have no merciful God to protect us?" Such doubt was not typical until his mental health faltered. In late 1855, he was in the infirmary with a new malady, "an attack of nervous weakness." Giles Avery later wrote that Isaac had "a slow, wasting nervous consumption, which induced great mental depression." His illness included "fearful forebodings," which were already evident in his journals in 1855.[13] In the last decade of life, his anxiety overwhelmed him.

Springtime, which Brother Isaac usually enjoyed for the blooming fruit trees and greening fields, brought him more ill health. In March 1856, he "went to the infirmary to be doctored on account of a difficulty in [his] neck or throat." The physician treated him with a purgative, but ten days later Isaac wrote, "I feel dubious about my neck." A week later, still "some unwell," he took a purgative again. And on April first, he wrote, "I went to the infirmary to doctor some—my stomach being out of order & something seems to ail my neck or throat—I can hardly tell what—it seems like a kind of hardening or as tho there was something in my throat." He was in the infirmary a week but the problem continued.[14]

Furthermore, Isaac, who appreciated all the seasonal foods he noted in his journals—strawberries, asparagus, watermelon, new potatoes, apple pie, clams, oysters—could no longer enjoy a good meal. In addition to his throat problem, he had probably lost his appetite; when he returned from Albany in late 1855, he noted that he had a good appetite for breakfast, a fact not worth mentioning unless his appetite had been low.[15] His health was poor, but, because many were sick in the New Lebanon Shaker village in the spring of 1856, one old brother's illness was probably not conspicuous. Isaac was in and out of the infirmary for months. In August, he lamented,

> O I feel sorrowful reflections—my health is not very good—I feel drawing to a close. My days of suffering feel near, my life feels uncertain. I have a difficulty in my neck. If it continues to increase, it seems to me it must close my mortal career. I may be mistaken but I do not feel prepared to die—my work does not feel done. I want when I leave this world, to leave my work well done.

Brother Isaac had good reason to fear the throat obstruction that afflicted him for almost six months. His former roommate, Luther Copley, had suffocated in 1851 from a throat stoppage. Though Copley's death was probably caused by an allergy or asthma attack, Isaac could not have known whether he had the same problem or something more benign.[16]

Isaac also revealed a new obsession, a growing dread of fire. This fear was well grounded. Over the years many Shaker buildings had been burned, some by accident and others by arson.[17] In early 1856, another society lost eleven buildings to fire in one conflagration. The news shook Isaac's confidence in the Almighty. "My faith & dependence in God's protection is sorely tried," he wrote. He reasoned that God "could either have averted the calamity or he could not & he either could not or would not—which was it. If he would not, there must be a cause, & if he could not, where is our security? Why trust in God?"[18] For the second time, Brother Isaac expressed doubt, a startling change in his outlook.

By August 1856, Isaac's anxiety was compounded by chronic depression. His journal entries became increasingly cantankerous in harangues about wayward youth, apostates, tin roofs, and tailoring. Even though he felt overwhelmed, he remained concerned that he might die with some task left undone. Such worries were reasonable for a conscientious Believer, but Brother Isaac dwelled on them.

At the end of August 1856, Isaac wrote four pages of "sorrowful Reflections" in his journal, obsessing on all things negative, reiterating his concern about the work that might be left when he died and touching on his ill health and Shakers' failed evangelism. He dwelled on their inability to retain young Believers and the need to hire outsiders. He brooded over the Shakers' becoming extinct. He wrote a page about their losses by fire, concluding, "O the dread of fire is a fearful thing—I feel sometimes almost hourly as if I should hear the cry of fire!" His fears enlarged to encompass natural disasters. "I suffer much in my feelings from a sense of the continual jeopardy we are in, with respect to outward calamities of storms, winds, fires and floods, drought," Isaac wrote. "It really seems as tho' the protection of God is withdrawn from Believers in that line." For the third time, he expressed doubt in God's protection.

Focused on his fears, Isaac could not help himself. For sixty years his faith had been unshaken, but his growing anxiety about "the sorrows and afflictions, the uncertainty and dangers of human life" made him question God's beneficence. "One could take but little comfort in this state of existence," he wrote; he felt "sorrow of soul." But Isaac apparently had second thoughts about questioning God, for he added, "I feel no doubt or discouragement in my own soul about the gospel. I feel it is my treasure, and I feel an assurance of future happiness." Perhaps he wrote that passage to reaffirm his faith after expressing misgivings. And he knew he had made personal progress in his travel toward salvation. "I feel I have gained much victory over evil," he wrote, "& especially over the great ruling passion <u>lust</u>, for I feel that is pretty much gone & dead—so far as I know. My self will no doubt remains yet as an object for further victory." [19] At age sixty-three, the perfectionist knew that he remained imperfect.

Despite the downward spiral of his emotions, Isaac must have appeared outwardly sound. When Benson Lossing visited the New Lebanon Shakers in mid-August 1856, Brother Isaac accompanied him as he sketched the village. Isaac may even have posed for the images of a balding man with grey hair. Ordinarily, he would have been fascinated by Lossing's camera lucida, a device used to speed sketching. But he was so consumed by his own problems that he barely mentioned Lossing's visit in his journal. [20] The Elders who assigned Isaac to accompany the visitor must not have realized the extent of his problems or they probably would not have permitted him to attend a visitor.

Isaac was unwell throughout September 1856. The hardening in his neck had not abated and he had also become dizzy and faint, complaining of having to sit down and rest by the time he got to the fourth floor of the dwelling. "If I do not get relief," he wrote, "I am short for this world." He made no more entries in his Personal Journal that fall but noted in his tailor's journal that he was still sick. Accompanied by the village physician, Barnabas Hinkley, Isaac consulted doctors in nearby Pittsfield, Massachusetts, and also saw Dr. Charity Vance, from New York. But he did not find a cure. In early 1857, he wrote that he was "not very well—nowadays." By then, Isaac literally felt shackled by old age and bodily infirmity. He knew he would never recover. His pleasures were dwindling. He was approaching the living death of old age and dependency, the "overaged" time that could come at the very end of life, when, according to contemporary accounts, many dreaded outliving their usefulness and becoming a burden to their caregivers. [21] And he was slipping into the depression characteristic of the chronically ill.

In 1857 Isaac worked as his health permitted, repairing clocks, injection pipe, and a rain gauge, making lampshades and garter clasps, remodeling his clock tool box, and writing. In May, he cleaned out the back room of his shop, probably to spare his successor the work. He closed the entry with, "I think I shall never do it again." He was right. He was sinking further into a long decline. But despite his depression, he did not fear death. His poetry was almost cheerful about being released. On his sixty-fourth birthday, he wrote, "Time rolls away—Soon I shall go—From this world below!" But on New Year's Day 1858, he penned another verse that focused less on impending death than on hopes for a better year ahead and his thankfulness for past blessings.

> Another year I've lived to see—
> I hope a happy year twill be—
> But whether it be good or bad
> I'm thankful for the good I've had.[22]

Isaac may have been feeling better. He still had good days, and he began writing A Concise View of the Church of God and of Christ On Earth, his 516-page history of the Shaker church. Isaac had not lost his intellect, and the Elders probably would not have entrusted him with the job if he had seemed mentally impaired.[23]

In late May 1858, however, Isaac was sick and again alluded to his "nervous affections, which brings on a disconsolate, bad feeling—and makes the final scene of dissolution seem near." A week later, he still felt "in poor condition for work." His latest problem, he wrote, was that his nose was "affected with a bad humor." He added, "I cannot help fearing that it will be a great affliction to me," but, in an effort to be optimistic, he noted, "I hope for the better."[24]

Because Shakers viewed diligence as a virtue, the Elders probably intended for old Believers, as far as possible, to have some sort of regular labor until life ended. By 1858, however, Isaac was no longer able to do all of his work to his former high standard. Midway through the year, his handwriting in the office ledgers, which he had been keeping in a neat, even script since 1844, became increasingly sloppy, as did some of his tailoring records. The Elders, unwilling to put their financial records at risk, relieved him of the bookkeeping responsibility in 1859.[25] But he continued to keep other records in his precise script until just weeks before his death, suggesting that his sloppy writing may have reflected his attitude toward those jobs rather than his mental or physical state. He also continued to tailor, but he made time to repair old journals and to fix his song books, to leave them in good order. Always the perfectionist, he wanted to correct the poor writing in some, but he knew his time was short.[26] Isaac tried to be useful even though his productivity had slipped. But he expected to be dead within months, not years.

By 1859, the Elders must have grown concerned about the elderly brother, too, because they sent him to a spa at Saratoga Springs, New York, to regain his health.[27] But three weeks away brought no improvement. Isaac ended his Private Journal, a "history of afflictions," with the note, "I myself am bro't into a scene of sorrow. I am afflicted & confined with a lame or sore leg, and it is very probable that my days of liberty & health are about at an end, & a terrible scene of suffering awaits me. I must try to be resigned—and may God have mercy on me." His closing "Adieu" began a trend that continued until he died. For six years, he was so certain that the end was near that he finished some journal entries with a farewell and signed his name to ensure that posterity would know who penned the words. He was also worried that his liberty was about to end.[28] The prospect must have been daunting, even for an old Believer who had lived under strictures that most Yankees found oppressive. But he would not lose liberty because he was lame. Though prescient, that fear was premature.

Isaac's leg improved, but he was not cured of all that ailed him. His adieux in several journals show that he knew it himself. When the Elders saw that the Saratoga treatment had been as unsuccessful as the outside physicians Isaac consulted, they sent him on a tour of the eastern Shaker villages. In May 1860, Elder Daniel Crosman wrote to the Shaker villages at Harvard and Shirley, Massachusetts, to explain why they were sending Isaac Newton Youngs and Nathan Williams, whom he described as "two aged Brethren, one aged in years, & the other more so by infirmities of body & mind."

> And now with Br Isaac O dear me, it is a very hard case, can any thing be done to regulate the machinery & make it last a little longer, if some one can discover the defect & cause the wheels to move with regularity again, they would perform a miracle in the latter days equal to former times. But this we do not expect or look for to any great extent; a little change may render temporary relief, & this is all that can be reasonably be expected. We would write more, but you will probably be informed better by them than we could communicate in any other way.

Elder Daniel ended with a postscript, "You will please counsel or direct them in any matters you feel will be for the best; they have goodness, love & many other virtues, but may need your wisdom to direct." [29] Isaac spent two weeks touring the east with Nathan Williams, thirteen years his senior. In addition to the Shaker villages, they visited Boston, Portland, New Gloucester, and Poland Spring, going part of the way by water.[30] The Elders held little hope for a miracle of healing. The old brother was beyond repair. The wheels of his machinery ran with regularity only at intervals.

As Isaac wrapped up his church history in December 1860, he looked back over his life at New Lebanon and compared the changes in the village to the changes in its residents, again, as he had in 1854, equating the loss of old buildings to the death of old friends.

> Not a building remains as it was at the beginning of the present century; all have been rebuilt, reformed or repaired, or demolished. And so with respect to the <u>inhabitants</u>, the occupants of those buildings, they have passed away,

and there are scarcely any, (only three, I think) here in the Church now,
that were here sixty years ago! So also with respect to the ways & manners,
habits and practices of the people, old & young. This is too much the case,
insomuch that the uniformity of those of our profession, is not so well
maintained, as it should be.[31]

He continued to lament the attitude of the younger generation. Believers
ostensibly vowed to lead a simple life, but, "The sense is continually aspiring
after more," he grumbled, "becoming more & more tasty, about clothing,
and articles of fancy, the use of high colors, of paint, varnish, &c. perhaps
more than is virtuous or proper." [32]

By 1861, everyone saw that Isaac was failing. After he visited the Hancock, Massachusetts, Shaker village, one of the deaconesses wrote, "Br. Isaac
Youngs takes dinner & takes home with him 10 thimbles to silver line, perhaps the last he will ever do, for he is quite feeble." [33] The sister may well have
wondered whether she would ever get those thimbles back. Isaac's disabilities
were multiplying. Several months later, the decision was made to replace him
as scribe for the Domestic Journal.

> Time brings to pass many events and produces many changes [Isaac wrote].
> This is even the case with me. It is now upwards of 27 years since I began to
> keep this domestic journal. And now, since thro' sorrowful disappointment
> I have met a serious decline of my health by nervous debility, I begin to feel
> unable to keep a journal like this, & do it justice. I have therefore sought for
> one who is able & willing to relieve me of the burden, viz. Brother John
> Brown.

The phrase "I begin to feel unable" suggests that Isaac removed himself from
the position. So on his sixty-eighth birthday, he handed his pen to the new
scribe, John Brown, adding, "I heartily wish him much success, & that he may
succeed me in correctness, beauty of execution, & matter of edification." [34]

In December, however, Isaac resumed responsibility for that Journal. John
Brown wrote, "N.B. By reason of the complicated cares attending the seed
department, and other duties incumbent on me, I resign this Journal in favor
of our Beloved Bʳ Isaac, whose health has improved, & is better qualified for
the office." In a note following Brown's comment, Isaac wrote, "Inasmuch as
Brother John has _favored_ me with a resignation of this journal, I therefore in
favor of him again resume the task; how long I shall continue, time must determine, but most probably not long." [35] Isaac may have been characteristi-
cally dissatisfied with Brown's record keeping and might have asked to

resume the job. He worked almost to the end. A dutiful Believer could have done no less.

In 1862, Isaac Newton Youngs continued to tailor as well as keep the Domestic Journal. He also composed verses, one each for eleven months of the year. In the verses he used rhyme and meter in a way he had not tried before, suggesting that his physical and mental problems did not impair either his composition skills or his critical view. The poem for July, when many of the world's people visited, reflects his view of them.

> Fear not to toil, tho' fashion sneer,
> And brainless fops, with lily hands,
> Deep stain'd with guilt, urge their demands,
> Toil on & keep your conscience clear.[36]

Those were strong words for a man who admonished the society's youth to not make fun of strangers. But because he did not expect the visitors to read his words, he freely expressed opinions that would have been rude if spoken to their faces. Isaac's own hands were probably callused from decades of cutting and sewing, and his conscience was clear.

At the end of the year, Isaac wrote another verse that sums up his feelings about the settled home where he had lived for so long.

> If all you need & more beside
> Is gain'd where home with all its ties
> Has bound your heart in any wise
> Roam not abroad, but there abide.[37]

At that moment, Isaac was reasonably content. Fifty-five years of Shaker life at the New Lebanon Church Family had bound his heart there, and he was not inclined to stray. He was again comfortable in his settled home because Horatio Stone had lightened his workload enough to be bearable and had not yet been transferred elsewhere.

Age, however, continued to eat away at him. The following summer, on July 4, 1863, Brother Isaac wrote,

> This is my Birth-day, the most uncomfortable birth-day I ever had, owing to
> poor health. I have now arrived to the full age of Man, Three-score and
> ten. I see no object in my living longer, unless I can have my health: all I do,
> hereafter, good or bad, seems extra: but I must live out the time Providence
> allots to me, & try to do what good I can—which seems to me very
> little. —I.N.Y.[38]

Soon afterward, Isaac gave up the honor of setting the pitch during worship. In one of his hymnals he wrote a note next to the song "Gospel Treasure": "The last song I pitched. I.N.Y. July 19, 1863." Isaac Newton Youngs had been one of the society's leading singers for more than forty years, and in this venue, as in all others, he was faltering. His seventy-year-old voice had apparently grown undependable. A nineteenth-century observer wrote that an aged man lived "among the ghosts of his former pleasures," and such was the case with Brother Isaac. His friends were dead. His productivity had dropped until he could no longer take pride in his accomplishments. Aches and pains racked his body. His appetite was gone, and so was his excellent voice. The changes were demoralizing, but Isaac continued to plug away at his work. Most men of his time labored until "judged less able than ever they were," and so too did Isaac Newton Youngs.[39]

In 1863, the burden of tailoring once again fell on him because his apprentice was needed elsewhere. Isaac was chagrined, but he accepted the blow with resignation. "I begin to do a little at tayloring—but I am in such poor health I shall get along very slowly," he wrote. "It is very contrary to my feelings to be bound to this business . . . but circumstances require that I should bear the burden awhile longer, if possible—so, for the general good, I am willing to try to do it. . . . But the time is short that I shall be here, I think, but a few days or weeks?"[40]

Brother Isaac remained true to form despite his poor health. In February 1864, he tried gymnastics, hoping it would combat his weakness. "William Calver & others have adopted the practice for some time to promote muscular strength," Isaac wrote. "It is much recommended for this purpose." Expecting to see proof of the hypothesis of the experiment, Isaac noted, "Let us see. There is much said about it; some ridicule, and others think it valuable to promote health and strength." His increasingly sedentary life in old age, when he was exempted from physically active chores, had probably promoted loss of muscle mass, and his other ailments had sapped strength that he hoped to regain. It may be hard to imagine the elderly Shaker doing calisthenics, much less tumbling, but that exercise, now known to benefit mental health as well as physical well-being, may have brought him some relief.[41]

Word of Brother Isaac's decline spread. Though Isaac Newton Youngs had not advanced to the position of Elder, he nevertheless was an influential man, known and respected throughout the society. He had visited and taught tailoring at almost every Shaker village. Letters of encouragement assured him of his honored place among Believers. The messages were comforting, but not enough to ease Isaac's mind. He wrote,

> The solemn day is hastening on, when I shall be unable to do any more,
> when some other one will occupy my place—and that will be a day of
> tribulation & much affliction! & they will wish me back again—but
> thankful shall I be when I get entirely free from it. But what a sorrowful
> scene I shall have to pass, before that day comes. O I dread it! Not <u>death</u>
> do I mean, but the sufferings. No one knows my feelings. Could they
> realize them, they would sympathize with me more than they do.

To judge from Isaac's words, he complained to no one but his journals. But
that coping mechanism was increasingly difficult because he was so weak, he
could barely move his pen across the page. Moreover, despite the encouraging letters from other villages, he thought that no one in the New Lebanon
Church Family understood or cared about his problems. His sympathetic old
friends were long gone, and the Elders had removed his support in the tailor's
shop, undoubtedly indicating to Isaac that they lacked empathy. He may
have dreaded tailoring alone more than he feared his own final dissolution.[42]

"And besides all this," Isaac wrote in March 1864, "I am sick. I have
much nervous distress, so that I can hardly write." He penned his tirade
about tailoring that month as he worked on summer clothes. By April, he was
"putting things in order—poor writing—feel very unwell now days—I think
every day this may be the last I shall have my liberty. Solemn tho't." He suspected that if his nervousness continued to escalate, he would be confined, a
prospect he must have dreaded. He probably remembered Seth Babbit, an insane Harvard Shaker who had to be locked up. And Isaac must have known
Oliver Train, a New Lebanon Believer who was "crazy as a bear" and had to
be chased down on a stormy winter night, and Harriet Hosford, a Shaker sister so deranged that she had to be chained. Even though the Shakers tried to
be humane, they could not cure mental illness.[43]

In 1864 Isaac wrote in his Tailor's Journal that he believed it "very probable" that he would "never do much more cutting in this shop." "My health is
gone," he wrote, "& it is not likely it will ever return. I suffer much from nervous distress, & feel as if I was short for this world. . . . I don't <u>know</u>, but so
I feel." Isaac's anxiety spiked that year. His entries in the Domestic Journal
became increasingly fearful. He seemed to fixate on calamities to the exclu-
sion of all else and to see catastrophe everywhere. He collected newspaper accounts of natural disasters and fires and clipped a notice warning hunters not
to hunt until it rained because the woods were so dry. Brother Isaac's mind
was slipping away into regions dark and frightening. His fears grew until his
only solace was the thought that his suffering would end with death.[44] In August 1864, dementia set in.

> I am very much out of health—I have very strange and wonderful experience
> in the night—there seems to be two of me—I am rational and irrational!
> I am wide awake and fast asleep—and no mortal knows the sorrows and
> sufferings I undergo. O could I know why this is so. Some say it is all Hypo!
> Well, be it so; who cares what name is attached, if it really is a disease, if it is
> really painful, if it be forced involuntarily on the patient, then it is a reality
> and the sufferer should be pitied & given sympathy, according to its degree
> of suffering.[45]

Despite his illness, Isaac was rational enough to understand the principle of
perceived reality. He realized that it mattered little whether he was ill or
whether he suffered from hypochondria, as someone had suggested. Indeed,
he may have had episodes of suspected hypochondria in the past, if we are to
give credence to that comment. But by 1864, he was hallucinating and he
knew it. He may have fallen prey to the mental debility that afflicted his parents and most of his siblings.

Another cause of his dementia must be considered, as well: thirty years of
exposure to lead. He had spent decades soldering tin, working close enough
to inhale fumes from melting solder. Occupational health experts now know
that the respiratory system is the primary pathway for lead absorption from
on-the-job exposure. Once inhaled, lead accumulates; continuing exposure
means that it builds up in the body. At low levels of exposure, headaches and
personality changes, such as irritability and depression, may be the only signs
of toxicity. Chronic lead poisoning can cause difficulty in sleeping, muscle
cramps, joint or muscle pain, convulsions, and loss of appetite, as well as im-
pairing the nervous system and reducing sex drive.[46] Brother Isaac exhibited
most of those symptoms.

Isaac Newton Youngs soldered tin roofs and pipe from 1823 until 1855,
the year he wrote that he lost sleep worrying about the tin roofs blowing off.
He may have been anxious and losing sleep (as well as his temper) because he
had spent more than 230 days working on roofs for the dwelling and meetinghouse, absorbing enough lead to cause irritability, insomnia, and depression. The comment he made about the good breakfast he had during his trip
to Albany in late 1855 suggests that he may have lost his appetite, as well.[47]
Some of those symptoms might be considered normal for an old man, but
Isaac showed most of the signs of lead poisoning. Definite diagnosis is unlikely without testing bone fragments, and since the Youngs family had a history of insanity and suicide, degenerative disease in addition to lead exposure
could have caused Isaac's decline. The irony remains, however, that by doing
his duty on the tin roofs so conscientiously, he jeopardized his health. He may
have suspected as much himself by the time he resigned from roofing.

Isaac's debility brought one boon: he was relieved of his tailoring duties in 1864. But his long-anticipated release did presage the loss of his liberty, as he had feared. By late October, he was in such poor health that he spent most of his time in his quarters in the Church Family dwelling. "Br. Isaac Youngs, very low indeed," Giles Avery reported. "Keeps his room mostly, very nervous, has nervous paroxysms." Finally Isaac's anxiety overcame his reason. His last, irregularly written and blotty entry in the Domestic Journal in July 1865 reported no news of the society's daily life but instead recorded the details of a disaster, a tornado in Wisconsin and "Plague Panic" in Europe. The Elders had to transfer the journal back to John Brown, who noted, "Brother Isaac N. Youngs has closed his labors as Journalist, after a term of 31 years faithful service." Two days later, Isaac "fell down in a fit, on the floor."[48] The seizure or convulsion was the last report on his condition while he lived. He died less than a month later.

Some details of Brother Isaac's death, however, remain a mystery. Confined to his room, he was attended by a brother watching over him full-time. But that system failed. On the night of August 7, 1865, at age seventy-two, Isaac Newton Youngs died from a fall out of the fourth-floor window of the dwelling.[49] Deaconess Betsy Crosman provided the most complete report:

> Isaac Youngs leaped from the 4th story window in the dwelling house, & struck first on the door cap, then on the stone walk; he was taken up senseless, & breathed an hour & half. He sent his attendant to call up the physician, & while he was gone he took his flight. He had been nervous & weak a long time bordering on insanity.[50]

The Shakers had mixed opinions on whether Brother's Isaac's death was an accident or suicide. A third, though remote, possibility, never mentioned, is that his caretaker lost patience with the needs of the demented old brother and took out his frustration on Isaac, who either fled out the window or was pushed over the sill. A fourth possibility is that Isaac jumped not because he was suicidal but because he was afraid. Considering his fear of fire, if he suffered the delusion that the building was burning, he could have feared he could not escape from the fourth floor before flames roared up the stairwells; he might have preferred a fall to being burned alive.[51]

Suicide was not unusual among the Shakers or in the Youngs family. In his youth, Isaac viewed suicide as a matter between the individual and God. He wrote that one "should not be so much condemned merely for the crime of self murder in such a condition . . . for he certainly can have no prospects of ever having better times—his sin is but against himself and his God."[52] Brother Isaac knew he had no prospects of better times.

Furthermore, for someone whose identity was bound up in his work, the loss of productivity was a sore trial. Because Isaac's sense of accomplishment was inextricably intertwined with his many employments, he was surely borne down in sorrow when he could not be useful. Another elderly man of the same era wrote, "You have no idea what a dreadful thing it is to be laid aside as good for nothing," and Brother Isaac may have felt the same way. Shakers, including Isaac Newton Youngs, valued a man according to his productivity, and when that was gone, he might have felt dispossessed of his reason for being. Worse yet, he knew he was a drain on the society. After his friend Garret Lawrence died, Isaac had written, "It is remarkable how little trouble he has made for others." Isaac admired Garret's ability to continue to be useful as he declined. He did not want his own care to be a burden on the society to which he had devoted his life. And he was suffering emotionally and physically. Old age, with its succession of losses—health, friends, occupation—could become a time of "inexpressible loneliness and desolation," according to one observer.[53] And so it was for Isaac Newton Youngs.

By August 1865, Isaac may have felt as the anguished David did in Psalm 55: 4–6, "Oh, that I had wings like a dove! I would fly away and be at rest." The window was Isaac's only way out. He may have literally taken flight from his fears. Though he was "bordering on insanity," he could have summoned the nerve to take a leap of faith into the afterlife to end his own suffering and relieve the society of the burden of his care. When one sister wrote that Isaac "jumped out of the window and killed himself this morning," she implied that his fall was deliberate.[54] He had been ready to die for several years. At the end, despite his dementia, Isaac Newton Youngs may have outsmarted his caretaker by sending him on a spurious errand; left alone, Isaac could finish his earthly travel. Some might view his death as a failure on the part of those tasked with safeguarding the elderly. But the old brother's death was not necessarily a failure of vigilance. In such a case, perhaps a kindly caretaker, with love and understanding, could have stepped out of the room to allow the old brother the opportunity to end his own life. As Isaac might have said, it was a matter between him and God.

Giles Avery wrote, "At half past 2 oclock INY eloped from the Southeast window west garret & landed on the stone path fatally injuring himself. Survived one and a half hours." By using the word *eloped,* a term applied to apostates and runaways, Avery also implied that the act was deliberate. But in another journal, he wrote in the margin, "Terrible Accident," and added, "Dear Br. Isaac N. Youngs, now exceedingly demented, jumped out of a fourth story window, at the south end of the great central house," suggesting that the fall was both accidental and purposeful. Emmanuel Jones, the farm deacon, also recognized that Isaac was insane when he went out the window. The Ministry may have believed Isaac committed suicide but realized that the act was not the product of a rational mind, because they noted, "No reflections are cast upon the poor demented & faithful Parent in Zion; but he is loved and blest forever and ever." [55]

Elisha Blakeman, one of Isaac's protégés, wrote the eulogy. He drew together the many threads of Brother Isaac's life to immortalize his "gospel Parent." He described the tailor as "meek, merciful, humble, forgiving, faithful, kind and upright. A stranger to <u>slander</u>." Among Isaac's contributions, Brother Elisha listed "Journals, Letters, Essays, Hymns and anthems." In worship, Isaac "distinguished himself as worthy of imitation," Elisha wrote. "Beautiful and exact in exercise, fervent in support of every gift, and in each devotional performance, manifesting correct and unadulterated faith in our religious creed. Zealous and devoted in singing, in which for many years, he occupied the leading gift." Isaac was "cleanly in his manners, affable, polite and well bred; but never <u>aped</u> the worldly Fop."

Elisha Blakeman recognized that Isaac's standard was perfection and quoted the hymn "New Year's Thoughts" to remind his audience of Isaac's aspiration to "be good thro' out the year." He mentioned Isaac's "superior education" despite his limited opportunity for schooling. Elisha had attended Isaac's school beginning in 1827 and wrote, "Tho' I have no claims to favoritism, on his part, yet I have been so far an object of his interest and attention, that in him I found a Father and friend, and can rise up and call him blessed." Elisha also mentioned Isaac's history of the millennial church and gave accolades to his work during the Era of Manifestations.

> Our Br. distinguished himself, during the great revival, termed <u>Mother's Work</u>. He entered into the spirit of it, with heart, soul and body. Volumes were filled with long and precious messages; delivered thro' instruments from our heavenly parents, thro' no other medium than the memory of our Brother. Yea, it seemed incredible, that so much could have been preserved, with meager assistance, and grasping all that nothing be lost; the smallest song, did not escape his vigilant eye, and his industrious pen.

Elisha Blakeman was eloquent in describing Brother Isaac's work life; the Shakers recognized and appreciated his industry, versatility, and inventiveness.

> His mechanical genius was remarkable. In him was combined, <u>The Carpenter</u>, <u>Cabinet maker</u>, <u>Clock</u> and <u>Watch-maker</u>; which obligation he

filled to the last. He many years did the Tayloring; and when needed, could turn machinist, mason or any thing that could promote the general good. Very many of our little conveniences, which added so much to our domestic happiness, owe their origin to Br. Isaac. After the decease of his Preceptor: Seth Y. Wells, he [was] clerk and scribe in the Church, till his mental and physical system became so impaired by the cruel ravages of disease, as to render him unable to fill his place.

Furthermore, Brother Isaac left behind "a name commendable, a character irreproachable, and an example of Christian virtue." [56] Isaac himself might have quibbled with parts of that description but he surely would have enjoyed the praise. The rising generation of Shakers appreciated Isaac's conveniences, the products of his versatility, and his concern for their well-being. John Brown, who succeeded Isaac in keeping the New Lebanon Domestic Journal, described his death as "a momentous catastrophe," a fair assessment of the loss of such a valued and trusted individual. [57] Isaac Newton Youngs was a man defined by his work and his faith. He was an exemplary Shaker; his standard was perfection. In the end, the Shakers remembered him not for the human failings he had struggled to conquer but for the virtues he labored to cultivate.

I shall however leave a plain trace by my pen.

Conclusion

ISAAC NEWTON YOUNGS'S determination to leave a plain trace by his pen was a poignant undertaking for a celibate with no descendants to perpetuate his memory. He consciously preserved information for posterity. His critical view and his position as scribe gave him motive and opportunity to write prolifically for fifty years. More than four thousand manuscript pages were his legacy, adding breadth and depth to today's understanding of nineteenth-century Shakers. Brother Isaac's journals provide a detailed account of life in a Shaker village and the daily work of the brethren. They also recount the personal battles of a man who struggled against his own human nature to try to achieve perfection, who suffered the agony of overwork and the sorrow of apostasy among his fellow Shakers.

We can draw several conclusions from Brother Isaac's depiction of the New Lebanon Church Family. In many respects, Isaac probably resembled those of his peers who remained in community. Like other Shaker boys, he went to work and became proficient in his trade. He internalized religious ideals, struggling to bring his attitude in line with his community's expectations and sometimes falling short. He learned to channel his affection toward sanctioned recipients—other brethren. As an adult, he overcame lust to live celibate. Isaac Newton Youngs supported the society with his time and talents. Believers were his family, friends, church, and economic support.

Few brethren recorded their reasons for choosing a celibate communal life, but many who persisted as Shakers may have had similar reasons for staying. Isaac craved security and order, perhaps beyond the norm, but that was not his only reason to remain a Believer. By the time he was grown, he may have been so thoroughly indoctrinated with fear of the world, the flesh, and the devil that he would have found it difficult to leave. Isaac believed that apostates were doomed to perdition. But he had more immediate concerns than the state of his immortal soul. Isaac saw the world's effects on his apostate brother James, who came to beg old clothes from the Shakers after a few years as a worldling. And their mother's impoverished dependency in old age was a sharp contrast to the lifelong support she would have had as a Believer.

Isaac's non-Shaker kin lived in loneliness and want. Within his communal society, Isaac had much more economic security than they did outside. Furthermore, because the rest of his family were Shakers, he would have had no support system if he left, regardless of his ability to find work among the world's people in perilous economic times. For emotional, financial, and religious reasons, Isaac Newton Youngs had incentive to remain a Believer. He chose to live overworked in Shaker society rather than going to the world impoverished, alone and damned. He stated often that he was set on salvation and made a conscientious effort to adhere to his faith. To him, adhering to his belief was more important than the reasoning behind it. In that, he may have resembled many persisting Shakers.

In other ways Brother Isaac could not be considered representative of his peers; one Shaker life cannot be entirely emblematic of others. Isaac was very bright, even gifted; his contemporaries remarked on his genius. And though he was not an Elder, he worked alongside Elders and Ministry for much of his life. Despite (or perhaps because of) that proximity, he was remarkably rebellious and highly critical. Other brethren did not record decades of complaints for posterity. Neither did they divulge details of their lust or their overwork. In those respects, Isaac diverged from the norm. But without his complaints, we would not know that superfluities ebbed and flowed, or that early nineteenth-century Shaker standards of humility and simplicity mutated through painted carpets and unpainted milking stools. More important, his journals show that removing the outward or visible symbols of pride was easier than reducing the inner man to obedience and humility.

Thus Isaac's complaints are historically valuable because they reveal new facets of Shaker life, some of them disturbing. Believers had more than one cross to bear. The society did not necessarily accommodate the individual. Indeed, a communal society could not always do so and prosper. But certain aspects of Shaker policy, such as assigning a boy to a trade he disliked and keeping him in it throughout his life, could blight an individual's happiness. And though we have seen some ways in which the Elders gave a frustrated young brother latitude—in allowing him the privilege of a secondary trade, such as clockmaking, for instance, or by removing an overcritical roommate—they withheld other types of relief. The needs of one Believer were not necessarily congruent with the needs of the group, and the power relations in a supposedly egalitarian society were skewed in the Elders' favor. Thus the path to Shaker salvation was a bumpy one.

In his twenties, Isaac had by "choice and understanding renounced the flesh," because the Shakers held that if sex "could be properly regulated, all other social problems could be brought under control as well."[1] But suppressing sexuality created new problems for the society even as it reduced others. Celibacy undoubtedly promoted apostasy, which brought despair to persisting Believers who feared losing the support of a younger generation. That support was the foundation of the Shaker covenant signed by celibate Believers who lacked children to care for them in old age. If Shakers' supply of young Believers failed, they would ultimately have to depend on the world's people, a daunting prospect.

Among persisting Shakers, however, the tension between desire and discipline was evident in areas other than celibacy. For instance, in an effort to adopt the official view on education—that learning was a clog to the soul— Isaac Newton Youngs did not openly express his longing to expand his knowledge. Nonetheless, he wanted more, and that desire persisted long after his sexual lust was gone. Moreover, his desire for autonomy within the communal society created problems. Painting stools, making silver pens, and signing his work may have provoked the Ministry to issue edicts, even Millennial Laws, against such misdeeds. And when he decided not to turn over his personal record of the church orders after being told to do so, he contravened the Elders' command, just as he did when he kept his supply of red ink. Isaac also circumvented their authority by sending a letter without going through the proper channels for approval. And there is no telling how many other minor misbehaviors slipped past the Shakers' domestic surveillance. Those acts of defiance show how strongly Isaac felt about his autonomy. At the same time, Isaac Newton Youngs served his society by maintaining outward union with Believers. This is not to suggest that he was a hypocrite. On the contrary, when Mother Lucy asked for his opinion, he was honest to a fault. But every disorderly journal entry and each act of rebellion, as well as his submission to duty, offers insight into the interior life of a nineteenth-century Shaker not only because Brother Isaac had these problems but also because others must have dealt with similar issues. The fact that Isaac repeatedly set out anew and wrote two autobiographies shows that he periodically evaluated his situation. Other Shakers may have done the same, whether they put their thoughts on paper or not.

Beyond these aspects of the individual's life in Shaker society, Brother Isaac's writings raise questions about the New Lebanon Church Family's workings, such as how Elders were chosen. When Elder Rufus Bishop died, his position had to be filled. That might have been a logical time for the Ministry to make Isaac Newton Youngs an Elder. Mother Lucy hinted early on that she was grooming him for a position of higher authority; that possibility may have been under consideration when Isaac was in his twenties. Despite his youthful rebellion, he proved himself an intelligent, steady, versatile performer in the 1830s and 1840s. But he was not promoted. Though we may never know for certain, we can see several reasons why. Brother Isaac's ego was a problem. He was too critical to automatically accept the Elders' arbitrary or inconsistent edicts. He picked apart their decisions in journals open to their reading and revealed that he did not entirely respect their decisions in temporal matters as well as in theological reasoning.[2] In fact, the qualities that made him such a good historian—analytical ability, confidence in his ideas, and a critical eye—could have made it difficult for others to work with him. He was too much of a perfectionist for comfort. His faultfinding might have divided rather than united the Elders. His criticism (or those he criticized) may have blocked his promotion, because Isaac was passed over on twelve occasions when new Elders were appointed between 1821 and 1861. And if he had been promoted, who would have run the tailors' shop? When Rufus Bishop became an Elder in 1808, he turned over most of the day-to-day tailoring to the master tailor David Slosson. Brother Isaac had no one to replace him.[3]

Isaac Newton Youngs was valuable as a member of the rank and file. His diligence was as exemplary as Mother Ann might have wished. Isaac was so hardworking that he was remembered, even revered, for his many contributions. But overwork made him unhappy, and the Elders exacerbated his workload rather than alleviating it. Further research might show the extent of overwork among Shakers. The line between enough work and too much work may have been thin indeed, and Isaac was pushed over that line. He felt increasingly overwhelmed in old age and the help he received was often inadequate. The Elders surely did not set out to overwork anyone—keep them humble and busy, yes, but not harassed into their graves by endless calls and chores, stuck in never-ending jobs that they hated. That, however, was how Brother Isaac felt.

Isaac Newton Youngs' overload stemmed from at least six factors. The first was declining membership. His work increased as the older generation died off and were not replaced by younger Believers. The resulting labor shortage led to a second factor: brethren's unwillingness to help one another beyond their own line of work. Reciprocity suffered as the numbers of able-bodied brethren declined. Their unwillingness was significant, because it suggests that other brethren resisted the Elders' demands. Withholding labor has long been a form of protest, and when Brother Isaac resigned from a job, or when the brethren refused to help each other, they made significant statements. Balking was disorderly, disobedient, undutiful, assertive rather than humble, and contrary to union. But they balked anyway, and on more than one occasion. We have to wonder how many Believers felt as Isaac did, and if overwork was a factor in apostasy—another question for future research.

Other brethren, however, may not have been hounded by their own desire to do everything perfectly, so the third factor in Isaac Newton Youngs' overwork was his own perfectionism. He could not do all things to his own high standards in the time available, even when he worked into the usual hours for sleeping. A perfectionist pays a price for perfectionism. Every detail left undone is an accusation of duty unfulfilled.[4] The cost of perfectionism is frustration, which was often evident in Brother Isaac's writings. And depression could follow as the frustrated perfectionist realized that he could never quite reach his own high standards or meet all his goals. A fourth factor was also related to perfectionism: Isaac added to his own workload when he took too much on himself. Every job he created meant less peace of mind—unless those tasks served another purpose, as well. Perhaps work filled an emotional void. The many conveniences he created may have brought him attention and approval that served as a substitute for love. Or he may have drowned his anxieties in work, staying so busy that he did not have time to be fearful. And some jobs he initiated were exercises in standardization, order and control, which may provide a clue to his willingness to do them. Perhaps controlling what he could regulate helped reduce stress caused by forces beyond his control.

A fifth factor promoting Isaac's overwork was that the Shakers were not only a religious group with values of humility and obedience. They also ran businesses, and the world's standards of time and profit had seeped into the society by the 1840s—thus the proliferation of clocks. In Isaac's adulthood, the Elders spent as little money as possible on outside help. They diverted personnel (including the younger tailor Benjamin Gates) to revenue-producing enterprises and handed more and more tasks to other Believers until they said "Enough!" But Isaac seemed generally unable to decline assignments. Thus a final factor in Isaac's overwork was his commitment to meekness, duty, and humility, in which he was outwardly successful, if we are to judge by other Shakers' comments.[5] Such qualities, of course, worked for the society; a humble Believer was far more tractable than an assertive one, even though he complained in the privacy of his journal. (The Elders did not necessarily practice the humility they preached; acceptance of a leadership role, in fact, suggests humility foregone even in the doing of duty.) But Isaac tried to preserve the standard of reciprocity. No matter how much he complained in writing, he felt he had to acquiesce to work assignments because Shakers had to support one another if they were to fulfill their covenant. Only when Isaac resigned from tin roofing did he refuse to work, and in that case, he may have felt that his survival depended on it.

Fortunately, Brother Isaac's journal-writing served for many years as an outlet for his frustrations. His disorderly pen may have enabled him to live as a good Believer, but finally his poor health and emotional problems outweighed his pen's ability to compensate. His need for a coping mechanism, however, does raise the question of how other Believers dealt with the pressures of communal life. Surely other brethren and sisters had similar problems, and we know little about how individuals adjusted to their circumstances short of leaving the society. Further research might address that question.

We can, however, be thankful for the trace Isaac Newton Youngs left with his pen. If Shaker society had permitted open dissent rather than viewing dissent as a threat to order and union (which it certainly was), Brother Isaac's complaints, spoken aloud, might have vanished into thin air. Given the freedom to voice all his objections, he might have felt no need to record them. Thus issues repressed were preserved for future generations. And despite his grievances, Isaac Newton Youngs persisted as a Shaker, enduring faithful to the end.[6] Thanks to his candor, we can glimpse the problems with utopia as well as the realities of one Shaker life.

Notes

Abbreviations

In citations, the number immediately following the repository refers to the microfilm reel number and the document designation.

BA	Berkshire Athenaeum, Pittsfield, Massachusetts
BSY	Benjamin Seth Youngs (older brother of Isaac Newton Youngs)
GKL	Garret K. Lawrence
HSV	Hancock Shaker Village, Pittsfield, Massachusetts
INY	Isaac Newton Youngs
LC	Shaker Papers, Library of Congress, Washington, D.C.
MCA	Shaker Collection printed documents on microfiche, Western Reserve Historical Society
NYPL	New York Public Library, New York, New York
NYSL	New York State Library, Albany, New York
SM	Emma B. King Library, Shaker Museum, Old Chatham, New York
SYW	Seth Youngs Wells (first cousin of Isaac Newton Youngs)
WM	Edward Deming Andrews Memorial Shaker Collection, Winterthur Museum Library, Winterthur, Delaware
WRHS	Western Reserve Historical Society, Cleveland, Ohio

Preface

1. INY, Family and Meeting Journal (1815–23), LC 3:42.

2. Jerry Grant and Douglas Allen, *Shaker Furniture Makers* (Hanover, N.H.: Published for HSV by University Press of New England, 1989).

3. [INY et al.], Records Kept By Order of the Church (1780–1855), 157, December 1, 1852, NYPL 2:7.

4. Rachel Coffey pointed out scholars' inability to individuate Shakers in her talk on Sister Polly Reed, April 29, 2000, for the HSV exhibit "Seen and Received," Sharon Koomler, curator.

5. INY, Family and Meeting Journal, July 8 and 26, 1820 (Wright), January 16, 1823 (Slosson), October 7, 1819 (Cogswell), LC 3:42.

6. Grant and Allen, *Shaker Furniture Makers,* 51.

7. INY, Family and Meeting Journal, March 27, 1818, LC 3:42.

8. Ibid., April 7, 1821; Elizabeth Lovegrove, Journal on the Revival in the Church, May 31, 1827, WRHS 33, V:B-94.

9. Pitchfork: INY, Domestic Journal, August 9, 1836, NYSL 10; roof repair: INY, Personal Journal, September 7, 1855, WRHS 35, V:B-134.

10. Tender-heartedness: INY [and Rufus Bishop], Tour thro the States of Ohio and Kentucky, in the Summer of 1834, October 1, 1834, SM 141; horse: INY, Domestic Journal, October 15, 1842, NYSL 10.

11. Lovegrove, Journal, April 16, 1827, WRHS 33, V:B-93.

12. Benny Gates to INY, March 26, 1826, SM 9547 (with thanks to Jerry Grant for pointing out the trip journal and this letter); Elisha D. Blakeman, Eulogical to Brother Isaac N. Youngs, September 1866, 355–61, WRHS 30, V:B-21.

13. INY, Domestic Journal (1847–55), June 11, 1850, WRHS 32, V:B-70; INY, Family and Meeting Journal, October 6, 1817, and March 31, 1819, LC 3:42.

14. Child bribed with sweets [Medcalf]: INY [and Bishop], Tour, June 26, 1834; working late: INY, Family and Meeting Journal, April 27, 1817, LC 3:42; INY, Personal Journal, September 7, 1855, WRHS 35, V:B-134; INY, Domestic Journal, September 24, 1855, WRHS 32, V:B-70.

15. Word play: INY, Autobiography in Verse (see also INY correspondence with Andrew Houston and GKL in Chapter 7); whistling: Benjamin Gates, Day Book, November 7, 1827, WM 819; blowing baskets and rat chase: INY, Domestic Journal, February 21, 1850, and July 2, 1852, WRHS 32, V:B-70; mimicry: Lovegrove, Journal, June 3, 1827, WRHS 33, V:B-94; Giles Avery, Journal of Times, Rhymes, Work & Weather, January 1, 1838, WRHS 34, V:B-106, in Sally Promey, *Spiritual Spectacles: Vision and Image in Mid-Nineteenth-Century Shakerism* (Bloomington: Indiana University Press, 1993), 54; INY, "if I should undertake to imitate all the odd motions of our assemblies: those of myself as well as others," Family and Meeting Journal, September 1, 1816, LC 3:42; and "rale ginerwine style" INY [and Bishop], Tour, September 4, 1834.

16. INY, Domestic Journal, March 31, 1836, NYSL 10.

17. Ibid., January 1, 1840.

18. Height and hair cap: ibid., January 1 and February 27, 1840; temperance: INY, Domestic Journal, December 31, 1850, WRHS 32, V:B-70; weight: INY, Family and Meeting Journal, November 1818 (cited in Grant and Allen, *Shaker Furniture Makers*, 55), and March 24, 1821, LC 3:42; hair: see Benson Lossing's drawings in [Lossing], *An Early View of the Shakers*, ed. Don Gifford (Hanover, N.H.: Published for HSV by University Press of New England, 1989).

19. [Lossing], *Early View*, 5, 13, 19.

20. [Daniel Myrick], Journal of a Visit to five societies of believers . . . 1846, SM 16,811, photocopy of Williams College original, #9779. I am indebted to Jerry Grant for finding the description of INY's shop.

21. INY et al., Taylor's Journal (1845–65), WRHS 36, V:B-139; Rebecca Johnson,

WRHS manuscripts assistant, to the author, March 8, 1991, re: outlines in WRHS 35, V:B-134.

22. INY, Domestic Journal, February 27, 1840, NYSL 10.

Chapter 1. Shaker Society

1. E. D. Andrews, *The People Called Shakers: A Search for the Perfect Society* (New York: Dover, 1963), 3–4; *New American Cyclopedia* (New York: Appleton, 1859–63), 544–46, University of Michigan Making of America collection online, www.moa.umdl.umich.edu; E. D. Andrews and Faith Andrews, *Fruits of the Shaker Tree of Life* (Stockbridge, Mass.: Berkshire Traveller Press, 1975), 121.

2. Andrews, *People,* 13–14; Rufus Bishop, *Testimonies of the Life, Character, Revelations and Doctrines of our Ever Blessed Mother Ann Lee . . .* (Hancock, Mass.: J. Talcott and J. Deming, Junrs., 1816), 214–15, 218–22, 226–27, 257–58, 278–80.

3. God's providence was a relic of Puritan thought. David Hackett Fischer, *Albion's Seed: Four British Folkways in America* (New York: Oxford University Press, 1989), 126–27. Andrews, *People,* 32–34; Stephen A. Marini, *Radical Sects of Revolutionary New England* (Cambridge: Harvard University Press, 1982), 53–53; J. E. A. Smith, *History of Pittsfield* (Boston: Lee and Shepard, 1869), 453; "A Short Account of the People known by the Name of Shakers, or Shaking Quakers," *Theological Magazine* 1 (September–October 1795): 83; Anna White and Leila Taylor, *Shakerism: Its Meaning and Message* (Columbus, Ohio: Shakers, 1905), 35–36.

4. White and Taylor, *Shakerism,* 100; [Matthew Patten], *Diary of Matthew Patten of Bedford, N.H., 1754–1788* (Concord, N.H.: Rumford, 1903), 414; Sarah A. (Smith) Emery, *Reminiscences of a Nonagenarian* (Newburyport, Mass.: W. H. Huse, 1879), 176; [Ebenezer Parkman], *Diary of Rev. Ebenezer Parkman of Westborough, Mass.,* ed. Harriette M. Forbes (Westborough: Westborough Historical Society, 1899), 235–36.

5. "Short Account," 84.

6. [Ezra Stiles], *Literary Diary of Ezra Stiles,* vol. 2 (1776–81), ed. Franklin Bowditch Dexter (New York: Charles Scribner's Sons, 1901), 558.

7. Daniel Goodrich, Narrative History of the Church, 1803, HSV 6140a, 3b-4. My thanks to Christian Goodwillie for pointing out this source.

8. Stephen Stein provides the most thorough treatment of the Shakers' expansion west. Stephen J. Stein, *The Shaker Experience in America: A History of the United Society of Believers* (New Haven: Yale University Press, 1992).

9. Andrews, *People,* 49. For discussions of Shaker theology, see Jane F. Crosthwaite, " 'A white and seamless robe': Celibacy and Equality in Shaker Art and Theology," *Colby Library Quarterly,* special issue: Women and Religion 25 (September 1989): 188–89; Priscilla Brewer, *Shaker Communities, Shaker Lives* (Hanover, N.H.: University Press of New England, 1986); Stein, *Shaker Experience.*

10. Brewer, *Shaker Communities,* 217; Watervliet Indentures, 1832–72, NYSL 5:367. See Stein, *Shaker Experience,* for a comparison of all investigators' statistics to date.

11. Brewer, *Shaker Communities,* 217.

12. Beverly Gordon, "Fossilized Fashion: 'Old Fashioned' Dress as a Symbol of a Separate, Work-Oriented Identity," *Dress* 13 (1987): 49–60; A few words respecting the brethren's wearing apparel, LC 22:306.

13. 1821 Millennial Laws, in John T. Kirk, *The Shaker World* (New York: Henry Abrams, 1997), 263; 1845 Millennial Laws, in Andrews, *People,* 254–55; Bishop, *Testimonies,* 265.

14. François Marquis de Barbé-Marbois, *Our Revolutionary Forefathers . . . 1779–1785,* trans. Eugene Parker Chase (New York: Duffield and Co., 1929), 181. The marquis visited on September 26, 1784. Bishop, *Testimonies,* 274, 306; BSY, *Testimony of Christ's Second Appearing,* 4th ed. (Albany, N.Y.: [for the Shakers, 1856]), 40.

15. Calvin Green and SYW, *Summary View* (1823), quoted in Lawrence Foster, *Religion and Sexuality* (New York: Oxford University Press, 1981), 46–47; Lawrence Foster, *Women, Family, and Utopia: Communal Experiments of the Shakers, the Oneida Community, and the Mormons* (Syracuse, N.Y.: Syracuse University Press, 1991), 35.

16. Issachar Bates, *Rights of Conscience,* quoted in Christian Goodwillie, *Shaker Songs: A Celebration of Peace, Harmony, and Simplicity* (New York: Black Dog and Leventhal, 2002), 18–19; 1845 Millennial Laws, 266–68; 1821 Millennial Laws, 262; Brewer, *Shaker Communities,* 93–94.

17. INY, Family and Meeting Journal (1815–23), March 14, 1818, LC 3:42; 1845 Millennial Laws: 266–68; 1821 Millennial Laws, 261–64.

18. Foster, *Women, Family, and Utopia,* 69.

19. INY, Family and Meeting Journal, November 17, 1816 and August 28–29, 1821, LC 3:42; Thomas Brown, *An Account of the People Called Shakers: Their Faith, Doctrines, and Practice* (Troy, N.Y.: Parker & Bliss, 1812; repr., New York: AMS, 1972), 58; Brewer, *Shaker Communities,* 94–95.

20. Confession: 1 John 1:9, James 5:16; *New American Cyclopedia,* 546; Brown, *Account,* 336; Alonzo Hollister, Book of Remembrances, March 1824 [selections copied from INY, Meeting Journal (1823–28)], 202, WRHS 58, VII:B-109.

21. Vincent Newton typescript, Duties of Children and Youth . . . 1842, 1, SM 21:9701; David Lamson, *Two Years' Experience among the Shakers* (West Boylston, [Mass.], 1848), 165–70; 1821 Millennial Laws, 261.

22. Mother Lucy's Sayings, Spoken at different times . . . , 18, 20–22, LC 5:88.

23. INY, Family and Meeting Journal, August 17, 1816, LC 3:42; Priscilla Brewer, " 'Tho' of the Weaker Sex': A Reassessment of Gender Equality among the Shakers," *Signs* 17 (Spring 1992): 609–35.

24. Daniel Patterson, *The Shaker Spiritual* (Princeton, N.J.: Princeton University Press, 1979), 16.

25. Mother Ann: Bishop, *Testimonies*, 265. Cleanliness: Frances Anne Kemble, "The Shakers," [1835], in *The Berkshire Reader*, ed. Richard Nunley (Stockbridge, Mass.: Berkshire House, 1992), 144; Lawrence Pitkethly, "Emigration," *Northern Star*, May 6, 1843, 7; "B," "The Shakers," *The Practical Christian*, February 1, 1845, 76; Marianne Finch, *An Englishwoman's Experience in America* (1853; repr., New York: Negro Universities Press, 1969), 119. New Lebanon: Elkanah Watson, *Men and Times of the Revolution*, ed. Winslow C. Watson (New York: Dana and Co., 1856), 288–89.

26. [Benjamin Silliman], *Remarks Made on a Short Tour Between Hartford and Quebec in the Autumn of 1819*, 2d ed. (New Haven: Converse, 1824), 42.

27. Newton typescript, Duties of Children and Youth, 3.

28. "The Shakers Worshiping," *Atkinson's Casket* 6 (February 1831): 74; Charles Nordhoff, *Communistic Societies of the United States* (1875; repr., New York: Dover, 1966), 216–17; Andrews, *People*, 287; Bishop, *Testimonies*, 273.

29. Elite views of work: Theodore Parker to Robert White, July 31, 1848, in *Life and Correspondence of Theodore Parker*, ed. John Weiss (New York: D. Appleton & Company, 1864), 384, University of Michigan journals online. INY, Domestic Journal (1834–46), August 12, 1840, NYSL 10; INY, Domestic Journal (1847–55), December 16, 1853, WRHS 32, V:B-70.

30. "B," "The Shakers."

31. Worn-out farm wife: Sally McMurray, *Families and Farmhouses in Nineteenth-Century America* (New York: Oxford University Press, 1988), chap. 4; Pitkethly, "Emigration," 7; INY, Personal Journal (1839–58), June 6–7, 1853, WRHS 35, V:B-134.

32. INY, Family and Meeting Journal, October 6, 1817, LC 3:42; Bishop, *Testimonies* 269; Hepworth Dixon, *New America*, vol. 2 (London: Hurst and Blackett, 1867), 85–86.

33. Frederika Bremer, *Homes of the New World*, vol. 2, trans. Mary Howitt (London: A. Hall, Virtue, 1853), 579; Dixon, *New America*, 86–88.

34. Elisha Blakeman, Journal of Occurances, January 28, 1839, WRHS 35, V:B-131.

35. "Life among the Shakers," *New York Times*, August 8, 1865, 5; Newton typescript, Duties of Children and Youth; Hervey Elkins, *Fifteen Years in the Senior Order of Shakers* (Hanover, N.H.: Dartmouth Press, 1853), 30; INY, Domestic Journal, June 11, 1850, WRHS 32, V:B-70. Glendyne R. Wergland, "Shaker Discipline and Bad Boys: 'more fit for the company of pirates than here' " (paper presented to the Dublin Seminar for New England Folklife, June 2002).

36. 1821 Millennial Laws, 262; INY, Domestic Journal (1834–46), October 23, 1843, NYSL 10; INY, Domestic Journal, July 23, 1847, WRHS 32, V:B-70.

37. A Correct Statement of the time When we are to lie down and to rise up, 1816, LC 22:305; INY, Concise View, 290, 295–96, WM 861; [A "winter Shaker" in 1842–43], "Four Months Among the Shakers," *The Circular*, May 10, 1869, 60.

38. INY, Concise View, 290, 295–96; Finch, *Englishwoman's Experience*, 145; Frederick Evans, *Autobiography of a Shaker* (1888; repr., Philadelphia: Porcupine

Press, 1972), 239–40; Pitkethly, "Emigration," 7; butter: "Rural Economy: The following is recommended to all Dairy Women," *Hampshire Gazette*, August 14, 1816.

39. Andrews, *People*, 179; Alonzo Hollister, Reminiscences by a Soldier of the Cross, written July 7, 1907, 162, WRHS 116, X:B-31; "Four Months," 60; INY, Concise View, 182–87, 189–93.

40. "C.B.," "Second Visit to the Shakers," *Lowell Offering* 1 (1841), 339.

41. "Four Months," 61; Elkins, *Fifteen Years*, 26.

42. Elkins, *Fifteen Years*, 26; Brewer, *Shaker Communities*, 72–73.

43. 1821 Millennial Laws, 262; INY, Family and Meeting Journal, April 27, 1817.

44. Hollister, Reminiscences by a Soldier of the Cross, 165–66; 1821 Millennial Laws, 262.

45. Marquise La Tour du Pin Gouvernet, *Recollections of the Revolution*, ed. and trans. Walter Geer (New York: Brentano's, 1920), 217–18; Finch, *Englishwoman's Experience*, 119.

46. Watson, *Men and Times*, 288–89.

47. Kemble, "The Shakers," 144; Horace Greeley, "A Sabbath with the Shakers," *The Knickerbocker, or New York Monthly Magazine*, June 1838, 533.

48. Bode, *American Life*, 191; INY, Family and Meeting Journal, October 14, 1820, LC 3:42.

Chapter 2. Isaac Newton Youngs's Childhood and Youth

1. Six of the ten Youngs children survived: Benjamin Seth, Wilson, Elizabeth, Henry, James, and INY. Selah Youngs Jr., *Youngs Family: A History and Genealogy* (New York, 1907), 117; Elizabeth Shaver, Shaker Heritage Society, letter to author, May 29, 1991; Montgomery County clerk, deed search, January 3, 2003; Kelly Yacobucci Farquhar, Montgomery County historian, e-mail message to author, October 1, 2001; Earlene Melious, Montgomery County Department of History and Archives, Fonda, N.Y., e-mail message to author, October 17, 2002.

2. INY [and Rufus Bishop], Tour thro the States of Ohio and Kentucky, in the Summer of 1834, SM 141; Penrose R. Hoopes, *Connecticut Clockmakers of the Eighteenth Century* (Hartford, Conn.: Edwin Valentine Mitchell, 1930), 127.

3. Abigail (Youngs) Wells was sister to Benjamin and Seth Youngs Jr. and wife of Thomas Wells. Her ten children included Seth Youngs Wells and Freegift Wells. Youngs, *Youngs Family*, 117; Shaver to Shaker Heritage Society, May 29, 1991; Jerry Grant and Douglas Allen, *Shaker Furniture Makers* (Hanover, N.H.: Published for HSV by University Press of New England, 1989), 36, 168–69n4. Wells-Youngs family: Shaker Names index, WRHS 123. A few wives fought for custody of their children. See Elizabeth A. DeWolfe, *Shaking the Faith: Women, Family, and Mary Marshall Dyer's Anti-Shaker Campaign, 1815–1867* (New York: Palgrave, 2002) or Eunice Chapman, *An Account of the People Called Shakers* (Albany, N.Y.: Eunice Chapman, 1817).

4. Putting out: Edmund S. Morgan, *The Puritan Family* (New York: Harper,

1966), 76–79; David Hackett Fischer, *Albion's Seed: Four British Folkways in America* (New York: Oxford University Press, 1989), 101–2; Watervliet indentures, NYSL 5:367.

5. INY, Family and Meeting Journal (1815–23), February 7, 1819, LC 3:42.

6. INY to Nancy Farrell, January 30, 1830, WRHS 20, IV:A-36.

7. Rufus Bishop, *Testimonies of the Life, Character, Revelations and Doctrines of our Ever Blessed Mother Ann Lee* . . . (Hancock, Mass.: J. Talcott and J. Deming, Junrs., 1816), 265–72.

8. INY to Molly Youngs, October 4, 1832, WRHS 20, IV:A-36; INY, Family and Meeting Journal, May 21, 1822, LC 3:42. Susan Matarese and Paul Salmon, "Assessing Psychopathology in Communal Societies," *Communal Societies* 15 (1995): 48, conclude that INY's later mental state resulted from early deprivation.

9. Thomas Brown, *An Account of the People Called Shakers* (Troy, N.Y.: Parker & Bliss, 1812), 58; INY, Private [Apostate] Journal (1837–59), August 29, 1837, SM 10,509. Shakers believed they fulfilled Revelations' prophecies. E. D. Andrews, *The People Called Shakers: A Search for the Perfect Society* (New York: Dover, 1963), 23, 29. Revelation, precognition, and healing: Bishop, *Testimonies*, 257–59, 214–15, 221–22, 227. Seth Youngs's suicide: INY, Family and Meeting Journal, May 20, 1815, LC 3:42.

10. Shaker Names index, WRHS 123; Youngs, *Youngs Family*, 87–88, 115–18.

11. INY, Autobiography in Verse, July 4, 1837, WM 818, reprinted in E. D. Andrews and Faith Andrews, *Fruits of the Shaker Tree of Life* (Stockbridge, Mass.: Berkshire Traveller Press, 1975), 129–34.

12. INY, Autobiography in Verse; INY, A Clock Maker's Journal, March 28, 1835, WRHS 33, V:B-86; Shaver to the author, May 29, 1991. Shaver's source was BSY's journal at SM.

13. INY, Autobiography in Verse; Hervey Elkins, *Fifteen Years in the Senior Order of Shakers* (Hanover, N.H.: Dartmouth Press, 1853; reprint, New York: AMS, 1973), 30; Philip Greven, *The Protestant Temperament: Patterns of Child-Rearing, Religious Experience, and the Self in Early America* (University of Chicago Press, 1977), 32–33.

14. SYW, A plain statement of the custom and manner of receiving, managing, teaching, governing and disciplining children . . . (1815), 10–11, WRHS 56, VII:B-62, quoted in Judith Graham, "The New Lebanon Shaker Children's Order" (Ph.D. diss., Iowa State University, 1996), 159, 178; Stephen J. Stein, *Shaker Experience in America: A History of the United Society of Believers* (New Haven: Yale University Press, 1992), 160; Alice Morse Earle, *Child Life in Colonial Days* (1899; repr., New York: Macmillan, 1927), 197–203. Wells's "plain statement" may have been aimed at new teachers or children's caretakers. Bagging may have been a Shaker practice: "Child Life in Shakerdom," *New York Times*, September 21, 1874, 3.

15. John Meacham journal extract, November 24, 1800, transcribed in Alonzo Hollister, Book of Remembrance, 381, WRHS 58, VII:B-109. Typescript of letter attributed to INY, ca. 1806, NYSL 3.

16. Earle, *Child Life in Colonial Days,* 305–8; Vincent Newton typescript, Duties of Children and Youth . . . 1842, 1, Mount Lebanon Records, SM 21:9701.

17. INY to BSY, October 22, 1807, SM 9573; Morgan, *Puritan Family,* 68–70.

18. INY, Family and Meeting Journal, March 27, 1818 and March 24, 1821, LC 3:42; INY, Autobiography in Verse.

19. Typescript of letter attributed to INY, ca. 1806, NYSL 3.

20. Graham, "Shaker Children's Order," 107.

21. INY to BSY, October 22, 1807, SM 9573; INY, Autobiography in Verse, 132.

22. INY in Watervliet South Family: Freegift Wells, Records of the Church at Watervliet, New York (1788–1851), March 23, 1807, WRHS 44, V:B-279. Scenery: Anne Royall, *The Black Book; or a Continuation of Travels in the United States* (Washington, D.C.: for the author, 1828), 41; [William Loughton Smith], "Journal of William Loughton Smith, 1790–1791," ed. Albert Matthews Massachusetts Historical Society *Proceedings* 51 (October 1917): 49; Eliza Williams Bridgham, "Journey through New England and New York in 1818," *Magazine of History* 2 (December 1905): 91.

23. INY, Family and Meeting Journal, September 6, 1819, LC 3:42.

24. Arthur Middleton and Henry Franklin [Priscilla Bell Wakefield, pseud.], *Excursions in North America, Described in Letters from a Gentleman and his Young Companion . . .* (London: Darton and Harvey, 1806), 201–3; INY, Personal Journal (1839–58), March 24, 1857, WRHS 35, V:B-134; [Nicholas Bennet], Journal Kept by Nicholas Bennet . . . 1807–14, March 24, 1807, WRHS 32, V:B-67.

25. [INY et al.], Records Kept by Order of the Church (1780–1855), 37–38, January–May 1813, NYPL 2:7; Freegift Wells, Records of the Church at Watervliet, February 25, 1813, WRHS 44, V:B-279.

26. INY to BSY, October 22, 1807, SM 9573. Tuberculosis killed a quarter of Shakers whose cause of death was listed, perhaps because they slept four or six to a room. John E. Murray, "A Demographic Analysis of Shaker Mortality Trends," *Communal Societies* 13 (1993): 22–44; Thomas R. Cole, *The Journey of Life: A Cultural History of Aging in America* (New York: Cambridge University Press, 1992), 88, 66; Christian Goodwillie, *Shaker Songs: A Celebration of Peace, Harmony, and Simplicity* (New York: Black Dog and Leventhal, 2002), 88–89.

27. Stein, *Shaker Experience,* 160; INY, Domestic Journal (1856–69), January 1, 1860, WRHS 32, V:B-71.

28. INY, Domestic Journal (1847–55), WRHS 32, V:B-70; Elisha Blakeman Jr., Boys' Journal of Work, 1844–65, WRHS 36, V:B-137; 1845 Millennial Laws, in Andrews, *People,* 280.

29. INY et al., Taylor's Journal (1846–65), March–April 1846, WRHS 36, V:B-139.

30. The previous year, the Tambora volcano (in what is now Indonesia) exploded, sending more ash and dust higher into the atmosphere than the usual volcanic event. As the heavy cloud of dust drifted around the world, it dimmed the sun, changing the climate. Sarah Snell Bryant diary, 1816 Remarks, original at Harvard University,

Cambridge, Mass.; Samuel Griswold Goodrich, *Recollections of a Lifetime* (New York: Auburn, Miller, Orton, and Mulligan, 1857), 2:78–79; Nicholas Bennet, Domestic Journal, May–September 1816, WRHS 32, V:B-68.

31. William G. Atkins, *History of Hawley* (West Cummington, Mass.: 1887), 86.

32. Goodrich, *Recollections,* 80; Priscilla Brewer, *Shaker Communities, Shaker Lives* (Hanover, N.H.: University Press of New England, 1986), 215.

33. Alonzo Hollister, Reminiscences by a Soldier of the Cross, written July 7, 1907, 160, WRHS 116, X:B-31; Linda Morton, "The Training of a Tailor," *Dress* 8 (1982): 22; INY, Concise View, 241, WM 861; Lawrence W. Towner, *A Good Master Well Served: Masters and Servants in Colonial Massachusetts, 1620–1750* (New York: Garland, 1998), 114; Bruce Laurie, *Artisans into Workers* (New York: Hill and Wang, 1989), 35–36. Apprentices' levels of work: Benjamin Gates's portions of INY et al., Taylor's Journal, 1841–46, WRHS 36, V:B-139.

34. Rufus Bishop, Records Book No. 2, 20–22, NYPL 2:6; INY, Family and Meeting Journal, January 16, 1823, LC 3:42; INY, Domestic Journal (1834–46), NYSL 10, notes on occupations at end. Though Graham ("Shaker Children's Order," 160) believes that Shaker children were segregated from adults, INY's journals suggest otherwise. Children, by the age of ten or so, were assigned to an adult for all their waking hours, whether at chores or in school or apprenticeship.

35. [J. Bennet and J. Walker], typescript of New Lebanon journal, 1795+, WRHS 33, V:B-72a; Sue Gibson Byrd and Mary Frances Drake, "Andrew Johnson, the Tailor President," *Dress* 13 (1987): 78; INY, Concise View, 317. This list seems generous. Probate inventories of the 1790s show that most nonelite men owned only two or three outfits. Two coats, vests, and shirts and two pairs of breeches were about average. Hampshire County, Mass., Probate Records, vol. 17.

36. INY to BSY, October 22, 1807, SM 9573. See also Benjamin Gates's portions of INY et al., Taylor's Journal, 1841–46, WRHS 36, V:B-139.

37. INY, Autobiography in Verse; GKL obituary, *Pittsfield Sun,* February 2, 1837; INY, Concise View, 366; Brewer, *Shaker Communities,* 212, 214.

38. Ministry Sisters' Journal, September 1832, WRHS 32, V:B-60; INY, Family and Meeting Journal, July 4, 1816 and March 27, 1818, LC 3:42.

39. INY, Concise View, 365–68; Family and Meeting Journal, August 27, 1816, LC 3:42. INY's students included later leaders Daniel Boler, Elisha Blakeman, and Benjamin Gates.

40. GKL was trained in medicine in Philadelphia and New York and became the village physician. Brown, *Account,* 249; GKL eulogy: INY, Domestic Journal, February 8, 1837, NYSL 10, courtesy of Andy Vadnais; BSY to SYW, February 25, 1839, BA V289.8 Un5.9 BB; INY, Concise View, 355; SYW, Remarks on Learning & the Use of Books, quoted in Brewer, *Shaker Communities,* 76.

41. William Dean Howells, *Three Villages* (Boston: Osgood, 1884), 104; *Scientific American:* INY, Personal Journal, June 1853, WRHS 35, V:B-134; INY, Family and Meeting Journal, April 8, 1819, LC 3:42.

42. INY, Spiritual Autobiography transcribed in Alonzo Hollister, Autobiogra-

phy of the Saints, or Stray Leaves from the book of Life, 291–305, WRHS 52, VI:B-36.

43. Middleton and Franklin, [Wakefield], *Excursions,* 201–3.

44. INY, Concise View, 83–90; INY, Family and Meeting Journal, April 14, 1822, LC 3:42; Anna White and Leila Taylor, *Shakerism: Its Meaning and Message* (Columbus, Ohio: Shakers, 1905), 96.

45. INY, "Good Believers' Character," printed for the dedication of the new meetinghouse at New Lebanon, 1824, MCA #515.

Chapter 3. Youth and Lust

An earlier version of this chapter was published as "Lust, 'A Snare of Satan to Beguile the Soul': New Light on Shaker Celibacy," *Communal Societies* 15 (1995): 1–23.

1. INY, "Good Believers' Character," printed for the dedication of the new meetinghouse at New Lebanon, 1824, MCA #515; [Lucy Wright], *Mother Lucy's Sayings* (Poland Springs, Maine.: United Society of Shakers, 1989); reprinted from *The Shaker Quarterly* 8 (Winter 1968): 104.

2. INY, Family and Meeting Journal (1815–23), March 24, 1821, LC 3:42.

3. INY, Autobiography in Verse, July 4, 1837, WM 818, reprinted in E. D. Andrews and Faith Andrews, *Fruits of the Shaker Tree of Life* (Stockbridge, Mass.: Berkshire Traveller Press, 1975), 132–33. The manuscript at WM reads, "New trials, I knew not before"; the reprinted version in Andrews contains an error: "New trails, I knew not before."

4. BSY, *Testimony of Christ's Second Appearing . . . ,* 4th ed. (Albany, N.Y.: [for the Shakers, 1856]), 40.

5. WRHS 121, XIV has lists of books owned by the New Lebanon Shakers. Dio Lewis, *Chastity, or, Our Secret Sins* (New York: Fowler and Wells Co., 1874), 27–37, 111, 264, 275–76, 279.

6. Stephen J. Stein, *The Shaker Experience in America: A History of the United Society of Believers* (New Haven: Yale University Press, 1992), 159.

7. Scholars have thoroughly examined the benefits of celibacy. For a discussion of Shaker celibacy and equality, see Jane Crosthwaite, "A white and seamless robe": Celibacy and Equality in Shaker Art and Theology," *Colby Library Quarterly* 25 (September 1989): 188–98. In the late 1700s, Shakers were harbingers of the feminist belief that the inequality of women was based on marriage, with its assumptions about men's authority. As Lawrence Foster writes in *Religion and Sexuality* (New York: Oxford University Press, 1981), sexual equality was connected with celibacy. Celibacy was also practiced by other communal societies who controlled sexuality. Of the thirty nineteenth-century U.S. communities Rosabeth Moss Kanter studied, six required celibacy. Kanter, "Family Organization and Sex Roles in American Communes," chap. 24 of *Communes: Creating and Managing the Collective Life* (New York: Harper and Row, 1973), chap. 24. Raymond Muncy, in *Sex and Marriage in*

Utopian Communities (Bloomington: Indiana University Press, 1973), maintains that successful communal societies used religious indoctrination and social censure of backsliders to enforce celibacy. Jeanette Lauer and Robert Lauer, in *The Spirit and the Flesh* (Metuchen, N.J.: Scarecrow Press, 1983), note that celibacy may have attracted women who wanted to avoid pregnancy. Moreover, as a man in the audience pointed out after my talk on Shaker sexuality at the Berkshire Family History Association meeting in Pittsfield, Massachusetts, March 27, 2004, some people are asexual, lacking sexual interest in anyone of either sex. Those people, he thought, might be ideal candidates for Shakerism.

8. INY, Family and Meeting Journal, July 7, 1815, LC 3:42.

9. Ibid., July 19, 1816.

10. Ibid., July 1816; on sinning and prayer, see INY, Spiritual Autobiography transcribed in Alonzo Hollister, Autobiography of the Saints, or Stray Leaves from the book of Life, 291–305, WRHS 52, VI:B-36. Priscilla Brewer, *Shaker Communities, Shaker Lives* (Hanover, N.H.: University Press of New England, 1986), 15; Louis J. Kern, *An Ordered Love: Sex Roles and Sexuality in Victorian Utopias—the Shakers, the Mormons, and the Oneida Community* (Chapel Hill: University of North Carolina Press, 1981), 89.

11. INY, Family and Meeting Journal, May 27, 1817, LC 3:42.

12. Daniel Patterson, *The Shaker Spiritual* (Princeton, N.J.: Princeton University Press, 1979), 167, 175, 191–92; INY to Alonzo Hollister, 1864 songbook: "Easy Yoke" and "Turning from Evil," WRHS 114, IX:B-413.

13. INY, Family and Meeting Journal, May 1 and December 18, 1817, LC 3:42.

14. Quoted in ibid., November 17, 1816.

15. Ibid., October 7 and December 30, 1819; [Rufus Bishop], Day Book, December 29, 1819, WRHS 33, V:B-85.

16. INY, Family and Meeting Journal, August 28, 1816, LC 3:42.

17. Ibid., May 1, 1818. The paw of Satan may have been a reference to Rebecca Slosson's testimony of Father James Whitaker, who said, "Let the devil once put his paw on you, and you will find yourselves under the power of the flesh." Testimony of Sixty, A Cloud of Witnesses, 97, WRHS 52, VI:B-40.

18. This order was shared in Saturday night meeting, which may not have been open to the public—and therefore was unlikely to cast suspicion on Shaker celibacy. INY, Family and Meeting Journal, March 14 and August 16, 1818, LC 3:42.

19. INY, Family and Meeting Journal, October 16, 1818, LC 3:42; Mark 1:13. INY's imagery resembles that of Jonathan Edwards in his *Personal Narrative* and his 1741 sermon, *Sinners in the Hands of an Angry God*, in *Anthology of American Literature*, vol. 1, 3rd ed., ed. George McMichael (New York: Macmillan, 1985): 237, 251–62.

20. INY, Family and Meeting Journal, December 20, 1818, LC 3:42.

21. BSY, *Testimony*, 40; INY, Family and Meeting Journal, October 16, 1818, LC 3:42.

22. INY, Family and Meeting Journal, December 10, 1818, LC 3:42.

23. Ibid., December 10 and 20, 1818.

24. Ibid., December 20, 1818.

25. Ibid., December 25, 1818.

26. Ibid., January 18, 1819.

27. Nicholas Gilman quoted in Philip Greven, *The Protestant Temperament* (Chicago: University of Chicago Press, 1977), 130.

28. In 1818, INY began experimenting with cryptography. Though translation is time-consuming, any Elder who exercised his right to peruse that journal could have translated it. In one cipher, numerals are substituted for vowels: a = 1, e = 2, i = 3, o = 4, u = 5. In another, all vowels were replaced by dots. In another, vowels are eliminated. Some entries are unnecessarily encrypted, such as the 1819 note that Mother Lucy had warned him against "letting his mind run with such unprofitable things" as a perpetual motion machine. She would just as soon see "a person would labor after a perpetual wife as after perpetual motion." In a December entry, he lambasted the apostate Clarissa Cogswell in encrypted language no different from what he used in plaintext entries in other journals. The last cipher on LC 3:42, ms. p. 266 (microfilm p. 466), however, I was unable to break. (See Chapter 4.) INY, Family and Meeting Journal, July 2, 1819, February 8, 1820, December 1822, January 16, 1823, LC 3:42.

29. INY, Family and Meeting Journal, February 29, 1820, LC 3:42. Shakers were not the only nineteenth-century Americans who suppressed masturbation. R. P. Neuman, "Masturbation, Madness, and the Modern Concepts of Childhood and Adolescence," *Journal of Social History* 8 (spring 1975): 1–27, points out that the genteel middle class tried to prevent it, as well, focusing instead on hard work and self-denial much as the Shakers did.

30. INY, Family and Meeting Journal, March 29, 1820, LC 3:42; 1821 Millennial Laws, in John T. Kirk, *The Shaker World* (New York: Henry Abrams, 1997), 261.

31. David R. Lamson, *Two Years' Experience among the Shakers* (West Boylston [Mass.], 1848), 165.

32. Kern, *Ordered Love,* 113; [Ralph Waldo Emerson], entry for June 15, 1844, in *Emerson in His Journals,* ed. Joel Porte (Cambridge Harvard University Press, Belknap Press, 1982), 327. My thanks to Jane Crosthwaite for her discussion of these issues in her Shaker seminar at Mount Holyoke College in 1990.

33. INY, Family and Meeting Journal, December 4, 1820. LC 3:42. Middle-class world's people "used a variety of chemical therapies, 'corrective surgery,' and mechanical devices" to prevent masturbation. Neuman, "Masturbation, Madness, and the Modern Concepts," 1, 12.

34. INY, Domestic Journal (1834–46), September 6, 1835, June 19, September 4, and December 8, 1836, NYSL 10; Jean M. Humez, ed. *Mother's First-Born Daughters: Early Shaker Writings on Women and Religion* (Bloomington, Indiana: Indiana University Press, 1993), 213. Ephraim Prentiss, caretaker of boys at Watervliet, claimed that a vegetable diet had made youngsters in his care remarkably tractable. Others thought he had starved them into submission on a diet lacking meat, butter, milk, and cheese. Freegift Wells said Prentiss had "restrained his boys altogether be-

yond the bounds of reason." (quoted in Brewer, *Shaker Communities* 111). New Lebanon waffled for years on dietary reform. Pork: INY, Domestic Journal (1834–46), November 27, 1841, January 6, 1846, NYSLIO; INY, Domestic Journal (1847–55), January 1, 1850, WRHS 32, V:B-70. Coffee and tea: "History of the Church of Mount Lebanon, New York," *The Manifesto* 20 (February 1890): 27.

35. John Woods, *Shakerism Unmasked* (Paris, Ky.: Western Observer, 1826), 18; "S.," "A Visit to the Shakers," *Blackwood's Magazine* [London], April 1823, 468; Thomas Brown, *An Account of the People Called Shakers*, 334–36.

36. Lewis, *Chastity*, 279–80. In the later nineteenth century, spiked belts and spermatorrhoea rings were marketed for men. The spermatorrhoea ring fit loosely around a flaccid member, but, as Rainer Engel, curator of the William P. Didusch Museum collection, explains, "when erection occurs, 50 steel teeth bite into the penis, and the erection disappears," www.citypaper.com/2001-12-12/nose.html (accessed March 29, 2004. See also Ornella Moscucci, "Male Masturbation and the Offending Prepuce," in *Clitoridectomy, Circumcision & Sexual Pleasure*, reprinted in *Sexualities in Victorian Britain*, www.cirp.org/library/history/moscucci/ (accessed February 5, 2004).

37. At Whitewater, the two Shaker boys seen skinny-dipping appeared to have no testicles. Outraged citizens demanded an investigation and Shakers were arrested. But physicians' examinations showed that one had undescended testicles and the other a congenital anomaly. Alfred G. Carter, *The Old Court-House: Reminiscences and Anecdotes of the Courts and Bar of Cincinnati* (Cincinnati, Ohio: P.G. Thompson, 1880), 299–305. My thanks to Christian Goodwillie for this reference. As Suzanne Thurman points out, the Shaker body was the focus of debate over celibacy. Thurman, "The Seat of Sin, the Site of Salvation: The Shaker Body and the Nineteenth-Century American Imagination," *Nineteenth Century Studies* 15 (2001): 1.

38. Castration has a long history among religious groups who saw eunuchs as a spiritual ideal. See Mathew Kuefler, *The Manly Eunuch: Masculinity, Gender Ambiguity, and Christian Ideology in Late Antiquity* (Chicago: University of Chicago Press, 2001). Laura Engelstein notes that at least seventeen hundred Skoptsy were castrated as part of their religion in nineteenth-century Russia. Engelstein, *Castration and the Heavenly Kingdom: A Russian Folktale* (Ithaca, N.Y.: Cornell University Press, 1999), 59. Gary Taylor points out that castration opens access to the divine, through the sacrifice of a part of one's self to a higher power that is valued more than the physical self. Taylor, *Castration: An Abbreviated History of Western Manhood* (New York: Routledge, 2000), 207.

39. Robley Dunglison, *Medical Lexicon: A Dictionary of Medical Science*, 7th ed. (Philadelphia: Lea and Blanchard, 1848), 156, 309. The HSV copy came from the Mount Lebanon Shakers' library.

40. Hervey Elkins, *Fifteen Years in the Senior Order of Shakers* (Hanover, N.H.: Dartmouth Press, 1853), 17; Stein, *Shaker Experience*, 51; John Hobart to INY, January 16, 1865, copied into Alonzo Hollister, Book of Remembrances, 154–55, WRHS 58, VII:B-109. The similarity of Elkins's and Rathbun's words, despite their

geographical distance, suggests that the reference "eunuch for the kingdom of heaven's sake" was common throughout the society. Suzanne Skees reports a historical rumor of castration in *God Among the Shakers* (New York: Hyperion, 1998), 77. And Christian Goodwillie points out several references to eunuchs in the Shakers' earliest printed hymnal, *Millennial Praises* (Hancock, Mass.: Josiah Tallcott Jr., 1813): "The Testimony of Eternal Truth," 3; "Resolution Against a Carnal Nature," 58; "There are Eunuchs," 244–45.

41. INY, Family and Meeting Journal, March 9, 1821, LC 3:42. Jonathan Wood became a Deacon. He was twenty-nine years old, on the verge of Shaker adulthood, when he had the surgery. He was censused in the Church Family in 1860. Names of the Brethren and the Sisters April 1835, LC 5:92; INY, Domestic Journal (1856–69), WRHS 32, V:B-71. Ciphers: Simon Singh, *The Code Book: The Science of Secrecy from Ancient Egypt to Quantum Cryptography* (New York: Random House, 1999).

42. Elkins, *Fifteen Years,* 26; Cancer BACUP, www.cancerbacup.org.uk/QAs /1126 (accessed December 8, 2002); "S.," "A Visit to the Shakers," *Blackwood's Magazine* [London], April 1823, 468.

43. Composed by INY, from Betsy Smith's Book, ca. 1828–34, WRHS 113, IX:B-385.

44. INY, Personal Journal, August 31, 1856, WRHS 35, V:B-134; INY, Spiritual Autobiography, in a letter to Oliver Hampton, November 1, 1848.

45. Diane Sasson, *The Shaker Spiritual Narrative* (Knoxville: University of Tennessee Press, 1983), 135. INY alluded to that lack of excitement, noting that he led a secluded life far from the bustling throng. INY, Spiritual Autobiography.

Chapter 4. Rebellion in Shaker Society

1. INY, Family and Meeting Journal (1815–23), August 16, 1818, LC 3:42.

2. Ibid., April 27, 1817; Molly McCarthy, "A Pocketful of Days," *New England Quarterly* 73 (June 2000): 291. His journals worked as the coping mechanism that Molly McCarthy attributes to many diarists.

3. INY, Family and Meeting Journal, September 1, 1816, LC 3:42.

4. INY, Family and Meeting Journal, March 16, 1818, LC 3:42.

5. Ibid., March 19, 1818.

6. Ibid., March 27, 1818.

7. Ibid. Later Mother Lucy amended the ban on silver pens to allow those who wrote a lot to use them. Ibid., August 16, 1820.

8. Ibid., March 27, 1818.

9. Ibid., March 28, 1818.

10. Ibid., April 20, 1820; *Mother Lucy's Sayings* (Poland Spring, Maine: United Society of Shakers, 1989), reprinted from *The Shaker Quarterly* 8 (Winter 1968): 103. INY as scribe for Lucy Wright's addresses: Calvin Green, Memoir of Lucy Wright, April 1, 1815, 114, WRHS 32, V:B-60.1.

11. INY, Family and Meeting Journal, February 27, 1820, LC 3:42.

12. Ibid., June 30, 1820.

13. Some Elders were old enough to be excused from milking, but others were not. Milking exemption at age sixty: INY, Personal Journal (1839–58), July 4, 1853, WRHS 35, V:B-134.

14. INY, Family and Meeting Journal, June 30, 1820, LC 3:42.

15. INY, Family and Meeting Journal, July 8 and 26, 1820, LC 3:42.

16. Ibid., July 26, 1820.

17. Ibid.; 1821 Millennial Laws, 264. There was also the matter of the work involved. If the Elders did not take turns at milking, then they may have avoided painting floors and carpets, as well. More references to painted carpets appear in Benjamin Gates, Journal (New Lebanon) (January 1839–April 1840, September 1846–January 1854), SM 10,450. Gates wrote that he, with "BC & TLps" "put new painted carpets on the stairs in the 2d & 3d lofts" on May 16, 1839, and he spent April 29, 1847, "Mending stair cloths."

18. *Mother Lucy's Sayings* 105.

19. INY, Family and Meeting Journal, July 26, 1820, LC 3:42.

20. Ibid., August 16, 1820.

21. Ibid., July 2, 1819.

22. Hervey Elkins, *Fifteen Years in the Senior Order of Shakers* (Hanover, N.H.: Dartmouth Press, 1853), 22; INY, Family and Meeting Journal, August 16, 1818, LC 3:42.

23. The New Lebanon Church Family read or recited the church orders at Wright's request on September 3, 1820, a task that took more than one meeting to complete. INY, Family and Meeting Journal, October 25, 1820, LC 3:42.

24. Ibid., March 24, 1821. Ministry edicts were not formalized as the Millennial Laws until after Mother Lucy died in 1821

25. Ibid., April 7, 1822. My thanks to Jane Crosthwaite for pointing out the biblical reference.

26. Ibid..

27. Ibid., October 14, 1820.

28. I am grateful to the historical cryptographers at the National Security Agency, Fort Meade, Maryland, for decoding this passage. Ibid., January 16, 1823. Clockmaking: ibid., April 20, 1820.

29. Elizabeth Lovegrove, Journal, May 31, 1827, WRHS 33, V:B-94.

30. INY, "New Year's Thoughts," January 1, 1824, MCA 269.

Chapter 5. Clockmaking

The first version of this chapter was written in 1991 for a Five College–Mount Holyoke College class in material culture.

1. I use the word *clock* to mean either a timepiece (a generic term for an apparatus for measuring time) or such an apparatus that also strikes the hours because INY in

his journals used *clock* in both contexts, and because some of the investigated clocks' descriptions do not mention whether or not they struck the hour.

2. An irony is that Shaker furniture collectors in the late twentieth century bid prices up so high that Shaker artifacts became precisely what Believers abhorred, a source of prideful display.

3. E. D. Andrews, *The People Called Shakers: A Search for the Perfect Society* (New York: Dover, 1963), 126.

4. E. D. Andrews and Faith Andrews, *Shaker Furniture* (New York: Dover, 1950), offprint from *New York History* (New York Historical Association), July 1950, 3.

5. Ibid..

6. June Sprigg and David Larkin, *Shaker Life, Work, and Art* (New York: Stewart, Tabori, and Chang, 1987), 110.

7. Chris H. Bailey, "Clocks and Instruments," catalogue no. 230, in *The Great River: Art and Society of the Connecticut Valley, 1635–1820*, William N. Hosley, project director (Hartford, Conn.: Wadsworth Atheneum, 1985), 345.

8. Ibid. The drawings of clocks that appear in figs. 8–12 are not quite to scale.

9. 1 John 2:16.

10. Robert Meader, *Shaker Furniture* (New York: Dover, 1972), 95; Post Road Gallery advertisement, *Maine Antique Digest,* November 1990.

11. A Benjamin Youngs tall clock in the Mount Lebanon Collection, dated 1806, is similar to the one shown in fig. 9 with worldly brass works. But it also has cut feet, an arched bonnet, and sculpting on the middle of the case. Tim Rieman, *Shaker: The Art of Craftsmanship* (Alexandria, Va.: Art Services International, 1995), 60; Charles L. Flint, *Mount Lebanon Shaker Collection* (New Lebanon, N.Y.: Mount Lebanon Shaker Village, 1987), 49; James W. Gibbs and Robert W. Meader, *Shaker Clock Makers* (n.p., n.d.), 11, 13. He had a son, Benjamin Jr. (1780–1821), who could have made clocks. Lacking information on the son's trade, however, the sources attribute them to Benjamin Senior.

12. [Rufus Bishop], *Testimonies of the Life, Character, Revelations and Doctrines of our Ever Blessed Mother Ann Lee* (Hancock, Mass.: J. Talcott and J. Deming, Junrs., 1816), 265; "Four Months among the Shakers" [1842–43], *The Circular* (Oneida), May 10, 1869, 62; Jacques Milbert, *Picturesque Itinerary of the Hudson River,* [1820], trans. Constance D. Sherman (New York: Gregg Press, 1968), 175. Most visitors' accounts mention Shaker cleanliness.

13. Robert Meader believed BSY made this clock about 1820. Meader, *Shaker Furniture* (New York: Dover, 1972), 98 (catalogue no. 194). Others assign it an earlier date. Milton C. Rose and Emily M. Rose, *A Shaker Reader* (New York: Universe Books, 1975), 83.

14. The evolution was not linear. An 1809 Benjamin Youngs clock (not shown) was eighty-one inches tall and retained the brass movement but also had simpler lines and glass windows in the sides of the bonnet for viewing the works. Tim Rieman, *Complete Book of Shaker Furniture* (New York: H. N. Abrams, 1993), 163.

15. INY, A Clock Maker's Journal (1815–35), March 28, 1835, WRHS 33, V:B-86.

16. INY, Autobiography in Verse, July 4, 1837, WM 818, reprinted in E. D. Andrews and Faith Andrews, *Fruits of the Shaker Tree of Life* (Stockbridge, Mass.: Berkshire Traveller Press, 1975), 131.

17. INY, Clock Maker's Journal, March 28, 1835; Rieman, *Complete Book of Shaker Furniture*, 140–41.

18. 1845 Millennial Laws, in Andrews, *People*, 274; Gibbs and Meader, *Shaker Clock Makers*, 14; Grant and Allen, *Shaker Furniture Makers*, 36–37, 42, 44–46, 169n7; June Sprigg, *Shaker Design* (New York: Whitney Museum of American Art; New York: W. W. Norton, 1986), 92–93. INY wrote "Oh where shall I my fortune find, / when this shall cease to measure time" on No. 19. Grant and Allen, *Shaker Furniture Makers*, 45. Tim Rieman reports that No. 18, dated May 12, 1840, has a rhyme on improving time. Rieman, *Complete Book of Shaker Furniture*, 141.

19. INY, Clock Maker's Journal, March 24, 1815.

20. Ibid., introduction, 1816, March 28, 1835.

21. INY, Family and Meeting Journal (1815–23), July 8 and 26, 1820, LC 3:42. Perhaps the clock with the "good cherry case" is the one at the Groton Historical Society. See n.37.

22. INY, Clock Maker's Journal, 1816–20; Family and Meeting Journal (1815–23), July 4 and 8, 1820, LC 3:42.

23. INY, Family and Meeting Journal, April 20, 1820, LC 3:42.

24. Ibid., March 24, 1821.

25. INY, Clock Maker's Journal, 1821. On shopping trips to Albany and Troy, Isaac could buy materials without close oversight. INY, Family and Meeting Journal, November 11, 1817, March 19, 1819, May 22, 1822, LC 3:42; Benjamin Gates, Day Book, May 14, 1828, October 27–10, 1835, WM 819; Freegift Wells, Memorandum of Events, Watervliet, May 14, 1834, WRHS 45, V:B-293; INY, Domestic Journal (1834–46), October 1835, January 17 and December 5, 1837, November 21, 1838, May 27, 1839, NYSL 10; Elisha Blakeman Jr., Journal of Occurances, November 21, 1838, WRHS 35, V:B-131; INY, Domestic Journal (1847–55), December 11, 1848, November 21, 1849, May 21, 1851, WRHS 32, V:B-70; INY, Personal Journal (1839–58), June 1853 (to New York City), November 5, 1855, WRHS 35, V:B-134.

26. INY, Clock Maker's Journal, 1822.

27. INY, Family and Meeting Journal, November 9, 1822, LC 3:42; INY, Concise View, 392–414, WM 861; INY, Domestic Journal, August 1836, NYSL 10. *Pittsfield Sun*, May 8, 1823. The New Lebanon brethren went just over the line each year for several days to establish their residence in Massachusetts. Mary Hazzard autobiography, 3, WRHS 49, VI:A-6.

28. INY, Family and Meeting Journal, August 18, 1821, May 20–23, 1822, January 16, 1823, LC 3:42; INY, Dedication (composed for the opening of the new New

Lebanon meetinghouse, June 20, 1824), MCA 515; John DeWitt, Memorandum, October 5, 1824, WRHS 33, V:B-92; INY, A Brief Collection of Hymns: Improved in Sacred Worship (1826–30), LC 16:230; Elizabeth Lovegrove, Journal on the Revival in the Church, April 16, 1827, WRHS 33, V:B-93; Selections from INY, Meeting Journal (1823–28) were copied into Alonzo Hollister, Book of Remembrances, April 29, 1827, WRHS 58, VII:B-109; Gates, Day Book, October–November 1827, March 1828, April–August 1829, March and November 1830, March 1831, August 1832, WM 819; Betsy Smith's Book, WRHS 113, IX:B-385; [INY et al.], Records Kept by Order of the Church (1780–1855), June 28, 1830, NYPL 2:7; Betsy Bates, Journal of Events, November 17, 1833, WRHS 35, V:B-128.

29. Freegift Wells, Records of the Church at Watervliet, New York (1788–1851), April 17, 1826, WRHS 44, V:B-279. INY was again sick in 1827. Lovegrove, Journal, April 16, 1827.

30. INY, Clock Maker's Journal, 1830.

31. Ibid., 1831, 1832; INY to BSY, December 1833, WRHS 20, IV:B-36, quoted in Grant and Allen, *Shaker Furniture Makers,* 37.

32. Clock Maker's Journal, 1835.

33. INY, Domestic Journal, July 13, 1837, NYSL 10; INY, Domestic Journal, July 5, 1847, WRHS 32, V:B-70. Jerry Grant reports that five of INY's 1840 clocks exist today, three at HSV, one in the Time Museum in Rockford, Illinois, and one in a private collection. Grant and Allen, *Shaker Furniture Makers,* 46. HSV also has No. 1, his "wag-tail" clock with pendulum exposed and no case. For INY's comments on clock maintenance, see INY, Domestic Journal, August 20, 1838, May 28, 1840, July 14, 1843, December 20, 1844, NYSL 10; INY, Personal Journal, June 1, 1844, WRHS 35, V:B-134; INY, Domestic Journal, June 16 and 18, July 5, August 17, November 17, 1847, May 15, 1848, WRHS 32, V:B-70. INY also earned money for the Shakers by repairing clocks for the world's people. Three accounts show nine repairs between 1856 and 1858. Edward Fowler, New Lebanon Church Family Account Book (1844–58), 267–69, HSV 361.

34. INY, Personal Journal, December 13, 1848 and January 31, 1849, WRHS 35, V:B-134.

35. Quotation by Mother Ann (source not cited): www.smithsonianmag.si.edu/journeys/01/apr01/images/slide_3.html. Grant and Allen, *Shaker Furniture Makers,* 45.

36. Gibbs and Meader, *Shaker Clock Makers,* 17. INY, Domestic Journal (1847–55), July 5, 1847, WRHS 32, V:B-70, describes No. 23 as a barn clock with one pointer, but No. 23 at HSV has two. Sprigg, *Shaker Design,* 95.

37. Grant and Allen, *Shaker Furniture Makers,* 44. Because INY's clock journal does not extend past No. 16 and because, except for No. 1, nothing that predates No. 18 is available for comparison, it is hard to tell what the interim clocks looked like. A wall clock at the Groton, Massachusetts, Historical Society is tentatively attributed to INY. This is a wall or shelf clock, about twenty inches by thirteen inches (front), with cherry case and wooden (possibly cherry) movement. Information courtesy of

Richard Dabrowski of Shaker Workshops and Isabel Beals of the Groton, Massachusetts, Historical Society, 1991.

38. Gibbs and Meader, *Shaker Clock Makers,* 18–19. Without Sharon Koomler's help on a blistering summer day at HSV in 2001, this question of access would have remained unanswered. Two 1840 clocks, Nos. 19 and 21, have been altered so that screws or nails hold the face in place. But on No. 23, the face appears to be removable, by first taking out the linch pin holding the hands in place, removing the hands, then sliding the face to one side so it can be lifted free of the supporting trim on the other side. In addition, a closely fitted molding at the back of each side window acts as a gate to hold the glass in place. Those moldings can be carefully slid toward the back and out of the case, which in turn frees the window glass for removal. All those features meant that the case had to be constructed with close tolerances and the same precision that the clockworks required.

39. The Narrow Path *ritual* was an 1840 gift of inspiration but the term *narrow path* dates from the 1700s. Elkanah Watson heard it in Shaker worship in 1790. INY, Family and Meeting Journal (1840–41), November 2, 1840, WRHS 77, VIII:B-138; Sally Promey, *Spiritual Spectacles: Vision and Image in Mid-Nineteenth-Century Shakerism* (Bloomington: Indiana University Press, 1993), chap. 5; Elkanah Watson, *Men and Times of the Revolution,* ed. Winslow C. Watson (New York: Dana and Co., 1856), 288.

40. Gibbs and Meader, *Shaker Clock Makers,* 16; INY, Concise View, 248, 506.

41. Giles Avery to Amos Stewart, WRHS 20, IV:A-37, quoted in Grant and Allen, *Shaker Furniture Makers,* 169 n. 8.

42. INY, Personal Journal, February 23, 1856, WRHS 35, V:B-134.

43. [Luther Tucker], "Visit to the Shakers," *The Cultivator,* n.s. 3 (October 1846): 305.

44. Gibbs and Meader, *Shaker Clock Makers,* 31.

Chapter 6. Journey to the Western Societies

1. SYW, in [INY et al.], Records Kept by Order of the Church (1780–1855), June 2, 1834, NYPL 2:7. Shaker politics: Stephen J. Stein, *The Shaker Experience in America* (New Haven: Yale, 1992), 124.

2. 1821 Millennial Laws, in John T. Kirk, *The Shaker World* (New York: Henry Abrams, 1997), 262–63. The following discussion is not a catalogue of everything Bishop and Youngs did. Rather, it selectively examines some of INY's views. INY's maps: Robert P. Emlen, *Shaker Village Views* (Hanover, N.H.: University Press of New England, 1987), chap. 4.

3. INY [and Rufus Bishop], Tour thro the States of Ohio and Kentucky, in the Summer of 1834, June 4–5, 1834, SM 141; Freegift Wells, Records of the Church at Watervliet, New York (1788–1851), February 22, 1817, WRHS 44, V:B-279.

4. INY [and Bishop], Tour, June 5, 1834; Freegift Wells, Memorandum of Events, Watervliet, June 5, 1834, WRHS 45, V:B-293.

5. INY [and Bishop], Tour, June 7, 1834.

6. Ibid., June 11, 1834; Stein, *Shaker Experience,* 107, 113; James Sullivan, ed., *History of New York State,* bk. 7, chap. 3 (n.p.: Lewis Historical Publishing Company, Inc., 1927), at www.usgennet.org/usa/ny/state/his/bk7/ch3.html, October 13, 2002. Sodus map: Emlen, *Shaker Village Views,* 66.

7. INY [and Bishop], Tour, June 11–14, 1834. Lockport stoneworks: [Author of *The Gray Champion*], "My Visit to Niagara," *New-England Magazine* 8 (February 1835).

8. INY [and Bishop], Tour, June 13, 1834.

9. Ibid., June 15, 1834.

10. Ibid., June 16, 1834.

11. Ibid., June 19, 1834. Master workman: Jerry Grant and Douglas Allen, *Shaker Furniture Makers* (Hanover, N.H.: Published for HSV by University Press of New England, 1989), 38; floors: Henry DeWitt, Journal (1827–67), April 21, 1834, WRHS 33, V:B-97; woodhouse: INY, Domestic Journal (1834–46), September 28, 1837, NYSL 10; Elisha Blakeman, Journal of Occurances, October 12, 1837, WRHS 35, V:B-131.

12. INY [and Bishop], Tour, June 24, 1834.

13. Ibid., June 26, 1834.

14. Ibid., June 28, 1834.

15. Warren Jenkins, *Ohio Gazetteer,* rev. ed. (Columbus, Ohio: Isaac N. Whiting, 1839), 442; INY [and Bishop], Tour, June 29 and July 4, 1834; Authority over western societies: Stein, *Shaker Experience,* 124. George Kendall copy of INY's Union Village map: Emlen, *Shaker Village Views,* 71.

16. Union Village to New Lebanon, July 3, 1826, WM 1048; Ministry Sisters' Book, August 2, 1826, WRHS 32, V:B-60; INY to Andrew Houston, May 18, 1827, LC 27: 347b; Andrew Houston to New Lebanon, September 29, 1834, WM 1048.

17. INY [and Bishop], Tour, July 5, 1834.

18. Ibid., July 6, 1834; Elizabeth Lovegrove, Journal on the Revival in the Church, 1827, April and May, WRHS 33, V:B-93 and 94.

19. INY [and Bishop], Tour, July 10–135, 1834.

20. Ibid., July 17, 1834; INY, Domestic Journals, year-end tallies of livestock 1841–63, NYSL 10 (1834–46) and WRHS 32, V:B-70 and -71 (1847–63).

21. INY [and Bishop], Tour, July 21–24, 1834.

22. Ibid., July 26 and 28, 1834.

23. Millennial Laws prohibited Shaker boys from using firearms, "and the longer they let guns alone the better." 1821 Millennial Laws, 263. Whitewater: Emlen, *Shaker Village Views,* 80–81.

24. INY [and Bishop], Tour, July 29, 1834.

25. Ibid., July 30, 1834.

26. Rufus Bishop, INY and GKL's prescriptive guide for Shaker youth, *Juvenile Monitor* (New Lebanon, N.Y.: for the Shakers, 1823) includes the admonition, "Never stand and gaze at strangers" as well as advice to treat visitors with civility and

kindness, being careful to give them correct information (9). My thanks to Jerry Grant for sharing his transcription.

27. INY [and Bishop], Tour, July 31, 1834.

28. INY [and Bishop], Tour, August 1, 1834; John E. Kleber, ed., *Kentucky Encyclopedia* (University Press of Kentucky, 1992): Georgetown, Harrodsburg, and Lexington. Wickliff quoted in E. D. and Faith Andrews, *Work and Worship: The Economic Order of the Shakers* (Greenwich, Conn.: New York Graphic Society, 1974), 196–97.

29. INY [and Bishop], Tour, August 6–16, 1834.

30. INY [and Bishop], Tour, vol. 2, August 19–20, 1834, SM 142.

31. Ibid., August 20, 1834.

32. Ibid.; aqueduct: Domestic Journal (1834–46), end of October 1837, NYSL 10.

33. INY [and Bishop], Tour, vol. 2, August 20, 1834.

34. Ibid., August 21, 1834.

35. Ibid., August 23–September 1, 1834. Map of South Union: Emlen, *Shaker Village Views,* 87.

36. INY [and Bishop], Tour, September 4–9, 1834.

37. Ibid., September 11–12, 1834.

38. Ibid., September 13, 1834. The 1845 Millennial Laws were very specific about language. Andrews, *People,* 268.

39. INY [and Bishop], Tour, vol. 2, September 13–15, 1834; Basil Hall, *Travels in North America in the Years 1827 and 1828* (1929; repr., Graz, Austria: Akademische Druck-v. Verlagsanstalt, 1964–65), 3:228–29; Harriet Martineau, *Retrospect of Western Travel* (New York: Harper and Brothers, 1838; repr., New York: Johnson,1968), 139–42. Travelers observed that the region was economically backward because of its reliance on slaves rather than free labor. James Stirling, *Letters from the Slave States* (London: J. W. Parker and Son, 1857), 175. Southern Ohio was "less generally hardworking than other areas" of the state. "Fifty Years of Ohio," *North American Review* 47 (July 1838): 33, Cornell University Making of America Collection online, cdl.library.cornell.edu/moa.

40. INY [and Bishop], Tour, vol. 2, September 15, 1834.

41. INY and Rufus Bishop to Ministry, September 26, 1834, WRHS 24, IV:A-71.

42. INY [and Bishop], Tour, vol. 2, October 1, 1834.

43. William Sharp and Andrew Houston to New Lebanon, September 29, 1834, WM 1048.

44. INY [and Bishop], Tour, vol. 2, October 1–5, 1834.

45. Ibid., October 6, 1834.

46. Ibid., October 8, 1834. Shaker table manners: Bishop, INY, and GKL, *Juvenile Monitor,* 11–17. Travelers' gluttony was confirmed by [Thomas Hamilton], *Men and Manners in America* (Edinburgh: Blackwood, 1833), 1:77.

47. INY [and Bishop], Tour, vol. 2, October 9, 1834.

48. Ibid., October 10, 1834.

49. Ibid., October 11, 1834; [INY et al.], Records Kept By Order of the Church, October 11, 1834, NYPL 2:7.

50. Union Village journal, November 1834, WRHS 40, V:B-230.

51. Stein, *Shaker Experience,* 131–32.

Chapter 7. Intimacy between Men in Shaker Society

1. Priscilla Brewer, *Shaker Communities, Shaker Lives* (Hanover, N.H.: University Press of New England, 1986), 74.

2. Susan Matarese and Paul Salmon, "Assessing Psychopathology in Communal Societies, *Communal Societies* 15 (1995), 39–43, make startling conclusions about INY's psychopathology. In my opinion, he was neither joyless nor friendless, as they suggest; he maintained decades-long bonds of affection with several individuals.

3. Donald Yacovone, " 'Surpassing the Love of Women:' Victorian Manhood and the Language of Fraternal Love," in *A Shared Experience: Men, Women, and the History of Gender,* ed. Laura McCall and Donald Yacovone (New York: New York University Press, 1998): 195–221.

4. 1821 Millennial Laws, in John T. Kirk, *Shaker World* (New York: Henry Abrams, 1997), 261. See Louis J. Kern, *An Ordered Love: Sex Roles and Sexuality in Victorian Utopias—the Shakers, the Mormons, and the Oneida Community* (Chapel Hill: University of North Carolina Press, 1981), 83–84, 89, on prohibitions against sexual activity including bestiality, homosexuality, and masturbation.

5. INY, Private [Apostate] Journal (1837–59), March 21, 1837, SM 10,509.

6. 1845 Millennial Laws, in E. D. Andrews, *The People Called Shakers: A Search for the Perfect Society* (New York: Dover, 1963), 267. Thomas Brown quoted the apostate Reuben Rathbun, "From the time I first knew the Shakers to this time, I never defiled myself with what is called among you effeminacy." Brown, *Account of the People Called Shakers: Their Faith, Doctrines, and Practice* (Troy, N.Y.: Parker & Bliss, 1812; repr., New York: AMS Press, 1972), 111. Kirk, *Shaker World,* 186–88, uses extracts from brethren's letters out of context.

7. Yacovone, "Surpassing the Love of Women," 197.

8. INY, Autobiography in Verse, July 4, 1837, WM 818, reprinted in E. D. Andrews and Faith Andrews, *Fruits of the Shaker Tree of Life* (Stockbridge, Mass.: Berkshire Traveller Press, 1975), 129–34; Arrival dates: Names of the Brethren and Sisters in the First and Second Order, April 1835, 1–2, LC 5:92.

9. School teaching: INY, Family and Meeting Journal, April 4, 1819, and August 24, 1820, LC 3:42; INY, Domestic Journal (1834–46), 1850 list at end, NYSL 10; Singing: INY, Family and Meeting Journal, March 20, 1819, March 1 and 18, 1821, LC 3:42; Betsy Bates, Journal of Events, September 13, 1835, WRHS 35, V:B-128. Social meetings: INY, Concise View, 370–71, WM 861.

10. Giles Avery, Historical Sketches or a Record of Remarkable Events (1834), January 1, 1834, LC 4:53; INY, Concise View, 357; 1821 Millennial Laws, 263.

11. Before July 1816, INY and GKL roomed together with several others. INY,

Family and Meeting Journal, July 4, 1816, LC 3:42. In 1832, INY and GKL shared a room with Eliab Harlow, Anthony Bruister, and Barnabas Hinkley, probably GKL's medical apprentice. Ministry Sisters' Journal, September 1832, WRHS 32, V:B-60. GKL and INY were still in the same room in 1833. INY to GKL, August 11, 1833, WRHS 20, IV:A-36. In 1835, INY's name was listed next to GKL's. Names of the Brethren and the Sisters, April 1835.

12. GKL to INY, April 3, 1826, WRHS 20, IV:A-35; INY, [Hymnal] Made for Edward Fowler, March 1833, BA: V289.8 Un3.3J, v. 10:17–20, 46–47.

13. INY to GKL, August 11, 1833, WRHS 20, IV:A-36.

14. 1821 Millennial Laws, 263; 1845 Millennial Laws, 273, 278.

15. INY and Rufus Bishop to Ministry and GKL, September 26, 1834, WRHS 24, IV:A-71.

16. INY to GKL, December 16, 1835, WRHS 20, IV:A-37. This is not to suggest that Shaker boys did not engage in sexual experimentation. But conclusions cannot be drawn without evidence.

17. Hymnal, letter p. 138, WRHS 98, IX: B-162; INY to Reuben Dickey and Abram Perkins, May 10, 1835, Daniel Boler to Beloved Br. Isaac, December 12, 1837, and INY to Beloved Brother, March 10, 1839, WRHS 20, IV:A-37; Union Village to New Lebanon Elders, July 3, 1826, WM 1048, SA-1249.23 and SA-1249.24; INY to Andrew Houston, May 18, 1827 and July 29, 1828, LC 27:347b.

18. INY, [Hymnal] Made for Edward Fowler, March 1833, BA, V298.8 Un3.3, 10:26–27; "Protecting Chain": Daniel Patterson, *The Shaker Spiritual* (Princeton, N.J.: Princeton University Press, 1979), 227.

19. Andrew Houston to INY, June 4, 1829, WRHS 24, IV:A-70; "old man": Ephesians 4:22–24, Romans 6:6, and Colossians 3:5–9. Guide posts are mentioned in Jeremiah 31:21.

20. INY to Andrew Houston, September 1, 1829, WRHS 20, IV:A-35.

21. Yacovone, "Surpassing the Love of Women," 197.

22. Andrew Houston to Ministry, October 10, 1835, WRHS 20, IV:A-71; Andrew Houston to GKL, November 25, 1835, WRHS 20, IV:A-71.

23. Andrew Houston to INY, May 1, 1836, WRHS 20, IV:A-71.

24. Andrew Houston to GKL, August 24, 1836, WRHS 20, IV:A-71.

25. INY to Andrew Houston, September 11, 1836, LC 27:347b.

26. Andrew Houston to INY, October 16, 1836, WRHS 20, IV:A-71.

27. GKL went to Saratoga to recuperate but gained little. Henry DeWitt, Journal (1827–67), June 8–17, 1833, WRHS 33, V:B-97; INY to GKL, August 8 and 11, 1833, WRHS 20, IV:A-36. Henry DeWitt's occupation: INY, Domestic Journal (1834–46), January 1, 1840, NYSL 10.

28. INY to Andrew Houston, September 11, 1836, LC 27:347b.

29. INY, Domestic Journal, December 30, 1835, February 22, August 2, September 1, November 29, December 18 and 31, 1836, NYSL 10; GKL obituary, *Pittsfield Sun*, February 2, 1837; Ministry Sisters' Journal, January 22 and 24, 1837, WRHS 32, V:B-60.

30. INY eulogized his friend, then described the autopsy on his body. As the village physician, GKL probably arranged the autopsy and asked INY to record the findings in hopes that someone might learn from them. Documenting the dissection of the corpse was the last office of friendship INY could perform for GKL. INY, Domestic Journal, January 24, 1837, NYSL 10.

31. Andrew Houston to INY, May 9, 1838, WRHS 20, IV:A-71. Andrew Houston corresponded with INY as late as March 1839, when he suggested in a letter to Austin Buckingham at Watervliet that Austin send the letter on to New Lebanon, to share the news from Union Village with one to whom Andrew owed a letter. The secondhand message suggests that personal contact was no longer a priority. Andrew Houston, Union Village to Austin Buckingham, Watervliet, March 21, 1839, WM 1048, SA-1249.29. Houston died in 1844. Elder Sisters' Domestic Journal, October 25, 1844, WRHS 32, V:B-61.

32. Thomas Hammond, Trip Journal (1816–53), October 1846, 97, WRHS 30, V:B-36; Bennet to Dean, March 3, 1839, and Avery to Barber, August 11, 1837, WRHS 20, IV:A-37; SYW to Rufus Bryant, October 30, 1837, BA, 289.8 Un5.9CC; Pelham to New Lebanon, November 29, 1852, BA, V289.8 Un5.9EE; Richard Pelham to INY, September 22, 1836, LC 18:245.

33. Brewer, *Shaker Communities,* 59–60; Elder H. Eads to INY, December 9, 1844, letter Alonzo Hollister transcribed in his Book of Remembrances, WRHS 58, VII:B-109.

34. William Sharp and Andrew Houston to New Lebanon, September 29, 1834, WM 1048,

35. Derobigne Bennet and INY, Journal of Inspirational Meetings (1840–41), January 19 and February 16, 1840, WRHS 77, VIII:B-138; Diane Sasson, *The Shaker Spiritual Narrative* (Knoxville: University of Tennessee Press, 1983), 96–97; INY [and Rufus Bishop], Tour thro the States of Ohio and Kentucky, in the Summer of 1834, July 10, 1834, SM 141, reported in Robert P. Emlen, *Shaker Village Views* (Hanover, N.H.: University Press of New England, 1987), 78.

36. Carroll Smith-Rosenberg, *Disorderly Conduct: Visions of Gender in Victorian America* (New York: Oxford University Press, 1985), 36.

37. Kirk misinterprets Benjamin Gates's 1826 letter by quoting only the part that agrees with his thesis. Kirk, *Shaker World,* 186. Gates, INY's apprentice, addressed INY as "daddy"; his affection was of a filial nature.

38. Andrews, *People,* 192.

39. INY, Family and Meeting Journal, September 15, 1818, LC 3:42; INY, Private [Apostate] Journal, March 21, 1837.

40. Emotional celibacy: Judith Graham argues that Mother Lucy intended to isolate children from adults in the Children's Order. Graham, "New Lebanon Shaker Children's Order" (Ph.D. diss., Iowa State University, 1996), 207–8. Elisha D. Blakeman, Eulogical to Brother Isaac N. Youngs, September 1866, 355–61, WRHS 50, VI:B-21; Benjamin Gates to INY, March 26, 1826, SM 9547.

41. Franklin Barber to INY, December 30, 1840, copied into Hollister, Book of Remembrances, 247–51, WRHS 58, VII:B-109.

42. Giles Avery to INY, appended to Franklin Barber to INY, December 30, 1840, copied into Hollister, Book of Remembrances, 247–52, WRHS 58, VII:B-109.

43. INY poem for Elder Benjamin Seth Youngs, June 20, 1818, WRHS 116, X:A-2.

Chapter 8. Shaker Worship, Isaac Newton Youngs, and the Era of Manifestations

1. INY as scribe: Calvin Green, Memoir, WRHS 56, VII:B-60.1. His reactions: INY, Family and Meeting Journal (1815–23), of Lucy Wright, 114, LC 3:42.

2. INY singing: INY, Family and Meeting Journal, March 1 and April 8, 1819, LC 3:42. Singing: [Andrew Bell], *Men and Things in America* (London 1838), 88; Richard Nunley, "Neumes and melismas," *Berkshire Eagle*, October 23, 2002, A7. Elisha D. Blakeman, Eulogical to Brother Isaac N. Youngs, September 1866, 357, WRHS 50, VI:B-21.

3. INY, *The Rudiments of Music Displayed and Explained* (New Lebanon, N.Y.: for the society, 1833); INY, *A Short Abridgement of the Rules of Music* (New Lebanon, N.Y.: for the society, 1843). INY in choir: INY, Family and Meeting Journal, September 17, 1816, LC 3:42; improving singing: INY, Family and Meeting Journal, March 1, 1819, LC 3:42; "the last song I pitched": INY, A Brief Collection of Hymns: Improved in Sacred Worship (1826–30), 77, LC 16:230; Horace Greeley, "A Sabbath with the Shakers," *The Knickerbocker, or New York Monthly Magazine* (June 1838), 534–37; "The Shakers at New Lebanon," *The Harbinger* 5 (August 14, 1847): 156–58; [Bell], *Men and Things in America*, 91; John S. Dwight, "Shakers at New Lebanon," *The Harbinger* 5 (August 14, 1847): 156–57.

4. Elizabeth Lovegrove, Journal on the Revival in the Church, May 3, 1827, WRHS 33, V:B-93.

5. 2 Samuel 7:13–16; Psalms 149:3.

6. François Marquis de Barbé-Marbois, *Our Revolutionary Forefathers . . . 1779–1785,* trans. Eugene Parker Chase (New York: Duffield and Co., 1929): 180–84; [Ezra Stiles], *Literary Diary of Ezra Stiles,* vol. 2 (1776–81), ed. Franklin Bowditch Dexter (New York: Charles Scribner's Sons, 1901), 558; Albert Matthews, "Journal of William Loughton Smith, 1790–1791," Massachusetts Historical Society *Proceedings* 51 (October 1917): 49–51; Elkanah Watson, *Men and Times of the Revolution,* ed. Winslow C. Watson (New York: Dana and Co., 1856), 289. Dancing subsided in the later 1790s; Mother Lucy Wright revived it in 1808. Jean Humez, *Mother's First-Born Daughters: Early Shaker Writings on Women and Religion* (Bloomington: Indiana University Press, 1993), 69, 72.

7. INY, Family and Meeting Journal, June 11, 1815, LC 3:42 (also told to shake May 2, 1819).

8. Thomas Brown, *An Account of the People Called Shakers: Their Faith, Doctrines, and Practice* (Troy, N.Y.: Parker & Bliss, 1812; repr., New York: AMS, 1972), 293, 322–23, 335–36.

9. "The Community of Shakers," *Chambers' Edinburgh Journal* 546 (July 16, 1842): 208; [Benson Lossing], "The Shakers," *Harper's New Monthly Magazine* 15 (July 1857): 168; Greeley, "A Sabbath with the Shakers," 534; Giles Avery, Journal of Times, Rhymes, Work & Weather, August 21, 1836, WRHS 34, V:B-106.

10. "A Visit to the Shakers," *Blackwood's Magazine* [London], April 1823, 467; Lawrence Pitkethly, "Emigration," *Northern Star,* May 6, 1843, 7.

11. Lovegrove, Journal, April 19, 1827, 17, WRHS 33, V:B-93, cited in Daniel W. Patterson, *Shaker Spiritual,* (Princeton, N.J.: Princeton University Press, 1979), 101.

12. John DeWitt, Memorandum, March 8, 1835, WRHS 33, V:B-92; Henry DeWitt, Journal (1827–67), January 28, 1835, November 29 and December 25, 1837, May 8, 1838, WRHS 33, V:B-97.

13. INY, Family and Meeting Journal, September 17, 1816, LC 3:42.

14. INY, Meeting Journal (1823–28), April 1827–October 1828, selections copied into Alonzo Hollister, Book of Remembrances, WRHS 58, VII:B-109; INY [and Rufus Bishop], Tour thro the states of Ohio and Kentucky, in the Summer of 1834, July 6, 1834, SM 141.

15. Giles Avery, Journal (1834–36), September 6, 1835, WRHS 33, V-B:105, quoted in Priscilla Brewer, *Shaker Communities, Shaker Lives* (Hanover, N.H.: University Press of New England, 1986), 115. At harvest, they may have been too tired to be lively in church.

16. INY, Concise View, 97, WM 861.

17. Rufus Bishop, A Daily Journal of Passing Events (1830–39), September 24 to October 8, 1837, NYPL 1:1.

18. Daniel Boler to INY, December 12, 1837, WRHS 20, IV:A-37.

19. INY quoted in Giles Avery, Historical Sketches (1832–55), [December 22, 1837], LC 4:53.

20. INY, Domestic Journal (1834–46), December 22, 1837, NYSL 10; Henry DeWitt, Journal, December 5, 1837, WRHS 33, V:B-97; INY quoted in Avery, Historical Sketches, [December 22, 1837]. Daniel the prophet also described his own vision of (and conversation with) a heavenly messenger (Daniel 10).

21. Aaron D. Bill, A Journal or Day Book [1834–40], January 4, 1838, WRHS 35, V:B-132; Avery, Journal of the Times, January 1, 1838, quoted in Sally Promey, *Spiritual Spectacles: Vision and Image in Mid-Nineteenth-Century Shakerism* (Bloomington: Indiana University Press, 1993), 54. Bill described both presentations. In a journal entry for November 1837, Bill mentioned hearing reports of visions from both Rufus Bishop and INY; his comments suggest that Brother Rufus did not make the impression that INY did: "Br. Rufus comes & read some visions that was seen at Watervliet"; INY "read & related a narrative of the Visions seen at Watervliet which is very interesting & remarkable."

22. INY, Sketches of Visions, 1838, 20, 21, 23, WRHS 75, VIII:B-113. The

Shaker village at Harvard, Massachusetts, was concerned about their participation in June 1841. Diane Sasson, *The Shaker Spiritual Narrative* (Knoxville: University of Tennessee Press, 1983), 51n15,53n20.

23. Philemon Stewart, Mother Ann's Message to the Church at New Lebanon, April 22, 1838, 1–2, WRHS 75, VIII:B-112.

24. Sally Promey describes the era as an "internal revival" or initiation for Shakers born after Mother Ann died. Promey, *Spiritual Spectacles,* 6, 131.

25. Stewart, Mother Ann's Message, 8; INY, Sketches of Visions, May 1838, 43, 45.

26. Henry DeWitt, Journal, May 2, 1838, WRHS 33, V:B-97; INY, Domestic Journal, May 1837 and 1838, NYSL 10; INY, Sketches of Visions, May 1838, 48.

27. INY, Sketches of Visions, May 14, 1838, 49, 50, 53.

28. Ibid., May 1838, 53.

29. INY, Concise View, 136; Charles Giles B. Daubeny, *Journal of a Tour Through the United States, and in Canada . . . 1837–1838* (Oxford: T. Coombe, 1843), 21. Horace Greeley attended a Watervliet service where a similar incident occurred. Greeley, "A Sabbath with the Shakers," 533–34.

30. INY, Concise View, 105, 136; Promey, *Spiritual Spectacles,* 275–76 n. 38; Stephen Stein, "Shaker Gift and Shaker Order: A Study of Religious Tension in Nineteenth-Century America," *Communal Societies* 10 (1990): 102–13. The phrase "a time for everything under heaven" is drawn from Ecclesiastes 3:1–8.

31. Alonzo Hollister, Reminiscences by a Soldier of the Cross, written July 7, 1907, 172, WRHS 116, X:B-31; Hervey Elkins, *Fifteen Years in the Senior Order of Shakers* (Hanover, N.H.: Dartmouth Press, 1853), 43, 72–76. Elkins was skeptical.

32. INY, Sketches of Visions, May 1838, 54.

33. Bishop, Daily Journal, October 8, 1837, NYPL 1:1; Greeley, "A Sabbath with the Shakers," 534–37; Fanny Appleton Longfellow, *Mrs Longfellow,* ed. Edward Wagenknecht (New York: Longmans, Green, 1956), 61–63.

34. Pitkethly, "Emigration," 7; New Hampshire Ministry to New Lebanon Ministry, April 1839, WRHS 17, IV:A-4; Brewer, *Shaker Communities,* 124–25. Brewer notes that some instruments tended to "run by their Lead" (125).

35. INY, Sketches of Visions, 1838, 52. Gifts were not just a phenomenon of youth. Though two-thirds of the visionists were under thirty years old, six were in their thirties or forties, and Elizabeth Lovegrove, who "beat everything for motion," was forty-six. Ages estimated from INY list of Church Family, Domestic Journal, January 1, 1840, NYSL 10.

36. INY, Sketches of Visions, May 1838, 53; Hollister, Reminiscences, 173, WRHS 116, X:B-31.

37. E. D. Andrews, *The People Called Shakers: A Search for the Perfect Society* (New York: Dover, 1963), 160–61; Anna White and Leila Taylor, *Shakerism: Its Meaning and Message* (Columbus, Ohio: Fred J. Heer for the Shakers, 1905), 234–35; Avery, Journal of the Times, February 4, 1843.

38. [Elder] Henry C. Blinn, *Manifestation of Spiritualism Among the Shakers,*

1837–1847 (1899), 26, 28, 29, 49–50, 59; INY, Sketches of Visions, 1838, 22; Stein, "Shaker Gift and Shaker Order," 103.

39. Derobigne Bennet and INY, Journal of Inspirational Meetings (1840–41), November 23, 1841, WRHS 77, VIII:B-138.

40. Visit from Mehomet, BA, V289.8 Un5.9J; Brewer, *Shaker Communities*, 124–25. Diane Sasson suggests that by 1839, the Ministry had asked Elders to designate visionists and pre-approve their messages. Sasson, *Shaker Spiritual Narrative*, 55. [Elder] Henry C. Blinn, *Manifestation of Spiritualism Among the Shakers, 1837–1847* (1899), 44, 48, 19; Brewer, *Shaker Communities*, 128–30; Bennett and INY, Journal of Inspirational Meetings, December 12, 1841, WRHS 77, VIII:B-138.

41. Bennet and INY, Journal of Inspirational Meetings, March 13, 1840, November 22, 1841, WRHS 77, VIII:B-138..

42. INY, Sketches of Visions, May 1838, 62–64. Ann E. may have been Ann Eliza Goodwin, who was returned to her parents. INY, Domestic Journal (1834–46), November 30, 1838, NYSL 10. In retrospect, other Shakers were also skeptical. Henry Blinn wrote that the manifestations were "not congenial to a well-disciplined mind" Decades later, he decided that "the unsubdued natures of the mediums led largely toward such peculiar manifestations." Blinn, *Manifestation of Spiritualism*, 49, 60–61. See also Elkins, *Fifteen Years*, 42–43.

43. Bennett and INY, Journal of Inspirational Meetings, November 8, 1840, WRHS 77, VIII:B-138.

44. Stewart, Mother Ann's Message, 8; Bennet and INY, Journal of Inspirational Meetings, March 15, 1840 WRHS 77, VIII:B-138; [INY et al.], Records Kept by Order of the Church (1780–1855), 191, NYPL 2:7.

45. Benjamin Gates, Day Book, November 7, 1827, WM 819; A True Record of Sacred Communications (April 1838–July 1839), November 1838, 109, WRHS 75, VIII:B-116.

46. According to Jean Humez, the best-known spirit-inspired expulsion was Richard McNemar from Union Village, Ohio, perhaps ousted by instrument Margaret O'Brien. Jean M. Humez, *Mother's First-Born Daughters: Early Shaker Writings on Women and Religion* (Bloomington: Indiana University Press, 1993), 215. At New Lebanon, after instrument Eleanor Potter identified Olive Gates as an "evil doer," and two other instruments attacked her as well, Gates had to leave. Bennet and INY, Journal of Inspirational Meetings, October 4, 7, 8, and 9, 1840, WRHS 77, VIII:B-138. Sally Dean was expelled after a similar attack. Bennet and INY, Journal of Inspirational Meetings, May 26, 1841, WRHS 77, VIII:B-138.

47. INY, Domestic Journal, December 1840, NYSL 10; Bennet and INY, Journal of Inspirational Meetings, October and December 1840, March 14 and December 1841, WRHS 77, VIII:B-138.

48. INY, Concise View, 136.

49. Andrews, *People*, 162.

50. Bennet and INY, Journal of Inspirational Meetings, March 3, 1841, WRHS 77, VIII:B-138.

51. INY, [Hymnal] Made for Edward Fowler, March 1833, BA, V289.8 Un3.3O, v. 10:28, 33, 35, 42, 57, 58, 59, 61, 62.

52. [INY et al.], Records Kept by Order of the Church, 229, NYPL 2:7. In 1842, Holy Mother Wisdom (perhaps Sarah Bates) presented him with a certificate that blessed Isaac's upright soul, his labors, hands, feet, eyes, and voice. He had "found favor in her sight" through his faithful service. [Sarah Bates?] to INY, Words on a Card, Sent from Holy Mother Wisdom, August 8, 1842, NYPL 9:122. My thanks to Jane Crosthwaite for pointing out this source. Sally Promey suggests that the Era of Manifestations made religion visible in new ways; I concur. Promey, *Spiritual Spectacles*, 131.

53. Polly Jane Reed, A Heart of Blessing for Isaac N. Youngs, April 14, 1844, NYPL, reproduced in Daniel Patterson, *Gift Drawing and Gift Song* (Sabbathday Lake, Maine: United Society of Shakers, 1983), 8. Gift drawings: Jane Crosthwaite, "The Spirit Drawings of Hannah Cahoon: Window on the Shakers and Their Folk Art," *Communal Societies* 7 (1987): 1–15; Sharon Koomler, *Seen and Received* (Pittsfield, Mass.: HSV, 1998).

54. [INY et al.], Records Kept by Order of the Church, March 31, 1841, 182–83, NYPL 2:7; Bennet and INY, Journal of Inspirational Meetings, December 14, 1840, January 14, March 3, and December 31, 1841, WRHS 77, VIII:B-138.

55. Bennet and INY, Journal of Inspirational Meetings, April 4, 1841, WRHS 77, VIII:B-138.

56. Blakeman, Eulogical.

57. Promey, *Spiritual Spectacles*, 161; Bennet and INY, Journal of Inspirational Meetings, December 14, 1840, WRHS 77, VIII:B-138; sacred writings: INY, Domestic Journal, June 30 and August 31, 1841, December 31, 1842, NYSL 10; INY, Personal Journal, December 30, 1842, WRHS 35, V:B-134.

58. John S. Dwight, "The Shakers at New Lebanon," *The Harbinger* 5 (August 14, 1847): 156–58.

59. "Godfrey Greylock," [J. E .A. Smith], *Taghkonic; or Letters and Legends about our summer home* (Boston: Redding, 1852), 120, 133, University of Michigan Making of America collection online, moa.umdl.umcih.edu; Frederika Bremer, *Homes of the New World*, trans. Mary Howitt (London: A. Hall, Virtue, 1853), 1:561.

60. INY, Domestic Journal, October 9 and November 6, 1851, WRHS 32, V:B-70; INY, Spiritual Autobiography, November 1, 1848, 296, transcribed in Alonzo Hollister, Autobiography of the Saints, or Stray Leaves from the book of Life, WRHS 52, VI:B-36; Susan Kendall letter, November 1, 1851, extract by Philemon Stewart, WRHS 52, VI:B-36; Jerry Grant and Douglas Allen, *Shaker Furniture Makers* (Pittsfield, Mass.: HSV, and Hanover, N.H.: University Press of New England, 1989), 51.

Chapter 9. Spiritual Autobiography

1. Sarah Bates, A Collection of Marching Songs (1853–64), 50, 77, BA, V289.8 Un3.3, vol. 18.

2. Matthew 5:48.

3. INY, Family and Meeting Journal (1815–23), April 7, 1821, LC 3:42. Pledge: Chap. 4. Language: Carroll Smith-Rosenberg, *Disorderly Conduct: Visions of Gender in Victorian America* (New York: Oxford University Press, 1985), 44–45.

4. Meridian age forty-five: Thomas R. Cole, *The Journey of Life: A Cultural History of Aging in America* (New York: Cambridge University Press, 1992), 63.

5. Priscilla Brewer, *Shaker Communities, Shaker Lives* (Hanover, N.H.: University Press of New England, 1986), 213–15.

6. [Rufus Bishop, INY, and GKL], *A Juvenile Monitor* (New Lebanon, N.Y.: for the Shakers, 1823); dialogue between flesh and spirit attributed to INY, transcribed ca. 1828–33 into Betsy Smith, Book of Poams of different Authers copied When She was in her teens . . . , WRHS 113, IX:B-385; INY, Idle Company: A Treatise on Disorderly Communication, particularly for boys and youth, 1854, WRHS 57, VII:B-103.

7. Later INY wrote, "The origin of the Devil is a topic of much conversation a[mong] the brethren and sisters." But he thought the discussion a waste of time. It did not matter how evil came to exist; as long as they recognized its existence. "All we have got to do," he wrote, "is, to overcome him." INY, Family and Meeting Journal, January 1 and 7, 1821, December 1, 1822, LC 3:42.

8. INY, Domestic Journal (1856–69), May 1862, WRHS 32, V:B-71. Lilies: Matthew 6:28. Lusts (see Chap. 4): 1 John 2:15–17. Israelites in the wilderness: book of Numbers.

9. INY, Spiritual Autobiography extracted from a letter to Oliver Hampton, November 1848, transcribed in Alonzo Hollister, Autobiography of the Saints, or Stray Leaves from the book of Life, 291–305, WRHS 52, VI:B-36.

10. Matthew 6:19–21.

11. This poem is from INY, Autobiography in Verse, July 4, 1837, WM 818, reprinted in E. D. Andrews and Faith Andrews, *Fruits of the Shaker Tree of Life* (Stockbridge, Mass.: Berkshire Traveller Press, 1975), 129–34. INY or Alonzo Hollister, the transcriber, changed the text of the lines quoted from INY's Autobiography in Verse.

12. Cole, *Journey of Life*, 40–43. Ownership of *Pilgrim's Progress*: Church Library at New Lebanon [ca. 1835–70], WRHS 121, XIV: 9 [third list]. According to school records, some of the books on this list were purchased between 1820 and 1834 when INY was keeping the records.

13. INY, Spiritual Autobiography, 297–98. See also Elisha Blakeman, Eulogical to Brother Isaac N. Youngs, September 1866, 355–61, WRHS 50, VI:B-21 for comments on INY's encouragement.

14. Matthew 6:19–21.

15. See INY, Private [Apostate] Journal (1837–59), SM 10,509, which includes his most vitriolic comments on apostates.

16. INY, New Year's Thoughts, January 1, 1824, MCA 269; INY, Spiritual Autobiography, 300–301.

17. [Lucy Wright], Mother Lucy's Sayings, Spoken at different times . . . , LC 5:88; 1845 Millennial Laws, in E. D. Andrews, *The People Called Shakers: A Search for the Perfect Society* (New York: Dover, 1963), 262, 268–69.

18. Luke 22:40.

19. INY, Personal Journal (1839–58), November 5, 1855, WRHS 35, V:B-134.

20. Genesis 2:9–3:4.

21. Tree known by its fruit: Matthew 12:33; not forsaking a mother's teachings: Proverbs 1:8.

22. INY, Personal Journal, March 23, 1857, WRHS 35, V:B-134.

23. Faith and works: The Shaker belief that works must accompany faith drew its authority from the apostle James (see James 2:18).

24. Aaron D. Bill kept a journal from 1834 to 1840 with temporal matters listed in the first part and a brief synopsis of Sabbath and special meetings in the back. Bill, A Journal or Day Book, WRHS 35, V:B-132. Elisha Blakeman and Benjamin Gates rarely mentioned spiritual matters in their journals. Blakeman, Boys' Journal of Work (1844–65), WRHS 36, V:B-137; Gates, A Day Book or Journal of Work and Various things (1827–38), WM 819.

Chapter 10. Perfectionism and Overwork in Middle Age

1. Jerry Grant and Douglas Allen, *Shaker Furniture Makers* (Hanover, N.H.: Published for HSV by University Press of New England, 1989), 45.

2. INY, Domestic Journal (1834–46), February 27, 1840, NYSL 10.

3. Peter Hoehnle, "Work and Labor in Three Communal Societies: Amana, Icaria, and Oneida" (paper presented at Communal Studies Conference, Oneida, N.Y., September 2002); Suzanne Thurman, " 'No idle hands are seen': The Social Construction of Work in Shaker Society," *Communal Societies* 18 (1998): 37, 40; David Hackett Fischer, *Albion's Seed: Four British Folkways in America* (New York: Oxford University Press, 1989), 158–60; E. D. Andrews and Faith Andrews, *Work and Worship: The Economic Order of the Shakers* (Greenwich, Conn.: New York Graphic Society, 1974), 44; Bread of idleness: Proverbs 31:27; 1845 Millennial Laws: E. D. Andrews, *The People Called Shakers: A Search for the Perfect Society* (New York: Dover, 1963), 288.

4. Frances Anne Kemble, "The Shakers," in *The Berkshire Reader,* ed. Richard Nunley (Stockbridge, Mass.: Berkshire House, 1992), 144; C. B., "Visit to the Shakers," *Lowell Offering,* n.s., 1 (1841): 279; [Benson Lossing], *An Early View of the Shakers,* ed. Don Gifford (Hanover, N.H.: Published for HSV by University Press of New England, 1989), 51; INY, Personal Journal (1839–58), August 18, 1856, WRHS 35, V:B-134.

5. Carl D. Arfwedson, Esq., *The United States and Canada in 1832, 1833, and 1834* (London: Richard Bentley, 1834, repr., New York: Johnson, 1969), 1:94.

6. INY to "Blvd Br," August 8, 1833, WRHS 20, IV:A-36. Staying up late: INY, Family and Meeting Journal (1815–23), April 27, 1817, LC 3:42; INY, Autobiography in Verse, July 4, 1837, WM 818, reprinted in E. D. Andrews and Faith Andrews, *Fruits of the Shaker Tree of Life* (Stockbridge, Mass.: Berkshire Traveller Press, 1975), 134. Men's work: Psalm 104:23.

7. Henry DeWitt, Journal (1827–67), September 30, 1836, WRHS 33, V:B-97. Suzanne Thurman reports that the Harvard and Shirley Shaker sisters felt they were overworked. *"O Sisters Ain't You Happy?" Gender, Family, and Community among the Harvard and Shirley Shakers, 1781–1918* (Syracuse, N.Y.: Syracuse University Press, 2002), 126. The relationships between business expansion, profits, aging, and worker discontent would provide ample material for further study.

8. INY to Andrew Houston, August 6, 1830, WRHS 20, IV:A-36.

9. INY, Family and Meeting Journal, March 24, 1821, LC 3:42.

10. INY, Autobiography in Verse, 129–34.

11. INY, Family and Meeting Journal, March 27, 1818 and April 8, 1819, LC 3:42; Elisha D. Blakeman, Eulogical to Brother Isaac N. Youngs, September 1866, 355–61, WRHS 50, VI:B-21.

12. INY, Family and Meeting Journal, July 26, 1820 (mechanic), LC 3:42; INY [and Rufus Bishop], Tour, September 27, 1834, SM 142 (mapmaker); Grant and Allen, *Shaker Furniture Makers,* 38 (new schoolhouse), 39, 42–43 (teacher's desk), 46 (tailoring counter, silver and steel pens, leveling instrument), 47 (stonecutter); INY, Personal Journal, November 30, 1843 (printer), February 8, 1844 (bookkeeper), December 31, 1850 (bone bodkins and stocking needles with ivory handles), August 1, 1853 (toneometer); INY et al., Taylor's Journal (1845–65), December 28, 1854 (soldering pipe), WRHS 36,V:B-139; Rufus Bishop, A Daily Journal of Passing Events (1830–39), July 31, 1839 (music pen), NYPL 1:1; Bishop, Daily Journal (1839–50), August 15, 1848 (tinsmith), NYPL 1:2; Charles L. Flint, *Mount Lebanon Shaker Collection* (New Lebanon, N.Y.: Mount Lebanon Shaker Village, 1987), app. C (sundial); Henry DeWitt, Journal, August 10, 1832, and April 21, 1834 (clothespins, floors), WRHS 33: V:B-97; John DeWitt, Memorandum, October 5, 1824 (table), WRHS 33, V:B-92; second half of WRHS 33, V:B-92, by Semantha Fairbanks, March 24, 1835 (weaver's reed); Lawrence Pitkethly, "Emigration," *Northern Star,* May 6, 1843, 7 (wash house).

13. INY's 1837 work was documented in these manuscripts: INY, Private [Apostate] Journal (1837–59), 1837, SM 10,509; INY, Domestic Journal, 1837, NYSL 10; Elisha Blakeman, Journal of Occurances, WRHS 35, V:B-131; Henry DeWitt, Journal, WRHS 33, V:B-97; Giles Avery, Historical Sketches, LC 4:53; Benjamin Gates to INY, December 17, 1837, SM 9558.

14. The conclusion that many farmers did a little of everything is based on one thousand western Massachusetts probate files, 1780–1860, as well as every Hampshire County probate inventory, 1700–92, which show that many farmers practiced

additional trades, such as blacksmithing, shoemaking, tinsmithing, carpentry, or joinery.

15. INY, Domestic Journal, July 1859, WRHS 32: V:B-71. Some of INY's journals must have been lost, destroyed, or misattributed. In addition, a spirit message required that journals be given up; according to Franklin Barber, INY went along with the gift. Barber to INY, December 30, 1840, in Alonzo Hollister, Book of Remembrances, 247–51, WRHS 58, VII:B-109.

16. Grant and Allen, *Shaker Furniture Makers,* 51; INY, Personal Journal, September 7, 1855. He wrote similar notes in other journals, as well. INY, A Clock Maker's Journal, conclusion, WRHS 33, V:B-86; INY, Private [Apostate] Journal, September 1853.

17. Grant and Allen, *Shaker Furniture Makers,* 37. Measurements: INY, Domestic Journal, March 31, 1836, NYSL 10; INY, Domestic Journal, January 1, 1860, WRHS 32,V:B-71. Firewood: Blakeman, Journal, April 1836; INY, Domestic Journal, March 31, 1850, WRHS 32, V:B-70.

18. INY was involved with the school as late as 1839. Benjamin Gates, Day Book (1827–38), March 12 and November 30, 1830, WM 819; Miranda Barber to INY, August 14, 1833, WRHS 20, IV:A-36; INY, Domestic Journal, March 15, 1836, and May 29, 1839, NYSL 10; Henry DeWitt, Journal, September 2, 1839, WRHS 33, V:B-97.

19. Blakeman, Eulogical; [Daniel Myrick], Journal of a Visit to five societies of believers . . . 1846, SM 16,811, photocopy of Williams College original, #9779.

20. INY, Family and Meeting Journal, July 26, 1820, LC 3:42.

21. Watervliet's ivory buttons: E. D. Andrews, *Community Industries of the Shakers,* New York State Museum Handbook 15 (Albany, 1932), 169; [Rufus Bishop], Day Book (1815–29), May and September, 1820, WRHS 33, V:B-85. Though this journal was attributed to Bishop, its handwriting, form, and content resemble INY's. INY, Family and Meeting Journal, April 20, 1820, LC 3:42; Andrews and Andrews, *Work and Worship,* 107.

22. INY, Concise View, 253, WM 861; Mount Lebanon Church Family Trustees' Account Book (1835–39), 11, 29, 36, HSV 9784.N5, #364; Gates, Day Book, November 1835, WM 819. Buttons estimated from INY [and Benjamin Gates], Tailor's Journal (December 1838–April 1845), SM 9657, and Hervey Eads, Tailor's Division System (Union Village, Ohio, 1849). INY also made buttons October–November 1848. See INY, Domestic Journal, WRHS 32, V: B-70. It is hard to say why the New Lebanon Shakers needed 24,000 buttons in 1835. The Church Family might have been selling them, supplying them to other orders, or stocking up for future needs. In 1836, they changed the brethren's apparel again and bought about 6,000 ivory, horn, and pearl buttons, but even that number seems large. In 1839, for instance, the brethren's 320 new garments might have required about 2,000 buttons. Their supply from 1835 to 1836 could have lasted for years unless buttons were sold.

23. INY, Personal Journal, October–November 1840.

24. Ibid., April–May 1851, August–September 1853.

25. Teaching: INY, Family and Meeting Journal, August 27, 1816, November 17, December 1, 1817, February 14, 1818, April 8, 1819, LC 3:42; [INY et al.], Records Kept by Order of the Church (1780–1850), December 1817, NYPL 2:7; INY et al., Memorandum of the Proceedings and Expenses of the School (1817–35), SM 21: 10,469; problems: INY, Family and Meeting Journal, March 19 and 31, 1819, February 14, 1820, LC 3:4.

26. INY, Family and Meeting Journal, April 8, 1819, LC 3:42.

27. Ibid., August 24, 1820.

28. Schoolhouse: INY, Personal Journal, July–November 1839; INY, Domestic Journal, July 13 and September 2, 1839, NYSL 10; Henry DeWitt, Journal, September 2, 1839, WRHS 33, V:B-97; arsonist: INY, Domestic Journal, November 10, 1837, NYSL 10; pirate: INY, Domestic Journal, June 11, 1850, WRHS 32, V:B-70. INY, Family and Meeting Journal, March 31, 1819 and October 14, 1820, LC 3:42.

29. [Rufus Bishop, INY, and GKL], *A Juvenile Monitor* (New Lebanon, N.Y.: for the Shakers, 1823), 3, 5, 9, 10, 13–14, 17–20. My thanks to Jerry Grant for sharing his transcription.

30. INY, Idle Company: A Treatise on Disorderly Communication, particularly for boys and youth (1851–54), 24–26, 28, 31, WRHS 57, VII:B-103; INY, Concise View, 362, 370; Priscilla Brewer, *Shaker Communities, Shaker Lives* (Hanover, N.H.: University Press of New England, 1986), 105. Written in 1854 when INY was in a precarious emotional state, Idle Company was a harangue. The Shakers did not publish it.

31. INY's songs "Victorious Love," "Gospel Blessings," "Mother's Notice," "Bowing," "Day of Thanksgiving," "Remember Each Other," "Parents' Notice," and "Sacred Worship" appear with less frequency. Elder Giles [Avery's] Tune Book [by INY, with music from 1782 to 1841], LC 14:190; Yaacov Oved, *Two Hundred Years of American Communes* (New Brunswick, N.J.: Transaction Books, 1988) 50; GKL, Millennial Praises; Being a collection of Gospel Hymns Improved in Sacred Worship (1829), 30, 32, 37, WRHS 91, IX:B-42; hymnal, 138–39, WRHS 98, IX:B-162; hymnal, 17, 24, 125, 131–132, 188, 234–235, WRHS 119, IX:B-383; Rhoda Blake, A Collection of hymns and Spiritual songs Improved in our general worship, 5–6, WRHS 100, IX:B-185; hymnal, 53–54, WRHS 103, IX:B-235; INY, songbook, 33, WRHS 114, IX:B-412; INY, Songbook for Alonzo Hollister, 10, WRHS 114, IX:B-413; Early Hymns of Shakers from 1810 on, 76–77, WRHS 113, IX:B-398.

32. INY, *The Rudiments of Music Displayed and Explained* (New Lebanon, N.Y.: for the society, 1833), 114, quoted in Daniel Patterson, *Gift Drawing and Gift Song.* Sabbathday Lake, Maine: United Society of Shakers, 1983, 26; INY, Family and Meeting Journal, April 8, 1819, LC 3:42; INY, A Brief Collection of Hymns: Improved in Sacred Worship (1826–30), LC 16:230; INY, Family and Meeting Journal (1840–41), May 10, 1840, WRHS 76, VIII:B-138; Betsy Bates, Journal of Events, March 7 and 15 and September 13, 1835, WRHS 35, V:B-128.

33. INY letter, September 1840, WRHS 98, IX:B-162; Patterson, *Gift Drawing,* 47–50.

34. INY, Personal Journal, February 28, 1843.

35. INY, *A Short Abridgment of the Rules of Music* (New Lebanon, N.Y.: for the society, 1843), 24, 38.

36. INY, Personal Journal, December 4, 1842, October 3, 1843, January 15, 1844.

37. INY et al., Taylor's Journal, September 14, 1846, WRHS 36, V:B-139.

38. INY, Private [Apostate] Journal, September 8, 1847.

39. INY, Domestic Journal, January 1, 1845, NYPL 10. *Granville Jubilee* (Springfield, Mass.: H. S. Taylor, 1845) 23; [Orville Dewey], *Autobiography and Letters of Orville Dewey*, ed. Mary E. Dewey (Boston: Roberts Brothers, 1883), 28.

40. INY, Personal Journal, February 28 and June 2, 1853.

41. INY, Domestic Journal, June 30, 1837, NYSL 10; Henry Colman, *Second Report of the Agriculture of Massachusetts, County of Berkshire, 1838* (Boston: Dutton and Wentworth, 1839), 18–19, 24–27, 31–34; Mount Lebanon Church Family Account Book (1828–43), 10, 101–2, 119, HSV 9784.N5, MtL #360. Nearby factories paid men between sixty-two cents and one dollar a day. [Louis McLane], *Documents Relative to the Manufactures in the United States* (1833), 1:126–53.

42. INY, Domestic Journal, end of October 1837, NYSL 10; INY, Private [Apostate] Journal, September 29, 1853.

43. INY, Domestic Journal, January 1, September 17, 1850, June 11, 1851, WRHS 32, V:B-70; INY, Personal Journal, September 30 and December 30, 1850; INY, Idle Company; [INY et al.], Records Kept by Order of the Church, December 1, 1852, NYPL 2:7. Susan Kendall letter to New Lebanon, November 1, 1851, extract by Philemon Stewart, WRHS 52, VI:B-36. Diary and List of Members, Canaan, N.Y., January 1850, LC 3:39.

44. Benjamin Gates worked on a tin roof for Eldridge and Hadsell in June 1848 and on Dr. Peirson's water cure's roof in Tarrytown, New York, in November 1849. INY, Personal Journal, September 7, 1855; [INY et al.], Records Kept by Order of the Church, 173, May–June 1830 and June 1831, NYPL 2:7; Gates, Day Book, October 20, 1827, June 6 and August 31, 1829, May 12 and July 16, 1831, December 1834–January 1835, WM 819; INY, Domestic Journal, October 7, 1837, September 22, 1838, September 19, 1839, NYSL 10; Benjamin Gates, Journal (January 1839–April 1840 and September 1846–January 1854), September 25–26, 1850, SM 10,450.

45. INY, Domestic Journal, September 1847, July 1, September 18, October 5, 1848, WRHS 32, V:B-70; Bishop, Daily Journal, August 15, 1848, NYPL 1:2; Gates, Journal, July 1848, SM 10,450; INY, A Collection of Spiritual Songs, WRHS 93, IX:B-70.

46. INY, Domestic Journal, May 6, September 17 and 30, August 4, 13 and 26, 1850, August 21 and 26, 1851, WRHS 32, V:B-70; Gates, Journal, May–June and August 1848, September 1850, August 1851, May–June 1852, SM 10,450. INY also soldered lead pipe, "a bad job indeed I don't like it." NY et al., Taylor's Journal, December 28, 1854, WRHS 36, V:B-139.

47. INY, Personal Journal, September 7, 1855. According to an archivist at WRHS, when a page was cut from this journal and by whom is unknown.

48. INY did not work on the brick shop roof when it was replaced in 1856 but was "unlucky" because while the roof was open over his shop, rain soaked all his belongings. INY, Domestic Journal, September 24, 1855, WRHS 32, V:B-70; INY, Personal Journal, September 13, 1856.

49. American Psychiatric Association's *Diagnostic and Statistical Manual* quoted in Loren Stein, "Workaholism," Blue Cross Blue Shield of Massachusetts Web site, "Healthy Me," www.ahealthyme.com/topic/workaholism, accessed January 23, 2003. Journal as coping mechanism: Molly McCarthy, "A Pocketful of Days," *New England Quarterly* 73 (June 2000): 274–96.

50. INY "forward": INY to "Brother," September 1840, p. 131 in collection of hymns, WRHS 98, IX:B-162. "Ambitious-looking figure": John S. Dwight, "The Shakers at New Lebanon," *The Harbinger* 5 (August 14, 1847): 158.

Chapter 11. Tailoring

1. Nicholas Bennet et al., Domestic Journal (1802–7), March 24, 1807, WRHS 32, V:B-66; [INY et al.], Records Kept by Order of the Church (1780–1855), NYPL 2:7

2. INY, Domestic Journal (1834–46), end, NYSL 10; INY et al., Taylor's Journal (1845–65), February 2, 1863, WRHS 36, V:B-139; INY, Family and Meeting Journal (1815–23), January 16, 1823, LC 3:42. Brethren hating their jobs: Priscilla Brewer, *Shaker Communities, Shaker Lives* (Hanover, N.H.: University Press of New England, 1986), 77, 85.

3. Arthur Middleton and Henry Franklin, [Priscilla Bell Wakefield, pseud.], *Excursions in North America, Described in Letters from a Gentleman and his Young Companion . . .* (London: Darton and Harvey, 1806), 201–3. "Spotted" probably meant streaked.

4. One Ministry order banned "any kind of coats, different from the uniform pattern at New Lebanon." The fact that edicts had to be issued suggests that some did have nonstandard apparel and had to be told not to wear it. A few words respecting the brethrens Wearing apparel, n.d., LC 22:306. Blue jackets were worn from the 1790s until 1806, when they switched to drab. Rufus Bishop said they changed because indigo was scarce, but working on drab was easier on the eyes. Colors changed again in 1822, 1836, 1840, and 1854. Some brethren had drab jackets dyed blue, which saved tailors labor. Bishop to Darrow, July 2, 1817, WRHS 20, IV:A-33; INY, Concise View, 317, 322–24, 334–35, WM 861; INY, Domestic Journal, November 24, 1836, NYSL 10. Believers' workday clothes could be colorful, including purple trousers, green waistcoats, red or blue frocks, red flannel drawers. INY et al., Taylor's Journal, March 27, 1856, WRHS 36, V:B-139; INY, Domestic Journal, December 6, 1836, NYSL 10; INY [and Benjamin Gates], Tailor's Journal (December 1838–April 1845), January 1842, SM 9657. See also [Henry Blinn], "Historical Notes About the

Change of Dress," *The World of Shaker* (Winter 1974): 2–3; Beverly Gordon, *Shaker Textile Arts* (Hanover, N.H.: University Press of New England, 1980), 160, 188–89; Gordon, "Fossilized Fashion," *Dress* 13 (1987): 49–60.

5. Tailor's Book of Measures (1830–69), WRHS 15, III:B-10; INY [and Gates], Tailor's Journal, SM 9657; rate of work: INY et al., Taylor's Journal, November 1853, WRHS 36, V:B-139.

6. INY, Family and Meeting Journal, March 14, 1820, 181, LC 3:42; 1821 Millennial Laws, in John T. Kirk, *Shaker World*. (New York: Henry Abrams, 1997), 263.

7. INY [and Gates], Tailor's Journal, SM 9657; Benjamin Gates, Day Book (1827–38), October 1838, WM 819; INY, Family and Meeting Journal, November 27, 1820, LC 3:42.

8. INY, Domestic Journal, end, NYSL 10; INY, Concise View, 508. Ages: Shaker names index, WRHS 123.

9. Benjamin Gates, Journal (January 1839–April 1840 and September 1846–January 1854), September 14, 1846, SM 10,450; Gates to INY, March 26, 1826, SM 9547. On January 21, 1826, INY left "on account of poor health." INY et al., Memorandum . . . School (1817–35), 41, SM 21: 10,469.

10. Judith A. Graham, "The New Lebanon Shaker Children's Order" (Ph.D. diss., Iowa State University, 1996), 207–8. INY violated the Millennial Law about nicknames if he called Benjamin Benny. And in the tailor's journal, either INY or Gates called John Bruce Johnny. INY [and Gates], Tailor's Journal (1838–45), November 4, 1844.

11. Gates, Day Book, November 7, 1827, WM 819.

12. Ibid., May 14, 1828, April 20, June and August 3, 1829; list of tailors, INY, Domestic Journal, end, NYSL 10.

13. Benjamin Gates to INY, December 17, 1837, SM 9558.

14. Gates, Day Book, September 16, 1833, WM 819; INY, Domestic Journal, end, NYSL 10; Benjamin Gates in INY et al., Taylor's Journal, August 8, 1846, WRHS 36, V:B-139; INY [and Gates], Tailor's Journal, SM 9657.

15. INY, Domestic Journal, September 9, 1839, NYSL 10.

16. INY et al., Taylor's Journal, September 14, 1846, February 2, 1863, WRHS 36, V:B-139; INY, Domestic Journal, October 1, 1845, NYSL 10; INY, Personal Journal, May 31, 1843, WRHS 35, V:B-134.

17. From 1839 to 1845, Rufus Bishop made only forty-one garments, about 465 hours of tailoring in six years. INY [and Gates], Tailor's Journal, SM 9657; Gates, Journal, September 14, 1846, SM 10,450.

18. INY et al., Taylor's Journal, beginning note, November 30, 1846 (surtout); October–December 1855 and May 1856 (numbers of garments recorded during two seasons' work), WRHS 36, V:B-139.

19. Ibid., January–June 1851.

20. INY, Domestic Journal, August 2, 1852, WRHS 32, V:B-70.

21. Ibid., January 1853; INY, Personal Journal, February 1853.

22. INY, Domestic Journal, May 26, 1853, WRHS 32, V:B-70; INY et al., Taylor's Journal, May 26, June and July 1853, WRHS 3, V:B-139; INY, Private [Apostate] Journal (1837–59), September 1853, SM 10,509.

23. INY et al., Taylor's Journal, May 26, 1853, WRHS 36, V:B-139.

24. INY, Private [Apostate] Journal, September 29, 1853.

25. INY et al., Taylor's Journal, September 4 and 26, 1853, WRHS 36, V:B-139.

26. INY et al., Taylor's Journal, September 26, 1853, WRHS 36, V:B-139; INY, Domestic Journal, end, NYSL 10; INY, Private [Apostate] Journal, September 4–29, 1853.

27. INY et al., Taylor's Journal, February 2, 1863, WRHS 36, V:B-139; Private [Apostate] Journal, September 29, 1853.

28. INY et al., Taylor's Journal, October 6, 1853, WRHS 36, V:B-139.

29. INY, Concise View, 502. Hired help: Mount Lebanon Church Family Account Book (1828–43), 10, 64, 94, 116, 119, 142, 159, 161, HSV 9784.N5, MtL #360; INY et al., Taylor's Journal, October 6, 1853, WRHS 36, V:B-139.

30. INY, Personal Journal, June–July 1853.

31. Rate of work: INY et al., Taylor's Journal, November 1 and 26, 1853, February 25, 1854, WRHS 36, V:B-139; INY, Concise View, 243. Speedups and stretchouts: Thomas Dublin, *Women at Work: The Transformation of Work and Community in Lowell, Massachusetts, 1826–1860* (New York: Columbia University Press, 1979).

32. INY et al., Taylor's Journal, January 11, May and July 1855, March 10 and May 1, 1857, WRHS 36, V:B-139.

33. Ibid., October 1, 1855. Illnesses: INY, Domestic Journal, January 8 and 26, March 7, 9, and 23, August 16, and September 18, 1855, WRHS 32, V:B-70; INY, Personal Journal, October 29, 1855.

34. INY, Personal Journal, October 29, 1855; David Hackett Fischer, *Albion's Seed* (New York: Oxford University Press, 1989), 104; Fischer, *Growing Old in America* (New York: Oxford University Press, 1977), 4. Ages: Rufus Bishop et al., Records Book No. 2, NYPL 2:6; INY, Domestic Journal, January 1, 1850; INY, Domestic Journal (1856–69), 1860, WRHS 32, V:B-71.

35. INY, Personal Journal, November 5–7, 1855; INY, Domestic Journal, November 8, 1855, WRHS 32, V:B-70.

36. INY, Personal Journal, November 7–8, 1855.

37. INY et al., Taylor's Journal, December 1855, WRHS 36, V:B-139.

38. INY, Personal Journal, December 22, 1855 and January 1, 1856; INY et al., Taylor's Journal, October–December 1855, WRHS 36, V:B-139.

39. INY et al., Taylor's Journal, May 1, 1857, WRHS 36, V:B-139; Benson Lossing, "The Shakers," *Harper's New Monthly Magazine* 15 (July 1857): 166.

40. INY et al., Taylor's Journal, February 2, 1863, WRHS 36, V:B-139.

41. Record keeping: [INY], Measures & Draughts of Trowsers & Jackets . . . 1846, WRHS 15, III:B-17; INY, Measures of Garments . . . 1859, WRHS 15, III:B-26; INY, Domestic Journal, July 4 and December 25, 1861, WRHS 32, V:B-71;

Deaconesses' Journal, March 26, 1861, HSV 1086a; James Prescott to INY, August 20, 1862, transcribed in Alonzo Hollister, Book of Remembrance, 3:170, WRHS 58, VII:B-109; INY et al., Taylor's Journal, May 14 and 24, 1862, WRHS 36, V:B-139.

42. Tirade: INY et al., Taylor's Journal, February 2, 1863, WRHS 36, V:B-139. Civil War: Shakers noted national events but INY mentioned only the war "raging between North & South," which was "enough to fill us with horror & distress," wartime inflation and Believers' avoiding the draft. INY, Domestic Journal, December 31, 1862, WRHS 32, V:B-71.

43. INY et al., Taylor's Journal, February 2, 1863, WRHS 36, V:B-139.

44. Ibid., March 23, and October 26, 1863; "i.n.y.," Measures of Garments, WRHS 15, III:B-26.

45. INY et al., Taylor's Journal, March 1 and 12, 1864, WRHS 36, V:B-139.

46. Ibid., April 13, 1864.

Chapter 12. The Final Years

1. INY, Personal Journal (1839–58), July 4, 1853, WRHS 35, V:B-134. When INY was born in 1793, less than 20 percent of the U.S. population survived to age seventy. David Hackett Fischer, *Growing Old in America* (New York: Oxford University Press, 1977), 3–4.

2. Henry, who had worked as a shoemaker, harness maker, and swineherd, may have had a longstanding disability; he was conspicuous as an underachiever in a family of outstanding performers and by 1855 he had "no definite branch" of employment. INY, Domestic Journal (1847–55), January 7, 1853 and March 23 and 29, August 16, 1855, WRHS 32, V:B-70; INY, Personal Journal, January 27, February 26, 1853; INY, Domestic Journal, January 1855, WRHS 32, V:B-70. Elizabeth Youngs: D. A. Buckingham, Records of the Church at Watervliet (1854–70), August 22, 1865, WRI IS 45, V:B 281. Seth Youngs cut his own throat. INY, Family and Meeting Journal (1815–23), May 20, 1815, LC 3:42. Martha was "quite deranged" by 1817, "middling rational" in 1822, and "rather wild" in old age. Freegift Wells, Records of the Church at Watervliet, New York (1788–1851), February 22, 1817, WRHS 44, V:B-279; INY, Family and Meeting Journal, May 20, 1822, LC 3:42; INY [and Rufus Bishop], Tour thro the States of Ohio and Kentucky, in the Summer of 1834, June 4, 1834, SM 141. INY's cousin Abraham also cut his own throat. INY, Family and Meeting Journal, May 27, 1817, LC 3:42. INY's grandfather, Seth Youngs, was jailed for public misbehavior, but it may have reflected his religious opinions more than his mental state. Penrose R. Hoopes, *Connecticut Clockmakers of the Eighteenth Century* (Hartford: Edwin Valentine Mitchell, 1930), 127.

3. Rowley: INY, Personal Journal, November 15, 1855; Jerry Grant and Douglas Allen, *Shaker Furniture Makers* (Hanover, N.H.: Published for HSV by University Press of New England, 1989), 17–21.

4. INY, Personal Journal, June–September 1853. Christian Goodwillie explained the use of a toneometer.

5. INY to Andrew Houston, August 6, 1830, WRHS 20, IV:A-36.

6. INY, Personal Journal, June 6, 1853.

7. Ibid., fall 1853; INY et al., Taylor's Journal (1845–65), WRHS 36, V:B-139.

8. INY, Personal Journal, April 3, 1854.

9. Ibid., July 4, 1855.

10. GKL had also chosen "Happy Change" in 1837. GKL funeral song: Giles Avery, Historical Sketches, December 1837, LC 4:53; [Anon.], Miscellaneous Collection of Very Old Shaker Hymns, n.d., WRHS 110, IX:B-333; also in INY, [Hymnal] Made for Edward Fowler, March 1833, BA, V289.8 Un3.3 10:47.

11. Samuel Houser in GKL, Millennial Praises . . . 1829, WRHS 91, IX:B-42; A Choice Selection of Sacred Hymns . . . , Laura Dole, Groveland, 1860, WRHS 91, IX:B-37.

12. Fischer, *Growing Old*, 67; Anne Bradstreet, "The Four Ages of Man," *The Tenth Muse Lately Sprung Up in America* (1650; repr., Gainesville, Fla.: Scholars' Facsimiles, 1965), 54–55.

13. Ulcerated tooth: INY, Personal Journal, February 4, 1854; fears: INY, Personal Journal, September 2, 1854 and July 4, 1855; sore eyes: INY, Personal Journal, July 16, 1855; nervousness: INY, Domestic Journal, September 18, 1855, WRHS 32, V:B-70; forebodings: Giles Avery in Ministry letter to Watervliet, October 1868, WRHS 52, VI:B-36.

14. The entry ends there, though not as written. A check of the original manuscript at WRHS revealed that a page was excised. Either INY himself tore it out—unlikely, considering what he had written before and left intact—or someone else removed it. INY, Personal Journal, March 29–April 1, 1856 (next page begins May 28); INY et al., Taylor's Journal, March 13–22, 1856, WRHS 36, V:B-139; INY, Domestic Journal (1856–69), April 7, 1856, WRHS 32, V:B-71. Another page may have been excised from his personal journal in the August 30, 1856 entry.

15. INY, Personal Journal, November 5, 1855.

16. Ibid., August 30, 1856; INY, Domestic Journal, April 8, 1851, WRHS 32, V:B-70.

17. INY, Personal Journal, August 30, 1856 and September 2, 1854.

18. INY, Private [Apostate] Journal (1837–59), April 15, 1856, SM 10,509.

19. INY, Personal Journal, August 30–31, 1856.

20. Ibid., August 1856; [Benjamin Lossing], *An Early View of the Shakers*, ed. Don Gifford (Hanover, N.H.: Published for HSV by University Press of New England, 1989), 66.

21. INY, Personal Journal, September 1856, February 7 and 28, 1857; INY et al., Taylor's Journal, October 1 and November 27, 1856, WRHS 36, V:B-139; INY, Domestic Journal, October 4 and 11, 1856, WRHS 32, V:B-71; W. H. Babcock, "In the Departments," *Putnam's Magazine* 15 (January 1870): 54; Fischer, *Growing Old*, 9; "Outlived Her Usefulness," *Littell's Living Age* 48 (February 2, 1856): 317–18.

22. INY, Personal Journal, January–May 23 and July 4, 1857, January 1, 1858.

23. INY, Concise View, WM 861. Concise View contains editorial comment and

redundancies, and the society did not publish it as INY wrote it. When Henry Blinn published it 1889–90, he drained all the life out of INY's writing. "History of the Church at Mount Lebanon," *Shaker Manifesto* 20 (January 1890).

24. INY, Personal Journal, May 22 and 29, 1858. Considering that many of his nose and throat afflictions occurred in springtime, he may have had seasonal pollen allergies.

25. INY's handwriting remained so good that as late as 1864, he transcribed a hymnal for Alonzo Hollister. INY, Day Book (October 1855–December 1858), HSV 372; INY [hymnal] to Alonzo Hollister, 1864, WRHS 114, IX:B-413.

26. INY, Personal Journal, February 13, 1858.

27. Grant and Allen, *Shaker Furniture Makers,* 50; [Anon.], Domestic Journal of Important Occurrences Kept for the Elder Sisters, New Lebanon, August 1 and September 1, 1859, WRHS 32, V:B-61; Buckingham, Records of the Church at Watervliet, August 15, 1859.

28. INY, Private [Apostate] Journal, May 10, 1859.

29. Elder Daniel Crosman to Harvard Ministry, May 21, 1860, WRHS 21, IV:A-43.

30. Giles Avery, Register of Incidents and Events, June 8, 1860, NYPL 1:4.

31. INY, Concise View, 485–86.

32. Ibid., 506.

33. Deaconesses' Journal, March 26, 1861, HSV 1086a.

34. INY, Domestic Journal, July 4, 1861, WRHS 32, V:B-71. His handwriting remained excellent, evidence that his debility did not involve a tremor.

35. INY and John M. Brown, Domestic Journal, December 25, 1861, WRHS 32, V:B-71.

36. INY et al., Taylor's Journal, March 28, May 14 and 24, 1862, WRHS 36, V:B-139; INY, Domestic Journal, July 1862, WRHS 32, V:B-71.

37. INY, Domestic Journal, November 1862, WRHS 32, V:B-171.

38. INY, Domestic Journal, July 4, 1863, WRHS 32, V:B-71.

39. INY, A Brief Collection of Hymns: Improved in Sacred Worship (1826–30), 77, LC 16:230. Ghosts: Babcock, "In the Departments," 54. Less able: Fischer, *Growing Old,* 44.

40. INY et al., Taylor's Journal, October 26, 1863, WRHS 36, V:B-139.

41. INY, Domestic Journal, February 15, 1864, WRHS 32, V:B-71; J. Kevin McNeil, Esther M. LeBlanc, and Marion Joyner, "Effect of Exercise on Depressive Symptoms in the Moderately Depressed Elderly," *Psychology and Aging* 6 (September 1991): 487–88.

42. INY et al., Taylor's Journal, March 1864, WRHS 36, V:B-139.

43. Babbit: ibid., March and April 1864; "Supreme Judicial Court," *Pittsfield Sun,* May 4, 1826. For the near-escape of Oliver Train, see [Rufus Bishop], Day Book (1815–29), December 7, 1828 and December 30, 1829, WRHS 33, V:B-85. Train was subdued by physical force, bleeding, and physick. Hosford: Freegift Wells, Memorandum of Events [Watervliet], March 7, 1826, WRHS 45, V:B-290.

44. INY et al., Taylor's Journal, April 1864, WRHS 36, V:B-139. At year end when he recorded brethren's occupations, he noted none for himself; he was "out of health." INY, Domestic Journal, July 28 and December 31, 1864, WRHS 32, V:B-71. The world's people created a literary genre of "gathered gems for the aged," which offered one consolation: that old age would soon end. Fischer, *Growing Old,* 121. And James Prescott consoled him, "So let us suffer a little longer & we shall soon be called." Prescott to INY, August 20, 1862, copied in Alonzo Hollister, Book of Remembrances, 170, WRHS 58, VII:B-109.

45. INY, Domestic Journal, August 16, 1864, WRHS 32, V:B-71, quoted in Priscilla Brewer, *Shaker Communities, Shaker Lives* (Hanover, N.H.: University Press of New England, 1986),175.

46. Philip Adamo, M.D., MPH, Medical Director, Berkshire Occupational Health, at Berkshire Medical Center, Pittsfield, Mass., discussed the illnesses of long-dead Shakers with me and presented INY as a case study in training other physicians about lead exposure. Kevin C. Staudinger and Victor S. Roth, "Occupational Lead Poisoning," *American Family Physician,* February 15, 1998: www.aafp.org/afp/980215ap/stauding; "Health Effects of Lead Exposure," NIOSH Publication No. 91–116: www.cdc.gov/niosh/91–116.

47. INY, Personal Journal, November 5, 1855; INY, Domestic Journal, September 1855, WRHS 32, V:B-70.

48. Giles Avery, Journal, October 20, 1864, WRHS 34, V:B-110; INY, Domestic Journal, July 8 and 10, 1865, WRHS 32, V:B-71; John M. Brown, Domestic Journal, July 14, 1865, WRHS 32, V:B-71; Avery, Register of Incidents and Events, July 16, 1865.

49. Emanuel Jones, Farm Deacon's Journal, August 2 and 8, 1865, HSV 401; Brewer, *Shaker Communities,* 175; Avery, Journal, August 7, 1865; Brown, Domestic Journal, WRHS 32, V:B-71.

50. Betsy Crosman, A Small Record Book, August 8, 1865, WRHS 36, V:B-143.

51. INY had obsessed over fire since 1856, when he wrote, "I feel sometimes almost hourly as if I should hear the cry of fire!" INY, Personal Journal, August 30, 1856. Since their carding mill had burned a few days earlier, such a fear was reasonable.

52. John E. Murray, "Demographic Analysis of Shaker Mortality Trends," *Communal Societies* 13 (1993): 30. INY on Joel Woods's suicide: INY, Family and Meeting Journal, December 30, 1819, LC 3:42.

53. INY, Domestic Journal, January 24, 1837, NYSL 10; Thomas R. Cole, *The Journey of Life: A Cultural History of Aging in America* (New York: Cambridge University Press, 1992), 58, 86.

54. Second Order Sisters' Journal, August 7, 1865, WRHS 36, V:B-158.

55. Giles Avery, Personal Journal, August 7, 1865, WRHS 34, V:B-111; Avery, Register of Incidents and Events, August 7, 1865, NYPL 1:4; Daniel Patterson, *Shaker Spiritual* (Princeton, N.J.: Princeton University Press, 1979), 260; Emmanuel

Jones, Farm Deacon's Journal, August 9, 1865, HSV 401; Brown, Domestic Journal, December 31, 1865, WRHS 32, V:B-71.

56. INY, Domestic Journal, December 8, 1840, NYSL 10; Elisha D. Blakeman Eulogical to Brother Isaac N. Youngs, September 1866, 355–61, WRHS 50, VI:B-21.

57. Brown, Domestic Journal, December 31, 1865, WRHS 32, V:B-71.

Conclusion

1. Lawrence Foster, *Religion and Sexuality* (New York: Oxford University Press, 1981), 47.

2. See INY's objections to their opinions on the origin of the devil: INY, Family and Meeting Journal (1815–23), January 1 and 7, 1821, and December 1, 1822, LC 3:42.

3. Rufus Bishop et al., Records Book No. 2, 20–22, NYPL 2:6.

4. Joann Larsen, "Today's Woman: All Things to All People?" in *LDS Women's Treasury: Insights and Inspiration for Today's Woman,* comp. Jay A. Parry (Salt Lake City: Deseret Book Co., 1997), 134, cited in Perfectionism: Friend or Foe?, the Church of Jesus Christ of the Latter-Day Saints, available at www.ldsdepression.com/Perfectionism (accessed May 2004). Mormons recognize the link between depression and perfectionism, even though it is hard to separate cause and effect.

5. Susan Kendall, in a letter to Mount Lebanon (November 1, 1851, extract by Alonzo Hollister, in Autobiography of the Saints, or, Stray Leaves from the Book of Life, 306–7, WRHS 52, VI:B-36) described INY as a model of meekness and humility, as did Elisha Blakeman in his Eulogical to Brother Isaac N. Youngs, September 1866, 355–61, WRHS 50, VI:B-21.

6. INY, When this you see, remember me (poem), WRHS 116, X:A-2.

Index

GLENDYNE R. WERGLAND was born in Okmulgee, Oklahoma, capital of the Creek Nation, and grew up in Texas and Colorado. She married at eighteen and attended five colleges as the trailing spouse of a field engineer, a corporate gypsy who moved nine times in their first eight years of marriage. After settling in the Berkshire hills of western Massachusetts, she worked as a Girl Scout executive for nine years while her children were in school. At age forty, she resumed her undergraduate work as a Frances Perkins Scholar at Mount Holyoke College, where she graduated with honors, Phi Beta Kappa, in 1992. She attended graduate school at University of Massachusetts Amherst and received her Ph.D. in U.S. history in 2001. Now an independent scholar, she occasionally teaches American history at nearby colleges. She lives with her husband and dogs on a hillside in western Massachusetts, where she snowshoes, knits, and makes maple syrup.